This book is available at a special
discount when ordered in bulk quantities.
For information, contact Special Sales Department,
AMACOM, a division of American Management Association,
1601 Broadway, New York, NY 10019.

ISBN: 0-8144-0469-3

Printing number

10 9 8 7 6 5 4 3 2 1

TABLE OF CONTENTS

PREFACE

Creating a dictionary for the computer world is like trying to swim through quicksand. As quickly as I found terms and incorporated them into the manuscript, new terms came along and replaced the ones already rapidly vanishing.

Nonetheless, this *Dictionary of Data Communications* is as complete and relevant as possible. The dictionary is not only for the computer technician nor entirely for the neophyte. Instead, this book should be used as a reference, a springboard to learn the ever-changing technological environment around us, especially in data communications. Because of this, I have included a list of accessible Web sites and addresses to discover the most up-to-date terms available. If you find discrepancies or updates, please let me know and I will incorporate these newer terms into future editions.

Now, and most important, I would like to thank certain people without whom this book would not have become a reality: Debbie Callahan, Mabel Castilla, and Leo Montes. I would like to thank Anne Grant for cleaning out the flotsam and jetsam. I would also like to thank Teresa Quick for all the work she put in to keeping track of the loose ends and slippery details. As you know, every technical writer and computer user has a guru without whom the world would collapse and the sky would fall; I would like to thank Grace McLoughlin for her expertise and insight. The woman's a genius - really.

Finally, I would like to thank Barbara Craig of the Glenlake Publishing Company for all of her assistance and for having the patience of a saint: Thank you for waiting.

ABOUT THE AUTHOR

Robert A. Saigh, a former software training instructor and technical writer with Metamor Technologies, has an extensive background in writing software training and communications manuals. Mr. Saigh received his B.S. and M.A. from Northwestern University.

A Programming Language (APL): A high-level programming language for mathematical and scientific uses. APL employs the Greek characters. Though the language is now available for IBM PC computers (and compatible computers), APL is predominantly used by the IBM mainframes.

AAL: *See* **Asynchronous Transfer Mode Adaptation Layer.**

A/B-Bit signaling: For T-1 transmission facilities. One bit, borrowed from every 6th and 12th frame of the 24 time slots, carries the control information. The control bit for the first six frames is the A bit, and the second six frames the B bit.

ABI: *See* **Application binary interface.**

ABM: *See* **Asynchronous Balanced Mode.**

ABR: *See* **Available Bit Rate.**

Access code: An identification number or password used to gain access to a network system or other computerized process.

Access control: Guarantees the security of a system or network. Users must supply a login name and then a password.

Access control list (ACL): In a network, a database with valid users and the allowed access level for each user.

Access fee: The fee a local telephone company levies to connect to any local communications network or network's system.

Access hole: The access hole (in the magnetic material and its casing) allows read/write operations.

Access line: A telecommunications line connecting switching exchanges and remote stations. Each access line has a unique telephone number.

Access method: The process for a note to send data. With Ethernet, the node determines if the line is available.

Access Nodes: Places to perform conversions of protocol and to concentrate access lines down to fewer feeder lines. Typical Access Nodes are

Digital Loop Carrier systems with cellular antenna sites, Private Branch eXchanges (PBXs), Optical network units, and Voice lines to T1 lines.

Access privileges: The privilege to open and, therefore, modify directories, files, and programs in a Local Area Network (LAN). In democratic or peer-to-peer networks, the owner grants the privileges and determines who gets the information and how this information will be employed. A similar procedure occurs in AppleTalk.

Access rate: The physical transmission speed, (bits per second or bps), between the user and the network.

Access time: The total time on an operating system between the data retrieval order and the data transfer order. Hard disk access times are measured in microseconds (ms) conventionally between 9 microseconds (ms) (considered fast) and 100ms (slow). The access time of a disk drive is affected by its Latency, Seek time, and Settle time. Additional Read Access Memory (RAM) will improve (decrease) access times. See Latency; Seek time; Settle time.

Account: A network contractual agreement between the service provider (often an Internet Service Provider or ISP) and its user. In return for access, the user often pays an access fee and is expected to follow the provider's rules and regulations (if any).

Accounting: Accounting allows owners to charge for the following network services: (1) the number of blocks read from and/or written to server hard disks; (2) the time the user was logged through the server; (3) the quantity of data stored on server hard disks; and (4) the requests the server takes care of.

Accumulator: A temporary storage location in the Central Processing Unit (CPU). The accumulator stores input/output information or intermediary calculation information. The accumulator holds this intermediary information as the calculations progress and empties its values when the process finishes.

ACD: *See* **Automatic Call Distribution.**

ACDunit: *See* **Automatic Call Distribution unit.**

Acknowledgement (ACK): The communications protocol which acknowledges the transmission receipt.

ACL: *See* **Access Control List.**

ACM: *See* **Association for Computer Machinery.**

Activation: In a network, the way the mode component is prepared to perform designed functions.

Active configuration: The process of modem configuration. The active configuration will override the factory configuration as long as the computer remains on or is not rebooted.

Active hub: A multiport device amplifying transmission signals for a Local Area Network (LAN).

Active line: A telecommunications line for data transmission.

Active matrix display: A complete color Liquid Crystal Display (LCD) with each pixel assigned its own transistor. An active matrix display can give a letter or picture higher contrast values and increased refresh rates. Compare to Passive matrix displays.

Active termination: The process which terminates links of Small Computer System Interface (SCSI) devices. Active termination can decrease interference in a series of SCSI devices.

Active version: The most current copy of a stored file. An active file can be replaced (with a Save As function) or can be deleted directly from the application or from some file management software.

Ada: An easily maintained programming language developed by the U.S. Department of Defense (DoD). Ada, named for Lady Augusta Ada Byron, employs structured programming and allows for program modules to be compiled separately.

Adapter card: A circuit board that plugs into an expansion bus. The motherboard of IBM's PS/2 computer, includes ports along with a Video Graphics Array (VGA) display adapter for higher resolution video output. Various cards allow for internal modems, game connections, increased speed, etc. Many of these cards or card options are being added as standard to the computer as the technology improves.

Adaptive Differential Pulse Code Modulation (ADPCM): Instead of encoding the actual values of a digital waveform, ADPCM allows for encoding the difference between the samples. With ADPCM, the sound quality and quantity increases and the amount of memory needed decreases. ADPCM is the storage technique used by Computer Disk Read Only Memory XA (CD-ROM XA) and CD-I disks and permits an increase of sixteen times the amount of information over a standard CD.

ADB: *See* **Apple Desktop Bus.**

ADC: *See* **Analog-to-Digital Converter.**

Address: A unique identifier assigned to networks, or other devices. With an assigned address, each device is designated to receive and reply to messages.

Address bus: An internal electronic channel to the Random Access Memory (RAM) location. The address bus is used by the microprocessor to locate program instructions and memory storage locations along with the actual data. The width of the bus (measured in bits) is proportional to the size of the main memory in the computer. For instance, a 24-bit bus can address 224 bits or 16 Megabits (Mb) of RAM.

Address Resolution Protocol (ARP): An Internet Protocol (IP) that maps Internet addresses dynamically to the actual addresses on a Local Area Network (LAN).

Addressable Service Area (ASA): A company delineates this geographical area which contains various special or switched services for access. Usually, an ASA is not as large as a Local Access and Transport Area (LATA) but is larger than the area covered by the end office of a telephone company.

Addressing characters: A computer transmits these characters to activate a station (or its component) to accept a message the computer has transmitted.

Adjacent channel interference: The interference caused by adjacent signals interfering with each other. Much of this can be reduced via filtration or by separating the channels.

ADPCM: *See* **Adaptive Differential Pulse Code Modulation.**

ADSL: *See* **Asymmetric Digital Subscriber Line.**

Advanced Intelligent Network (AIN): A type of network architecture that can change quickly to offer custom telecommunications services, such as procuring local number routing information.

Advanced Interactive eXecutive (AIX): This UNIX Operating System (OS), created by IBM, runs on a PS/2 with the Intel 80386 chip. AIX can also interface with various workstations, minicomputers, and mainframes.

Advanced Mobile Phone System (AMPS): An analog system for cellular Frequency Modulation (FM) with 30 KiloHertz (KHz) channels and superaudio signaling (used in North America).

4

Advanced Peer-to-Peer Networking (APPN): Meant to be a replacement for a Systems Network Architecture (SNA), this type of network architecture permits the creation of dynamic routing across various network topologies.

Advanced Program-to-Program Communications (APPC): This permits internetwork communication by creating the conditions within the Systems Network Architecture (SNA) and involves LU6.2 and its associated protocols without a common host system or terminal emulation.

Advanced Run-Length Limited (ARLL): A process that controls the storage and retrieval of hard disk information. ARLL increases Run-Length Limited (RLL) storage density and offers a 9-Megabits/sec (Mbit/sec.) data-transfer rate.

Aerial cable: A telecommunications cable connected to a variety of overhead structures.

AFP: *See* **AppleTalk Filing Protocol.**

Agent: The agent prepares and exchanges information for a client or server application in a client/server environment.

AIN: *See* **Advanced Intelligent Network.**

Airline reservation system: An online application used to track flights, passengers, seats, and other information. This reservation system maintains current data files and must quickly respond to remote ticket agent queries.

AIX: *See* **Advanced Interactive eXecutive.**

Alarm: Audible (beeping, etc.) signal or visible (dialog box, etc.) warning signal indicating to a network administrator of an error or a problem on a network.

Alert: Lets administrators know that thresholds have been attained or discrepancies are occurring on a network.

Alert box: A visible cautionary window in a Graphical User Interface (GUI) warning the user of a bad command.

Algorithm: A defined set of rules or processes to aid in solving a problem.

All-points-addressable (APA): A Video Display Terminal (VDT) or printer characteristic for addressing each dot or pixel on the screen.

Alphanumeric: Pertains to letters, digits, and other characters, such as punctuation marks. Synonymous with alphameric.

Alternate Buffer: A memory area reserved to receive and hold data after the primary buffer is full.

Alternate Mark Inversion (AMI): The T1 line signal sending consecutive 1-bits through polarity inversion. Note: Zeros are represented by time and not by voltage.

ALU: *See* **Arithmetic Logic Unit.**

Am386: A 32-bit microprocessor developed by Advanced Micro Devices (AMD). An Am386 is 100 percent compatible with the Intel 80386DX.

Am386DXL: The Am386DXL uses only one-third the power required to fuel the Intel 80386 in the 20 MegaHertz (MHz) and 25MHz versions and two-thirds the power in the 33MHz version. This power reduction was done so the Am386DXL could be used in portable or laptop computers.

American National Standards Institute (ANSI): A U.S.-based organization for establishing many data communications and terminal standards and standards for the information processing industry such as the standard versions of COmmon Business-Oriented Language (COBOL) and FORmula TRANslator (FORTRAN). A member of International Standards Organization (ISO) and is the U.S. representative in the ISO and the Consultative Committee for International Telephony and Telegraphy (CCITT).

American Standard Code for Information Interchange (ASCII): An alphanumeric American National Standards Institute (ANSI) 7-bit code (created in 1968) meant to increase compatibility and communication between products from a disparate group of companies. ASCII uses 96 uppercase and lowercase letters and 32 non-displayed control characters. ASCII uses seven bits along with one parity bit for error checking.

American Standard Code for Information Interchange (ASCII) file: An ASCII character set file.

American Standard Code for Information Interchange (ASCII) sort order: The sort order determining the sequence of the standard ASCII character set. The sort order is: words or lines with spaces or punctuation, words or lines with uppercase letters, words or lines with lowercase letters.

American Wire Gauge (AWG): A wire size system. The gauge varies inversely with the wire diameter size.

America Online®: An Internet Service provider who provides the program one needs for connection to the Internet, an easy setup program, a local service number, and frequently a free trial membership.

AMI: *See* **Alternate Mark Inversion.**

Amplifier: A device increasing the analog signal strength.

Amplitude: The voltage or analog waveform magnitude.

Amplitude Modulation (AM): The modulation of the alternating current amplitude.

Analog: A continuously variable waveform (as opposed to discretely variable). The public telephone communication system is in analog form. Contrast with digital signals. Analog is also continuously varied form of measurement reflecting the represented environment.

Analog channel: A data communications channel on which the information transmitted can take any value between the limits defined by the channel. Voice-grade channels are analog channels.

Analog device: A computer peripheral that handles information in continuously variable quantities rather than digitizing the information into discrete, digital representations. An analog monitor, for example, can display thousands of colors with smooth, continuous gradations.

Analog/Digital Converter: An adapter that enables a digital computer (such as an IBM Personal Computer) to accept analog input from laboratory instruments. Analog/digital converters are frequently used for the real-time monitoring of temperature, movement, and other continuously varied conditions.

Analog monitor: A monitor that accepts a continuously varied video input signal and consequently can display a continuous range and infinite number of colors. In contrast, a digital monitor can display only a finite number of colors. Enhanced Graphics Adapter (EGA) monitors are digital; Video Graphics Array (VGA) monitors are analog. Most analog monitors are designed to accept input signals at a precise frequency; however, developments in display adapter technology will ensure that higher frequencies will be required to carry higher-resolution images to the monitor (the higher the frequency, the greater the on-screen resolution). For this reason, multisync monitors have been developed that automatically adjust themselves to the incoming frequency.

Analog signal: A signal, such as voice or music, that varies in a continuous manner.

7

Analog-to-Digital Converter (ADC): A device that converts analog signals to digital signals.

Analog transmission: A communications scheme that uses a continuous signal varied by amplification.

Analysis: The methodological investigation of a problem. The separation of the problem into smaller related units for further detailed study.

Analyst: A person who defines problems and develops algorithms and procedures for their solution.

ANSI: *See* **American National Standards Institute.**

ANSI.SYS: In Microsoft Disk Operating System (MS-DOS), a configuration file containing instructions needed to display information, following recommendations of the American National Standards Institute (ANSI).

Answerback: The response of a terminal to remote control signals.

Answer/originate: In data communications, the property of a communications device such that the device can receive (answer) and send (originate) messages.

APA: *See* **All-Points-Addressable.**

API: *See* **Application Program Interface; Application Programming Interface.**

APL: *See* **A Programming Language.**

APPC: *See* **Advanced Program-to-Program Communications.**

Apple Desktop Bus (ADB): An interface standard for connecting keyboards, mice, trackballs, and other input devices to Apple's Macintosh SE, Macintosh II, and Macintosh IIGS computers. These computers come with an ADB port capable of a maximum data transfer rate of 4.5 Kilobits per second (Kbps). You can connect up to 16 devices to one ADB port.

Apple Desktop Interface: A set of user interface guidelines developed by Apple Computer and published by Addison-Wesley, intended to ensure that all Macintosh applications appear and work in similar ways.

AppleShare: AppleShare is Apple Computer's networking solution. It requires a Macintosh computer as a network server and includes both server and workstation software. It uses the AppleTalk Filing Protocol (AFP). Novell's Macintosh connectivity solution teams NetWare for Macintosh server software with AppleShare workstation software.

AppleShare File Server: In an AppleTalk Local Area Network (LAN), a Macintosh computer that runs AppleShare File Server software which allows network users can employ this machine to store and retrieve shared programs and data.

AppleTalk: A **Local Area Network (LAN)** standard developed by Apple Computer. AppleTalk is capable of linking as many as 32 Macintosh computers, IBM PC-compatible computers, and peripherals such as laser printers. Every Macintosh computer has an AppleTalk port, through which you can connect the machine to an AppleTalk network using a bus topology. AppleTalk networks are slow compared to high-speed systems like EtherNet or AppleTalk.

AppleTalk Filing Protocol (AFP): Allows distributed file sharing across an AppleTalk network.

Application: A software program or program package that makes calls to the operating system and manipulates data files, thus allowing a user to perform a specific job (such as accounting or word processing).

Application binary interface (ABI): A specification defining the interface between an operating system and a certain hardware platform, particularly the calls between applications and the operating system.

Application heap: In a Macintosh computer, the area of memory set aside for user programs (synonymous with base memory).

Application interface: A set of software routines and associated conventions that permits application programmers to use that interface as a part of any application. In general, an application interface is used to access system or networking services that would otherwise require significant development effort to create from scratch. For example, the ManageWise application interface lets a programmer use ManageWise file structures and services within an application.

Application layer: The seventh layer in the Open System Interconnection (OSI) model which is ultimately responsible for managing communication between application processes.

Application Program Interface (API): System software that provides resources on which programmers can draw to create user interface features, such as pull-down menus and windows, and to route programs or data to a Local Area Network (LAN). The Macintosh was the first personal computer to use the API concept.

Application Programming Interface (API): A means by which an application gains access to system resources, usually for the purpose of communication (the sending and receiving of data), data retrieval or other system services. In the specific area of terminal emulation, an API provides for the simulation of keystrokes and for writing into and reading from the presentation space (device buffer). It may also provide for the sending and receiving of structured fields.

Application server: A server in a client-server network that runs one or more applications that can be shared by client stations and which also shares the data processing burden with client stations. This shared application and shared data processing model contrasts with the model used for other servers, such as file servers, that simply send, receive, and store files, requiring client stations to run all applications and process all data. Either model can be most advantageous, depending on circumstances. In many circumstances the application server model allows for faster data processing, faster throughput to client stations, greater data reliability, and increased data security.

Application software: Programs that perform specific tasks unlike system software that maintains and organizes the computer system and utilities that assist you in maintaining and organizing the system.

APPN: *See* **Advanced Peer-to-Peer Network.**

Architecture: The overall design by which the individual hardware components of a computer system are interrelated. The term architecture is frequently used to describe the internal data-handling capacity of a computer. The 8-bit architecture of the Intel 8088 microprocessor, for example, is determined by the 8-bit data bus that transmits only one byte of data at a time.

Archive: To create a redundant copy of computer file data, typically to create a backup copy of that data to protect it if the original copy is damaged or otherwise irretrievable. By some definitions, an archive is required to contain copies of every version of particular file. In this case, to archive means to save a copy of every object in a file system with a separate copy of all changes made to that file. In addition to protecting files from loss, this approach also permits any previous version of a file to be restored, typically by date and time.

ARCnet: *See* **Attached Resource Computing Network.**

Arithmetic Logic Unit (ALU): The portion of the Central Processing Unit (CPU) devoted to the execution of fundamental arithmetic and logical operations on data.

ARLL: *See* **Advanced Run-Length Limited.**

ARP: *See* **Address Resolution Protocol.**

ARPANET: A Wide Area Network (WAN) supported by the U.S. Defense Advanced Research Projects Agency (DARPA) and intended to support advanced scientific research. Access to ARPANET is restricted to a small group of advanced researchers because its broader communication functions are being taken over by National Science Foundation NETwork (NSFNET).

ARQ: *See* **Automatic Request-Repeat.**

AS: *See* **Autonomous System.**

AS/400: An IBM minicomputer.

ASCII: *See* **American Standard Code for Information Interchange.**

ASE: *See* **Application Service Element.**

ASIC: *See* **Application Specific Integrated Circuit.**

ASM: *See* **Association for Systems Management.**

ASR: *See* **Automatic Send/Receive.**

Assembler: A program that transforms an assembly language program into machine language so that the computer can execute the program.

Assembly language: A low-level programming language in which each program statement corresponds to an instruction that the processing unit can carry out. Assembly languages are procedural languages; they tell the computer what to do in precise detail. The languages are only one level removed in abstraction from machine language, the language of 0s and 1s that the processing unit actually reads to carry out its operations. Assembly language differs from machine language only in the use of codes that represent the major functions the machine carries out.

Association for Computer Machinery (ACM): The oldest professional society for computer experts. ACM was founded in 1948 and sponsors conferences, journals, book publishing, and student groups at colleges and universities. The ACM is known for its annual Computer Science Conference.

Association for Systems Management (ASM): A professional society for systems analysts and other computer professionals. The ASM has chapters in most cities and offers many short courses in systems analysis and other information-systems topics. The ASM was formerly known as the Systems and Procedures Association (SPA).

Asymmetrical Digital Subscriber Line (ADSL): An emerging technology developed by the telephone companies that transmits data at 1.5 MegaBytes Per Second (MBPS) to 9 MBPS over standard copper telephone wires and twisted pair cabling. A dedicated connection service, it requires two ADSL modems: one on the user's end and one at the central office. Several different types of data can be transmitted over the connection at the same time, e.g., voice and television broadcasts.

Asynchronous: Variable transmission rate without a predictable time relationship to a specified event.

Asynchronous Balanced Mode (ABM): A communication mode used in High-level Data-Link Control (HDLC) that allows either of two workstations in a peer-oriented point-to-point configuration to initiate a data transfer.

Asynchronous Transfer Mode (ATM): A new type of cell switching technology which uses fixed-length packets to transmit data from source to destination. ATM uses fixed-length 53-byte cell-switching to transmit data, voice and video over both a Local Area Network (LAN) and a Wide Area Network (WAN). Also referred to as Broadband-Integrated Services Digital Network (B-ISDN) and Cell Relay.

Asynchronous Transfer Mode (ATM): A transmission protocol that segments user traffic into small, fixed size cells. Cells are transmitted to their destination where the original traffic is re-assembled. During transmission, cells from different users are intermixed asynchronously to maximize utilization of network resources. Used to transmit multiple types of information such as voice, video, and data. Can be ATM25 (at 25.6 Megabits per second or 25.6 Mbps) or ATM155 (155 Mbps).

Asynchronous Transfer Mode Adaptation Layer (AAL): Layer 3 of the ATM architecture. Adapts user traffic into and from ATM 48-byte payloads.

Asynchronous Transfer Mode (ATM) Layer: Layer 2 of the ATM architecture. Responsible for the creation and management of ATM cells, including routing and error checking. Sometimes informally called the "Cell Layer."

Asynchronous Transfer Mode Adaptation Layer Type 1 (AAL1): Functions in support of constant bit rate, time-dependent traffic such as voice and video.

Asynchronous Transfer Mode Adaptation Layer Type 2 (AAL2): Functions in support of variable bit rate traffic but with the same timing requirements as voice and video.

Asynchronous Transfer Mode Adaptation Layer Type 3/4 (AAL 3/4): Functions in support of variable bit rate, delay tolerant data traffic requiring some sequencing and/or error detection support. Originally, two AAL types (connection-oriented and connectionless) which have been combined.

Asynchronous Transfer Mode Adaptation Layer Type 5 (AAL5): Functions in support of variable bit rate, delay tolerant, connection-oriented data traffic requiring minimal sequencing or error detection support.

Asynchronous Transmission (AT): Data transmission one character at a time with intervals of varying lengths between transmittals. Start and stop bits at the beginning and end of each character control the transmission. Transmission in which each information character is individually synchronized usually by the use of start and stop elements.

AT: *See* **Asynchronous Transmission.**

AT-ADAPT-2: A harmonic-style adapter that allows direct conversion from a 50-pin Telco connector to Registered Jack 45 (RJ45) receptacles

ATCON: A diagnostic tool used in Novell NetWare environments; provides information about a server or router's AppleTalk stack, and about other AppleTalk networks on the Internetwork.

ATM: *See* **Asynchronous Transfer Mode Layer.**

ATM25: *See* **Asynchronous Transfer Mode.**

ATM155: *See* **Asynchronous Transfer Mode.**

Attach: To access a network server, particularly to access additional servers after logging in to one server.

Attached Resource Computing Network (ARCnet): A proprietary token-bus networking architecture developed by Datapoint Corporation in the mid-1970s. Currently, ARCnet is widely licensed by third-party vendors and was a popular networking architecture, especially in smaller installations. It has a bandwidth of 2.5 Megabits per second (Mbps), is reliable, and supports coaxial, twisted pair, and fiber optic cable-based implementations. *See next.*

Attached Resource Computing Network (ARCnet): A popular Local Area Network (LAN) for IBM Personal Computers and compatibles originally developed by Datapoint Corporation and now available from several vendors. ARCnet interface cards are inexpensive and easily installed. ARCnet networks employ a star topology, a token-passing protocol, and coaxial or twisted-pair cable. The network is capable of transmitting data at speeds of 2.5 Megabits per second (Mbps).

Attachment Unit Interface (AUI): The branch cable interface located between a Media Access Unit (MAU) (a transceiver) and a Data Terminal Equipment (DTE) (typically a workstation). Includes a 15-pin D-sub connector and sometimes a 15-conductor twisted pair cable. Maximum length is 50 meters (164 feet).

Attachment Unit Interface (AUI) Cable: An Institute of Electronic and Electrical Engineers (IEEE) 802.3 cable connecting the Media Access Unit (MAU) to a networked device. An AUI may also refer to the host backpanel connector to which an AUI cable attaches.

Attention interruption: An Input/Output (I/O) interruption caused by a terminal user pressing an attention key or its equivalent.

Attenuation: A decrease in magnitude of current, voltage, or power of a signal in transmission between points. It is normally expressed in decibels (dBs)

Attenuation distortion: The deformation of an analog signal that occurs when the signal does not attenuate evenly across its frequency range.

@TeX: A free typesetting created by Donald Knuth.

Attributes: A technique for describing access to and properties of files and directories within a filing system. For NetWare files, attributes include Read, Write, Create, Delete, and Execute Only (prevents files from being deleted and copied). For NetWare directories, attributes include Read, Write, Create, Execute and Hidden (hides information about the directory from file listings, preventing unauthorized access, deletion, or copying).

Audio frequencies: Frequencies that can be heard by the human ear. These frequencies are approximately 15 Hertz (Hz) to 20,000 Hertz (or 20KHz).

Audio response unit: An output device that provides a spoken response to digital inquiries from a telephone or other device. The response is composed of a prerecorded vocabulary of words and can be transmitted over telecommunications lines to the location from which the inquiry originated.

Audiotex: A voice messaging system that can access a database on a computer.

Audit: To review and examine the activities of a system, mainly to test the adequacy and effectiveness of control procedures.

Audit trail: A manual or computerized means for tracing the transactions affecting the contents of a record.

AUI: *See* **Attachment Unit Interface.**

Authorization code: A code typically made up of the user's identification and password, used to protect against unauthorized access to data and system facilities.

Auto-answer: *See* **Automatic answering.**

Autoauthentication: In a client-server environment, a utility that lets users access unrestricted network resources without password verification. Only when a user attempts to access a restricted resource does the utility prompt for a password.

Auto-dial: *See* **Automatic dialing.**

Auto-dial/auto-answer modem: A modem capable of generating tones to dial the receiving computer and of answering a ringing telephone to establish a connection when a call is received.

Autologin: In a network environment, a utility that regulates user login attempts.

Automatic answering (Auto-answer): Answering in which the called Data Terminal Equipment (DTE) automatically responds to the calling signal; the call may be established whether or not the called DTE is attended. *See next.*

Automatic answering (Auto-answer): A machine feature that allows a transmission control unit or a station to respond automatically to a call that it receives over a switched line.

Automatic Call Distribution (ACD): (1) Service which allows automated routing and reporting of calls for customers with multiple locations. (2) A system to distribute a high volume of calls evenly or according to priority to minimize waiting time, or to route calls to appropriate parties.

Automatic Call Distribution (ACD) unit: A device attached to a telephone system that routes the next incoming call to the next available agent.

Automatic dialing (Auto-dial): A capability that allows a computer program or an operator using a keyboard to send commands to a modem, causing it to dial a telephone number.

Automatic mode switching: The automatic detection and adjustment of a display adapter's internal circuitry to adjust the video output of a program on an IBM PC-compatible computer. Most Video Graphics Array (VGA) adapters, for example, switch to adjust to Color Graphics Adapter (CGA), Enhanced Graphics Adapter (EGA), Monochrome Display Adapter (MDA), or VGA output from applications.

Automatic Request-repeat (ARQ): Error-correction technique where the receiver may detect an error and request the sender to retransmit.

Automatic Send/Receive (ASR): A teletypewriter unit with keyboard, printer, paper tape reader/transmitter, and paper tape punch. This combination of units may be used online or offline and, in some cases, online and offline concurrently.

Automount: A graphical utility that provides an iconical tree structure to simplify the user's task of locating and using a server, file system, or volume.

Autonomous System (AS): Part of the Internet layer that routers use to relate to network connectivity and packet addressing. The router checks the network address and only routes on the host address if the source and destination are on the same network.

Auto-poll: A machine feature of a transmission control unit or front-end processor that permits it to handle negative responses to polling without interrupting the processing unit.

AUX: *See* **Auxillary port.**

A/UX: Apple Computer's version of the UNIX operating system. To use A/UX, you need a Macintosh with a Motorola 68020 or 68030 microprocessor and 4 MegaBytes (MB) of Random Access Memory (RAM).

Auxillary port (AUX): The COMmunications (COM) port that a Disk Operating System (DOS) uses by default; the default port is normally COM1.

Available Bit Rate (ABR): One of five Asynchronous Transfer Mode (ATM) Forum-defined service types. Supports variable bit rate data traffic with flow control, a minimum guaranteed data transmission rate and specified performance parameters.

AWG: *See* **American Wire Gauge.**

Backbone: In a Wide Area Network (WAN) such as the Internet, a high-speed, high-capacity medium that is designed to transfer data over hundreds or thousands of miles and connect usually shorter, slower circuits. A variety of physical media are used for the backbone services, including microwave relays, satellites, and dedicated telephone lines.

Backdoor: An undocumented way to gain access to a program, data, or an entire computer system, usually known only to the programmer who created it. Backdoors can be handy when the standard way of getting information is unavailable, but usually they constitute a security risk.

Back-end: The portion of a program that accomplishes the processing tasks that the program is designed to perform. In a Local Area Network (LAN) with client/server architecture, the back-end application may be stored on the file server while front-end programs handle the user interface on each workstation.

Background: In computers that can perform more than one task at a time, the environment in which low-priority operations (such as printing a document or downloading a file) are carried out while the user works with an application in the foreground. In computer systems that lack multitasking capabilities, background tasks are carried out during brief pauses in the execution of the system's primary (foreground) tasks Many word processing programs use multitasking to provide background printing. *See* **Multitasking.**

Background communication: Data communication, such as downloading a file, performed in the background while the user concentrates on another application in the foreground. *See* **Multitasking**.

Background noise: Random or extraneous signals that infiltrate a communications channel, as opposed to the signals that convey information.

Background pagination: *See* **Pagination.**

17

Background printing: The printing of a document in the background while a program is active in the foreground. Background printing can bring major productivity benefits if you frequently print long documents or use a slow printer. Background printing enables you to use your computer system while a document is printing. Background printing can work four ways: a program can include a background printing command that enables you to print one document while editing another; a separate commercial print spooling program can add this ability to all or most of your applications; the capability can be part of the operating system (for example, OS/2); you can use a print buffer peripheral. A print buffer is a hardware device that connects between your computer and the printer. The buffer contains memory chips that store the computer's output until the printer is ready. The computer offloads the print job, freeing your computer for other uses. *See* **Multitasking; Print queue.**

Background process: In a multitasking operating system, the operations occurring in the background (such as printing or downloading from a bulletin board) while your work with an application program in the foreground.

Background program (background mode): A program that performs its functions while the user is working with a different program. Communications programs often operate in background mode. They can receive messages while the user works with other programs. The messages are stored for later display.

Background tasks: In a multitasking operating system, the operations occurring in the background (such as printing, sorting a large collection of data, or searching a database) while you work in another program in the foreground.

Backhaul: An earth-based communications channel linking an earth station to a local switching network.

Backlight display: A Liquid Crystal Display (LCD) commonly used in notebook and laptop computers. The back of the screen is illuminated to improve the screen's legibility over those that rely only on ambient light, but at the cost of decreased battery endurance.

Backplane: A motherboard. Originally, the term described a main circuit board mounted vertically at the rear of the case.

Backup: A copy of installed application software or of data files you've created. Regular backup procedures are imperative if you want to protect the data files you have created. Also, make copies of all software installation disks whenever you buy new software. Use the copies to install the program and keep the originals in a safe location away from your computer. Also, the act of copying files to another disk. *See* **Global backup; Incremental backup.**

Backup/Archive Client: A client to a backup/archive process. Usually there is an agent code resident on the client that allows the controlling application to provide backup/archive services.

Backup file consolidation: The ability for the backup software to re-create a full backup every time an incremental backup is performed.

Backup procedure: A regular maintenance procedure that copies all new or altered files to a backup storage medium, such as floppy disks or a tape drive. Hard disks fail, and a catastrophic disk failure can cause a business disaster. If you use your computer for business or professional purposes, you should back up your hard disk on a regular basis-at least weekly. If you do not, you expose yourself to the possibility of professional embarrassment, loss clients and lost profits. You can manually back up important files to floppy disks, but this approach is inconvenient, time-consuming and liable to error. It is best used for archiving small data files. The best solution to backing up an entire hard drive is to purchase a backup utility program. Perform a full backup of your entire hard drive. Later, at regular intervals (daily, weekly), perform an incremental backup. The backup utility automatically detects any files you have created or altered since the last backup. Some users prefer to back up only those subdirectories that contain the data they have created. If the hard disk fails, programs can be reinstalled from the original program distribution disks. Two flaws mar this reasoning. If your hard disk fails, you will lose all your program configuration choices. When you reinstall your software on your new (or repaired) disk, you must choose all these configurations options again. Installing programs can be very tedious process. If you back up your entire hard disk, you can use the restore operation to re-create your entire hard disk-program files and configuration files included - in about the time it would take to install one, huge application. Quarter-inch cartridge tape drives are now very inexpensive, and you should consider equipping your system with a drive whose capacity matches that of your hard drive. Backing up with a tape drive is much more convenient than backing up with floppy disks; you don't have to swap disks in and out. Most backup utilities include a scheduler program that lets you schedule automatic backup operations. *See* **Backup utility; Incremental backup; Quarter inch cartridge (QIC); Save.**

Backup utility: A utility program designed to back up programs and data files from a hard disk to a backup medium such as floppy disks or a tape drive. Backup utility programs include commands to schedule regular backups, to backup only selected directories or files, and to restore all or only a few files from a backup set. Rather than use floppy disks for backups, consider buying a more convenient Quarter-Inch Cartridge (QIC) or Digital Audio Tape (DAT) tape drive. Tape drives with a 250-MegaByte (MB) capacity are available for less than $200. *See* **Backup procedure; Incremental backup; Quarter-Inch Cartridge.**

Backward chaining: In expert systems, a commonly used method of drawing inferences from IF/THEN rules. A backward chaining system answers a question by searching through the system's rules to determine which one allows it to solve the problem and to determine what additional data is necessary. A backward-chaining expert system asks questions of the user, engaging him or her in a dialogue. *See* **Forward chaining; Knowledge base.**

Backward compatible: Compatible with earlier versions. Microsoft Windows '95, for example, is backward compatible with application programs designed to run on earlier versions of Windows. This is primarily so that a user can retain the value of their original software investment.

Backward search: In a database, spreadsheet, or word processor document, a search that begins at the cursor's location and proceeds backward toward the beginning of a document (rather than proceeding from the original cursor to the end of the document).

Bad break: An improperly hyphenated line break.

Bad sector: An area of a floppy or hard disk that won't reliably record data. Most hard disks have a certain percent of bad sectors as a result of manufacturing defects. The operating system locks these sectors out of reading and writing operations so that they are ignored. *See* **Bad track.**

Bad track: A hard disk or floppy disk track that contains a bad sector. Marked as unusable in the File Allocation Table (FAT), bad tracks are harmless. If Track 0 (which contains all the information on how the drive is organized) is bad, the disk must be replaced.

BAK: The Microsoft Disk Operating System (MS-DOS) file name extension usually attached to a file containing backup data. Many application programs assign the .BAK extension to the old version of a file any time you change the file's name.

Ball bat: In UNIX, a common slang term for an exclamation point (!). Also called a bang character or an astonisher.

Balun (BaLanced Unbalanced): An impedance-matching device that connects a balanced line (such as a twisted-pair line) and an unbalanced line (such as a coaxial cable).

Band: A range of radio frequencies between two defined frequencies. For example the so-called 'audio' band of frequencies audible to a human being is from 20 Hertz (Hz) to 20 KiloHertz (KHz).

Band pass filter: A circuit that allows signals of a desired frequency to pass though while impeding the passage of signals outside that frequency.

Bandit mobile: An illegal or invalid mobile communications subscriber.

Bandwidth: The capacity of a communication channel. In analog channels, bandwidth is the difference between the high and low frequencies that the channel can accommodate. In digital channels, bandwidth is the rate at which data can be transmitted.

Bandwidth: The difference between the two limiting frequencies of a band, expressed in Hertz (Hz).

Bang: *See* **Ball bat**

Bar code: A printed pattern of wide and narrow vertical bars used to represent numerical codes in machine-readable form. Computers equipped with bar-code readers and special software can interpret bar codes. Supermarkets use bar codes conforming to the Universal Product Code (UPS) to identify products and ring up prices, while the U.S. Postal Service uses POSTNET bar codes to make ZIP codes machine-readable. The latest version of word processing programs such as WordPerfect and Microsoft Word include options to print POSTNET bar codes on envelopes.

Bar code reader: An input device equipped with a stylus that scans bar codes; the device then converts the bar code into a number displayed on-screen. *See* **Bar code.**

.BAS: The Micorsoft Disk Operating System (MS-DOS) file name extension usually attached to a file containing Beginner's All-purpose Symbolic Instruction Code (BASIC) source code.

Base address: The first address in a series of addresses in memory, often used to describe the beginning of a network interface card's Input/Output (I/O) space.

Base station: In cellular communications, the station in the center of a cell that generates and receives radio signals. It communicates with the mobile switching office using a land line.

Baseband: In a Local Area Network (LAN) a communications method in which the information-bearing signal is placed directly on the cable in digital form without undergoing any modulation. A computer's signals can be conveyed over a cable in two ways: using analog signals or using digital signals. Analog signals are continuous signals that vary in a wave-like pattern. Digital signals are discrete signals that alternate between high current or low currents. Because a computer's signals are digital, they must be transformed by a process called modulation before they can be conveyed over an analog network such as an ordinary telephone line link. A modem performs this task. Digital communication networks are called baseband networks. The advantage of a baseband network is that relatively little circuitry is required to convey the signal to and from the computer. Many baseband networks can even use twisted-pair (ordinary telephone) cables. However, a baseband system is limited in its geographic extent and provides only one channel of communication at a time. Most personal computers LANs are baseband networks. *See* **Broadband.**

Baseband: Form of transmission in which the entire bandwidth of a channel is devoted to one signal.

Baseband transmission: Transmission using baseband techniques. The signal is transmitted in digital form using the entire bandwidth of a circuit or cable. Typically used in Local Area Networks (LANs).

Base font: The default font a word processing program uses to create a document. You can choose a default base font for all new documents or for just the document you are currently editing. You can subsequently assign other fonts to individual words and paragraphs within the document.

Base level synthesizer: In multimedia, the minimum capabilities of a music synthesizer required by Microsoft Windows '95 and its Multimedia Personal Computer (MPC) specifications. A base level synthesizer must be capable of playing at least six simultaneous notes on three melodic instruments, and three simultaneous notes on three percussion instruments.

Baseline: In typography, the lowest point that characters reach (excluding descenders). For example the baseline of a line of text is the lowermost point of letters like a and x, excluding the lowest point of p and q.

BASIC: *See* **Beginner's All-purpose Symbolic Instruction Code.**

BASICA: *See* **Beginner's All-purpose Symbolic Instruction Code A.**

Basic Input/Output System (BIOS): A set of programs encoded in Read Only Memory (ROM) on IBM PC-compatible computers programs handle startup operations such as the Power-On Self Test (POST) and low-level control for hardware such as disk drives, keyboard, and monitor. The BIOS programs of IBM personal computers are copyrighted, so manufacturers of IBM PC-compatible computers must create a BIOS that emulates the IBM BIOS or buy an emulation from companies such as Phoenix Technologies and American Megatrends, Inc. Some system components have a separate BIOS. The BIOS on a hard disk controller, for example, stores a table of tracks and sectors on the drive. *See* **Flash Basic Input/Output System.**

Basic-Rate Interface (BRI): The Integrated Services Digital Network (ISDN) standard governing how a customer's desktop terminals and telephones can connect to the ISDN switch. It specifies to B-channels that allow 64-Kilobit-per-second (Kbps) simultaneous voice and data service, and one D-channel that carriers call information and customer data at 16 KiloBytes Per Second (KBPS).

Basic services: Services performed by the common carriers to provide the transportation of information. Basic services are regulated. Contrast with enhanced services.

.BAT: The Microsoft Disk Operating System (MS-DOS) filename extension attached to a batch file.

Batch file: A file containing a series of Microsoft Disk Operating System (MS-DOS) commands executed one after the other, as though you had typed them. The mandatory .BAT file extension causes COMMAND. COM to process the file one line at a time. Batch files are useful when you need to type the same series of MS-DOS commands repeatedly. Almost all hard disk users have an AUTOEXEC.BAT file, a batch file that MS-DOS loads at the start of every operating session and establishes operating parameters.

Batch processing: A mode of computer operation in which program instructions are executed one after the other without user intervention. For example, batch processing is an efficient use of computer resources to print out large jobs during off-hours in a business. In interactive processing, you see the results of your commands on-screen so that you can correct errors and make necessary adjustments before completing the operation. Batch processing, on the other hand, does not allow you to catch errors. Reserve batch processing for well-tested routines such as system backups.

Battery pack: A rechargeable battery that supplies power to a portable computer when an external power source, such as a wall socket, is not available. Most battery packs use NIckel-CADmium (NiCad) batteries, which have two drawbacks: they're prone to becoming incapable of accepting a full charge, and, because of their cadmium content, are extremely toxic. Increasing in use are Nickel Metal Hydride (NiMH) and lithium-ion battery packs, which provide increased capacity without either drawback.

Baud: A unit of signaling speed in analog communications equal to the number of signal events per second. Not necessarily the same as Bits Per Second. *See* **Bits Per Second.**

Baud rate: The maximum number of changes that can occur per second in the electrical state of a communications circuit. Under RS-232c communications protocols, the baud rate equals the bits per second (bps) rate on an analog line until the maximum feasible 2400 changes per second is reached: 2400 baud is equal to 2400 bps. Higher signaling rates such as 9600 bps, 14.4 Kilobits per second (Kbps), and so forth are achieved by using increasingly complex modulation techniques to encode more data bits in the basic 2400 baud signal. These higher rates are properly referred to in terms of bps or Kbps.

BBS: *See* **Bulletin Board System.**

B-channel: A "bearer" channel that carriers voice or data at 64 Kilobits per second (Kbps) in either direction and is circuit-switched.

BCD: *See* **Binary Coded Decimal.**

BCI: *See* **Binary Coded Information.**

Beacon: The low-power signal transmitted by a satellite that contains status information for the engineers on the ground.

Beamwidth: The diameter of the signal a satellite antenna transmits. A wider beamwidth covers a greater area; a narrower beamwidth targets a smaller area. The narrower a beamwidth, the better it pinpoints a station and the more accurate its signal is.

Because It's Time NETwork (BITNET): A Wide Area Network (WAN) that links mainframe computer systems at approximately 2,500 universities and research institutions in North America, Europe, and Japan. BITNET (an acronym for Because It's Time NETwork) does not use Transmission Control Protocol/Internet Protocol (TCP/IP) protocols, but can exchange electronic mail with the Intent. BITNET is operated by the Corporation for Research and Education Networking (CREN), headquartered in Washington, D.C. To become a member of the network, an organization must pay for a leased line that connects to the nearest existing BITNET site-and it must also agree to let another institution connect with this line in the future.

Beginner's All-purpose Symbolic Instruction Code (BASIC): An easy-to-use high-level programming language popular on personal computers. Developed in 1965, BASIC is a procedural language that allows you to write step-by-step instructions. BASIC is easy to learn for those new to programming, although programs written in it execute slowly. C is far more popular for professional program development. Object-oriented programming techniques are giving BASIC a new lease on life. For example, Microsoft's Visual BASIC, designed for Microsoft Windows '95 programming, uses the Windows Graphical User Interface (GUI) and event-oriented programming to create impressive applications. *See* **Beginner's All-purpose Symbolic Instruction Code A; Compiler; Control structure; Debugger; GW-BASIC; Interpreter; Pascal; QuickBASIC; Spaghetti code; Structured programming.**

Beginner's All-purpose Symbolic Instruction Code A (BASICA): An interpreter for the Microsoft BASIC programming language. BASICA is supplied on the Microsoft Disk Operating System (MS-DOS) disk provided with IBM-manufactured personal computers.

Bell System: The collection of companies headed by AT&T and consisting of the 22 Bell Operating Companies and the Western Electric Corporation. The Bell System was dismantled by divestiture on January 1, 1984.

Benchmark: A standard measurement, determined by a benchmark program, that is used to test the performance of different brands of equipment. In computing, standard benchmark test (such as Dhrystones and Whetstones) do not provide accurate measures of a system's actual performance in an end-user computing environment. Most of these tests are Central Processing Unit-intensive (CPU-intensive); that is, they put the CPU through a mix of instructions, such as floating-point calculations, but do not test the performance of system components such as disk drives and internal communications. The speed of these components greatly affects the performance of end-user application programs. Benchmarks developed for personal computers, such as the Norton SI, include the performance of peripherals. *See* **Throughput.**

Benchmark program: A utility program used to measure a computer's processing speed so that its performance can be compared to that of other computers running the same program. Benchmark programs provide some indication of the number-crunching prowess of a Central Processing Unit (CPU), but the results generate may be close to meaningless. What counts for users is a system's throughput, its capability to push data not only through the CPU but also through all the system's peripheral components, including its disk drives. A computer with a fast processor (and a numeric coprocessor) performs well on benchmarks, but if the computer is equipped with a sluggish hard disk and lacks cache memory, the performance may disappoint the user. *See* **Cache memory, Central Processing Unit; Throughput; Utility program.**

Benchmark test: A test used to measure system speed or throughput.

BER: *See* **Bit Error Rate.**

Berkeley Software Distribution (BSD): A version of the UNIX operating system that was developed and formerly maintained by the University of California, Berkeley. BSD helped to establish the Internet in colleges and universities because the distributed software included Transmission Control Protocol/Internet Protocol (TCP/IP).

Berkeley UNIX: A version of the UNIX Operating System (OS) developed at the University of California at Berkeley, that takes full advantage of the virtual memory capabilities of Digital Equipment Corporation (DEC) minicomputers.

Beta site: The place where a beta test occurs. When developing a program or a version of an existing program, a company chooses beta sites where the program is subjected to demanding, heavy-duty usage. This process reveals the program's remaining bugs and shortcomings.

Beta software: In software testing, a preliminary version of a program that's widely distributed before commercial release to users who test the program by operating it under realistic conditions. *See* **Beta site; Beta test.**

Beta test: The second state in the testing of computer software, after alpha test but before commercial release. Beta tests are performed at beta sites. Also used as a verb, as in, the software is ready to be beta-tested.

Bezier curve: A mathematically generated line that can take the form of non-uniform curves. In a Bezier curve, the locations of two midpoints-called control handles - are used to describe the overall shape of an irregular curve. In graphics applications, by dragging the control handles (shown as small boxes on-screen), you can manipulate the complexity and shape of the curve.

Bid: In the contention form of invitation or selection, an attempt by the computer or by a station to gain control of the line so that it can transmit data. A bid may be successful or unsuccessful in seizing a circuit in that group. Contrast with seize.

Bi-directional parallel port: A parallel port, capable of both sending and receiving detailed messages, that can transfer data much faster than a standard parallel port. In its standard Institute of Electronic and Electrical Engineers (IEEE) 1284, the IEEE established the technical rules governing bi-directional parallel ports. Both the

Enhanced Parallel Port (EPP) and the Extended Capabilities Port (ECP) conform to IEEE 1284, and one of the two standards - probably the ECP, experts say-will replace the standard parallel port in the next few years.

Big Blue: An informal term for International Business Machines (IBM) Corporation, which uses blue as its corporate color.

Bin: Common abbreviation for a binary (program) file.

Binary: A method of representing data using two possible states. Binary numbering systems use digits with values of 1 (mark) and 0 (space).

Binary Coded Decimal (BCD): A method of coding long decimal numbers so that they can be processed with greater precision. Most personal computers work with binary numbers in 8-bit chunks called bytes. The biggest number that can be represented with 8 bits is 256, but that size causes problems for number crunching. BCD notation gets around this limitation by coding decimal numbers in binary form without really translating them into binary. For example, you cannot fit the binary equivalent of the number 260 into 8 bits, but you can fit the codes for 2, 6, and 0 into 3 adjacent bytes. A 3-digit decimal number takes up 3 bytes of storage. Increasing the number of bytes set aside in memory to store the number can accommodate larger numbers. Therefore, you have no limit to the precision that can be achieved in coding and processing numbers. Also, a very early code, similar in function to American Standard Code for Information Interchange (ASCII), that was used in the early 1960s to enable printers to print numeric characters. *See* **Binary Coded Information; Extended Binary-Coded Decimal Interchange Code; Precision.**

Binary Coded Information (BCI): An improvement on Binary Coded Decimal (BCD) that included codes for capital letters and some punctuation. *See* **Extended Binary-Coded Decimal Interchange Code.**

Binary compatible: In microprocessors, the capability to run software originally written for another company's Central Processing Unit (CPU). In software, a program that will run on any microprocessor with which it is binary compatible.

Binary digit: In binary notation, either the character 0 or 1. Synonymous with bit.

Binary file: A file containing data or program instructions in a computer-readable format. You cannot display the contents of a binary file using the Disk Operating System TYPE (DOS TYPE) command or a word processing program: they appear as happy faces, spades, clubs and other symbols.

Binary newsgroup: In Usenet, a newsgroup in which the articles contain (or are supposed to contain) binary files such as sounds, graphics, or movies. These files have been encoded with UUencode, a program that transforms a binary file into coded ASCII (American Standard Code for Information Interchange) characters so it can be transferred via the Internet. In order to use these files it is first necessary to decode them using a program called UUdecode.

Binary numbers: A number system with a base (radix) of 2, unlike the number systems most of us use, which have bases of 10 (decimal numbers), 12 (measurements in feet and inches), and 60 (time). Binary numbers are preferred for computers for precision and economy. Building an electronic circuit that can detect the difference between two states (high current and low current, or 0 and 1) is easy and inexpensive; building a circuit that detects the difference among 10 states (0 through 9) is much more difficult and expensive. The word bit derives from the phrase Binary digit.

Binary search: A search algorithm that avoids searching through every record by starting in the middle of a sorted database and determining whether the desired record is above or below the midpoint. Having reduced the number of records to be searched by 50 percent, the search proceeds to the middle of the remaining records, and so on, until the desired record is found.

Binary Synchronous Communications (BSC; BiSync): A communications protocol developed by IBM that has become an industry standard. It uses a defined set of control characters and control characters sequences for synchronized transmission of binary coded data between stations in a data communications system.

Binary transfer: A file transfer protocol that allows you to transfer binary files to a remote computer using terminal software.

Bindery: A database maintained by Novell's NetWare operating system that maintains information on users, servers and other elements of the network.

Binding: A process during which a protocol driver and Medium Access Control (MAC) driver exchange information, via the Network Driver Interface Specifications (NDIS) interface library, about identities, capabilities, function addresses, and binding context.

BinHex: A method of encoding binary files so that the coded file contains nothing but the standard American Standard Code for Information Interchange (ASCII) characters, and can therefore be transferred to other computers via the Internet. The receiving computer must decode the file using BinHex-capable decoding software. BinHex is popular among Macintosh users.

BIOS: *See* **Basic Input/Output System.**

Bis: Meaning "second" in Latin this term is used as a suffix to denote a secondary version of an International Telecommunications Union-Telecommunications (ITU-T) modem standard.

B-ISDN: *See* **Broadband Integrated Services Digital Network.**

BiSync: *See* **Binary Synchronous Communications.**

Bit: The smallest unit of information in a digital signal, 0 or 1, it is the basic unit of information in a binary numbering system. Computers work well with binary numbers because the internal circuitry can easily represent the two digits in a binary system: 1 is represented by a high current and a 0 is represented by a low current. Because this process is relatively easy and inexpensive, computers are very accurate in their internal processing capabilities. Computes typically make less than one internal error in every 100 billion processing operations. *See* **Byte.**

Bit Error Rate (BER): The number of bits in a data stream that is incorrect.

Bit map: The representation of an image stored in a computer's memory as a matrix of bits. Because each tiny dot on the screen (pixel), is controlled by an on or off code stored as a bit in the computer's memory, bit-mapped graphics consume very large amounts of memory—both in Read Access Memory (RAM) and on the hard drive. *See* **Bit; Block graphics; Pixel.**

Bit-mapped font: A screen or printer font in which each character is composed of a pattern of dots, and is designed to look best at one particular resolution. To display or print bit-mapped fonts, the computer or printer must keep a full representation of each character in memory. When referring to bit-mapped fonts, the term font should be taken literally as a complete set of characters of a given typeface, weight, posture, and type size. If you want to use Palatino Roman 12 and Palatino Italic 14, for example, you must load two complete sets of characters into memory. You can not re-size bit-mapped fonts without producing distortions (aliasing) in the appearance.

Bit-mapped graphic: A graphic image formed by a pattern of pixels and limited in resolution to the maximum resolution of the display or printer on which it is displayed. Bit-mapped graphics are produced by paint programs such as MacPaint, SuperPaint, GEM Paint, PC Paintbrush, as well as some scanning programs. Considered inferior to object-oriented graphics for most applications, bit-mapped graphics may have aliasing caused buy the square shape of pixels. Irregularities are visible when the image includes diagonal lines and curves. Additionally, resizing a bit-mapped graphic image without introducing distortions is almost impossible, and bit-mapped graphics require large amounts of memory. *See* **Encapsulated PostScript file; Object-oriented graphic.**

BITNET: *See* **Because It's Time NETwork.**

Bit-oriented protocol: A communications protocol that uses only one special character called the flag character, to mark the beginning and end of a message. All other combinations of bits are treated as valid data characters.

Bit rate: The speed at which bits are transmitted, usually expressed in bits per second (bps). At high speeds, not equal to the baud rate.

Bit stuffing: A technique of inserting redundant bits into a data stream to avoid confusing data with control symbols.

Bit synchronization: A method of ensuring that a communications circuit is sampled at the appropriate time to determine the presence or absence of a bit.

Bit time: The duration of one bit symbol (1/BR). Ethernet specifies 10 million bits per second or 10 Megabits per second (Mbps).

Bits per second (bps): In asynchronous communications, a measurement of data transmission speed based on the number of bits that can be encoded into a signal change. Bits per second (bps) rates are used to measure the performance of serial ports and, particularly, modems. In modems, transmission speeds faster than 2400 baud are described in terms of bps for the sake of accuracy. On an analog line the signaling itself rate never exceeds 2400 signals per second (baud); however, sophisticated modulation techniques enable each signal to carry multiple bits per second.

Blanking: In video communications, the part of the signal transmitted between picture frames.

Bleed: In desktop publishing, a photograph, text box, or other page-design element that extends to the very edge of the page. This usually isn't possible if you're printing with a laser printer, which can't print in a 1/4-inch strip around the page's perimeter.

Bleed capacity: The ability of a printer to print bleeds.

Blessed folder: The Macintosh folder containing a System file and a Finder file. The blessed folder acts like a Microsoft Disk Operating System (MS-DOS) directory named in the PATH command because the System Folders is the only folder the System consults when it can't find a file.

Macintosh users, therefore, are obliged to place all the configuration files required by their application programs in this folder, which can quickly grow so large that keeping track of its contents is difficult. Moving the System and Finder files into another folder is called 'blessing' a folder.

Blind carbon copy (BCC): In electronic mail, a copy of a message that is sent to one or more persons without the knowledge of the recipient.

Block: A string of records, words, characters or bits which, for technical or logical reasons, is treated as an entity. A set of things, such as words, characters, or digits, handled as a unit. A group of bits, or characters, transmitted as a unit. An encoding procedure is generally applied to the group of bits or characters for error-control purposes. The portion of a message terminated by an EOB or ETB line-control character or, if it is the last block in the message, by an EOT or ETX line-control character.

Block Check Character (BCC): In longitudinal redundancy checking and cyclic redundancy checking, a character that is transmitted by the sender after each message block and is compared with a block check character computed by the receiver to determine if the transmission was successful.

Block graphics: When working with IBM PC-compatible computers, graphics formed on-screen by standardized graphics characters in the extended character set. The graphic characters in the IBM extended character set are suitable for creating on-screen rectangles but not for fine detail. Because the block graphics characters are handled the same way as ordinary characters, the computer can display block graphics considerably faster than bit-mapped graphics. *See* **Bit-mapped graphic; Graphics character.**

Block operation: The act of transferring a chunk, or block of information from one area to another. In word processing, an editing or formatting operation—such as copying, deleting, moving, or underlining—performed on a marked block of text.

.BMP: In Microsoft Windows '95, an extension indicating that the file contains a Windows-compatible bit-mapped graphic.

BNC connector: A small coaxial connector with a half-twist locking shell.

Board: *See* **Adapter; Circuit board.**

Body type: The font (usually 10- to 12-point) used to set paragraphs of text, distinguished from the font used to set headings, captions, and other typographical elements.

Boilerplate: A block of text used over and over in letters, memos, or reports. You can use boilerplates to achieve big speed gains in your writing. For example, if your job involves answering routine inquiry letters, develop boilerplate responses to questions and save the text in a file. Then you can write a letter just by inserting one or two boiler-plate files and adding a few personalized touches.

BOM: Beginning of Message.

Bomb: *See* **Crash.**

Bookmark: In general, a code inserted at a particular point in a document so that it can easily be found later. You typically insert book-marks on often-used pages of an application program Help file. In Netscape or other Web browser, a bookmark is used to make note of your favorite places on the World Wide Web (WWW).

Boolean search: A search that involves the use of Boolean operators (AND, OR, and NOT). In a Boolean search, you can use these opera-tors to refine the scope of your search. OR increases the data set, AND narrows the data set. NOT ignores an item. A search for "Chardonnay OR Cabernet" returns all the items that mention either Chardonnay or Cabernet. A search for "Chardonnay AND Cabernet" returns only those documents that mention both wines. A search for "Chardonnay and Cabernet NOT Merlot" returns only those items that mention both Chardonnay and Cabernet, but omits those that also mention Merlot. Boolean searches are often used in bibliographic retrieval serv-ices and on the World Wide Web (WWW).

Boot: To initiate an automatic routine that clears the memory, loads the operating system, and prepares the computer for use. Included in the computer's Read Only Memory (ROM) is the Power On Self-Test (POST) which executes when the power is switched on (a cold boot). After a system crash or lockup occurs, you usually must initialize the computer again, or reboot, by pressing the Reset button or Ctrl+Alt+Del (a warm boot).

BOOTP: Bootstrap Protocol.

Boot Protocol (BOOTP): A Transmission Control Protocol/Internet Protocol (TCP/IP) network protocol that lets network nodes request configuration information from a BOOTP "server" node.

Boot Read Only Memory (Boot ROM): A Read Only Memory chip that allows a workstation to communicate with the file server and to read a DOS boot program from the server. Stations can thus operate on the network without having a disk drive.

Boot record: The first track on an IBM PC-compatible hard or floppy disk (track 0). After you turn on the power, the boot-up software in Read Only Memory (ROM) instructs the computer to read this track to begin loading the Microsoft Disk Operating System (MS-DOS). *See* **Boot.**

Boot ROM: *See* **Boot Read Only Memory.**

Boot sector: The first track on an IBM PC-compatible hard or floppy drive (track 0). During the boot process, Read Only Memory (ROM) tells the computer to read the first block of data on this track and loads whatever program is found there. If system files are found, they direct the computer to load the Microsoft Disk Operating System (MS-DOS).

Boot sequence: The order in which a computer's Basic Input/Output System (BIOS) searches disk drives for operating system files. Unless programmed otherwise, IBM PCs and compatibles look for the operating system on drive A first, then search the C drive. To speed up your computer's boot procedure you can use the BIOS setup program to make it search drive C first. The ability to boot from either drive assures you will be able to boot from the A drive in case of a hard drive failure.

BOOTP: Bootstrap Protocol.

BOT: In Multi-User Dungeons (MUDs) and Internet Relay Chat (IRC), a character whose on-screen actions stem from a program rather than a real person. The term is a contraction of robot. The most famous of all bots, Julia, inhibits a MUD called LambdaMoo, and has tricked thousands into thinking that she is a real human being.

Bottleneck: A point within a communications link where the data flow is slowest.

BPS: See **Bits per second.**

Branch control structure: In programming, a control structure that tells a program to branch to a set of instructions only if a specified condition is met. If a program detects that a vital data file has been irretrievably corrupted, for example, the program branches to display a message that says something like, "The file you want to open is corrupted." Synonymous with selections. *See* **IF/THEN/ELSE.**

Break: A user-initiated signal that interrupts processing or receiving data.

Break-out box: A testing device inserted into a communications cable or between a serial port and a serial cable that allows each wire to be tested separately.

Breakpoint: A location in a program where it pauses to let the user decide what to do next. If you're writing a complex macro, include several breakpoints so that you can check your progress and decide whether to continue.

BRI: *See* **Basic-Rate Interface.**

Bridge: In a Local Area Network (LAN) a device that allows two networks (even ones dissimilar in topology, wiring or communications protocols) to exchange data as through a single network existed.

Broadband: In Local Area Networks (LANs), a communications channel with a bandwidth greater than 64 KBPS. Broadband communications channels often use coaxial cabling, and analog as well as digital signaling to support intensive data communications applications such as video and multimedia. The signal is usually split, or multiplexed, to provide multiple communications channels. Broadband communications can extend over great distances and operate at extremely high speeds. A broadband network can, like a cable TV network, convey two or more communication channels at a time (the channels are separated by frequency). Therefore, a broadband network can handle both voice and data communications. *See* **Analog; Analog transmission; Bandwidth; Baseband; Local Area Network.**

Broadband Integrated Services Digital Network (B-ISDN): Another term used for a cell relay digital network using Asynchronous Transfer Mode (ATM). B-ISDN operates at data rates in excess of 1.544 MegaBytes Per Second (MBPS) or 2.048 MBPS, and enables transport and switching of voice, data, image, and video over a single infrastructure.

Broadband signaling: A method of signaling in which multiple signals share the bandwidth of the transmission media by the subdivision of the bandwidth into channels based on frequency (multiplexing).

Broadband transmission: A transmission technique of a Local Area Network (LAN) in which the signal is transmitted in analog form with frequency division multiplexing.

Broadcast: The simultaneous transmission of a message to multiple stations.

Broadcast band: The range of radio frequencies between 550 KiloHertz (KHz) and 1600 KHz used for commercial Amplitude Modulation (AM) broadcasting.

B-router: A network device that can perform the functions of both a bridge and a router.

Brownout: A period of low-voltage electrical power caused by unusually heavy demand, such as that created by summertime air-conditioner use. Brownouts can cause computers to operate erratically or to crash, either of which can result in data loss. If brownouts frequently cause your computer to crash, you may need to buy a line-interactive uninterruptible power supply to work with your machine.

Browse: To use a dialog list box to look for a documents or directory. In a database management program, to use a dialog or list box to look for a data record. When you use a Browse dialog box, you can restrict the number of files shown at one time by selecting a single file type in the List Files of Types list box.

Browser: *See* **Web browser.**

Browsing: On the World Wide Web (WWW), an information-seeking method that involves manually searching through linked documents. Browsing is rarely as effective for finding information on a specific topic as using a subject trees or a search engine. Synonymous with surfing. *See* **Search engine; Subject tree.**

Brute force: In programming, a crude technique for solving a difficult problem by repeating a simple procedure many times, for example, 'multiplying' two numbers by performing a long series of additions.

BSC: *See* **Binary Synchronous Communications.**

BSD: *See* **Berkeley Software Distribution.**

BSD UNIX: *See* **Berkeley UNIX.**

Bubble-jet printer: A variation on the ink jet printer concept that uses heating elements instead of piezoelectric crystals to shoot ink from nozzles.

Buffer: A temporary storage space for data. A buffer is ordinarily used to as a timing coordination device to compensate for the difference in the speeds of two or more processes.

Buffer description: A data structure containing information about a buffer, such as a pointer to the buffer's physical location, the number of bytes, and the size. This does not include actual data in the buffer.

Buffering: The storage of bits or characters until they are specifically released. For example, a buffered terminal is one in which the keyed characters are stored in an internal storage area or buffer until a special key such as the CARRIAGE RETURN or ENTER key is pressed. Then all of the characters stored in the buffer are transmitted to the host computer in one operation.

Bug: A programming error that causes a program or a computer system to perform erratically, produce incorrect results, or crash. The term bug was coined when a real insect was discovered to have fouled up one of the circuits of the first electronic digital computer, the Electronic Numerical Integrator And Calculator/Computer (ENIAC). A hardware problem is called a glitch.

Built-in font: A printer font encoded permanently in the printer's Read Only Memory (ROM). All laser printers offer at least one built-in typeface, also called a resident font. You should consider buying a printer with several typefaces, including a Roman-style, font with serifs such as Times Roman, and a clean sans serif font such as Helvetica. Check a printer's literature for a list of the built-in fonts and whether they're scalable. *See* **Cartridge front; Downloadable font; Screen font.**

Built-in function: In a spreadsheet program, a ready-to-use formula that performs mathematical, statistical, trigonometric, financial, and other calculations. A built-in function begins with a special symbol (usually @ or =), followed by a keyword, such as AVG or SUM, that describes the formula's purpose. Most built-in functions require one or more arguments enclosed in parentheses and separated by commas (argument separators).

Bulk-storage: Magnetic media that can store data. Synonymous with mass storage. *See* **Secondary storage.**

Bullet list chart: In presentation graphics, a text chart that lists a series of ideas or items of equal weight.

Bulletin Board System (BBS): A telecommunications utility usually set up by a personal computer hobbyist for the enjoyment of other hobbyists.

Bulletproof: Capable, because of high fault tolerance, of resisting external interference and recovering from situations that would crash other programs.

Bundled software: Software included with a computer hardware system as part of the system's total price. Bundled software is also considered several programs that are packaged and sold together.

Burn-in: A power-on test of a computer system, performed on behalf of the customer. Semiconductor components such as memory chips and microprocessors tend to fail either very early or very late in their lives. Responsible computer retailers, therefore, run systems continuously for 24 to 48 hours before releasing the systems to customers. Defective chips are likely to fail during the burn-in period.

Bus network: In a Local Area Network (LAN), a decentralized network topology used by AppleTalk and EtherNet, for example, in which a single connecting line, the bus, is shared by a number of nodes, including workstations, shared peripherals, and file servers. In a bus network, a workstation sends every message to all other workstations. Each node in the network has an unique address, and its reception circuitry monitors the bus for messages being sent to the node, ignoring all other messages. Bus networks have a significant advantage over competing network designs (star topology and ring topology) since the failure of a single node doesn't disrupt the rest of the network. Extending a bus network also is a simple matter; just lengthen the bus and add nodes, up to the system's maximum (about 1,000 feet without a repeater).

Bus topology: The structure used in Local Area Networks (LANs) whereby connection between devices is accomplished by connecting all devices to a single transmission medium such as fiber or wire.

Button: In a Graphical User Interface (GUI) a dialog box option used to execute a command, choose an option, or open another dialog box. *See* **Pushbutton; Radio button.**

Bypass: Installing private telecommunications circuits to avoid using those of a carrier.

Byte: Eight contiguous bits, the fundamental data unit of personal computers. A unique combination of bits represents a specific character or number. The meaning of each of the 256 unique 8-bit combinations has been codified by the American Society of Information Interchange (ASCII). The term Kilo (thousand, as in KiloByte, abbreviated KB) and Mega (million, as in MegaByte, abbreviated MB) are used to count multiple bytes. Because they are derived from decimal (base 10) numbers, one KB is actually 1,024 bytes, and one MB is actually 1,048,576 bytes.

C: A high level programming language preferred by most major software publishers. C combines the advantages of high-level programming languages with the efficiency of an assembly language. Many larger programs are written in C or C++; shareware programs are usually written in Visual Beginner's All-purpose Symbolic Instruction Code (Visual BASIC). Because the programmer can embed critical instructions, C programs run significantly faster than other high-level programming languages.

C: In most personal computers, the drive letter assigned to the first (default) hard disk dive.

C++: A high-level programming language developed by Bjarne Stroustrup at AT&T Bell Laboratories. C++ is considered the standard programming language for several major software vendors, such as Apple Computers, because it combines C languages virtues with the advantages of object-oriented programming.

C band: The radio communications band between 4 billion Hertz (GigaHertz or GHz) and 8 GHz. The 4 Ghz band is the down link wavelength, and the 6 GHz band is the uplink wavelength.

Cache: A storage area holding quickly available information so that it doesn't have to be accessed from slow storage sources. Caches improve performance by storing data in faster sections of memory and by using efficient design to anticipate data needed in the next cache. Access speeds are determined by the amount Random Access Memory (RAM). *See* **Hardware cache.**

Cache controller: A chip, (for example, Intel 82385), using from 32 KiloBytes (KB) to 256KB and controlling the retrieval, storage and delivery of data to and from cache memory on a hard disk. The cache controller handles the request from the Central Processing Unit (CPU) and the delivery of data from the Random Access Memory (RAM) area. The cache controller determines the storage, delivery, delivery timing, management, etc. of data to be accessed. The cache controller also keeps an up-to-date table of the addresses of its held data. *See* **Disk cache; Disk drive controller.**

Cache memory: Also called external cache. Fast memory chips controlled by the cache controller chip; these chips set aside to store most frequently accessed information from the Random Access Memory (RAM) area. Cache memory is usually 32 KiloBytes (KB) to 512 KB of Static Random Access Memory (SRAM) chips with its own bus (connection) to the Central Processing Unit (CPU). Cache memory is distinguished from software caches, a slower area of RAM for storing information retrieved from disk drives. Cache memory frees the computer from having to wait for the Dynamic Random Access Memory (DRAM) chips to catch up. *See* **Wait state.**

CAD: *See* **Computer-Aided Design.**

CADD: *See* **Computer-Aided Design and Drafting.**

Caddy: A plastic tray used to carry Compact Disks (CDs) into the compact disk's read-only drive area and protects the surface of the disk from human intervention or dust.

CAI: *See* **Computer-Assisted Instruction.**

Call: An instruction within the program that transfers a program execution to a subroutine and after execution returns to the next command after the call statement.

Callback: A very popular technique that determines which user is allowed to connect to the network. It is used mostly for security reasons. The connection is made after a user calls and identifies himself or herself. Then, the computer breaks the connection and calls the user back.

Call For Votes (CFV): A newsgroup's (such as USENET) control procedure that allows voting for or against a new newsgroup's creation. The voting period is between 21 days and 31 days. There is, however, no way to push USENET administrators to stop or accelerate the decision or decision-making process.

Call packet: Data that contain information (along with addresses) required to set the characteristics of an X.25 Switched Virtual Circuit (SVC).

Call record: The record of each data such as a dialed number, a time stamp, or the mobile numbers needed to bill cellular phone call users.

Call set up time: The total elapsed time needed to connect a switched phone call; this equals the time between the start (dialing) and end (answering) of the sequence for the receiver.

Call waiting: An option offered by most telephone companies where an incoming call is put on hold while you are answering another one.

Camera-ready copy: Any variety of illustrations ready to be reproduced as a picture or illustration in a finished publication.

Campus-Wide Information System (CWIS): A system that connects students, universities, and its staff to an on-line service containing vital information such as registration information, class lists, faculty and department phone numbers, etc.

Cancelbot: An Internet program that locates and removes those users who post (or spam) unwanted messages to USENET newsgroups.

Cancelmoose: In USENET, an individual that uses a cancelbot. Therefore, a cancelmoose has the ability/permission to cancel any other user's unwanted articles or insertions.

Capture: To record an activity and store it in a file which can be opened later within the modem communications field. Also, captures represent all or part of an image on-screen. This image can be converted to a graphics file in order to save it to a disk.

Caret: A symbol commonly used in spreadsheet programs, (for example, Excel, Lotus 1-2-3, etc.), for exponent functions. Also, this symbol is used in computer documentation as a representative of the Control key. So, for example, CTRL + F is seen on the screen as ^F.

Carpal Tunnel Syndrome: *See* **Repetitive Strain Injury.**

Carpet bomb: *See* **Spamming.**

Carriage return: A special command that forces a printer head to move to the left margin. Some printers perform a line feed while carrying out the carriage return command.

Carriage Return (CR) character: A character displayed or printed that is moved by a format command to the first position on the same line. Contrast with line feed character.

Carrier: A signal that consolidates information to be transmitted (in an analog system). Also, a company that provides telecommunications networks. *See* **Carrier wave.**

Carrier detect signal: A signal that indicates a successful connection sent from a modem to the computer.

Carrier-Sense Multiple Access/Collision Avoidance (CSMA/CA): A network transmission method allowing one carrier at a time on the line. Colli-sion Avoidance (CA) reduces the frequency with which collisions can occur.

Carrier Sense Multiple Access with Collision Detection (CSMA/CD): In a Local Area Network (LAN), a network transmission method in which the network randomly decides which computer can use the network. This method is employed by small-sized to medium-sized networks. Larger networks use token passing or polling. *See* **AppleTalk; Ethernet; Local Area Network; Node; Polling; Token passing.**

Carrier System: A system which contains a number of channels where each channel is modulated on a different frequency and demodulated to restore the original signal.

Carrier wave: A signal in analog communication without any information within it.

Cartesian coordinate system: A mathematical method for locating a point in a two-dimensional space characterized by a vertical and horizontal axis. The system is used to locate the position of the mouse on the computer display. In some applications (for example, Flow, Visio), the pointer position is described by coordinates.

Cartridge: A removable part of a system. In a computer, this could be a magnetic tape or disk; in the printer, this could be the ink container. A cartridge is also a module that expands the memory of computers or expands a printer's font capabilities.

Cartridge font: Fonts written in the Read Only Memory (ROM) cartridge that is used as a portable and immediate source of fonts and their characteristics. Another advantage of cartridge fonts is that they are not impinging upon the printer's Random Access Memory (RAM).

Cascading menu: A menu's system that instructs a submenu to appear (cascade) when the right-pointing triangle in the drop-down or pop-up menu; is activated. Synonymous with submenu.

Cascading window: A window viewing option (one of at least three) that allows several windows to overlap. With this option, the user can see the titles of all of the opened windows and the contents of the front selected window. The windows usually cascade up and to the left.

Case-sensitive search: A type of character or word search in which matching is based on the exact pattern of the original string of characters. Upper case and lower case letters must be typed exactly as seen in the original form or string.

Case-sensitivity: Upper case and lower case letter sensitivity of the operating system. The Disk Operating System (DOS) is not case-sensitive. Therefore, the user can type commands in both lower-case and upper case letters. UNIX is, however, case-sensitive, so all commands must be typed as specified.

Catalog: In database management (dBASE), a list of related files grouped together by the user in order for ease in retrieving of similar items. *See* **dBASE; Join; Relational DataBase Management System.**

Cathode Ray Tube (CRT): Another term for monitor (though monitor is more popular). A CRT contains a vacuum tube with an electron gun to emit electrons that illuminate the phosphor on the inside of the screen. *See* **Monitor; Phosphor; Refresh.**

CAV: *See* **Constant Angular Velocity.**

CBDS: *See* **Connectionless Broadband Data Service.**

41

CBT: *See* **Computer-Based Training.**

CCITT: *See* **Consultative Committee for International Telephony and Telegraphy.**

CCP: *See* **Certified Computer Programmer.**

CD: *See* **Compact Disk.**

CD-DA: *See* **Compact Disk-Digital Audio.**

CDEV: *See* **Control panel DEVice.**

CD-I: *See* **Compact Disk-Interactive.**

CDMA: *See* **Code Division Multiple Access.**

CDPD: *See* **Cellular Digital Packet Data.**

CD-ROM: *See* **Compact Disk-Read Only Memory.**

CD-ROM/SD: *See* **Compact Disk-Read Only Memory Super Density.**

CD-ROM XA: *See* **Compact Disk-Read Only Memory eXtended Architecture.**

Cell: In calculation programs, an intersection of a row and a column that contains text and/or numbers. In Asynchronous Transfer Mode (ATM), the transmission unit that contains a five-byte header and a 48-byte payload.

Cell Error Ratio: The ratio of errored cells in a transmission in relation to the total cells sent in a transmission. The measurement is taken over a time interval and is desirable to be measured on an in-service circuit.

Cell Loss Ratio (CLR): An Asynchronous Transfer Mode (ATM) performance parameter that specifies the ratio of nondelivered cells to the total number of cells transmitted over a given circuit.

Cell protection: In calculation programs, (for example, Excel, Lotus 1-2-3, etc.), an option applied to one or many cells preventing the user from changing the contents of a cell. Either cells, entire worksheets, or entire workbooks can be protected.

Cellular Digital Packet Data (CDPD): Transmission of digital packets over free (not busy) analog lines of an Advanced Mobile Phone System (AMPS).

Cellular Geographic Service Area (CGSA): The area where the cellular service is being performed.

Cellular telephone service: A service provided by companies responsible for handling phone calls to and from moving vehicles. These phone calls are transmitted to and from radio transmitters in each geographic area and passed from transmitters each time the vehicle leaves one area and enters another.

Centa call seconds: A typical measurement of a circuit utilization which is 100 seconds of utilization.

Central office (CO): The nearest office to the user's facility telephone switching office that serves private and corporate users to their own loop lines.

Central office switch: A device that allows connection of any circuit to another circuit.

Central Processing Unit (CPU): The functional brain of a computer. The CPU is an essential part of the computer system. The CPU contains the processing and control circuitry and contains the Arithmetic Logic Unit (ALU), the Read Only Memory (ROM), Random Access Memory (RAM), and the Control Unit. *See* **Arithmetic Logic Unit; Control Unit; Expansion bus; Microprocessor; Motherboard; Primary storage.**

Centralized network: A synonym for star topology network or star network.

Centrex: The telephone equipment located in the central office that serves users on a private automatic branch exchange basis.

Centronics Interface: The parallel port on the back of all Personal Computers (PCs) and PC-compatible computers. Its name was taken from the company that designed the first parallel port. Synonymous with parallel port.

CERN: *See* **European Laboratory for Particle Physics.**

CERT: *See* **Computer Emergency Response Team.**

Certified Computer Programmer (CCP): A title received from the Institute for Certification of Computer Professionals (ICCP) after passing exams in programming rules and concepts.

CGA: *See* **Color Graphics Adapter.**

CGI: *See* **Common Gateway Interface.**

CGM: *See* Computer Graphics Metafile.

CGSA: *See* Cellular Geographic Service Area.

Chain printing: The printing option that allows printing separate files as one unit by positioning commands at the end of the first file that calls the second file which calls the third and so on. *See* **Master document.**

Challenge Handshake Authentication Protocol (CHAP): A protocol (Point-to-Point Protocol or PPP) in which a password is required to begin a connection as well as during the connection. If the password fails any of these requirements, the system breaks the connection.

Change coordination meeting: A meeting in which system changes are approved and passed to all interested members.

Change management: The use of principles set by administrators that prohibits system changes by unauthorized users. The only allowed users to make changes are those who administrate the computer systems.

Channel: A path information travels on established between a sender and receiver.

Channel access: In a Local Area Network (LAN) a networking method for gaining access through the nodes to the data communication channels that link computers. *See* **Contention; Local Area Network; Polling; Token-Ring network.**

Channel Service Unit (CSU): *See* **Data Service Unit.**

Channel, voice grade: A communication channel used to transmit speech or data in analog form; the frequency range is from 300 Hertz (Hz) to 3400 Hz.

CHAP: *See* **Challenge Handshake Authentication Protocol.**

Character: Any symbol produced by keying in. A character takes about one byte of information.

Character graphics: *See* **Block graphics.**

Character-mapped display: A display method wherein an image is set in a section of memory and can be modified anywhere on-screen. *See* Teletype display.

Character mode: A display mode that shows only characters held in the computer's built-in character (font) set. Also, a communications protocol that uses special characters at the beginning and end of messages.

Character set: The set of codes that a computer system uses such as the American Standard Code for Information Interchange (ASCII). *See* **American Standard Code for Information Interchange; Code page; Extended character set.**

Character string: Any series of symbols or spaces.

Characters Per Inch (CPI): The number of characters per inch for each given font. The standard typewriting CPI is 10 CPI (Pica) and 12 CPI (Elite).

Characters Per Second (CPS): The number of characters transmitted per second via the modem.

Charge-Coupled Device (CCD): A device that is used to convert reflected light into an electrical signal. The number of CCDs packed in a row determines a resolution of a scanner.

Chart forum: A conference or forum that allows users (single or group) to communicate with each other. Usually, the forum is used to exchange information about games, software, etc.

Check bit: A binary digit responsible for checking for errors within the associated character or block.

Check box: The box that specifies if the option is on or off. The check box may be alone or with list of check boxes. *See* **Dialog box; Graphical User Interface; Radio button.**

Checkpoint restart: The process of restarting a data processing job within a process that shuts down abnormally. Checkpoint restarts may be automatic or deferred.

Checksum: A field created by adding bits or characters for a result that claims for error checking.

Chief Information Officer (CIO): The highest executive in charge of a company's information resources.

Child: Any object or process that is secondary or subordinate to (or springs from) a main object or process.

Child node: A node at the next lower level of the hierarchy that is contained in the peer group represented by the logical group node currently referenced.

Child peer group: A child peer group of a peer group is any one containing a child node of a logical group node in that peer group.

Chip: An electronic circuit produced on a thin wafer made mostly of silicon as a semiconducting material. *See* **Integrated circuit; Microprocessor.**

Chip set: A group of chips that performs similar functions, for example, generating video displays. A common chip set is the Rockwell chip set used for modems. Synonymous with chipset.

Chooser: A Macintosh Desktop Accessory (DA) supplied by Apple Computer. As part of the operation system of the Macintosh, the chooser is in charge of programs that control communication within the network and printer environments.

Chrominance: In multimedia, the part of the video signal that contains color information.

Ciphertext: An encrypted message readable only by the receiver who knows how to decode the message. *See* **Encryption; Public key cryptography.**

CIR: *See* **Committed Information Rate.**

Circuit: An electrical channel or path that allows communication between two or more devices.

Circuit board: A plastic board with built-in circuits. Synonymous with printed circuit boards. *See* **Motherboard.**

Circuit grade: The level of information-carrying circuits. There are several circuit grades such as voice, subvoice, broadband, and telegraph that varies with the speed of the system.

Circuit switching: A data transmitting method that sets up an unbroken circuit path between communicating devices.

Circuit switching network: A type of Wide Area Network (WAN) characterized by transmitting and receiving stations hooked up in a single circuit by using switching mechanisms.

CISC: *See* **Complex Instruction Set Computer.**

Cladding: The glass that surrounds a fiber optic cable.

Clari: In USENET, a hierarchy that contains read only newsgroups. The Clari is open to every user who pays a fee the ClariNet organization that combines copyrighted and registered wire articles in one place.

Class 1 fax: A standard class for sending faxes that takes care of the physical process of transmitting faxes while the preparation of faxes for transmission are the software's job.

Class 2 fax: A standard class for sending faxes that takes care of the physical process and preparation of transmitting faxes. Class 2 faxes are more expensive than Class 1 types since the Class 2 types also take care of the preparation phase.

Class A Certification: A U.S. Federal Communications Commission (FCC) certification for specific computer models. Class A certification limits Radio Frequency Interference (RFI) which is set for the commercial environment.

Class A network: A network that makes up to 16,777,215 separate Internet addresses (called Internet Protocol addresses or IP addresses) accessible. Current limitations are for 128 Class A networks.

Class B Certification: A U.S. Federal Communications Commission (FCC) certification for specific computer models. Class B certification limits Radio Frequency Interference (RFI) which is set for the home environment. The Class B standards are more likely to interfere radio and television signal reception.

Class B network: On the Internet, a network allocating up to 55,535 distinct Internet addresses (called Internet Protocol addresses or IP addresses). Current Internet addressing defines a maximum of 16,384 Class B networks.

Class C network: On the Internet, a network allocating up to 256 distinct Internet addresses (called Internet Protocol addresses or IP addresses). Current Internet addressing defines a maximum of 2,097,152 Class C networks.

Clear packet: A defined size of data that contains a command performing a function similar to hanging up the telephone.

Clear To Send/Request To Send (CTS/RTS): Also called hardware handshaking. A method of data flow control that prevents the computer from sending more information than the modem can handle.

Client: A workstation which can request information from a file server. *See* **Client/Server network; File server; Local Area Network.**

Client application: In Object Linking and Embedding (OLE), an application wherein the user places a linked or embedded object.

Client-based application: An application that is located on the computer's hard drive and is accessible only by the user even though the computer system is in the client/server network. *See* **Client/Server network; File server; Local Area Network; Server-based application.**

Client/Server architecture: A model of back-end and front-end processing where back-end operations can handle the processes on a server and the front-end operations communicates with the user on the workstation. *See* **Local Area Network; Wide Area Network.**

Client/Server computing: A system that divides processing between workstations (clients) and servers (servers). Typically, clients use data taken from the servers. The system allows for stand-alone versions and, of course, provides for true client/server work. Structured Query Language (SQL) is the processing language.

Client/Server model: *See* **Client/Server architecture.**

Client/Server network: The Local Area Network (LAN) that allows computing power to be distributed but centralizes shared resources in a file server. *See* **Client/Server architecture; Peer-to-peer network.**

Clip art: A graphic file used in presentation programs (PowerPoint, etc.), word processing programs (Word, etc.), or desktop publishing programs (PhotoShop, etc.) and other applications. The file contains a picture or graphic ready to be located on letters, brochures, cards, etc.

Clipboard: A temporary memory area where cut or copied data is stored for later use when pasted. The clipboard holds only one entry at a time and all data are lost when the computer is turned off.

Clipper Chip: A U.S. encryption technology on a semiconductor that might give individuals the opportunity to encrypt their messages successfully and completely. A backdoor is included in the chip that allows law enforcement agencies to read the encryption if necessary and if they have a warrant.

Clock: A tiny circuit generating equal impulses with a speed of millions of Hertz which are used to synchronize the flow of information throughout the computer. *See* **Clock speed.**

Clock cycle: The time measured between two impulses of the system's internal clock.

Clock doubled: A microprocessor with twice the speed of the motherboard system clock. The double speed, however, does not improve speeds outside of the microprocessor.

Clock speed: The speed of the internal clock that sets all the speeds at which operations are performed. The speed of the clock affects performance yet is not the only factor.

Clone: A hardware copy of an existing device that works and performs its function as well as or often better than the original.

Close box: A control box that may include a pull-down menu. This mainly used to close a window. Also called a control menu box.

CLR: *See* **Cell Loss Ratio.**

Cluster: A unit containing sectors of information on the hard drive. If a floppy or hard drive contains bad clusters, Scandisk (software) will mark the bad clusters in order to correct them or allow the system to bypass them. *See* **File fragmentation; File Allocation Table; Sector.**

Cluster controller: A computer between terminals and a mainframe that collects all the messages from the terminals and amplifies them over a single link to the mainframe.

CLV: *See* **Constant Linear Velocity.**

CMIP: *See* **Common Management Information Protocol.**

CMOS: *See* **Complementary Metal-Oxide Semiconductor.**

CMYK: A model creating colors from combinations of Cyan, Magenta, Yellow, and blacK. The CMYK model handles various color devices better than the Red-Green-Blue (RGB) and HSB models.

Coaxial cable: A cable built up of a conductor surrounded by a polyethylene insulator and encased within a sheath. Coaxial cable is more expensive telephone wire (twisted-pair) and can carry more data. *See* **Bandwidth; Broadband; Local Area Network; Twisted pair cable.**

COBOL: *See* **COmmon Business-Oriented Language.**

Co-channel interference: Interference during transmission at the same frequency.

Code: A set and/or conventions of rules that describe the form of data, transmission flow, receiving and processing methods. *See* **Algorithm.**

Code Division Multiple Access (CDMA): A data communication rule that allows multiple voice channels identified by a unique code being sent in one direction to be rebuilt at the receiver end based on the unique code.

Code efficiency: The use of the fewest bits possible to get the characters' meaning with a high degree of accuracy.

Code-independent data communications: Data communications with character-oriented link protocol independent from the data source's character set or code.

Code page: One of the standard code sets used to express different languages.

Code transparent data communication: Data communications with a bit-oriented link protocol independent from the data source's bit sequence.

Codec: An audio, video, or graphic file compression program that decompresses the file during playback. Codec is an abbreviation of compression/decompression. *See* **Lossless compression; Lossy compression.**

Codes: *See* **Hidden codes.**

Cold boot: Turning on a computer with the system's power switch. *See* **Boot; Warm boot.**

Collate: *See* **Sort.**

Collating sequence: *See* **Sort order.**

Collision: The impact of data when two units simultaneously try to send a message on a single channel. In the event of a collision, all senders may stop transmission or the receiving station could fail to acknowledge the data.

Color depth: In monitors, the number of colors a video adapter can simultaneously display dependent on the amount of video memory. In scanners, the number of data bits used to record the pixels of an image. A 24-bit scanner can render an image with 16.7 million colors and 256 shades of gray. A 30-bit scanner can record more than a billion colors and 1,024 levels of gray.

Color Graphics Adapter (CGA): A graphics display adapter for IBM PC-compatible computers. The CGA adapter can show four colors simultaneously with a horizontal resolution of 200 pixels and a vertical resolution 320 lines; or one color can be displayed with a horizontal resolution of 640 pixels and a vertical resolution of 200 lines. *See* **Bit-mapped graphic; Enhanced Graphics Adapter; Red-Green-Blue Monitor.**

Color ink jet printer: Ink jet printers producing color renditions. Most can render all colors from cyan, magenta, and yellow inks, but higher quality printers use blank ink, to adhere to the Cyan Magenta Yellow blacK (CMYK) model.

Color laser printer: A laser printer with color capability. The quality is good but cannot surpass the quality of dye sublimation, thermal wax transfer, or thermal dye transfer printers.

Color model: The description and alteration process of colors. The popular color models are: the HSB model, the Red-Green-Blue (RGB) model (used in monitors) and the Cyan Magenta Yellow blacK (CMYK) model which supports device-independent color systems.

Color scanner: A scanner recording color and shades of gray. Color scanners have more color depth, and are not much more costly than grayscale scanners.

Color separation: The separation of a multicolor graphic into several layers of color, with each layer corresponding to one of the colors printed when professionally reproduced. *See* **Pantone Matching System.**

.com: On the Internet, a top-level name assigned to businesses. These names come last in a given Internet computer's domain name (such as www.apple.com).

.COM As a file name extension, .COM indicates an executable program file no larger than 64 KiloBytes (KB).

COM port: *See* **COMmunications port.**

COMDEX: *See* **COMputer Dealers Exhibition (COMDEX).**

Comma-delimited file: A data file, often in the American Standard Code for Information Interchange (ASCII) format, for which the data items are separated by commas to speed data transfer to another program. *See* **American Standard Code for Information Interchange; File format; Tab-delimited file.**

Command: A signal given to a program that starts, stops, or controls a specific operation. The signal can be a typed command or selected command. *See* **Graphical User Interface; Menu-driven program.**

Command button: In a Graphical User Interface (GUI) such as Macintosh Finder or Microsoft Windows '95, a button in a dialog box starting an action such as Okay, Cancel, Help, etc. Choose the default button by pressing Return (for Macintosh) or Enter (for Windows).

COMMAND.COM: In Microsoft's Disk Operating System (MS-DOS), an essential system file containing the command processor. This file must be present for MS-DOS to operate.

Command key: On Macintosh keyboards, a key marked with a quotation mark frequently combined with alphabetical keys for menu option shortcuts.

Command language: *See* **Software command language.**

Command-line operating system: A command-driven Operating System (OS), such as Microsoft's Disk Operating System (MS-DOS), requiring typed keyboard commands. *See* **Graphical User Interface.**

Command mode: A modem mode taking instructions from other computer devices instead of immediately transmitting the data. Communication programs are assigned to distinguish command communication modes.

Command processor: The part of an Operating System (OS) accepting user input and displaying prompts and messages. Also called the command interpreter. *See* **Command-line operating system.**

Comment out: In programming, placement of a symbol (for example, semicolon) or a command at a line's beginning to mark the line as documentation and not a command. Compilers or interpreters will ignore lines with this symbol. *See* **Remark.**

Commercial Internet Exchange (CIX): An organization of Internet Service Providers (ISPs) collaborating to provide an Internet backbone service exempt from Acceptable Use Policies (AUPs) and having no restrictions for commercial use of the CIX backbone network.

Committed Information Rate (CIR): The information transfer rate that a network with Frame Relay Service (FRS) is committed to transfer.

COmmon Business-Oriented Language (COBOL): A high-level programming (and compiled) language released in 1964 designed for business applications. COBOL can store, retrieve, process, and automate business and accounting information and functions. COBOL is popular in corporate mainframe programming. *See* **dBASE; High-level programming language.**

Common carrier: A regulated company furnishing communication services to its own backbone network and to the public.

Common Gateway Interface (CGI): How HyperText Transfer Protocol Daemon-compatible (HTTPD-compatible) World Wide Web (WWW) servers should access external programs. If this process is followed, data will be returned to the user as a generated Web page. CGI programs or scripts are commonly employed as a user fills out an on-screen form. The form generation or search process then brings other programs into play. After completing the on-screen form, the user sees a new Web page with a secondary form, a confirmation, feedback, another Web page, etc.

Common Management Information Protocol (CMIP): An Open System Interconnection-based (OSI-based) structure designated ICO 9596 to format messages and transmit data between receiving programs and reporting devices.

Common User Access (CUA): A Windows interface methodology deciding the default menu items, menu arrangement, item arrangement, and basic keystrokes. *See* **Application Program Interface.**

Communication endpoint: An object associated with a set of attributes that are specified at the communication creation time.

Communications: Data transfer data between two devices.

Communications Access Method (CAM): *See* **TeleCommunications Access Method.**

Communications adapter: A hardware feature on some processors permitting attachment of telecommunication lines to the processor

Communications controller: A front-end programmable computer serving data communication processes in the IBM Systems Network Architecture (SNA) network.

Communications medium: A physical communications connection consisting of bounded or unbounded media.

Communications parameters: In telecommunications and serial printing, the customizable settings for the contacted hardware. *See* **Baud rate; Communications protocol; Full DupleX; Half-dupleX; Parameter; Parity bit; Stop bit.**

COMmunications port (COM port): In Microsoft's Disk Operating System (MS-DOS), a name designating the serial ports available in a computer. Most computers can have up to four COMmunication (COM) ports: COM1, COM2, COM3, and COM4.

Communications program: An application program converting a computer into a terminal to transmit data to and receive data from other non-Local Area Network (non-LAN) computers. This program can automate log-on procedures, file-transfer protocols (such as XMODEM and Kermit), mainframe terminal emulation (such as the DEC VT 100), on-screen timing, and telephone number storage and retrieval.

Communications protocol: The standards for transfer of information on a network or telecommunication lines. The computers involved must be set and standardized identically to avoid errors. Many communications services use eight data bits and one stop bit; full duplex is also common.

Communications settings: *See* **Communications parameters; Communications protocol**

Comp hierarchy: In USENET, one of the seven standard newsgroup hierarchies. For instance, the comp.binaries newsgroups contain freeware and shareware programs.

Compact disk (CD): A read-only plastic disk with up to 72 minutes of audio data or 650 Megabytes (650Mb) of digitally encoded computer data. *See* **Compact Disk-Read Only Memory disk drive; Erasable optical disk drive; Optical disk; Secondary storage.**

Compact Disk-Digital Audio (CD-DA): A Compact Disk Read Only Memory (CD-ROM) disk bought in a music store. CD-DA is one of the most available music-recording media.

Compact Disk-Interactive (CD-I): A Compact Disk (CD) standard for interactive viewing of audiovisual recording shown on television with a CD-I player.

Compact Disk-Read Only Memory (CD-ROM): A compact disk read-only optical storage technology. CD-ROM disks are often used for encyclopedias and software libraries. New compression techniques enables storage of 250,000 text pages on one CD-ROM disk.

Compact Disk-Read Only Memory (CD-ROM) disk drive: A compact disk read-only disk drive reading CD-ROM data within a computer. CD-ROM drives can detect and read data faster than a typical compact disk player dedicated to playing audio CDs.

Compact Disk-Read Only Memory eXtended Architecture (CD-ROM XA): A compact disk data storage standard developed by Microsoft, Phillips, and Sony for simultaneous access to audio and visual data in a compact disk.

Compact Disk-Read Only Memory Super Density (CD-ROM/SD): A rare standard for compressing 9.6 GigaBytes (9.6GB) onto a CD-ROM. The CD-ROM/SD standard uses both sides of a CD-ROM disk and cannot used by any common CD-ROM disk drives.

Compaction: The elimination process of redundant characters from data before storage or transmission.

Compandor (compression-expander): A device to compress the transmitted speech range and expand the receiving speech range on a telephone circuit for more efficient use of voice telecommunications channels.

Comparison operator: *See* **Relational operator.**

Compatibility: The capability of a computer, device, or program to complement or substitute another computer, device, or program. True compatibility means no modifications are necessary.

Compiler: A program able to read statements from a user-friendly programming language such as Pascal or Modula-2 and capable of translating the statements into an executable program. Compiled programs operate more quickly than interpreted programs. *See* **Machine language.**

Complementary Metal-Oxide Semiconductor (CMOS): An energy saving chip used in battery powered laptops and in applications.

Complex Instruction Set Computer (CISC): A Central Processing Unit (CPU) capable of executing most computations directly. Most microprocessors are CISC chips. Reduced Instruction Set Computer (RISC) technology is becoming more popular in home and professional workstations. *See* **Central Processing Unit; Reduced Instructions Set Computer.**

Composite video: A video signal broadcast method in which the red, green and blue components, as well as horizontal and vertical synchronization signals are mixed together. Composite video, regulated by the U.S. National Television Standards Committee (NTSC), is used for television. Some computers have composite video outputs that use a standard RCA phono plug and cable such as on the backplane of a hi-fi or stereo system. *See* **Composite color monitor; Red-Green-Blue monitor.**

Compound document: In Objects Linking and Embedding (OLE), a single file created by two or more applications, such as a Microsoft Excel chart in a Microsoft Word document, and the compound document is a file larger than normal in size. *See* **Object Linking and Embedding.**

Compress: A UNIX compression utility creating *.Z extension files. Since Compress is copyrighted and undistributable, UNIX users prefer to use Open Software Foundation's gunzip.

Compressed file: A file converted by a compression utility that minimizes required disk storage space. *See* **File compression utility.**

Compression: The process of reducing a file's size by means of a compression utility. The two types of compressions are lossless compression and lossy compression. Lossless compression allows for decompression with no loss of the original data files or programs. Lossy compression removes some data not obvious to the user such as for sound, animation, and video.

Compression ratio: A measurement of compaction defined by the ratio of bits before compaction to the number after.

CompuServe: An Internet service provider who provides the program one needs for connection to the Internet, an easy setup program, a local service number, and frequently a free trial membership.

Computer-Aided Design (CAD): The use of a computer and CAD program to design various industrial products. CAD is now used in architecture, engineering, and interior design. CAD applications require fast microprocessors and high resolution (high res) video displays.

Computer-Aided Design and Drafting (CADD): The use of a computer system for industrial design and technical drawing. CADD software resembles Computer-Aided Design (CAD) software, but allows for adherence to engineering conventions.

Computer-Assisted Instruction (CAI): The use of programs to instruct and teach, such as drills, practice, tutorials, and tests.

Computer-Based Training (CBT): The use of Computer-Assisted Instruction (CAI) techniques to train for specific skills whether they are industrial or computer-oriented.

Computer Branch Exchange (CBE): *See* **Private Branch Exchange.**

Computer Dealers Exhibition (COMDEX): A computer-industry trade show wherein hardware manufacturers and software publishers display their newest products for customers, the computer press, and their peers. COMDEX appears twice: in the spring in Atlanta and in the fall in Las Vegas with the Las Vegas show considered more important.

Computer Emergency Response Team (CERT): An Internet security task force detecting and responding to security threats. CERT was formed in 1988 by the Defense Advanced Research Project Agency (DARPA) in response to the infamous Internet Worm.

Computer Fraud and Abuse Act of 1984: A U.S. Federal law criminalizing U.S. government computer or network abuse crossing state boundaries.

Computer Graphics Metafile (CGM): An international graphics file format storing object-oriented graphics in device-independent form. With this form, the files can be exchanged among different computer systems or programs. Harvard Graphics and Ventura Publisher can read and write to CGM files. *See* **Windows Metafile Format.**

Computer-Telephony Integration (CTI): The standardized integration of voice with data networks.

Concatenation: To link two or more units of information so they become one unit. In spreadsheet programs, this technique combines text in a formula by placing an ampersand between the formula and text.

Concentrator: In data transmission, a device permitting a common transmission medium to serve more data sources than there are available channels. The device combining incoming messages is the concentrator.

Concurrency management: On a Local Area Network (LAN), an application's capability to guarantee that data files are not corrupted by modification or multiple inputs.

Concurrent processing: *See* **Multitasking.**

Conditioning: Additional equipment for a leased voice-grade circuit providing minimum values of line characteristics required for transmission.

Conditioning line: Additional equipment for a leased voice-grade channel improving the transmission's analog characteristics to permit higher rates of transmission.

CONFIG.SYS: In Microsoft's Disk Operating System (MS-DOS), an American Standard Code for Information Interchange (ASCII) text file in the root or parent directory containing configuration commands. This file is necessary for system start up. Without the CONFIG.SYS, DOS will fall back on the default configuration values. The most frequent configuration commands are BUFFERS, DEVICE, DEVICE-HIGH, DOS=HIGH, and FILES.

Configuration: The manual or automatic choices for setting up a computer system or an application program. After the choices are decided upon, the configuration is saved to a configuration file.

Configuration file: A file created by an application program storing manual and automatic choices when installing the program. After the choices are fixed, they will be available each time the program is activated.

Conformance Test (CT): A test used to determine if an implementation complies with the specifications of and the behavior within a standard.

Connection-oriented: A type of communication wherein a connection is established between the sender and receiver before transmission occurs.

Connection-oriented protocol: In a Wide Area Network (WAN), a protocol establishing a procedure so two or more computers can establish a physical connection activated until all data has been exchanged. Handshaking is the accepted method to ensure a complete exchange of data. *See* **X.25.**

Connectionless Broadband Data Service (CBDS): A connectionless service similar to Bellcore's Switched Multi-megabit Data Services (SMDS) defined by the European Telecommunications Standards Institute (ETSI).

Connectionless protocol: In a Wide Area Network (WAN), a standard enabling data transmission from one computer to another. No analysis is made to determine if the receiving computer is on-line or connected. In the Internet, the connectionless protocol is the Internet Protocol (IP) which deconstructs data into packets which are reassembled after having been received. A connection-oriented protocol on the Internet (Transmission Control Protocol or TCP) assures all packets are received. *See* **Transmission Control Protocol.**

Connectivity platform: A program or utility enhancing and allowing an exchange of data with other similar or dissimilar programs through a Local Area Network (LAN). Oracle is used for the Macintosh. *See* **HyperCard; Local Area Network.**

Constant Angular Velocity (CAV): In data storage media (for example, floppy and hard disk drives), a playback process in which the disk rotates at a constant speed. The data is retrieved more quickly as the read/write head nears the spindle; the opposite occurs as the read/write head moves toward the perimeter of the disk. *See* **Constant Linear Velocity.**

Constant Linear Velocity (CLV): In Compact Disk-Read Only Memory (CD-ROM) disk drives, a playback technique altering the disk's rotation speed ensuring the disk's velocity is constant where the disk is being read. The closer the head is to the spindle, the slower the speed. In contrast to CLV devices, Constant Angular Velocity (CAV) devices such as hard disk drives access data at different rates, depending on the distance of the read/write head from the drive spindle. *See* **Constant Angular Velocity.**

Consultative Committee for International Telephony and Telegraphy (CCITT): A defunct international organization that designed analog and digital communications standards involving modems, computer networks, and fax machines, such as V.21, V.22, V.32bis, and V.34. The CCITT has been replaced by the International Telecommunications Union-Telecommunications Standards Section (ITU-TSS).

Consumables: The supplies a printer uses as it operate, such as ink cartridges, paper, etc., and expressed as cost per page.

Contact head: In a hard disk drive, a read/write head skating on the surface of a platter instead of flying over it.

Contention: In a Local Area Network (LAN), a channel access method using the dial network or the port selector in which communication channel access is on a first-come, first-served policy. *See* **Carrier Sense Multiple Access with Collision Detection.**

Context-sensitive help: In an application program, assistance displaying documentation to aid understanding the action to be executed. Without context-sensitive help, the desired information may not be immediately available or apparent.

Context switching: The ability to change from one program to another without closing either program. Context switching can occur in a true multitasking environment (for example, Microsoft Windows '95) or in a multiple-loading program (which does not allow background programs to continue their processes).

Contiguous: Adjacent; placed one next to or after the other, such as files selected in Windows Explorer or File Manager. Windows' ability to create virtual system memory is limited to the contiguous sectors available.

Continuous Automated Repeat reQuest (ARQ): An error correction technique in which data blocks are transmitted through the forward channel, and ACKnowledgements (ACKs) and No AcKnowledgements (NAKs) are sent over the reverse channels.

Contrast: In monitors, the degree of distinction between dark and light pixels.

Control: In a Microsoft Windows '95, a dialog box feature (for example, a check box, radio button, or list box) allowing user options to be chosen.

Control character: A character for initiating, modifying, or stopping a control function or special signaling, such as printer paper movement, handshaking, display screen blinking, etc. A control character may be recorded in a subsequent action and may have a graphic representation.

Control code: In American Standard Code for Information Interchange (ASCII), one of 32 codes specifically for hardware-control purposes, such as advancing a printer page.

Control key (Ctrl): In IBM PC-compatible computing, a key employed in combination with other keys to execute program commands.

Control menu: In Microsoft Windows '95, a pull-down menu containing options for managing the active windows. The menu usually includes commands to move, size, maximize, and minimize windows as well as to close the current window or switch to another application window or the next document window.

Control panel: In Lotus 1-2-3, the top three lines of the screen. The top line contains the current cell indicator and the mode indicator. The second is the entry line and the third line is blank. In the Macintosh and Microsoft Windows '95 operating environment, the control panel is a utility window that lists options for hardware devices, such as the mouse, monitor and keyboard.

Control panel DEVice (CDEV): Any Macintosh utility program placed in the System Folder appearing as an option in the Control Panel.

Control station: A station on a network assuming control of the network's operation. A typical control station exerts its command by polling and addressing. Contrast with slave station.

Control structure: A logical algorithm organization governing the sequence wherein program statements are executed. Control statements govern a program's control flow by specifying the sequence of steps in a program or macro. Control structures include branch structures and procedure/function structures. The use of control structures tends to make a program more readable. Readability is enhanced by avoiding GOTO statements producing an untrackable program interconnection, called spaghetti code. To avoid spaghetti code, use the basic control structures: sequential, branch and loop. *See* **Branch control structure; DO/WHILE loop; FOR/NEXT loop; High-level programming language; IF/THEN/ELSE; Structured programming.**

Control terminal: Any active network terminal in which a user is authorized to enter commands altering system operation.

Control unit: A component of the Central Processing Unit (CPU) procuring program instructions and emitting signals to carry out the programs. *See* **Arithmetic Logic Unit; Central Processing Unit.**

Controller: A device directing data transmission over the network links. A controller's operation may be handled by a program executed in a connected processor or may be controlled by an executed program within the device. *See* **Communications controller; Hard disk controller; Floppy disk controller.**

Controller card: An adapter connecting hard and floppy disk drives to the computer.

Conventional memory: In any IBM computer or IBM-compatible computer, the first 640 KiloBytes (KB) of Random Access Memory (RAM). This 640 KB of RAM was made accessible to programs and the remaining 1 MegaBytes (MB) memory space was reserved for internal system functions.

Convergence: In a packet-switching network, an automatic network mapping process occurring after a router is switched on. A router reads each incoming packet and determines where to send it. Convergence software allows a router to detect network changes.

Cookie: Information sent by Web Server to a Web browser. The browser software saves this information and sends it back to the server whenever additional requests come from the server. The browser may or may not accept the cookie and may save the cookie for either a short or long time.

Cooperative multitasking: In an Operating System (OS), a means of running more than one program at a time. In cooperative multitasking, one application's task is independent of another.

Cooperative network: A Wide Area Network (WAN) such as Because It's Time Network (BITNET) or UNIX-to-UNIX Copy Program (UUCP), in which the linked organizations carries some of the participating costs. *See* **Research network.**

Copper pair: Standard telephone cable unable to handle high-speed digital communications services such as an Integrated Services Digital Network (ISDN). *See* **Twisted pair.**

Coprocessor: A microprocessor support chip controlling a specific processing operation such as handling mathematical computations or displaying video images. *See* **Microprocessor; Numeric coprocessor.**

Copy fitting: In DeskTop Publishing (DTP) a method determining the copy (text) amount in a specific font fitting onto a given area on a page or in a publication.

Copy protection: Hidden instructions included in a program intended to prevent unauthorized duplication. Copy protection is still common, in recreational and educational software.

Core: The glass or plastic conductor of an optical fiber enabling the transmission carrying capabilities.

Core dump: In a mainframe, a debugging technique employing printing out the entire contents of the computer's core or memory. *See* **Dump.**

Corona wire: In laser printers, a wire applying an electrostatic charge to paper.

Corrupted file: A file with scrambled and unrecoverable data. Files become corrupted due to bad sectors, disk drive controller failures, or software errors.

Courseware: Software created especially for Computer-Assisted Instruction (CAI) or Computer-Based Training (CBT) applications.

CPE: *See* **Customer Premise Equipment.**

CPI: *See* **Characters Per Inch.**

CPU: *See* **Central Processing Unit (CPU).**

Crash: An abnormal termination of a program or programs often resulting in a frozen keyboard and mouse or an unstable state.

CRC: *See* **Cyclic redundancy check.**

Creator type: In the Macintosh, a four-letter code identifying the program creating a document. The code associates the document and the application. Apple Computer maintains a registry of creator type codes that no two applications use the same code.

Creeping commitment of resources: Project management concepts suggesting the dedicated project resources should increase as the project scope becomes defined by its creators. The reason for this to avoid duplication of resources.

Crippled version: A freely distributed program version lacking disabled crucial features to introduce the user to the program so the user will want to purchase the full version. Synonymous with working model.

Cropping: A graphics editing operation wherein the graphical edges are trimmed to remove unnecessary image parts or to fit them into a given space.

Cross-linked files: In Microsoft Windows '95, a file-storage error occurring when the File Allocation Table (FAT) shows two files designating the same disk cluster as their own. Cross-linked files can occur after a computer is interrupted by a crash or a power failure. ScanDisk may repair a cross-lined file. *See* **Lost cluster.**

Cross-platform computing: Using nearly identical user interfaces for programs running on various and/or incompatible computer architectures. The Microsoft Windows '95 and Macintosh versions of Microsoft Word resemble each other closely in many ways.

Cross-post: In a computer newsgroup such as EchoMail (Fidonet) or UserNet (Internet), the process of simultaneously mailing a contribution to two or more discussion groups.

Crosstalk: Interference or spillover generated by cables too close to one another. Crosstalk often prevents error-free data transmission.

CRT: *See* **Cathode Ray Tube.**

Cryptoanalysis: The science of breaking encrypted messages determine the strength of encryption techniques and to provide the nation with a military advantage.

Cryptography: The science of coding messages so they cannot be read by any other than the intended recipient. Public key cryptography eliminates the need to send a key via a separate, secure channel, and enables two people who have never before communicated to exchange virtually unbreakable messages. *See* **Cryptoanalysis.**

CSMA/CD: *See* **Carrier Sense Multiple Access with Collision Detection.**

CT: *See* **Conformance Test.**

CTI: *See* **Computer-Telephony Integration.**

Ctrl: *See* **Control key.**

CTS/RTS: *See* **Clear To Send/Request To Send.**

CUA: *See* **Common User Access.**

Current directory: The directory Microsoft's Disk Operating System (MS-DOS) or an application program uses by default to store and retrieve files. Synonymous with default directory.

Current drive: The hard or floppy disk drive used by the Operating System (OS) for a used-defined operation. Synonymous with default drive.

Current loop: An electrical interface sensitive to changes of current rather than voltage swings.

Cursor: An on-screen blinking character indicating where the next character will appear. *See* **Pointer.**

Cursor control key: The key or key s controlling the cursor movement.

Cursor-movement keys: The keys moving the onscreen cursor. Synonymous with arrow keys. Arrow keys can be used as auto repeat keys. Some programs choose additional keys to affect the cursor. These keys include Home, End, Tab, Shift-Tab, PgUp, and PgDn.

Customer Premise Equipment (CPE): A term for telephones, computers, private branch exchanges and other hardware located on the end user's side of the network boundary, established by the U.S. Federal Communications Commission (FCC).

Cut-sheet feeder: A paper-feed mechanism feeding separate sheets of paper into the printer; a friction-feed mechanism draws the paper through the printer.

CWIS: *See* **Campus-Wide Information System.**

Cyberspace: The virtual space created by computer systems. *See* **Virtual Reality.**

Cycle stealing: Interrupting a computer to store each character coming from a telecommunications line in the computer's memory.

Cyclic redundancy check (CRC): An automatic error-checking method used by Microsoft's Disk Operating System (MS-DOS) when writing data to a hard or floppy disk in its drive mechanism. Later, upon reading, the same error-check is conducted and the results of the two checks are compared to make sure the data hasn't been altered.

Cylinder: In hard and floppy disk drives, a storage unit consisting of the tracks set occupying identical positions on opposite sides of the platter.

D/A converter: *See* **Digital-to-Analog converter.**

Daemon: A Unix process designed to handle a specialized function (such as handling Internet server requests) and requiring a limited user interface.

Daisy chaining: Linking two or more devices together in a series using specific cabling and protocols, for example, a series of Small Computer System Interface (SCSI) devices.

DASD: *See* **Direct Access Storage Device.**

Data: Items such as facts, text, numbers, sounds, video, and images that can be shaped by an application program such as a database into meaningful and cohesive information. The word 'data' is technically plural, but commonly used as either singular or plural.

Data Access Arrangement (DAA): Equipment that permits a privately owned data terminal equipment and telecommunications equipment to be attached to the public telephone network.

Database: A collection of facts about a subject (for example, CUS-TOMERS) that has been is organized to yield meaningful information such as that required to make critical business decisions. These facts are organized in such a way that questions (queries) can be posed, figures can be totaled, and reports can be generated. The cornerstone of a database is the record, a complete collection of Information about one data entity. The essence of a database is the ability to collect several pieces of information about one entity. For example, a CUS-TOMER record might include such specific information (attributes) as First Name, Middle Initial, Last Name, Address, Apartment Number, Telephone Number, City, State, ZIP Code, e-mail address, and so forth.

Database design: The logical selection and arrangement of data entities and descriptive attributes required to solve a specific business problem. For example, a company might see a good database as the answer to improving its help desk services. In order to accomplish this, a strict analysis of the problem must be performed. Not only do the specific data entities have to be determined, but the pertinent attributes must be selected as well. These choices must then conform to certain logical rules (also known as normalization), and be placed correctly in a relational hierarchy (if necessary) to assure that the desired information can be obtained from queries. These steps assure that all records will be unique and meaningful, and that the entire database will appear and act as a cohesive whole. Finally, the designer must take into account ease-of-use issues. *See* **Data redundancy; Repeating fields.**

Database Management System (DBMS): A database application program that runs on a server or mainframe and provides the tools for data retrieval, modification, deletion and insertion to a community of users working on a network. Ordinarily, a portion of the program on the user's end (the 'front-end') allows queries to be posed using a data extraction language like Structured Query Language (SQL), while the process of data retrieval is performed at the server (on the 'back-end'). This method is relatively quick as only the query results are passed back to the user. A DBMS also controls user access to individual records thus ensuring data integrity and record security. *See* **Band.**

Data bits: The number of bits a computer uses to represent a character of data. In order for two computers to communicate by modem they must both use the same number of data bits which is ordinarily eight. *See* **Parity; Stop bit.**

Data bus: The internal electronic pathway in a computer that allows the microprocessor to exchange data with Random Access Memory (RAM). The width of the data bus, usually 16 bits or 32 bits, determines how much data can be sent in one clock cycle. *See* **Bus network; Microprocessor; Random Access Memory.**

Data circuit: A two-way data communications circuit formed by a pair of send and receive channels.

Data communications: The transmission, reception and validation of data between a data source and data sink via one or more data links using standard hardware and standard communications protocols. This includes point-to-point, LAN (Local Area Network), and WAN (Wide Area Network) communications architectures.

Data Communications Equipment (DCE): In the RS232 specification, a communications device such as a modem (analog) or a Data Service Unit (DSU) that resides between a computer, terminal, printer, bridge, or router, and a communications circuit.

Data Communications Equipment (DCE) speed: The speed measured in bits per second (bps) at which a DCE device communicates over a telephone line.

Data compression protocol: In modems, a protocol that automatically compresses data as it is sent and decompresses data as it is received. For files containing redundant characters (graphics, database files) data compression can improve the transmission speed dramatically. The two most common data-compression protocols are the international V.42bis and the domestic Microcon Network Protocol-5 (MNP-5).

Data dependency: The requirement of a Central Processing Unit (CPU) using superscalar architecture and multiple pipelines to receive the results of one calculation before beginning another.

Data dictionary: In a database management program, a detailed description of all the elements of a database: the database files, indexes, views, data structures, including any other information pertinent to the maintenance of that database.

Data-encoding scheme: One of several schemes used to encode data on to the surface of a hard drive or other magnetic media. *See* **Advanced**

Run-Length Limited; Disk drive controller; Modified Frequency Modulation; Run-Length Limited.

Data encryption equipment: A device encrypting the data stream running through a communications circuit.

Data Encryption Standard (DES): A private key encryption scheme developed by IBM in the 1970s which has been adopted by the National Institute of Science and Technology (NIST) as the U.S. government standard.

Data-entry form: A user-friendly data-entry format which allows a user to enter data into a database by working with one, easy-to-read record at a time. Otherwise, data must be entered directly into a table or must be viewed as part of a large, hard-to-read table.

Data field: In a database management program, the space reserved for a specified piece of information in a data record, for example, FIRST-NAME, LASTNAME, ADDRESS, CITY, ST, and ZIP. In a table-oriented database program composed of rows and columns, each vertical column represents a data field. The data field usually has a particular type of data which can be entered into it, for example, long integers. The database designer can specify whether data fields are mandatory or optional, for example, a record is not saved unless all mandatory data fields have the appropriate data entered into them.

Data file: The file created as the result of an application program, for example, a letter, monthly payroll statement, or newsletter design.

Datagram: A self-contained packet used in connectionless transmission protocols such as Transmission Control Protocol/Internet Protocol (TCP/IP). Because it includes a complete destination address, it can be transmitted independently of other packets. It sends no acknowledgment to the transmitting station. If a packet is corrupted or lost, and error message is generated requesting a retransmission of that packet.

Datagram model: A connectionless (non-interactive) networking model.

Datagram Network Services: A set of services that assures a datagram or series of datagrams is correctly received if transmitted using a connectionless network service such as Novell's Internetwork Packet Exchange (IPX) or Transmission Control Protocol/Internet Protocol (TCP/IP). A datagram contains address information in its header that is referred to when determining if a retransmission has to be requested.

Data highway: A synonym for the National Information Infrastructure (NII). The NII is a proposed national computer network that will provide electronic information as well as voice and video to anyone with a computer or other device that can connect to a computer network. Libraries, universities and commercial providers provide resources on the network. The system is being built on existing interstate fiber-optic backbones and using the coaxial TV cable system. The existing Internet, which was developed with federal funding, not only serves as a model, but is one of the primary components on the network infrastructure.

Data independence: In database management, the storage of data in such a way that you can access it without knowing exactly where it is located or how it's stored. Newer database management programs include query languages that allow you to phrase queries based on data content rather than on data location. *See* **Structured Query Language.**

Data insertion: In a database management program, an operation that adds new records to any point in the database table, as opposed to having to append them to the end.

Data integrity: The accuracy, completeness, and internal consistency of the information stored in a database. Data integrity rules and data normalization prevents records from being entered multiple times, and assures that each record is unique.

Data Interchange Format (DIF) file: A standard file format used to make it easy to import and export data between different brands of spreadsheet and database programs.

Data link: The physical connection between a transmitter at one location and a receiver at another location.

Data-link Control Layer: Level 2 of IBM's proprietary System Network Architecture (SNA). It corresponds closely in function to Open System Interconnection's (OSI) Data Link Layer. *See* **Data-Link Layer.**

Data-Link Layer: Level 2 of the Open System Interconnection (OSI) reference model. Directly above the Physical Layer, it is concerned chiefly with defining the logical structure of data packages that are transported over various physical media, and determining the protocols that work directly with the different network hardware systems.

Data-Link Protocol Data Unit (DLPDU): The Open System Interconnection (OSI) term for a package of data and control symbols as it is transmitted by the Data-Link Layer protocol. A frame.

Data management: Data management includes the control, distribution, maintenance, security, and migration of data in an organization.

Data manipulation: Inserting, deleting, modifying, and retrieving data in a database.

Data mask: In database management programs, a field template specifying the format of the data you can enter in the data field. For example, MM/DD/YYYY suggests a specific format for entering a date. If the data entered does not match the structure of the field template, an error message appears.

Data migration: Archiving older, seldom-used, or unused files by transferring them off the computer's hard drive to a secondary of-line storage system, such as a separate magnetic tape or optical disk. Files can be as easily accessed as if they were local, but hard drive space is conserved.

Data modification: In database management, any operation that updates one or more records according to specific criteria. For example, you can use a query language such as Structured Query Language (SQL) to raise a product line's cost by 3 percent throughout the database.

Data packet: A logically organized package of data that is accompanied by all necessary control information.

Data-Phone: A service of AT&T and the Bell System that permits the transmission of data over the telephone network.

Data privacy: The limitations of access to a file so that only those users who have proper authorization can view or alter it. *See* **Encryption; File privilege; Password protection.**

Data Public Branch Exchange: A switch designed exclusively for handling data calls as opposed to voice calls.

Data processing: Preparing, storing or manipulating information. Synonymous with information processing.

Data record: A collection of related data items (fields) which are stored as a unit. Records are usually stored by subject in grids, or tables, each column of which represents a descriptive fact, or attribute about the subject of the table. Each attribute has its own field name. For example, the subject of the table (entity) might be CUSTOMERS, and the field names might include such things as MAILING_ADDRESS, TELEPHONE_NUMBER, and LAST_NAME. Each record fills an entire row and includes as many fields as required. Records can be viewed in two ways: as data-entry forms and as data tables. *See* **Relational DataBase Management System.**

Data redundancy: The existence of identical information in more than one record in a database. An example of this would be if the same customer were listed three times, as B. Smith, Elizabeth Smith, and

B. SMith. Among other reasons, data redundancy is caused by misspelling, or by changes in letter case. Data redundancy makes it difficult, if not impossible, to obtain accurate results from queries, or to maintain accurate business records. For example, a query to see the total sales to Elizabeth Smith would not be likely to include the sales from either of the other two names under which she is listed.

Data retrieval: Using a query to filter database records and to reveal a subset of records based on specific criteria. For example, you might create a query listing all customers from the 312 area code in Illinois that were under 5'5" and owed you more than $100 for a period of 90 days or more. Queries can also be used to sort records and create new fields based on numeric calculations.

Data security: Protecting data from unauthorized disclosure, transfer, modification, and destruction.

Data Service Unit/Channel Service Unit (DSU/CSU): A device, very much like a modem in function, designed to connect an organization's communications equipment directly to a digital communication line like a T1. As a device designed for higher-grade digital equipment, it is less concerned with analog-to-digital conversion than it is with shaping, multiplexing, and regenerating the digital data stream.

Data sink: The part of a Data Terminal Equipment (DTE) device that continues to accept data after transmission and is the source error control signals.

Data striping: A RAID (Redundant Arrays of Inexpensive Disks) backup technique in which a single file is stored in sections across a series of hard drives. Theoretically, it is very unlikely more than one drive will fail at one time; the failed drive can be changed ('hot-swapped') without shutting down the remaining drives; and the data on the failed drive can be entirely reconstructed using information from a separate 'parity drive.'

Data switch: A hardware device that acts as a concentrator, allowing multiple computing devices to be physically connected to a host computer.

Data Terminal Equipment (DTE): The part of a computer, terminal, printer, bridge, or router that serves as a data source and/or data sink.

Data Terminal Equipment (DTE) speed: The speed measured in Bits Per Second (bps) at which a DTE device such as a computer, terminal, printer, bridge, or router sends data to a Data Communications Equipment (DCE) device which is often a modem or Data Service Unit (DSU).

Data transfer rate: A measurement of the amount of digital information that can be transmitted through a communications channel (data source to data sink) in one second. Bandwidth is a measurement of line capacity, while throughput (bit rate) is a measurement of speed. For example, transferring a compressed video file requires a bandwidth more than 8 million bits (Megabits or Mbits) wide because it requires the ability to transmit at a speed of from 2 to 10 Mbits per second. The overall rate is affected by several factors including the interface transfer rate, the computer bus bandwidth, and file compression.

Data type: The form in which data is entered and manipulated in a data field. For the sake of accuracy and consistency, a database often limits the type of data that can be entered into a field. Common data types include alphanumeric (a combination of letters and numbers), numeric (numbers that can be mathematically calculated), memo (non-sortable text fields ignored by the database), logical (yes/no, true/false), date, and media object (graphics, photos or videos).

dBASE: A popular DataBase Management System (DBMS) originally created by Ashton-Tate for the personal computer. Its command language was widely imitated and was the basis of many later database management programs. In 1992, Borland International bought Ashton-Tate and assumed responsibility for the product. *See* **Software command language.**

DB-25: A standard plug used in RS-232C wiring. It uses a 25-pin connectors: 13 pins in the top row and 12 in the bottom.

DBMS: *See* **Database Management Systems.**

DC: Direct current.

DCA: Distributed Communications Architecture (Spree/Unisys).

DCE: *See* **Data Communications Equipment.**

D-Channel: The channel that transmits control and signaling information (for example, the phone number to which a call is being placed) for the B-channels in an Integrated Service Digital Network (ISDN) environment, In the Basic Rate Interface (BRI) the D-channel operates at 16 Kilobits per second (kbps). In the Primary Rate Interface (PRI), the D-channel operates at 64 kbps.

DCS: Digital Cellular System.

DDCMP: Digital Data Communications Message Protocol.

DDE: *See* **Dynamic Data Exchange.**

Debugger: A programming utility that helps programmers to find and fix various errors in source code. *See* **Compiler; Interpreter; Source code.**

DEC: Digital Equipment Corporation.

Decibel (dB): A unit that expresses the ratio of two sound levels on a logarithmic scale.

Decimal tab: A tab stop designed to allow a user to correctly line up columns of numbers with decimals.

Declarative language: A programming language that frees the programmer from specifying the exact procedure the computer needs to follow to accomplish a task. *See* **Data independence; Procedural language.**

Declarative Markup Language (DML): A logical system of codes for formatting text so that it can be transmitted electronically. Markup languages are primarily concerned with conveying the structure of the text rather than the format. Consequently, a document is tagged in a way that specifies its structure, for example, <RETURN ADDRESS>,<DATE>, <SALUTATION>, <PARAGRAPH>. Paired tags act as container labels indicating how the contents inside are to be parsed at the receiving end. An international standard is Standard Generalized Markup Language (SGML), a loose subset of which HyperText Markup Language (HTML) is popularly used to create pages for the World Wide Web (WWW).

DECnet: A communications protocol and line of networking products from Digital Equipment Corporation (DEC) compatible with Ethernet and a wide range of systems. A family of hardware and software implementing Digital Network Architecture (DNA).

DEC PATHWORKS: See Digital Equipment Corporation PATHWORKS.

Deconcentration: The process of extracting individual messages from a multiplexed data stream.

Decrement: In programming, to decrease a value. *See* **Increment.**

Decryption: The process of decoding previously encrypted data. Contrast with encryption.

Dedicated file server: A networked computer whose sole purpose is to provide various network services. For example, it runs the Network Operating System (NOS).

Dedicated line: A leased telephone line that has been specially conditioned and essentially acts as a private communications line. Available from either the regional telephone company or a Public Data Network (PDN).

Default extension: The conventional three-letter extension an application program uses to name files when it saves them. For example, a Word document is saved with a .DOC extension, while a Lotus 1-2-3 spreadsheet is saved with the extension .WKSX by default. File extensions make it easier to determine what program created a particular file. Files can also be viewed by extension, making it easier to find specific files. *See* **Extension.**

Default home page: In a Web browser such as Netscape Navigator or Microsoft Internet Explorer, the document that appears when you start the program. You return to it at any time in your web travels by clicking the 'Home' button. Any World Wide Web (WWW) page you wish can be configured as your home page.

Default numeric format: In a spreadsheet program, the number format the program uses for all cells unless you choose a different one. Ordinarily, the default is a right-justified general number format, although it can be changed to decimals, monetary units, and dates among others. *See* **Numeric format.**

Default setting: A global configuration setting for a program. Virtually every application program has this feature. Usually, it is to be found under the 'Options' or 'Preferences' menu. The setup or installation program establishes the defaults when the program is first installed, but you can change most settings at any time. You might want to change a default setting, for example, if you feel the default font is too small.

Defense Advanced Research Projects Agency (DARPA): An agency of the U.S. Department of Defense (DoD) assigned to fund basic research. DARPA funded most of the basic research for the Transmission Control/Internet Protocol (TCP/IP) protocol suite and the Internet in the early 1970s. DARPA does not conduct its own research. It funds universities and commercial or nonprofit organizations to do the research the DoD needs.

Defragmentation: The process of re-writing files to a hard drive so that they are written to contiguous sectors, thereby improving the speed with which a file is retrieved from the drive. Ordinarily, a file is written to the first available sectors it finds regardless of location on the disk. While this makes for a quick save operation, it ultimately slows down the file retrieval time. Defragmenting a hard drive is a part of regular computer maintenance.

Delay: Commonly a pause in activity. Delay can be a kind of distortion on a communications circuit. Specifically it is the property of an electrical circuit that slows down and distorts high-frequency signals. Devices called equalizers slow down the lower frequencies and "equalize" the signal.

Delay equalizer: A corrective network that is designed to make the phase delay or envelope delay of a circuit or system substantially constant over a desired frequency range.

Delay propagation: The time required for a signal to travel from one point to another on a component circuit or system.

Delete key (DEL): A key that erases the characters to he right of the cursors. Use the backspace and delete keys to correct mistakes as you type.

Delimiter: A code such as a space, tab or comma that marks the end of one sector of a command and the beginning of another. Delimiters are used to separate data into fields and records when you want to export or import data using a database format.

Demarcation point: The physical and electrical boundary between the telephone company responsibility and the customer responsibility.

Demodulation: The process of retrieving data from a modulated data stream after it has been transmitted. This typically involves changing it from analog to digital format at the receiving end. The reconstruction is performed on the data using the same logic (protocol) with which it was originally modulated. The reverse of modulation.

Density: A measurement of the number of data bits that can be reliably stored within a square inch of magnetic media such as that found in hard drives, magnetic tape, and floppy disks.

DES: *See* **Data Encryption Standard.**

Descender: The portion of a lowercase letter that extends below the baseline, for example, g, p, q, y, and j.

Descending sort: A reverse-order sort that lists the data in order from highest value to lowest value, for example, D,C,B,A or 4,3,2,1.

Descriptor: In a database management, a word used to classify a data record so that all records containing the word can be retrieved as a group. *See* **Identifier; Keyword.**

Desktop presentation: A slide show feature available in a presentation graphics programs enabling you to create a display of charts or other illustrations that can be run on a desktop computer. *See* **Presentation graphics program; Slide show.**

Destination code: A code in a message header containing the name of a terminal or application program to which the message is directed.

Destination document: In Object Linking and Embedding (OLE) the document in which you insert or embed an object. When you embed a Microsoft Excel object (such as a chart) into a Microsoft Word file, the Word document is the destination document. *See* **Object Linking and Embedding; Source document.**

Destination file: The file into which data or program instructions are copied.

Device: Any hardware component or peripheral such as a printer, modem, monitor or mouse than can receive and/or send data.

Device contention: In a multitasking environment, a technique to handle simultaneous requests to access peripheral devices. If two programs try to access the same peripheral device at the same time, one of the programs is given preference.

Device driver: A program that provides the operating system with all the information needed for it to work with a specific device, such as a printer or a monitor. A handful of basic drivers are included with the operating system; however, the most up-to-date drivers must be obtained separately. Manufacturers make them easily available to their customers, usually including them with the product.

Device independence: The ability of a program, operating system or programming language to work on a variety of hardware platforms. *See* **C; Portable; PostScript; UNIX.**

Device independent color: The ability of an output device such as a printer or plotter to reproduce an exact color created by the software. Often, a great difference exists between the two. A method of describing colors in a standard way, such as the Pantone Matching System (PMS), is one solution to this problem. Software and hard conforming to this standard allow you to faithfully reproduce colors.

Device name: In the Disk Operating System (DOS), a three-letter abbreviation that refers to a peripheral device. *See* **Auxillary port; COMmunications port.**

Device node: In Microsoft Windows '95, an object in the hardware tree that represents a piece of hardware. Synonymous with Plug and Play object.

Diagnostic program: A utility program that tests computer hardware to determine whether it is operating correctly. Most computers initiate a diagnostic memory check at the start of every operating session. If any errors occur, an error message is generated and the computer stops at that point.

Dialer program: In a Serial Line Internet Protocol (SLIP) and Point-to-Point Protocol (PPP), a program that dials an Internet service provider's number and establishes the connection. A dialer program establishes the connection that fully integrates your computer into the Internet. Many service providers distribute preconfigured dialer programs that enable users to connect to their service without configuring or programming the dialer.

Dialing directory: A feature in a communications program that acts as a telephone book. The program dials the modem of any number you select.

Dial line: Synonym for switched connection.

Dialog: In an interactive system, a series of interrelated inquiries and responses analogous to a conversation between two people.

Dialog box: In a Graphical User Interface (GUI) an on-screen message box that requests information from the user.

Dial tone: An audible signal indicating that a device is ready to be dialed.

Dialup access: A means of connecting to another computer or a network like the Internet, with a modem-equipped computer. If terminal emulation is involved, this may mean that certain programs which access the web directly can not be used, effectively eliminating the possibility of being able to see graphics.

Dialup IP: A method of accessing the Internet over a regular phone line by dialing up an Internet host using the protocols Point-to-Point Protocol (PPP) or Serial Line Internet Protocol (SLIP). Graphical web browsers such as Netscape Navigator can then be used.

Dial-up line: A communications circuit established by dialing a destination over a commercial telephone system. As soon as the call is terminated, the connection is dropped.

Dialup modem: A modem that can dial a telephone number, establish a connection and close the connection when it is no longer needed. Most personal computer modems are dialup modems.

Dial-up terminal: A terminal on a switched line.

Dibit: A pair of two bits. In four-phase modulation, such as Differential Phase Shift Keying (DPSK) each possible dibit is encoded as one of four unique carrier phase shifts. The four possible states for a dibit are 00, 01, 10 and 11.

Dictionary sort: A sort that ignores the case of characters. *See* **Sort; Sort order.**

DIF: *See* **Data Interchange Format.**

Differential Phase Shift Keying (DPSK): In modems, an enhanced phase modulation technique in which the relative degrees of change in a carrier signal phrase are coded into bits.

Digital camera: A portable camera, incorporating one or more Charge-Coupled Devices (CCDs) that records images in a machine-readable format. Though digital cameras are expensive and generate output of far lesser quality than that of film-based cameras, they eliminate the potentially expensive and time-consuming film-processing and photo-scanning steps involved in putting photos into computer-readable form.

Digital cash: A proposed method of ensuring secure electronic cash transactions. In digital cash commerce, a person could have an electronic bank account and use it to make on-line purchases, which would be automatically debited automatically and transferred to the payee. The transaction would be secure for all three parties: the bank, the payer and the payee.

Digital data: Data in the form of discrete data bits.

Digital Equipment Corporation (DEC) PATHWORKS: A DEC family of products creating a client-server environment where multivendor PCs, diverse communication protocols, networks and applications can work together.

Digital modulation: Translating analog signals into digital signals. Analog signals can be analyzed and encoded into a binary format consistent with modern telecommunications processing equipment. The result is a more reliable, cleaner data stream that can be manipulated to produce a wider variety of data services.

Digital monitor: A monitor that requires digital output from the display adapter. For example, the IBM Monochrome Display Adapter (MDA), Color Graphics Adapter (CGA) and Enhanced Graphics Adapter (EGA) standards all require a digital monitor. Digital display modes have been superseded by analog modes such as VGA (Video Graphics Array) and XGA (Extended Video Graphics Array) which are capable of reproducing a much wider palette of colors. *See* **Analog monitor;**

Color Graphic Adapter; Enhanced Graphics Adapter; Mono-chrome Display Adapter.

Digital Network Architecture (DNA): Digital Equipment Corporation Network Architecture.

Digital signal: A discrete or discontinuous signal; one whose various states are pules that are discrete intervals apart. Contrast with analog signal.

Digital Signal Level 0 (DS0): The standard 64-KiloBytes Per Second (KBPS) digital telecommunications channel that is devoted to voice transmission. It is equivalent to 1/24th of a T1 channel, or one voice circuit.
Other digital signal levels are:
DS1 = 1.54 MBPS, or one T1 channel (24 voice circuits)
DS1C = 3.152 MBPS, or two T1 channels (24 voice circuits)
DS2 = 6.312 MBPS, or four T1 channels (96 voice circuits)
DS3 = 44.736 MBPS, or 28 T1 channels (672 voice circuits)
DS4 = 274.760 MBPS, or 168 T1 channels (4032 voice circuits)

Digital Signal Processor (DSP): A programmable sound-processing circuit used in both modems and soundboards. Soundboards use DSPs to handle a variety of sound resolutions, formats and sound-altering filters without requiring separate circuits for each one, while modems use DSPs to handle several modulation protocols.

Digital switching: A process in which connections are established between digital transmissions without converting them to analog signals.

Digital transmission: A data communications technique that transmits information encoded in the form of discrete bits. See **Analog transmission.**

Digital-to-Analog (D/A) converter: A device that converts a digital value to an analog signal.

Digitize: The process of transforming analog data into discrete bits of digital data. For example, a scanner converts continuous-tone images into a bit-mapped graphic. Compact Disk-Read Only Memory (CD-ROM) disks contain many digital measurements of the pitch and volume of sound. See **Digitizing tablet; Scanner.**

Digitizing tablet: An electronic sketch pad. A peripheral device, usually measuring 12x12 inches or 12x18 inches and 1/2-inch thick, used with a pen-like device called a stylus that allows freehand images to be drawn to the screen. The location of the stylus point on the tablet is identical to the location of the cursor on the screen, allowing a user maximum control over an image. Synonymous with graphics tablet.

Dimmed: The grayed appearance of a menu command, icon or dialog box option indicating that the menu selection is not available.

Dingbats: Ornamental characters such as bullets, stars, pointing hands, scissors and flowers used to illustrate text, especially as bullets. *See* **Zapf Dingbats.**

DIP: *See* **Document Image Processing.**

Direct Access Storage Device (DASD): Any auxiliary storage device such as a hard disk, that offers random access or direct access to stored data; in contrast to a sequential access device (such as a tape drive). *See* **Random access; Sequential access.**

Direct Distance Dialing (DDD): A telephone exchange service that enables the telephone user to call subscribers outside the user's local service area without operator assistance.

Direct Inward Dialing (DID): A telephone service that allows a telephone call to pass through the system directly to an extension without operator intervention.

Direct Memory Access (DMA) Channels: A channel used to transfer data from Random Access Memory (RAM) memory to peripheral devices such as hard disk controllers, network adapters and tape backup equipment. Requests for data are handled by a special chip called a DMA controller, which operates at half the microprocessor's speed. When data is transferred using DMA channels, the microprocessor is bypassed completely, leaving it free to process other requests.

Direct Memory Access (DMA) conflict: A problem that results when two peripherals try to use the same DMA channel. A DMA conflict usually causes a system crash and can be solved by assigning one of the conflicting peripherals a new DMA channel.

Direct Outward Dialing (DOD): A telephone service allowing an internal caller at an extension to dial an external number without operator assistance.

Direct-map cache: A means of organizing cache memory by linking it to locations in Random Access Memory (RAM). Though direct-map caches are simpler than other types of cache and easier to build, they are not as fast as other cache designs. *See* **Full-associative cache.**

Directory: An index of the files stored on a disk. The operating system keeps an up-to-date record of the files stored on a disk, with ample information about the file's contents, time of creation and size.

Directory of servers: In Wide Area Information Servers (WAIS), a directory of WAIS-accessible public databases and a short description of their contents. The first step in searching WAIS is to access the directory of servers. Several copies are available on the Internet. Search using very general key words, such as "business" or "gardening." The directory of servers then lists the databases that contain information about to your topic.

Directory sorting: The organized display of the files in a directory, sorted by name, extension, date, and time of creation.

Directory tree: A graphical representation of a disk's contents showing the hierarchy of directories and subdirectories.

Disk: *See* **Floppy disk.**

Disk buffer: *See* **Cache controller.**

Disk cache: A portion of your hard disk that has been set aside to temporarily store documents. Documents are retrieved from a disk cache much faster than they are if they are stored on a hard drive. World Wide Web (WWW) pages, for example, are stored in a disk cache so that when you return to a page you have accessed recently, it reappears quickly.

Disk capacity: The storage capacity of a floppy disk measured in KiloBytes (KB) or MegaBytes (MB). The capacity of a floppy disk depends on the size of the disk, the density of the magnetic particles on its surface, and the coating used in its manufacture. The most popular size is currently 3 1/2 inches. Also popular are high-density and extra high-density disks. Also important are the capabilities of the disk drive you're using. For example, a 1.44 MB floppy drive is not compatible with a 2.88 MB floppy disk.

The following table shows the capacity of several popular disks after they have been formatted:

3 1/2 inch MS-DOS Double Density (DD):	720 KB
3 1/2 inch MAC Double Density (DD):	800 KB
3 1/2 inch MAC Superdrive High Density (HD):	1.44 MB
3 1/2 inch MS-DOS High Density (HD):	1.44 MB
3 1/2 inch MS-DOS Extra High Density (EHD):	2.88 MB
5 1/4 inch MS-DOS Double Density (DD):	360 KB
5 1/4 inch MS-DOS High Density (HD):	1.2 MB

Disk drive controller: The circuitry that controls the coding and decoding of information on a hard drive. Originally, the controller was a separate add-in adapter, but later came to be included in the system board or on the drive. Integrated Drive Electronics (IDE) drives, for example, incorporate the controller circuitry into the drive itself.

Disk duplexing: A fault-tolerant technique that writes simultaneously to two hard disks using different controllers. *See* **Disk mirroring.**

Diskette: *See* **Floppy disk.**

Diskless workstation: In a Local Area Network (LAN) a workstation that has a Central Processing Unit (CPU) and Random Access Memory (RAM) but lacks its own disk drives. Diskless workstations ensure that everyone in an organization produces compatible data and helps reduce security risks. *See* **Personal computer.**

Disk mirroring: A data security method that protects against the chance of disk failure by duplicating the contents of a one hard drive on to a second hard drive. Both drives are attached to the same controller, and the operating system writes data to both disks simultaneously. A disk duplexing scheme, on the other hand, uses a separate controller for each drive for added protection.

Disk Operating System (DOS): *See* **Operating System.**

Disk Operating System (DOS) prompt: In the Microsoft Disk Operating System (MS-DOS), a letter representing the current disk drive followed by the greater-than-symbol (>) which together informs you that the operating system is ready to receive a command. For example, C:\> *See* **Prompt.**

Disk optimizer: *See* **Defragmentation.**

Disk server: A mass storage device capable of sharing its resources.

Dispersion: In a fiber optic cable, the difference in arrival time between signals traveling straight through the core, and those traveling a slightly longer path because they have reflected off the cladding.

Display: *See* **Monitor.**

Display adapter: *See* **Video adapter.**

Display card: *See* **Video adapter.**

Display device: An output unit that shows a visual representation of data, for example, a monitor, terminal, plotter, microfilm viewer or printer.

Display Power Management Signaling (DPMS): A system in which a specially equipped video adapter sends instructions to a compatible monitor telling it to conserve electricity. The video adapter can tell the monitor to assume any of three levels of power conservation.

Display type: A typeface usually 14 points or larger and differing in style from the body type, used for headings and subheadings. *See* **Body type.**

Distinctive ringing: A ringing tempo that indicates whether a phone call is internal or external.

Distortion: A change to a transmitted signal caused by crosstalk, delay, attenuation or other factors.

Distortion delay: The distortion resulting when the various frequencies of a signal travel at different speeds. Also called Group delay.

Distributed control: A network-control method where individual nodes develop their own routing tables based on information from adjacent nodes.

Distributed database: A distributed database is stored on multiple servers over a network, but viewed and accessed as a single database by users.

Distributed Data Processing (DDP): Data processing in which some or all of the processing, storage and control functions in addition to input/output functions are situated in different places and connected by communications facilities.

Distributed Relational Database Architecture (DRDA): An IBM database strategy to establish universal access to relational databases across both the IBM and non-IBM platforms.

Distribution cable: The grouping of individual telephone lines as they approach a central office.

Dithering: In color or grayscale printing and displays, combining dots or colors to produce what appears to be a new shade of gray or a new color.

.DLL: *See* **Dynamic Link Library.**

DNA: Digital Network Architecture.

Docking station: A structure which can house a portable computer. It may contain a hard drive, video circuitry for a full-sized monitor, a Compact Disk (CD) player, additional Input/Output (I/O) ports, or a network interface adapter. When the portable is inserted into the docking station, it can use all the devices attached to the docking station, in essence, becoming a desktop computer.

Document: A term meaning any data file created with an application program, such as a business report, a memo or a worksheet. Because of the collective nature of the creation and maintenance of electronic documents, and the advent of dynamic data exchange, (DDE) the definition of what constitutes a document is changing. *See* **Dynamic Data Exchange; Groupware; Word processing.**

Documentation: The instructions, tutorials and reference information that provide you with the information you need to use a program or computer system effectively. Documentation can appear in printed form or electronically in on-line help systems.

Document format: In a word processing program, a set of formatting choices that affects the entire document (i.e., margins, headers, footers, page numbers and columns). You can also format a document by selecting formats at the paragraph level, the sentence level, the word, or the individual character.

Document Image Processing (DIP): A system for the imaging, storing and retrieving text-based documents. It include scanning documents, storing the files on optical or magnetic media, and viewing them on a monitor, printer or fax. The goal of a document image processing system is to create a paperless office.

Document window: A window within an application program that displays the document you're creating or editing. You can open more than one document window within an application window. *See* **Microsoft Windows.**

Domain: In networks, the resources that are under the control of one or more associated host processors.

Domain name: On the Internet, a system of easily identifying individual servers or sites using a single word or abbreviation. The domain name farthest to the right of an address is the most general or top-level domain. For example, .edu (educational) and .com (commercial) are top-level domain names. Lower level, more specific names are placed to the left. The farther left, the more specific. For example, einstein.physics.illinois.edu would be the address of a server named 'einstein' residing in the Physics Department at the University of Illinois. See Domain Name System.

Domain Name System (DNS): Because the actual unique Internet Protocol (IP) address of a web server is in the form of a number difficult for humans to work with (for example, 128.143.8.187), text labels separated by dots (domain names) are used instead. The DNS is responsible for mapping these domain names to the actual IP numbers in a process called resolution. A major benefit of the DNS is that an organization can retain a familiar address even if the actual IP number changes.

DOS: *See* **Operating System; Microsoft Disk Operating System.**

Doskey: A utility provided with Microsoft Disk Operating System (MS-DOS) (version 5.0 and later) that enables you to type more than one MS-DOS command on a line to store and retrieve previously used MS-DOS commands to create stored macros and to customize all MS-DOS commands.

DOS prompt: *See* **Disk Operating System prompt.**

Dot matrix printer: An impact printer that forms text and graphic images by pressing the ends of fine pins against a ribbon in a pattern (matrix) of dots. Some dot matrix printers use 24 pins instead of 9 to improve print quality, but the output is still not considered to be true letter quality. They are an excellent and inexpensive choice for utility printing, especially for producing high-speed copy and printing multi-part forms. *See* **Font; Near Letter Quality; Non impact printer.**

Dot pitch: On a monitor, the distance between the center of two adjacent pixels. It is an effective gauge of a monitor's clarity. The smaller the distance, the crisper the image. A monitor with a dot pitch of .26 millimeters or .28 millimeters is an exceptionally good one from which to read text.

Dots Per Inch (DPI): The number of dots an output device such as a printer can place in a linear inch.

Double-click: To click a mouse twice in rapid succession. Double clicking is used primarily to open program, files, or icons in one step.

DO/WHILE loop: A program flow structure that repeats a series of steps until a pre-determined condition is satisfied. Once the condition is met, the program proceeds to the next instruction. *See* **Sequence control structure; Software command language; Syntax.**

Downlink: The rebroadcast of a microwave radio signal from a satellite back to earth.

Download: To transfer a file from another computer to your computer by means of a modem and a telephone line. *See* **File Transfer Protocol; Modem; Upload.**

Downloadable font: Also known as a soft font, a printer font that must be transferred from the computer's hard disk drive to the printer's Random Access Memory (RAM). Downloading fonts is time-consuming and uses a lot of your printer's memory. In fact, you may have to add additional megabytes of expensive printer RAM to print certain jobs without difficulty. Despite this, soft fonts are available in a wide variety of typefaces and make up in versatility what they lack in convenience. You download fonts using a downloading utility or a word processing or page layout program (such as Microsoft Word, Word Perfect or PageMaker) which is capable of downloading fonts. *See* **Built-in font; Cartridge font; Font; Font family; Page description language; PostScript font.**

Downward compatibility: The ability of hardware and software to operate with earlier versions. For example, you can still use many of the internal cards designed for your old computer with a computer you would purchase today. And the latest edition of your favorite word processing program can read all the files you created with the previous edition. Downward compatibility allows users to retain their investments in earlier technology.

DPSK: *See* **Differential Phase Shift Keying.**

Drag: To move a mouse pointer while holding down the mouse button.

Drag-and-drop: In Graphical User Interface (GUI) environments such as Microsoft Windows '95 and Macintosh programs running under System 7.5, the ability to perform operations on objects by dragging them with the mouse. For example, you can open a document by dragging its icon to an application icon and releasing the mouse button.

Drag-and-drop editing: An editing feature in a word processing program allowing you to move or copy a block of text by highlighting it and then using the mouse to drag it to a new location on the page. When you release the mouse button, the text appears in the new location.

DRAM: *See* **Dynamic Random Access Memory.**

Draw program: A graphics program that uses object oriented graphics to produce line art. A draw program stores the components (primitives) such as lines, circles, curves, as mathematical formulas rather than as bit patterns like paint programs do. Line art created with a draw program can be sized and scaled without distortion and will produce output that uses a printer's maximum resolution. *See* **Object-oriented graphic; Paint program.**

Drive activity indicator: A small light on the front of a disk drive indicating that it is in use.

Drive array: Synonym for Redundant Array of Inexpensive Disks (RAID).

Drive bay: A space in a computer's chassis into which peripherals can be installed, for example, hard drives floppy drives, Compact Disk (CD) players, internal tape backup units.

Drive designator: In the Disk Operating System (DOS), an argument that specifies the drive to be affected by the command. For example, C:\ or A:\.

Driver: A utility file containing all the information needed by a program to correctly operate a peripheral such as a Compact Disk (CD) player, monitor, or printer. *See* **Device driver.**

DriveSpace: A disk compression utility included with Microsoft Windows '95.

Drop cap: An initial letter of a chapter or paragraph, enlarged and positioned so that the top of the character is even with the top of the first line, and the rest of the character descends into the second and subsequent lines.

Drop Down list box: A graphical user interface device that allows a user to see many command options in a relatively small area. Clicking on one command causes a list of all available options to appear. When an option is chosen, the list box disappears.

Drop out: In data communication, a momentary loss in signal usually due to the effect of noise or system malfunctions.

Dropouts: Characters lost during a data transmission.

Drop wire: The wire running from a residence or business to a telephone pole or its underground equivalent.

D-Shell connector: The connector used primarily for hooking up monitors to video adapters. The video adapters of analog video modes such as VGA (Video Graphic Array) use 15-pin D-shell connectors. Older digital standards such as Enhanced Graphics Adapter (EGA) uses 9-pin D-shell connectors.

DSU/CSU: *See* **Data Service Unit / Channel Service Unit.**

DTE: *See* **Data Terminal Equipment.**

DTMF: *See* **Dual-Tone Multiple Frequency.**

Dual actuator hard disk: A hard disk design incorporating two read/write heads. Dual actuator hard disks have better access time than standard hard disks because the platters are always less than half a revolution away from one of the heads, instead of almost a full revolution away as in a standard hard disk.

Dual issue processor: A type of Central Processing Unit (CPU) that can process two instructions simultaneously, each in its own pipeline.

Dual-scanned passive matrix: An improved passive-matrix Liquid Crystal Display (LCD) design that refreshes display twice as fast as standard ones. This type has better brightness and contrast than passive-matrix LCDs.

Dual-Stripe Magneto-Resistive (DSMR) head: A new read/write head design for hard disks that reduces their sensitivity to interference form the outside environment. DSMR heads have separate portions for reading and writing and pack data tightly onto disks.

Dual-Tone Multiple Frequency (DTMF): A method of telephone signaling which uses two sets of standard frequencies to create unique values. For example, pressing a button on a touch-tone telephone combines two frequencies into a third, usable, frequency. Commonly known as touch-tone. Most dialup modems generate DTMF tones, as well.

Dumb terminal: A non-programmable terminal having little or no memory. It relies on a host computer for all processing capabilities.

Dump: To transfer the contents of memory to a printing or secondary storage device. Programmers use memory dumps when debugging programs to see exactly what is in memory at the time the program fails. *See* **Screen dump.**

Duplex: In communication circuits, the ability to transmit and receive at the same time; also referred to as full duplex. For example, during a telephone call both callers can speak at the same time. Half duplex circuits, like Citizens' Band (CB) radios, can only receive or only transmit. *See* **Full-dupleX; Half-duplex.**

Duplex printing: Printing a document on both sides of the paper so it can be bound as a book.

Dvorak keyboard: An alternative keyboard layout in which 70 percent of the keystrokes take place on the home row (compared to 32 percent with the standard QWERTY layout). A Dvorak keyboard is easier to learn and faster to use.

Dynamic beam forming: A monitor design that ensures that electron beams are perfectly round when they strike the display no matter where on-screen the yoke steer them. Without dynamic beam forming, electron beams would be elliptical at the edge of the display.

Dynamic Data Exchange (DDE): Part of Microsoft's Object Linking and Embedding (OLE) technology, DDE is a messaging protocol that allows data to be transferred between conforming applications individually or over a network. It is simple to do as it relies on the copy and paste feature of Windows. The application supplying data acts as a server while the application receiving data acts as a client. Most DDE capable applications can be either client or server. A server application can supply data to more than one client application. If the client application isn't running when the server document is updated, an alert appears the next time the client document is opened prompting you to update it. *See* **Client application; Dynamic link; Object Linking and Embedding; Server application; System 7.**

Dynamic link: The ability of two programs to dynamically exchange data. For example, a chart created in a spreadsheet can be inserted into a word processing document such as a letter. Every time the figures on which the chart is based are changed in the spreadsheet program, the appearance of the chart in the letter changes. *See* **Hot link.**

Dynamic Link Library (.DLL): The Microsoft Disk Operating System (MS-DOS) file name extension attached to a collection of library routines.

Dynamic object: A document or section of a document conforming to Microsoft's Object Linking and Embedding (OLE) technology. OLE-compliant programs can transfer data among themselves using special properties of the copy and paste feature of Windows. A linked object automatically updates whenever changes are made in the source document. For example, a chart created in a spreadsheet can be inserted into a word processing document such as a letter. The chart graphic as it appears in the letter reflects the most recent changes made on it by the spreadsheet program. An embedded object, on the other hand, actually allows you to open the source program and edit the object in place. *See* **Object Linking and Embedding.**

Dynamic Random Access Memory (DRAM): Random Access Memory (RAM) chips that must be constantly electronically refreshed because the capacitors in them holding the electrical charge eventually lose their charges, DRAM chips have different speeds at which they transfer data (access times). Access times are measured in billionths of a second or nanoseconds (ns) and are clearly marked on the chip. A chip marked - 8, has an access time of 80 ns. *See* **Static Random Access Memory.**

Dynamic Range: The ability of a scanner to accurately detect colors at the extreme edge of the color spectrum, for example, the lightest yellows and the darkest blues.

Dynamic routing table: A frequently updated list of available routers that assures the fastest possible transference of packets.

E1: Also known as CEPT1. A 2.048-MegaByte Per Second (MBPS) rate used by a European CEPT carrier to transmit thirty 64 KiloByte Per Second (KBPS) digital channels for voice or data calls. This includes a 64 KBPS signaling channel and a 64 KBPS channel for maintenance and framing.

E3: Also known as CEPT3. A 34.368 MegaByte Per Second (MBPS) rate used by European CEPT carriers to transmit sixteen CEPT1 channels.

E.164: A public network addressing standard utilizing up to a maximum of 15 digits. Most Asynchronous Transfer Mode (ATM) networks use the E.164 addressing for public network addressing.

E Rate: See Vertical frequency.

Easter egg: An inaccessible message/screen within a program made available only by an undocumented or special procedure.

EBCDIC: *See* **Extended Binary Coded Decimal Interchange Code.**

Echo: A reverse signal (e.g., voice) caused by an electrical wave bouncing back from the circuit's intermediate or end point.

Echoplex: A method of transmission whereby the transmitting station receives and confirms that the message was sent by echoing it back to the sender. *See* **Full-duplex; Half-duplex.**

Echoplexing: A method of echoing back signals to check the sender's message.

Echo suppressor: A device eliminating long distance voice echoes. In order to transmit full-duplex data, the suppressor is automatically turned-off by a modem.

ECMA: *See* **European Computer Manufacturers Association.**

ECPA: *See* **Electronic Communications Privacy Act.**

Edge connector: The section of an adapter board that plugs into the expansion slot. See Adapter; Expansion slot.

Edge device: A physical device capable of forwarding packets of information between legacy interworking interfaces (e.g., Ethernet, Token Rings) and Asynchronous Transfer Mode (ATM) interfaces based on data-link information and network layer information. This device does not participate in managing any network layer routing protocol.

Edgelighting: The shining lights around the border of the Liquid Crystal Display (LCD), improving the readability of the LCD yet are less effective that backlighting.

EDI: *See* **Electronic Data Interchange.**

Edit mode: An application mode editing text and data.

Editor: *See* **Text editor.**

EDLIN: A word processing program of the Disk Operating System (DOS) that edits line-by-line on the text. Primarily used for creating small bath files, EDLIN is difficult to use and is out-dated.

Edu: The extension denoting a higher educational institution.

EEMS: See Enhanced Expanded Memory Specifications.

EFF: See Electronic Frontier Foundation.

Effective data transfer rate: The rate of an average number of characters, blocks, or bits per unit from a data source to a data sink.

Effective resolution: The output resolution of a printer utilizing resolution enhancement to improve printing quality.

Effective transmission rate: The compressed data communication rate from one modem to another. The compression of data enables it to be sent rapidly within a given short amount of time.

EFS: *See* **Error Free Seconds.**

EGA: *See* **Enhanced Graphics Adapter.**

EINet Galaxy: A subject tree service within the World Wide Web (WWW) controlled by Enterprise Integration Network (EINet).

EISA: *See* **Enhanced Industry Standard Architecture.**

ELAN: *See* **Emulated Local Area Network.**

ElectroMagnetic Interference (EMI): Interference that occurs when sufficient power from signals escapes equipment enclosures or transmission data. These signals are found in the radio frequency portion of the electromagnetic spectrum.

Electron gun: An electron emitter located within a Cathode Ray Tube (CRT) utilizing a yoke to guide the emittance of electrons to make an image on the display area of the CRT.

Electronic Communications Privacy Act (ECPA): A U.S. federal law passed in 1986 protecting all electronic mail (e-mail) that is temporarily held within the storage device from being read by agencies, unless they have a warrant.

Electronic Data Interchange (EDI): The electronic transmission of business documents (invoices, billing, etc.), that utilizes field codes to format data.

Electronic data transfer rate: The valid transfer rate from a data source to a data sink as computed by the average number of characters per unit time. *See* **Effective data transfer rate.**

Electronic Frontier Foundation (EFF): A nonprofit pubic advocacy organization formed to maintain privacy in computer and electronic transmissions.

Electronic mail: Communication sent and received electronically utilizing an electronic mail (e-mail) software program, modem and information network service, such as CompuServe, Microsoft Network (MSN) or American OnLine (AOL). Electronic mail can be utilized within a private or public network.

Electronic mail address: Characters and/or number allowing the identification and location of an electronic mailbox.

Electrostatic printer: A computer printer which utilizes the magnetic attraction between opposite particles to apply toner to the paper. Laser printers are an example of an electrostatic printer.

Element: A title, heading, or list component within the HyperText Markup Language (HTML). Head elements within HTML are the document title while the body elements are structures such as headings, text, paragraphs, etc.

Elevator Seeking: A procedure for optimizing the motion of the hard disk drive heads of a file server.

E&M Signaling: A switch, Private Branch Exchange (PBX), or trunk electronic signal sent on two-state wires by way of a two-state voltage.

Emac: A LISt Processing (LISP) language programmed text editor within a UNIX-based computer system allowing the configuration of a defined editor.

E-mail: *See* **Electronic mail.**

Embedded chart: A chart within the Microsoft Excel program created within a standard Excel worksheet instead of a short document.

Embedded formatting commands: Hidden text formatting commands located directly in the text on-screen.

Embedded objects: A file linked to another without a dynamic link between the original source file and the destination file. Object Linking and Embedding (OLE) actually insert one file into another, if the user is using OLE programs.

EMI: *See* **ElectroMagnetic Interference.**

EMM386.EXE: An emulator of expanded memory enabling the user to input device drivers and application software into the upper memory area. Computers equipped with 80386 or higher require this emulator. *See* **Device driver; Expanded memory; Expanded memory emulator; Extended memory; Upper memory area.**

Emoticon: A group of American Standard Code for Information Interchange (ASCII) characters allowing messages from electronic mail and newsgroups to be converted in context.

EMS: *See* **Lotus-Intel-Microsoft Expanded Memory Specification (LIM EMS).**

Emulated Local Area Network (ELAN): A logical network initiated by using the mechanisms defined by Local Area Network (LAN) emulation. This could include Asynchronous Transfer Mode (ATM) processes or legacy attached end stations.

Emulation: A copied functional capability from one device to another. For example, a dumb terminal, one without a microprocessor, is emulated by a personal computer, allowing communication to another distant personal computer. *See* **Dumb terminal.**

Encapsulated PostScript (EPS) file: A graphic image of high-resolution stored on the postscript page description file. These graphics print at the quality or 300 Dots Per Inch (DPI). A postscript-compatible printer is required to print all EPS files. They are only viable on the computer when the EPS file has a PICT or Tagged Image File Format (TIFF) formatted image attached. *See* **PostScript**.

Encryption: A system of rules for changing computer data into unintelligible symbols so that they are not deciphered by others unless they have the password.

End office: A local telephone exchange allowing the subscriber loop to terminate.

End user: A computer user directly performing tasks located on a computer server.

Energy Star: A program symbol developed by the U.S. Environmental Protection Agency (EPA) in order to encourage computer equipment manufacturers to lower the amount of electrical consumption utilized by their equipment. This is done by putting the device in a temporary sleep mode when not in use.

Enhanced 101-key keyboard: A keyboard designed with two distinct parts: a keypad and cursor controls.

Enhanced CD: A compact disk standard designed by Microsoft allowing audio Compact Disk (CD) publishers to incorporate digital information on the CD.

Enhanced Expanded Memory Specifications (EEMS): An expanded memory improved from the original version of the Lotus-Intel-Microsoft Expanded Memory Specifications (LIM EMS), allowing all Disk Operating System (DOS) application to utilize more than 640 kilobytes (Kb) of memory.

Enhanced Graphics Adapter (EGA): A graphics adapter developed to enable a color digital monitor. An adapter for IBM compatible computers, it can display up to 16 colors simultaneously, allowing a resolution of 640 horizontal lines by 350 vertical ones.

Enhanced Graphics Display: A color digital monitor for IBM Enhanced Graphics Adapter (EGA).

Enhanced Industry Standard Architecture (EISA): A bus architecture supportive of 32-bit peripherals compatible with 16-bit peripherals, transferring data at 33 M/s. *See* **MicroChannel**.

Enhanced Industry Standard Architecture (EISA-2): A new version of an expansion bus that has improvements from the earlier EISA stand.

Enhanced Integrated Drive Electronics (EIDE)

It can transfer data at 132 M/s. Although it remains in several sophisticated Ethernet Servers, it has been mostly superseded by Peripheral Component Interconnect (PCI) standard.

Enhanced Integrated Drive Electronics (EIDE): An Integrated Drive Electronics (IDE) enabling the connection of hard drives and Compact Disk-Read Only Memory drives (CD-ROMs). The EIDE has been improved to allow one to connect up to two-primary hard drives and two-slave hard drives to a computer with an 8.4 GigaBytes (GB) capacity for each.

Enhanced National Center for Supercomputing Applications (NCSA) Mosaic: A specific commercial Web browser application created by Spyglass, Inc.

Enhanced Parallel Port (EPP): Currently the most popular two-way communication port. It enables the communication of a computer and printer, as well as other two-way communications.

Enhanced Parallel Port/Extended Capabilities Port (EPP/ECP): A rapid parallel port which is a newly improved version of the Enhanced Parallel Port (EPP) and Extended Capabilities Port (ECP) standards.

Enhanced Serial Port (ESP): A serial port employing specifically dedicated Random Access Memory (RAM) to rapidly transfer data.

Enhanced services: Services of processing information being transmitted.

Enhanced System Device Interface (ESDI): A hard disk drive interface standard allowing the rapid transfer of data at 10 Megabits per second (Mbps). *See* **Interface standard; Seagate Technology 506/412.**

Enterprise Management Architecture (EMA): A specific architecture conforming to International Standards Organization's (ISO) Coded Mark Inversion (CMI), which is utilized by the Digital Equipment Corporation (DEC).

Enterprise Network: All business Internet sites can be connected from this network.

Enterprise Storage Management: A family of suite of related processes and applications including management of storage devices plus files and data as enterprise resources across heterogeneous environments.

Entity: Software applications or other active elements supplying the service of a physical Open System Interconnection (OSI) layer.

Entry level system: A small computer system using minimal programs such as word processing software or spreadsheet programs.

Entry line: The line in an application program on which characters appear after they are types or entered.

Envelope delay distortion: An electrical phenomenon of distortion resulting from an unequal propagation of frequencies through a communication circuit.

Environment variable: A memory string located within reserved memory allowing specified programs to be configured.

EPP: *See* **Enhanced Parallel Port.**

EPROM: *See* **Erasable Programmable Read Only Memory.**

Equal access: The requirement for local telephone companies to provide all long distant telephone companies with services that are equal in type, quality, and prices of those to AT&T.

Equalization: The balancing of circuit for frequencies to transmit equally, thereby with less distortion. Equalization is achieved by inserting networks.

Equation typesetting: Codes in a document enabling symbols, such as mathematical signs, and characters to be printed.

Equivalent four-wire system: A system of transmission utilizing the division of frequency, thus allowing full-duplex operation through one pair of wires.

Erasable optical disk drive: A disk drive that can store large amounts of data by using a laser to write, edit and store data using the binary system (0-1). Using an optical disk is both efficient and economical.

Erasable Programmable Read Only Memory (EPROM): A programmable Read Only Memory (ROM) chip.

Ergonomic keyboard: A keyboard designed in a curved layout so that there is less strain on hands and wrists while typing.

Ergonomics: The science of designing office equipment, machines computers, etc. to adapt better to the human body and be more comfortable, thus making them healthier and less straining for people to use.

Erlang: A measure of one hour of circuit usage or communication equipment.

Erlang B Capacity table: A table of the number of circuits needed for various levels of telephone communication traffic. The table assumes that failed call attempts were not retried (e.g., that a user does not radial numbers).

Error: The difference between the computed value and the actual one.

Error correcting code: A code of rules for the construction of data signals that are read in the receiving end, in order for departures from it, or errors, to be corrected automatically.

Error correcting system: A system in which errors are corrected before a signal is received at the receiving end.

Error-correction protocol: The process of filtering line noise and if needed, sending transmissions again for modems to link to others that use the same error-correction protocol. The most commonly used ones are Microcon Network Protocol-4 (MNP-4) and V.42.

Error detecting code: A code of construction rules established so those elements transmitted not conforming to the code will be detected.

Error detection: The identification of errors.

Error Free Seconds (EFS): A unit used to specify the error performance of T carrier systems and usually expressed as EFS per hour, EFS per day, or EFS per week. This method more accurately indicates the bit error distribution than other performance measurements such as bit error rate methods.

Error handling: How a program handles errors. Better programs anticipate errors and thus are equipped to help the user overcome them while those of lower quality might not be as efficient. *See* **Error trapping.**

Error message: The message appearing on the computer screen that indicates when a program occurs with the operation.

Error rate: The rate or number of errors occurring per 100,000 characters used to measure the quality of a system.

Error ratio: The ratio of errors to the total number of units.

Error recovery: The procedure or correcting errors in order to return to the computer program.

Error trapping: A software program detecting and responding to errors.

ES: *See* **End System.**

ESC: *See* **Escape.**

Escape (ESC): The key allowing the user to escape a screen or cancel a command.

Escape character: A command disconnecting the Telnet server so the user can directly communicate with the Telnet client.

Escape code: Also referred to as an escape sequence. A code combining the Esc code with an American Standard Code for Information Interchange (ASCII) character that communicates printing functions such as bold typeset.

Escape mechanism: A special code used to provide alternative meanings for characters. *See* **Escape character.**

Escape sequence: *See* **Escape code.**

ESDI: *See* **Enhanced System Device Interface.**

ESP: *See* **Enhanced Serial Port.**

Ethernet: A networking protocol linking up to 1,024 nodes in a bus topology, currently used by Digital Equipment Corporation (DEC) and 3Com.

EtherTalk: The linking adapter for a MacIntosh computer to access Ethernet; the computer needs a compatible Network Interface Card (NIC). It uses a bus topology sending data at a rate of 10 Megabits per second (Mbps).

ETX/ACK handshaking: *See* **Handshaking.**

Eudora: An electronic mail (e-mail) program connecting to the Internet, primarily used on MacIntosh computers. Eudora also uses Multipurpose Internet Multimedia Extensions (MIME) so messages can include files and various multimedia objects.

European Computer Manufacturers Association (ECMA): The association assisting in the setting of international computer standards.

European Laboratory for Particle Physics (CERN): The physics and nuclear research lab in Switzerland where the World Wide Web (WWW) was started. It is also known as CERN (Counseil European pour la Recherche Nucleaire).

Even parity: In a 1-byte data item, adding an extra (parity) bit to 1 if there is an even number of bits, and setting the parity bit to 0 if the number is 0. This is done to stop errors. *See* **Odd parity; Parity checking.**

Event: A signal, such as mouse clicking or a keyboard input, that issues a command code. *See* **Event handler; Event-driven program.**

Event-driven environment: A program executing an event, or signal code, and then returning to an idle mode, or loop.

Event-driven language: A programming language for event-driven programs, which respond to events (signals) to execute a code and then return to an idle mode.

Event-driven program: *See* **Event-driven environment.**

Event handler: A program code managing events in an event-driven environment. *See* **Event; Event-driven environment.**

Exchange: A location where telecommunication lines connect, end, or switch using automatic or manual equipment.

Exchange code: The first three numbers in a seven-digit telephone number, which indicate the customer's exchange server.

.EXE: *See* **Executable.**

Executable (.EXE): The character extension indicating a file is executable, or able to be run, in a given computer. It is used in the Disk Operating System (DOS).

Executable file: *See* **Executable program.**

Executable program: A computer program that can be executable, or carried out, on a computer. Programs not translated are not executable.

Execute: To carry out, or put in effect, programmed instructions.

Expand: A directory listing all the sub-entities in a directory.

Expandability: The capability of hardware to carry additional drives and memory.

Expanded memory: The process of acquiring Read Access Memory (RAM) on an IBM-compatible personal computer that has only 640 Kilobytes (Kb), typically an earlier model computer that can't accommodate extended memory. A bank swaps in data and switches out the chunks not in use. This process can be slow, but later model computers can use extended memory instead if the software has an extended memory manager. *See* **Extended memory.**

Expanded memory board: In IBM-compatible computers, a board which gives additional Read Access Memory (RAM).

Expanded memory emulator: A Disk Operating System (DOS) program that, like expanded memory, extends the memory in earlier modal computers so that more than 640 Kilobytes (Kb) memory can be accessed. This is used in place of installing an adapter board, which is more costly.

Expanded memory manager: The Disk Operating System (DOS) utility program managing expanded memory, which is above 640 Kilobytes (Kb).

Expanded type: Type set that is expands to a larger lateral size, with fewer character units per inch.

Expansion board: *See* **Adapter card.**

Expansion bus: A bus containing extra slots for adapter boards.

Expansion bus bottleneck: Lags in the operation of a computer in which the processor is more efficient that the expansion bus. There are fast expansion bus standards that can solve this, such the Peripheral Component Interconnect (PCI) standard.

Expansion card: *See* **Adapter card.**

Expansion slot: A location where adapters are installed.

Expert system: A computer program helping a non-expert find a solution to a problem. An expert system's answer or response ranges from speculation to a firm, definite conclusion. Relying on IF/THEN rules, many expert systems are lacking in performance since a large number of rules can become confused with each other due to similarities with one another.

Expiration date: The data an article expires set by the author or a UseNet administrator. Expiration allows disk space for new articles. *See* **Expired article.**

Expired article: An article deleted from the UseNet system software because its expiration data has passed, although the name is still listed. *See* **Expiration date.**

Export: To send out data for another program to read.

Extended Binary Coded Decimal Interchange Code (EBCDIC): A code reading characters (alphabet, letters, numbers, or symbols) from the 8-bit string of 0s and 1s used in IBM computers larger than a personal computer.

Extended Capabilities Port: *See* **Enhanced Parallel Port/Extended Capabilities Port.**

Extended character set: A set of characters consisting of 128 American Standard Code for Information Interchange (ASCII) character codes, foreign language and technical characters as well as block graphics.

Extended Graphic Array (XGA): Within IBM, a video display allowing high-resolution mode (1,024 x 768) to display 256 colors and low resolution mode (640 x 480) to display 65,536 colors, provided there is at least 1 Megabytes (MB).

Extended-level synthesizer: A synthesizer playing 16 simultaneous notes on 9 melodic instruments or on 8 percussion instruments in Microsoft Windows' Multimedia Personal Computer (MPC). *See* **Multimedia Personal Computer.**

Extended memory: Random Access Memory (RAM) beyond 1 Megabyte (MB) (or 1,024 KB) installed directly on the motherboard of a computer that is 80286 or a later model. It is accessed with an extended memory manager, which follows eXtended Memory Specifications (XMS) guidelines. *See* **Conventional memory; Expanded memory; Extended memory manager; eXtended Memory Specifications; Microsoft Windows; Upper memory area.**

Extended memory manager: A utility program allowing access to extended memory, that above 1 Megabyte (MB). *See* **Conventional memory; Extended memory; eXtended Memory Specifications.**

eXtended Memory Specifications (XMS): The set of rules a memory manager uses to access extended memory. Memory managers are in the CONFIG.SYS file before XMS memory is accessed. *See* **CONFIG.SYS; Extended memory; HIMEM.SYS; Memory management program.**

Extended VGA: *See* **Super VGA.**

Extension: The three letters added at the end of a file name after the period to describe its contents.

External command: In the Disk Operating System (DOS), a command for a program that is not internal; thus, the program needs to be inserted into the drive. *See* **Internal command.**

External command (ECMD): A command written in the C or Pascal language using built-in MacIntosh routines not available in Hyper Card.

External data bus: Channels managing communication between the Central Processing Unit (CPU) and other components on the hard drive.

External function (XCFN): A software application returning values to a program with HyperTalk. It is written in a language like Pascal or C.

External hard disk: A portable hard disk installed in the case.

External modem: A portable modem attaching to the outside port of a computer.

External reference formula: A formula enabling a cell in a spreadsheet to obtain a value from a cell in another spreadsheet. *See* **Dynamic Data Exchange.**

Extraction: The process of decoding a file encoded for network transmission by using UUEncode by UNIX.

Extra high density floppy disk: A floppy disk containing up to 2.88 Megabytes (MB). Extra High Density (EHD) floppy disks use a driver with two heads.

Extremely Low Frequency (ELF) emission: A magnetic filed emitted from electrical appliances, including computer monitors. These emissions have cause fetal and tissue changes in laboratory animals.

Fall back: The decreased rate of data transfer in order to maintain communications with older, slower modems.

Fall forward: Data, sent by modems, transfer faster because line conditions have improved.

Fall-over: The process of shifting operations from an on-line system to an alternative or redundant system after a failure. The fall-over process may be automatic (as in fault-tolerant systems) or manual (as in high availability systems).

False dependency: A condition within a superscaler microprocessor construction wherein two calculations are written to the same register while separate pipelines simultaneously perform the calculations.

False drop: An error occurring in search systems. The user receives information that is not what was requested.

Family: Members of a group, with higher and lower units of rank, in a windowing system.

FAQ: *See* **Frequently Asked Question.**

FAT: *See* **File Allocation Table.**

Fatal error: A mistake in processing that discontinues the programs and prohibits the user from retrieving unsaved data. Usually the user restarts the computer. Few programs can prevent this occurrence.

Fatware: A term used to describe inadequately developed software applications that inefficiently utilize a large amount of the computer's memory.

Fault tolerance: The design of a computer to maintain its system's performance when some internal hardware problems occur. This is done through the use of back-up systems.

Fax: (1) A printed transmission sent through the telephone lines from one device to another. (2) To send a printed communication through a machine that operates on a telephone line.

Fax machine: A machine that transmits and receives written information via telephone lines.

Fax program: A program that makes using a fax board possible, which functions like a fax machine. Documents can be read as text if the program has Optical Character Recognition (OCR).

Fax server: The computer providing fax capabilities to other workstations in a Local Area Network (LAN).

Fax switch: A mechanism directing telecommunications, which makes having additional telephone lines unnecessary.

FCC: *See* **Federal Communications Commission.**

FCS: *See* **Frame Check Sequence.**

FDD: *See* **Floppy Disk Drive.**

FDDI: *See* **Fiber Distributed Data Interface.**

FDM: *See* **Frequency Division Multiplexing.**

FDX: *See* **Full DupleX.**

FEC: *See* **Forward Error Correction.**

Federal Communications Commission (FCC): Also, the U.S. Federal Communications Commission. The board of commissioners that regulate all electrical telecommunications systems within or from the United States. The FCC is assigned by the President and originated from the Communications Act of 1934.

Federal Communications Commission (FCC) certification: Certification of the FCC that approves the limits of a computer's radio frequency emission. Computers used in commercial settings fall under Class A Certification while those used in homes must meet Class B Certification standards, which dictate lower amounts since high emissions would affect radio and television receptions.

Federal Information Processing Standards (FIPS): A U.S. government computer processing standard for automatic data processing and telecommunication for all government agencies.

Federated database: A collaborative, scientific database enabling scientists to communicate and share their knowledge.

Feeder cable: A set of many electrical distribution cables located near the entrance of a building.

Female connector: Receptacles from a computer cable and connection device developed to receive the pins of a male connector cable.

Femto: The prefix for the quantity of one millionth of one-billionth (1015).

FEP: *See* **Front End Processor.**

Fiber channel: A standard high-speed, fiber-optic connection between several computers (mainframes, mass storage systems, etc.) within a local area, such as a corporation or university. The speed of this communication ranges from 133 Megabits per second (Mbps) to 1 Gigabits per second (Gbps) through many different cable types such as co-axial cable, glass fiber or shielded twisted pair wire.

Fiber Distributed Data Interface (FDDI): Fiber-optic networks running at 100 Megabits per second (Mbps), utilizing wiring hubs as prime servers for network monitoring and control devices. Also a standard for transmitting data on optical fiber cables and is ten times faster than Ethernet but only twice as fast as T-3 lines.

Fiber optic cable: This glass fiber used to transmit data at very high speed, utilizing the guidance laser light. This very expensive medium can transmit data at speeds of 100 Megabits per second (Mbps).

Fiber Optic Inter Repeater Link (FOIRL): A fiber optic signaling method based on the Institute of Electronic and Electrical Engineers (IEEE) 802.3 standard governing fiber optics and their technology. This link allows up to 1,000 meters of multimode duplex fiber optic cable, especially in a point-to-point link.

Fiber optics: The use of light signals to transfer data through glass fibers.

Fidonet: Procedures and standards of data exchange allowing a computer Bulletin Board System (BBS) to exchange information across the global telephone system.

Field: A message frame position, indicated as control field, flag field, etc.

Field definition: A group of attributes within a database management program defining the type of information a user inputs into a data field.

Field name: A name of a datafield within a database management program which assists the user in identifying the contents of the field.

Field privilege: A database definition within a database management program controlling the use of the contents of a data field in a protected database.

FIFO: *See* **First In First Out**.

50-Pin Telco: See Registered Jack.

File: Data stored as a unit on a storage medium.

File Allocation Table (FAT): An area on a disk indicating the arrangement of files in the sectors.

File attribute: A file directory code hidden and which contains read-only information.

File compression utility: A software program compressing files not being used to make extra room on the hard disk. Files are later returned to their original length.

File conversion utility: A program converting files into another format for them to be read in a different program.

File defragmentation: *See* **Defragmentation.**

File deletion: The process of removing and terminating a file because it is no longer useful or because more room is needed. There are two steps to this process. The first is deleting a file that is recoverable, such as putting is in the Macintosh trash can or Windows recycling bin. The file can be retrieved if needed. The second step in this process is deleting it permanently, such as emptying the trashcan or recycling bin. Failure to permanently delete many files can slow the processing time of a computer. It is possible to retrieve a deleted file of which the space has not been used with a utility, such as North Utilities (IBM) or Symantec (Macintosh).

File/Disk grooming: The maintenance and management of files and disk space on servers and workstations.

File extension: *See* **Extension.**

File format: Standards a program utilizes to store information on a disk.

File fragmentation: The inefficient placement of data in non-contiguous sections on a disk. This develops from multiple file deletions and other operations. By defragmenting the disk, much efficiency can be gained. Defragmentation locates file groups together on the same contiguous clusters so that the drive's read/write head must travel longer distances to retrieve. *See* **File defragmentation.**

File locking: This command ensures that no more than one user is accessing a file and altering it.

File management program: A program easing the management of files. It shows the structure of a disk's directory and a list of files. The commands allow one to manage files. *See* **Flat-file database management program.**

File name: A unique name given to an application at some entity on the Operating System (OS). The Disk Operating System (DOS) and early versions of Operating System/2 (OS/2) have two parts, the name and program application extension.

File privilege: An attribute in the dBase language allowing the operation of a protected database on a network.

File recall: The return of migrated files from the lower level of the storage hierarchy to a higher level in response to user access request or in accordance with preset rules.

File recovery: A previously erased file which has been found and placed back into the file system.

File server: A computer within a Local Area Network (LAN) allowing access to a main system of files for all computers on the network.

Filespec: A complete specification for a file's location within a computer system.

File Transfer Access and Management (FTAM): A procedure enabling the transfer of files on another system.

File Transfer Protocol (FTP): An Internet allowing the exchange of files. A program enables the user to contact another computer on the Internet and exchange files.

File transfer utility: A software application that can switch files from one type of computer to another.

Fill: A function entering a series of formulas and numbers on a spreadsheet.

Filter: A computer network developed to send electrical signals with frequencies on nearby bands. All other signals are attenuated.

Filter command: In a Disk Operating System (DOS), a command altering and transferring data information to a printer or other device.

Finder: A file and memory management utility provided by Apple for Macintosh computers. This utility enables you to run one application at a time.

FinePrint: Effective Apple Laser printers resolution of 600 by 600 Dots Per Inch (DPI).

Finger: A utility on the Internet allowing someone to obtain information about a user's electronic mail (e-mail) address. This information is limited to a user's full name, job title, and address.

FIPS: *See* **Federal Information Processing Standards.**

Firewall: A utility preventing unauthorized users from entering a restricted database or server via a Local Area Network (LAN) and/or the Internet for security reasons.

Firmware: Permanently stored software within the Read Only Memory (ROM), which cannot be modified.

FIRST: *See* **Forum of Incident Response and Security Teams.**

First In First Out (FIFO): Placing calls in the order in which they arrive.

Five-level code: A telegraph code utilizing five impulses to indicate a character.

Fixed disk: This is a hard disk in an IBM system.

Fixed frequency monitor: A monitor-receiving analog inputting data signals at one frequency.

Fixed length: A fixed length of a field within a DataBase Management System (DBMS). The field cannot accommodate the changing size of data entries.

Fixed numeric format: A numeric format in spreadsheet programs utilizing rounded values as specified by the user.

F-key: A Macintosh utility command enabled by depressing a number key from 0-9 and the Shift key. This is similar to the function keys on IBM computer keyboards.

Flag: A variable normally utilized for indicating a true or false statement.

Flame: Inappropriate language used in electronic mail.

Flame bait: A posted topic within a newsgroup or the World Wide Web (WWW) that may prompt abusive remarks or inappropriate language.

Flash Basic Input/Output System (BIOS): A Read Only Memory (ROM) computer chip that a user can simply alter with an encoded disk in lieu of substituting a new chip.

Flat: Computer system files without subdirectories in which to group similar files.

Flat address space: A non-restrictive and efficient procedure of organizing a computer's memory in order to allocate portions of the memory. Microsoft Windows '95 utilizes this design of flat memory through the use of the 32-bit memory addresses.

Flatbed scanner: An electronic digitizer utilizing optical scanning to transform a graphic sheet into a digitized file.

Flat-file database management program: A program for database management allowing the retrieval, storage and organization of files, one at a time.

Flat panel display: A display screen in small, portable computers; to make such a thin, flat display, special technology is used. A gas plasma display, Liquid Crystal Display (LCD), and Thin Film Transmission (TFT) are all examples of flat panel displays.

Flat rate service: One monthly fee service allowing the user an unlimited number of local calls.

Flat square monitor: A gently curved monitor screen that decreases most, but not all, spherical distortion.

Flat tension-mask monitor: A Zenith flat display monitor that, unlike the others, has no distortion but is costly.

Flicker: An on-screen distortion develop from the scrolling of a low refresh rate.

Floating graphic: A non-fixed picture or graph within a program allowing it to move up or down the page as the user deletes or inserts text above the graphics.

Floating point calculation: The procedure of having a decimal point that can move freely so that large numbers and calculations can be stored, thus increasing accuracy.

Floating Point Unit (FPU): A component within a computer allowing operations of moving the decimal point to create a very high precision for large numbers.

Flood search: The process of sending the same data transmission or call request to many outgoing circuits.

Floppy disk: A removable, optical disk utilizing a magnetically sensitive, flexible plastic disk to store data in. The disk rotates within the disk drive, which reads for written data. They vary in terms of size and density. The most common disks used are the high-density and smaller 3 1/2-inch disks. They are encased in protective plastic. An access hole allows protection from changes in the files.

Floppy disk controller: The electronics controlling a floppy disk, which operates the spindle motor and read/write head.

Floppy Disk Drive (FDD): An acronym for a floppy disk drive; the device operating the software disk.

Floppy Drive High Density (FDHD): An acronym for a high density floppy drive, the device operating high density software disks.

Floptical drive: A storage device utilizing lasers to illuminate tracks on a disk. The read/write heads are precisely positioned from the photo-detector signals of the reflected light.

Flow: The word processing command enabling written text to line up in columns and be placed around graphics and photos for newspapers.

Flowchart: A chart that shows how a computer program works with symbols and graphics.

Flow control: A procedure of enabling a modem, computer or other data device to regulate the flow of data. The flow between modems is term-ed software handshaking while the flow between a computer and modem is called hardware handshaking.

Flush: A function correcting errors by turning off a printer to clear the operation.

Flush left: Justifying text within a word document to the left margin and leaving an uneven right margin.

FM: *See* **Frequency Modulation.**

FOIRL: *See* **Fiber Optic Inter Repeater Link.**

Folder: A graphic of a file folder on the screen of the Macintosh finder or Microsoft Windows '95 that organizes computer files.

Follow-on post: A public message posted within an on-line newsgroup in response to a previous posting.

Font: The style of typeface, size, and weight of written text in which all the characters (for example, letters, numbers, symbols) pertain to.

Font cartridge: This read-only memory cartridge contains text fonts and inserts into a printer.

Font/DA Mover: Within a Macintosh system, a program allowing extra accessories (font and Desk Accessory) to be added to the system file of the computer's start-up disk.

Font family: Fonts sharing the same typeface but vary according to weight (Roman or bold), posture (vertical or italics), and size.

Font ID conflict: A system error in Macintosh resulting from conflicts between the identification assigned to screen fonts and those stored within the system folder.

Font metric: The size of characters located within the width table.

Font smoothing: The reduction of distortions of text or graphics from high resolution printers.

Font substitution: The substitution of an outline font for a bit-mapped font when printing documents.

Footer: Written text at the foot or bottom of all the pages in a document. Footers usually indicate information such as the title or author of the document.

Footprint: The amount of floor area utilized by a printer, monitor, computer or other type of equipment.

Forced page break: A permanent page break created by the computer user.

Foreground task: The priority task within a multi-taxing computing job.

Foreign exchange: A telephone line represented by a local phone number that is actually located in another area, usually for business purposes.

Form: *See* **Forms.**

Format: A procedure for arranging data for displaying, printing, or storage. Examples of formatting within spreadsheets programs include values, constants within a cell, labels, etc.

Format effector character: A character setting the location of data on the computer display or paper.

Formatted mode: A Video Display Terminal (VDT) display mode allowing the screen to be transmitted at once instead of one line at a time.

Formatting: A computer operation setting up the configuration of patterns for the display, storage, or the printing of data.

Form factor: The hard or floppy disk physical height.

Form feed: A printer command instructing the ejection of the current page and the loading of a new page.

Forms: On the World Wide Web (WWW) or within Hypertext Markup Language (HTML), a set of document commands allowing the user to connect with a Web page.

Forms capable browser: An Internet Web Browser capable of creating on-screen interactive forms within Hypertext Markup Language (HTML). The Mosaic and Netscape Navigator browsers are both capable of this feature.

FORmula TRANslator (FORTRAN): A computer programming language developed by IBM in mid-1950s for scientific, mathematical, and engineering applications.

FOR/NEXT loop: A computer loop control command that is capable of initiating an instruction a specific number of times.

FORTH: A computer programming language allowing control of hardware devices. FORTH denotes FOURTH-generation programming language. It is usually preferred for laboratory data acquisition, such as machine control, automation, and patient monitoring.

FORTRAN: *See* **FORmula TRANslator.**

Forum: *See* **Newsgroup.**

Forum of Incident Response and Security Teams (FIRST): A staff of several worldwide Computer Emergency Response Teams (CERT), which are a part of the Internet Society. Their goals are to assemble, coordinate, and promote the security of the Internet.

Forward chaining: An interface procedure for expert systems requiring the user to state all relevant data before the processing may begin. It begins with input data and progresses through its rules in order to determine if additional data is required and determine the interface.

Forward channel: The forward or primary direction data travels in a circuit.

Forward Error Correction (FEC): A procedure of sending extra characters with a data block to resolve errors in transmission.

For Your Information (FYI): Guidelines clearly written explaining Internet standards for the average user, frequently distributed in electronic mail; these useful instructions can be obtained from a Network Information Center (NIC).

Four-way set-associated cache: A set-associated cache design that is faster yet costlier than two-way set-associative caches.

Four-wire circuit: A circuit of four wires arranged in pairs that make one duplex circuit.

Four-wire terminating set: An electrical circuit layout with four-wire circuits leading to a two-wire circuit in order to connect with other two-wire circuits.

FPU: *See* **Floating Point Unit.**

FQDN: *See* **Fully Qualified Domain Name.**

Fragmentation: *See* **File fragmentation.**

Frame: (1) A Logical Data block that can be forwarded utilizing data link protocols. (2) Data packet on a network, such as Token Ring, X.25, or Systems Network Architecture (SNA). (3) A message block. (4) The vehicle for every command, response, procedures within the Synchronous Data Link Control (SDLC). (5) A sequence of contiguous characters bracketed by a band, including the closing and opening flag sequence. (6) A rectangular area containing text, graphic or both located on the page within desktop publishing and word processing applications.

Frame buffer: An area of the display monitor holding the data of the image on-screen. The Central Processing Unit (CPU) sends the data to the frame buffer allowing the video controller to read it.

Frame Check Sequence (FCS): A term corresponding to Cyclic Redundancy Check (CRC), an error-checking protocol for linking modems.

Frame relay: A packet switching communication service that neither detects nor corrects routing relays. It typically provides for a bandwidth within the range of 56 Kilobits per second (Kbps) to 1.544 Megabits per second (Mbps) rates emerging.

Frame synchronization: A data link condition describing the start and end frames a receiver recognizes.

Framing bits: Bits or characters that do not carry information in order to provide separation within a bit stream.

Freenet: A Bulletin Board System (BBS) devoted to helping communities easily reach resources, which include access to the Internet, information on community groups and organizations, card catalogs of libraries, notes and transcripts of city council meetings, etc. Freenet's services can be used at little or no cost; they are normally housed in a local library.

Free Software Foundation (FSF): A not-for-profit group, located in Massachusetts, that is committed to the idea that software should be freely shared. FSF supports computer system utilities under FSF's General Public License (GPL).

Freeware: Software programs that anyone can use at no cost. They are copyrighted and cannot be resold.

Freeze frame television: Television frames changing when necessary, about 30 to 90 seconds.

Frequency: The rate of analog signal cycles per second measured in Hertz.

Frequency-agile modem: A modem that can change frequencies for different broadband systems to communicate.

Frequently Asked Question (FAQ): In USENET, postings designed to help newcomers and keep all users informed. They answer commonly asked questions and give updated information.

Frequency converter: A tool translating frequencies in broadband cable systems.

Frequency Division Multiplexing (FDM): A method of combining signals on a cable circuit by separating frequency bandwidth, or altering frequencies, so signals can operate individually as channels.

Frequency Modulation (FM): Modulation in which the frequency is the measured variable, not amplitude.

Frequency Modulation (FM) recording: Single-density recording on computer disks and tapes more commonly used in the past.

Frequency Modulation (FM) synthesis: A way of simulating musical instruments in sound boards using Musical Instrument Digital Interface (MIDI) that is less economical yet poor in quality.

Frequency response: An alteration in frequency; an attenuation distortion.

Frequency Shift Keying (FSK): A modem method of altering frequencies to signify the digital 0s and 1s. In a modem, modulation of frequencies so that signals are transmitted separately.

Friction feed: Insertion of sheets paper into a printer using friction of the paper. Pages are normally fed by hand.

Front-end: The interactive section of a program, which can be sent to workstations in a Local Area Network (LAN) for users to interact with the back end programs on the file server.

113

Front End Processor (FEP): A computer situated between the mainframe and terminals. It processes tasks of the host computer, including line and error control, and other application functions. Thus, the host computer can operate more efficiently.

Front-end systems: A computer providing information on a back-end server system in a commercial setting.

FSF: *See* **Free Software Foundation.**

FSK: *See* **Frequency Shift Keying.**

FTAM: *See* **File Transfer Access and Management.**

FTP: *See* **File Transfer Protocol.**

Full-associative cache: A cache design that instructs the Central Processing Unit (CPU) to conduct a full search for requested information. It is considered between the direct-map cache design and the stronger set-associative cache design.

Full bleed: Design graphics or characters that extend the full length of a page.

Full-DupleX (FDX): Communications operations in which data is sent and received at the same time; bi-directional communication.

Full justification: Text is justified, or aligned, on both the left and right margins.

Full motion television: The rate of 30 television pictures transmitted every second.

Full motion video adapter: A practical video adapter that can play live images from a camcorder as well as recorded tapes. It is equipped for multimedia presentation, using techniques such as animation, sound and fades.

Full-page display: The display of a full page of text on a screen.

Full-screen application: In Microsoft Windows, a non-Windows application that takes up the entire screen after you launch it from Windows.

Full-screen editor: A word processing utility assisting the user with creating and editing text. The cursor can scroll the full length of the created document.

Fully Qualified Domain Name: A full site name of a system rather than just its host name.

Function: A built-in procedure that returns a value while programming spread sheets and computer languages.

Functional-management layer: In Systems Network Architecture (SNA), a communications layer outlining formal presentations.

Function key: A key, such as ENTER or numbered F1, F2, etc., transmitting signals for special functions.

Fuser wand: A device heating toner on the paper in laser printers.

FYI: *See* **For Your Information.**

FX: Foreign exchange.

Game port: A socket connecting a joystick or game devices to play various games.

GAP: *See* **Generic Address Parameter.**

Garage: An inkjet printer bracket for storing an unused ink cartridge without the ink drying.

Garbage collection: A process deciding what information is no longer needed in Random Access Memory (RAM). This prevents useless data collecting in RAM and causing a crash.

Garbage In Garbage Out (GIGO): What goes in badly or incorrectly will come out in the identical condition.

Gas plasma display: *See* **Plasma Display**

Gateway: A gateway acts as an interface and connects two dissimilar Local Area Networks (LANs) or connects to Wide Area Network (WAN) or mainframe. A gateway may have its own memory and processor and can perform protocol and bandwidth conversion along with translation of different protocols.

Gaussian noise: *See* **Background noise.**

Gb: Abbreviation for Gigabyte.

GCID: Global Call IDentifier.

GCID-IE: Generic Call IDentifier-Information Element.

GCRA: Generic Cell Rate Algorithm.

GDI: See Graphical Device Interface.

General Musical Instrument Digital Interface (MIDI) (GM): In multimedia, a MIDI Manufacturers' Association (MMA) standard defining a set of 96 standard voices of musical instruments along with non-melodic percussive instruments. See **Musical Instrument Digital Interface.**

General Public License: See **Free Software Foundation.**

Generic Address Parameter (GAM):

Geometry: The physical layout of a hard disk's surface as delineated by the number of tracks and sectors and also the landing zone locations.

GFC: Generic Flow Control.

Ghost: Characters or images burned onto the back of the screen phosphors creating a faint yet recognizable reproduction of those characters or image. See **Screen savers.**

GHz: An abbreviation for GigaHertz.

GIF: See **Graphics Interchange Format.**

Giga (G): One billion. For example, 1 GigaHertz equals 1,000,000,000 hertz. One GigaHertz also equals 1000 MegaHertz (MHz) and 1,000,000 KiloHertz (KHz).

Gigabit (Gb): A unit of measurement equal to slightly more than one billion bits (1,073,741,824). This is used to show transmission of bits per second.

GigaByte (GB): A unit of memory measurement slightly more than one billion bytes (1,073,741,824).

GIGO: See **Garbage In Garbage Out.**

Glitch: A momentary power interruption or electronic fluctuation such as those caused by power surges or bad connections. In computer slang, a glitch can be a hardware problem; a software problem is usually called a bug.

Global backup: A hard disk backup procedure in which all data is backed up onto another medium such as a tape drive or floppy disk. See **Incremental backup.**

Global format: In a spreadsheet program, a type of format or alignment applying to all worksheet cells. Most global formats can be overridden.

Global kill file: In UseNet, a file containing words, phrases, or network addresses identified as unwanted message signals. The signals activate a process that automatically deletes the article before it arrives.

Global Naming Service: A naming service for users and services on a network.

Global network: A network created and connected between countries and/or continents.

Glossary: A utility program with often-used phrases that can be used when needed in a document. *See* **Boilerplate.**

Glossy finish: A quality of paper that reflects light more completely than matte paper.

GM: *See* **General Musical Instrument Digital Interface.**

Gopher: In Internet to UNIX-based systems, a menu-based program used as an adjunct for finding files, definitions, and resources. Gopher was developed at the University of Minnesota. Gopher is slowly becoming obsolete.

Gopherspace: In Gopher, the computer-based "space" created by disseminating Gopher-accessible resources. Veronica, a search tool, can search Gopherspace for titles and resources to match supplied key words.

GOSIP: *See* **Government Open System Interconnection Profile.**

.Gov: An Internet domain name for a government office or agency.

Government Open System Interconnection (OSI) Profile (GOSIP): The U.S. government's OSI protocols version.

Grabber hand: In graphics programs and HyperCard, an on-screen hand positioned to move selected on-screen text or graphics.

Grade of service: A traffic handling capability measurement of a network in terms of sufficiency of equipment and trunking throughout all nodes.

Graphical Device Interface (GDI): A Graphical User Interface (GUI) programming resource enabling programmers to generate consistent dialog boxes and other visual elements. GDIs simplify the programming work; the programmer simply has to instruct what element to draw and its position.

Graphical User Interface (GUI): An overall and consistent for the interactive and visual program that interacts (or interfaces) with the user. GUI can involve pull-down menus, dialog boxes, on-screen graphics, and a variety of icons.

Graphical Web browser: A program allowing access to documents and information on the World Wide Web (WWW) containing in-line images and various document layouts. Some Web browsers can include Enhanced National Center for Supercomputing Applications (NCSA) Mosaic and Netscape Navigator.

Graphic character: A character displayed on a terminal screen or printed page.

Graphics: There are two types of computer-produced graphics: 1) object-oriented graphics or vector graphics and 2) bit-mapped graphics or raster graphics. Object-oriented graphics (often called draw programs) store graphic images as mathematical formulae and are adaptable for architecture, computer aided design, and interior design. Bit-mapped graphic programs (referred to as paint programs) store graphic images as screen pixels. Paint programs can work with subtlety yet may be missing some precision whereas draw programs are usually more precise with fewer artistic effects. *See* **Bit-mapped graphic; Draw program; Object-oriented graphic; Paint program.**

Graphics accelerator board: An expansion board containing a graphic coprocessor and all other circuitry found on a video adapter. The accelerator board does the graphics job for the Central Processing Unit (CPU) freeing it to do other processes and so speeds the display speeds of the computer. *See* **Central Processing Unit; Graphic coprocessor; Microsoft Windows; Video adapter.**

Graphics character: A character is composed of lines, rectangles or other shapes. Graphic characters can be combined to form graphics or images, illustrations, and borders. *See* **Block graphics.**

Graphics coprocessor: A microprocessor which accelerates the processing and display of high-resolution video images. Popular graphics coprocessors include the Weitek W5086 and W5186 as well as S3 Inc.'s 86C911. *See* **Graphic accelerator board.**

Graphics Interchange Format (GIF): A bit-mapped graphics file format for IBM and IBM-compatible computers. GIF is often employed for graphics exchange on a Bulletin Board System (BBS) and networks and uses a high resolution graphics compression technique.

Graphics mode: In video adapters, a display mode with both text and graphics displayed on the screen. Conversely, a character mode runs more quickly since the computer uses ready-made characters as opposed to creating them one at a time.

Graphics primitive: In an object-oriented or vector graphics program, the unit of visual creation, such as an arc, circle, line, oval, or rectangle.

Graphics scanner: A graphics input device that analyzes and then transforms a physical image into an electronic one.

Graphics table: A graphics input device permitting drawing with an electronic pen on an electronically sensitive table with each movement of the pen mimicked on the screen.

Graphics view: In some Disk Operating System (DOS) applications, a process switching the display circuitry to its graphic mode to display bit-mapped graphics. The graphics mode is slower than a computer's character mode.

Gray code: A binary code as sequential numbers differing from the preceding expression by only one place.

Gray scale: A series of graphical shades from white to black.

Grayscale monitor: A monitor displaying a full range of shades from white to black. Gray-scale monitors are expensive. Color monitors are usually more than adequate for most users.

Grayscale scanner: An output scanner generating 256 levels of gray. Grayscale scanners are less expensive than color scanners, with the price difference diminishing.

Greeking: The simulated version for a page layout showing an approximation of what the layout will look like without displaying all the graphics and details.

Greek text: Simulated text or lines representing the positioning and point size identical to the compositor's page design. Typesetters use standard Greek text that actually looks more like Latin.

Green Book: A standard (by Philips) for combining text, sound and video onto a Compact Disk-Read Only Memory (CD-ROM) disk. Also known as Compact Disk-Interactive (CD-I).

Green PC: An energy-efficient computer system drawing 40 watts less than the usual system. For instance, in sleep mode, green PCs draw between 28 watts and 36 watts.

Ground: An electrically neutral contact point.

Group: Program icons stored together inside a group icon, such as the Accessories, Main, and Games groups.

Group: Twelve 4-KiloHertz (KHz) voice signals multiplexed as a 48 KHz signal.

Group 2: An obsolete and also slow standard for fax machines.

Group 3: A fax machine and fax modem standard published by the International Telecommunications Union-Telecommunications Standard Section (ITU-TSS). The Group 3 standard specifies how a fax is sent.

Group 4: A fax transmission standard interfacing with digital transmission networks such as Integrated Services Digital Network (ISDN).

Group coding: A modem process to transmit data by altering the carrier characteristics. Unlike Frequency Shift Keying (FSK), group coding increases the modem's sending ability and uses quadrature (and other) modulation techniques for character modification.

Group icon: An icon containing a collection of program icons with each program icon usually pointing to individual applications.

Groupware: Application programs able to increase the joint productivity of groups of coworkers.

Guard band: *See* **Guard channel.**

Guard channel: The intervening space between the primary signal and the edge of an analog channel.

Guest: In a Local Area Network (LAN), non-password access privilege allowing connection to another computer on a network. *See* **Local Area Network.**

Guide: An on-screen nonprinting line. The dotted line can indicate the location of margins, gutters and other layout elements.

Gutter: In word processing and desktop publishing programs, an inside margin indicating the binding margin for a book, pamphlet or booklet. *See* **Duplex printing.**

GW-BASIC: A version of the Beginner's All-purpose Symbolic Instruction Code (BASIC) programming language almost the same as IBM's BASIC interpreter but able to be customized. *See* **Beginner's All-purpose Symbolic Instruction Code.**

H0 channel: A 384-KiloByte Per Second (KBPS) channel with six adjacent Digital Signal O (DSO) channels each being 64 KBPS on a T1 line.

H10 channel: A 1472-KiloByte Per Second (KBPS) channel supplied by a T1 carrier or a primary rate carrier. The H10 channel is analogous to twenty-three 64-KBPS channels.

H11 channel: A primary rate employed as one 1536-KiloByte Per Second (KBPS) channel with 24 adjacent Digital Signal O (DSO) channels or, often, a T1 line.

H12 channel: A primary rate (used in Europe) with one 1920-KiloByte Per Second (KBPS) channel which is equivalent to thirty 64-KBPS channels.

Hacker: This term originally meant a technologically adept individual who explored and expanded computers to their limits. Now, the term means a person with an illegal and potentially intention to slip past a computer security system or firewall in order to change data, destroy data, insert viruses, or execute other unauthorized functions.

Hacker ethics and security: A set of moral principles known to the first-generation hacker community as highlighted by Steven Levy. Hacker ethics insisted all technical information should be available to all. Therefore, with such a viewpoint, entering a system to explore and increase knowledge cannot be unethical. Of course, destroying data remains unethical. In fact, breaking into database systems is against the law. *See* **Cyberspace; Hack; Phreaking.**

Half-DupleX (HDX): A singular transmission over one medium and in one direction during transmission.

Half-duplex transmission: A two-way transmission process wherein information is carried in one direction at a time as with the transmissions between two Citizens' Band (CB) radios.

Half-height drive bay: A mounting rack area for devices (not with full height dimensions) such as a half-height drive in a computer. A half-height drive bay is 1.625 inches tall.

Halftone: A series of noncontinuous dots prepared from a photograph or print. The higher the number (density) of dots, the darker the reproduced area. *See* **Tagged Image File Format.**

Handle: In memory management, access to a block of extended memory. When a program requests extended memory, the High-MEMory SYStem file (HIMEM.SYS) gives the program a handle (access) to an extended memory block. *See* **Draw program; Object-oriented graphic.**

Handler: In an object-oriented graphics program, a set of instructions or script placed inside an object used to hold messages inside the object. A handler is also a driver, utility program or subroutine designed to manage a task. For instance, an A20 handler is a controlling routine for access to extended memory in a computer using a Disk Operating System (DOS). *See* **Event-driven program; Object-Oriented Programming language.**

Handshake: An automatic dial-up circuit security technique that requires terminal hardware to make a self-identification sending a predetermined identification code. The handshake technique is not terminal-operator controlled.

Handshaking: This method controls the serial communication flow between two devices; one device transmits when another device is ready to receive.

Hard copy: Printed output as opposed to data stored on a floppy disk or in the computer's memory.

Hard disk backup program: A utility program designed to back up disk data and/or programs onto floppy disks in case of damage or data loss to the primary data and/or drive.

Hard disk controller: The circuitry controlling both the hard disk drive spindle motor and head actuator. Using host adapter instructions, the hard disk controller searches and communicates the needed information to the computer. An Integrated Drive Electronics (IDE) hard disk controller, which is actually part of the hard drive, must be configured differently, depending on whether the drives are acting as master or slave drives.

Hard Disk Drive (HDD): A storage device and medium using one or more nonflexible disks and housed, together with the recording heads, in a sealed mechanism. Storage capacities can range up to several gigabytes (a number which is increasing with the advancing technology). A hard disk is a complex storage device including the disks, the read/write head assembly, and the electronic interface between the drive and the computer. *See* **Access time; Backup; Integrated Drive Electronics; Secondary storage.**

Hard disk interface: An accepted standard controlling and managing the connection of a Hard Disk Drive (HDD) to the computer. *See* **Enhanced System Device Interface; Hard Disk Drive; Integrated Drive Electronics; Small Computer System Interface.**

Hard drive: *See* **Hard Disk Drive.**

Hard hyphen: In word processing programs, a formatted hyphen that prevents a program from introducing a line break between hyphenated words. Synonymous with nonbreaking hyphen. *See* **Soft hyphen.**

Hard page break: An active user-added page break effective even after the user later adds or deletes text above the break. In contrast, a program-inserted soft page break automatically shifts with text addition or deletion. Synonymous with forced page break.

Hard return: An active manually inserted page break even after text addition or deletion above the break. In contrast, a program-inserted soft return may move after text alteration. Synonymous with forced page break.

Hard space: In word processing programs, a specially formatted space preventing the introduction of a line break. Hard spaces are often employed to keep two-word proper nouns together.

Hardware: The electronic components (boards, peripherals, etc.) comprising a computer system. In contrast, the software or programs tells these components what to do.

Hardware cache: Temporary storage cache memory placed on a disk drive controller or a disk drive. The cache memory stores frequently accessed programs, instructions and data. A computer accesses required data more quickly from a hardware cache than from a disk. Both 32-bit and 16-bit cache disk controller cards are currently available. *See* **Disk drive controller.**

Hardware error control: Error-correction protocol, such as Microcon Network Protocol-4 (MNP-4) or V.42, encoded in the modem rather than in the communications program. The hardware error control frees the Central Processing Unit (CPU) from error catching and error correction.

Hardware panning: A video adapter feature enabling a larger-than-allowed video display. By creating additional display memory and altering the frame buffer display memory area, the video adapter allows the mouse to move to the edge of the screen and/or scroll to other areas of a "virtual" display.

Hardware platform: A computer hardware/software standard such as IBM PC-compatible or Macintosh. Devices or programs created for one

123

platform cannot typically run on others. *See* **Device independence; Platform independence.**

Hardware reset: A system restart performed with the reset button. A hardware reset may be necessary after a system crash if Ctrl-Alt-Del cannot be used to restart the computer. *See* **Programmer's switch; Warm boot.**

Hardware sprite: A video adapter feature allowing a cursor or mouse pointer to be drawn without redrawing the entire screen. Hardware sprites, included as part of all video standards after eXtended Graphics Array (XGA), make programming easier since programs can move the cursor or printer with simpler commands.

Hardware tree: In Microsoft Windows '95, a graphical representation of the path and connections of devices and adapters installed in a computer.

Hardware windowing: A video performance improvement technique employed by graphic accelerator boards. A hardware windowing design is good for multitasking environments like Microsoft Windows '95 or IBM's Operating System/2 (OS/2). Hardware windowing systems frees the Central Processing Unit (CPU) from windows management chores and enables the graphic accelerator board to improve performance since it only has to change a window and not a whole screen.

Hard wired: A built-in processing function instead of a process activated by program instructions. The specialized math functions in a math coprocessor, for example, are hard wired. The term hard-wired also refers to the program instructions contained in the computer's Read Only Memory (ROM) or firmware.

Harmonic Adapter: An efficient method for converting a 50-pin Telco connection to a Registered Jack-45 (RJ45) connection.

Harmonics: The presence of harmonic frequencies/overtones (due to nonlinear characters of a transmission line in response to an applied sine wave).

Hayes command set: A standardized instruction set for controlling modems. *See* **Modem.**

The Hayes commands include:

AT: Attention (starts all commands)
ATDT: Attention (dial in tone mode)
ATDP: Attention (dial in pulse mode)
+++:   Enter command mode during communications session
ATH: Attention, Hang up.

Hayes compatible modem: A modem capable of recognizing the Hayes command set. All asynchronous modems have this ability.

H-Channel: Integrated Services Digital Network (ISDN) bearer services with pre-defined speeds along with starting and stopping locations on a Primary Rate Interface (PRI).

HDD: *See* **Hard Disk Drive.**

HDLC: *See* **High-level Data Link Control.**

Head access aperture: A floppy disk shell opening enabling the read/write head to work in conjunction with the recording medium. In a 31/2-inch floppy disk drive, a sliding metal shutter covers the head access aperture, but a 51/4-inch disk drive exposes the head access aperture when the disk is moved out from its protective sleeve.

Head crash: A hard disk drive read/write head and floppy disk surface collision; this often results in damage to the disk surface and to the head.

Header: Part of the data message (with protocol control information) with information about a message such as destination, sequence number and perhaps a date and time stamp. Also, repeated text, such as a page number and/or document title information appearing on each document page. Some programs, such as Word, allow odd and even headers for mirror-image headers. First-page headers can be suppressed and other options are available depending on the software. Synonymous with running head. *See* **Footer.**

Head-Mounted Display (HMD): A stereoscopic set of head-mounted goggles that produce a sensation of three-dimensional space and openness. Head-mounted displays have become important for virtual reality systems.

Head parking: Positioning the read/write head over a zone for head crash prevention and disk surface contact avoidance. Older hard disk drives require an outside command to park the head; newer hard disk drive functions feature automatic head parking. *See* **Head crash.**

Head Seek time: *See* **Access time.**

Head slot: A floppy disk case opening. This access hole exposes the necessary disk surface so a read/write head can read or write information.

Heap: In earlier versions of Microsoft Windows, a heap was a specified storage area saved for critical resources. The heaps (local heap, menu heap, and user heap) were called the system resources and were limited to 64 KiloBytes (KB). When they became full, the user would encounter the message "Not enough memory" when attempting to begin another program.

Heat sink: A metal assembly with fins atop a hot component, such as a Pentium microprocessor. The heat sink prevents overheating by pulling the heat away.

Help desk: The single point of user contact (via phone, fax, or e-mail) when problems occur not immediately remediable.

Helper program: In a Web browser, an additional program allowing the browser to handle multimedia files. Most helper programs are shareware or freeware (available at little or no cost) and are downloaded at the time of downloading the file. Setup usually tries to match or configure the program with the file type, such as the Multipurpose Internet Multimedia Extension (MIME), to be displayed.

Hertz (Hz): A unit of measurement for frequency or electrical vibrations; one Hz equals one cycle per second. *See* **MegaHertz.**

Heterogeneous network: A Local Area Network (LAN) with computers and devices from several manufacturers. Many firms have created heterogeneous networks able to link Macintosh and Window systems. *See* **Local Area Network.**

Heuristic: A problem-solving method using rules acquired from experience. Heuristics are rarely formally stated, but are knowledge human experts use in problem solving. *See* **Expert system; Knowledge base.**

Hewlett-Packard (HP): A manufacturer of computers, plotters, laser printers and other scientific and technical instruments.

Hewlett-Packard-compatible printer: A printer able to understand the Hewlett-Packard Control Language (HPCL), the de facto standard for IBM and IBM-compatible laser printers.

Hewlett-Packard Control Language (HPCL): Hewlett-Packard's printer control language introduced in 1984 with their first LaserJet printer. HPCL has now become the industry standard for all laser printers and the language acts as a "universal driver." *See* **Printer Control Language.**

Hewlett-Packard Graphics Language: A Page Description Language (PDL) and file format for printing with HP LaserJet printers. This process is now emulated by HP-compatible laser printers. *See* **Hewlett-Packard Control Language.**

Hex: *See* **Hexadecimal.**

Hexadecimal (Hex): A numbering system employing a base (radix) of 16. Unlike decimal numbers (base 10), Hex numbers require 16 digits: 0 1 2 3 4 5 6 7 8 9 A B C D E and F. Programmers find Hex convenient for representing binary numbers since binary numbers grow in length quickly and Hex numbers do not grow as quickly. For example, the base-10 number 16 is represented as 1-0-0-0-0 in the binary system but simply as the letter F in Hex.

HFC: *See* **Hierarchical File System.**

Hidden codes: Hidden text formatting codes in a document. Even a What-You-See-Is-What-You-Get (WYSIWYG) word processing program will generate and embed a code or codes in text because of formatting commands. The codes are necessary because the screen imaging technique needs to communicate with the printer even though most formatting operations are completely transparent to the user.

Hidden file: A file with file attributes so the file name is not listed in the disk directory. Hidden files cannot be copied, displayed, or erased; hidden files are typically used by the computer's operating system.

Hierarchical: A host interconnecting topology with increasing data processing capabilities.

Hierarchical File System (HFC): A Macintosh disk storage system designed for hard disk drive use and for file storage within folders so a short file list appears. With the Disk Operating System (DOS), default paths can be defined to locate data and program files; in HFC, such path definitions do not exist with the exception of the Search Folder within an application. Mac users must manually guide applications through the folder structure if a program cannot find a file. To automate the process, purchase a file-location utility such as Findswell or Boomerang.

Hierarchical network: A network in which process and control functions perform at several levels by computers suited for the performed functions.

Hierarchical storage management: An automatic data storage process in which the software manages more than one storage hierarchy level.

Hierarchy: In UseNet, a category of newsgroups and their subjects. Seven hierarchies exist: comp, misc, news, rec, sci, soc, and talk. *See* **Standard newsgroup hierarchies.**

High density: A floppy disk storage technique. High-density disks are more expensive to manufacture than double-density disks but have become the standard and can store 1 MegaByte (MB) or more on one disk. Synonymous with quad density.

High density disks: *See* **Floppy disk.**

High-Level Data-Link Control (HDLC): A standard bit-oriented communication line protocol developed by the International Standards Organization (ISO). It is also considered a bit-oriented link-layer protocol.

High-level format: A formatting operation that creates the boot record, File Allocation Table (FAT), and root directory on a floppy disk. *See* Boot sector.

High-Level Language Application Program Interface (HLLAPI): A scripting language allowing programmers to construct transparent interfaces between 3270 terminals and various applications on IBM mainframes.

High-level programming language: A programming language such as Beginner's All-purpose Symbolic Instruction Code (BASIC) or Pascal somewhat resembles human language. A high-level language allows the programmer to concentrate on the problem, instead of concentrating on how the to type in the commands to carry out the program. Each statement in a high-level language can equal one or more machine language instructions. The downside is that high-level language programs run more slowly. *See* **Assembly language; Low-level programming language; Machine language.**

Highlight: A character, command, text block, or word reverse-displayed on a video screen.

Highlighting: Marking characters or commands in reverse video for on-screen use.

High memory: *See* **Upper memory area.**

High Memory Area (HMA): In a Disk Operating System (DOS), the first 64 KiloBytes (KB) of extended memory above 1 MegaByte (MB). Programs conforming to the eXtended Memory Specifications (EMS) can use HMA as an extension of conventional memory. *See* **Conventional memory; Extended memory; eXtended Memory Specification.**

High Performance Computing Act of 1991: A U.S. federal legislative act intended to promote gigabit networking development within a Wide Area Network (WAN) capable of transferring a billion or more bits of information per second. A National Research and Education Network (NREN) will have to be constructed and NREN is to link several supercomputer research centers. This act created the High Performance Computing and Communications (HPCC) program and will bring together many federal agencies to support high-performance computing.

High resolution: In computer monitors and printers, a visual definition producing characters evenly as large type sizes and with smoothly defined curves in graphic images. A high resolution video adapter and monitor can display 1,024 pixels horizontally by 768 lines vertically; a high resolution printer should be able to print at least 300 Dots Per Inch (DPI). *See* **Low resolution.**

High speed circuit: A circuit designed to carry data at speeds greater than voice grade circuits. The amount being carried depends on many variables. Synonym for wideband circuits.

High Speed Technology (HST): A U.S. Robotics proprietary modem data transmission standard. HST allows data transmission at 14,400 Bits Per Second (BPS) in the direction the data is moving and 450 BPS in the other direction. The universally accepted V.32bis protocol has replaced HST.

HIMEM.SYS: A Disk Operating System (DOS) function (supplied with Microsoft Windows and DOS) configuring the upper memory area, extended memory, and high memory area so properly written programs can access it. Programs must conform to the eXtended Memory Standard (XMS). See CONFIG.SYS; Device driver; eXtended Memory Standard; High Memory Area; Upper memory area.

Hinting: In digital typography, weight reduction of a typeface so small-sized fonts print without blurring or losing detail on 300-Dots Per Inch (DPI) printers.

HLLAPI: *See* **High-Level Language Application Program Interface.**

HMA: *See* **High Memory Area.**

HMD: *See* **Head-Mounted Display.**

Holding time: The duration of a switched call. This measurement is often applied in traffic studies in relation to the duration of a telephone call.

Home page: In any hypertext system, including the World Wide Web (WWW), a document intended to serve as an initial point of entry to a web of related documents. A home page usually contains introductory information and often hyperlinks to related resources. Synonymous with Home page.

129

Homogeneous: A description of a network with hosts and communication software from one manufacturer.

Hook: In programming, an Operating System (OS) or Application Programming Interface (API) feature permitting programmers to access operating system features. This feature allows hobbyists and programmers to add their own custom features.

Hop-by-Hop Route: A route created by having each path switch use its own routing capability to determine the next hop (or jump) of the route. A Private Network-Network Interface (PNNI) does not use hop-by-hop routing.

Horizontal retrace: The process of directing an electron beam in a Cathode Ray Tube (CRT) from one end of a horizontal scan line to the beginning of the next. Video adapters must allow time for a horizontal retrace to prepare the video signal.

Horizontal scroll bar: *See* **Scroll bar/scroll box.**

Host: In a computer network, the computer performing centralized functions such as program or data file creation and making them available to workstations in the network. A host can share processing resources with other devices on a network. In the Internet, a host is any computer functioning as the beginning and end point of data transfers. An Internet host has a unique Internet address, called an Internet Protocol (IP) address, and a unique domain name.

Host adapter: The adapter transferring data and/or instructions between a hard or floppy disk drive controller and the Central Processing Unit (CPU). Usually, the host adapter plugs into the expansion bus and complies with Integrated Drive Electronics (IDE), Enhanced IDE (EIDE) or Small Computer System Interface (SCSI) specifications.

Host backup server: The backup server designed to be a repository employing enterprise data management architecture.

Host computer: In a network, a computer providing computation processes, data base access, or special programs or programming languages.

Hot key: A keyboard shortcut accessing a menu command. Alt+key combinations are considered hot keys; function key assignments are called shortcut keys.

Hot link: An information copying method so the link remains active between the source and target documents. In Microsoft Windows, create a hot link by using the Paste Link command that will allow updating the target document after the source document is changed.

Hot list: In a Web browser, a list of favorite World Wide Web (WWW) sites saved for future browsing use. In Netscape Navigator, hot list items are called bookmarks, and a hot list is called a bookmark list.

Hot standby: A standby computer or telecommunications line kept ready to take command in case other computers or telecommunications lines fail.

Hot swapping: Replacing a failed hub module while keeping the network active. This process occurs by placing an active module into a fully powered-up concentrator.

HP: *See* **Hewlett-Packard.**

HPCL: *See* **Hewlett-Packard Control Language.**

HTML: *See* **HyperText Markup Language.**

HTTPD: *See* **HyperText Transfer Protocol Daemon.**

HTTPS: *See* **HyperText Transport Protocol Server.**

Hub: A centralized point on a network through which all traffic flows.

Hub Management Information Base (Hub MIB): A specification defining an experimental portion of the Management Information Base (MIB). The MIB can be used with network managing protocols in Transmission Control Protocol/Internet Protocol-based (TCP/IP based) Internets and defines various objects for managing Institute of Electronics and Electrical Engineers (IEEE) 802.3 10Megabit per second (Mbps) baseband repeaters.

Hub/Repeater: The central signal distributor used for wiring topologies with point-to-point segments from a central point. The term hub is considered with the term repeater. Multiport 10BASE-T, 10BASE2, and fiber optic repeaters, such as a 10BASE-FL or Fiber Optic Inter Repeater (FOIRL), are often called hubs.

Hub ring: The ring in the center of a 51/4-inch floppy disk. The hub ring can protect the disk from spindle contact wear.

Hung system: A system that has failed to be able to continue its processes. If a computer crashes frequently, eliminate any Terminate and Stay Resident (TSR) programs. Reload the TSRs to see which is causing any problem. *See* **INIT; Terminate and Stay Resident program.**

Hybrid network: A network combined as various network topologies.

HyperCard: An authoring language inside a Macintosh enabling storage processes and retrieving on-screen cards with different types of data. HyperCard contains a collected stack of one to several thousand cards. Each interactive button is associated with a HyperTalk script with a specific procedure. HyperCard allows for the creation of customized HyperCard applications or stand-alone applications. *See* **Front-end; Hypermedia; HyperTalk; Script; Stack.**

Hyperlink: In a hypertext system, an underlined or otherwise emphasized word or phrase. When the word or phrase is clicked, the user is taken to another document.

Hypermedia: A hypertext system with multimedia resources, such as graphics, video, etc.

HyperTalk: A event-oriented HyperCard-included scripting language inside each Macintosh. HyperTalk programs are implemented with HyperCard to create screen objects and then scripts to connect to the screen objects. HyperTalk is considered too slow for professional program development. *See* **Object-oriented programming language; SmallTalk.**

Hypertext: A process for creating hyperlinks within text to be read on a computer. The text is collected into nodes, and then hyperlinks, or anchors, are embedded in the text. A hyperlink takes the reader to the associated node; this is called browsing. On a larger scale, a group of interconnected nodes is called a web. On a global scale, the World Wide Web (WWW) is a vast hypertext system.

HyperText Markup Language (HTML 1.0): The original (now obsolete) HTML specifications from 1990. The HTML 2.0 specification superceded HTML 1.0. HTML 1.0 is also known as HTML Level 1.

HyperText Markup Language (HTML 2.0): A revised HTML specification describing HTML practice as of the mid-1990s. Forms were included and various tags were added, amended, or deleted. The HTML 2.0 specification does not include tables and Netscape Navigator functions.

HyperText Markup Language (HTML 3.0): A revised HTML specification supporting advanced features, such as tables. HTML 3.0 was not used since its change was too radical. Instead, version 3.2 was adopted by the World Wide Web Organization (W3O) in 1997.

HyperText Markup Language (HTML) Editor: A document preparation assistance program for the World Wide Web (WWW) with HTML. A simple editor is a word processing program to type text and manually add HTML tags. Add-on packages are usually slow and cumbersome with HTML codes. *See* **Microsoft Internet Assistant; WebAuthor.**

HyperText Transfer Protocol (HTTP): An Internet standard supporting World Wide Web (WWW) exchanges. By creating the definitions for Universal Resource Locators (URLs) and their retrieval usage throughout the Internet, HTTP allows Web authors the ability to embed hyperlinks and also allows for transparent access to an Internet site.

HyperText Transfer Protocol Daemon (HTTPD): A Web server developed at the Swiss Center for Particle Research (CERN) and called CERN HTTPD. HTTPD was also developed at the National Center for Supercomputing Applications (NCSA). Unlike the CERN version, the NCSA version allowed for authentication, clickable imagemaps, forms, and word searches.

HyperText Transport Protocol Server (HTTPS): A Web server designed for interacting with Microsoft Windows NT. HTTPS was created and is maintained by the European Microsoft Windows NT Academic Centre (EMWAC). The server has the capability to search Wide Area Information Server (WAIS) databases.

Hytelnet: An Internet hypertext-based guide to the Telnet-based resources which includes Bulletin Board Systems (BBSs), freenets, and libraries.

Hz: *See* **Hertz.**

I-beam pointer: In Macintosh and Windows applications, the cursor or pointer in the shape of an I-beam when editing text.

IBM: International Business Machines.

IBM 3X-AS/400: A computer system allowing a host controller port to support up to seven devices on a twinaxial cable.

IBM 3270: A mainframe environment with a 2.358 MegaBytes Per Second (MBPS) data rate and features 3174/3274 cluster controllers either connected locally or remotely to a host Central Processing Unit (CPU).

IBM 8514/A display adapter: A video adapter designed for an IBM Personal System/2 (PS/2) computer producing a maximum resolution

133

of 1,024 pixels horizontally and 768 lines vertically. The adapter has its own processing circuitry that frees the Central Processing Unit. (CPU) for other functions. *See* **Super VGA; Video adapter.**

IBM PC-compatible computer: A personal computer clone capable of running most or all software for an IBM personal computer. Compatible computers can accept IBM adapters, computer cards, and peripheral devices. *See* **Clone.**

IBM Personal Computer (PC): An IBM personal computer employing the Intel 8088 microprocessor. The release of the PC in 1981 increased personal computer industry revenue dramatically in the business community. The 1981 machine was manufactured with 16 KiloBytes (KB) of Random Access Memory (RAM) and could be expanded to 64KB on the motherboard. The next model had four times more RAM with disk drives capable of storing up to 320 KB of memory.

IBM Personal Computer Advanced Technology (AT): An IBM personal computer employing the Intel 80286 microprocessor. The AT was introduced in 1984. The AT improved the PC's and XT's performance, in some cases with an increase in throughput by approximately 50 percent to 75 percent.

IBM Personal Computer eXtended Technology (XT): An IBM personal computer employing the Intel 8088 microprocessor and a hard disk drive. The XT included more expansion slots, power, and Random Access Memory (RAM) capability of up to 640 KiloBytes (KB) on the motherboard. The Turbo XT offers a clock speed of approximately 10 MegaHertz (MHz) or nearly twice the original XT speed. *See* **Intel 8088.**

IBM Personal System/2: IBM's personal computer series employing the Intel 8088, 80286, and 80386 microprocessors. Most PS/2s contained a proprietary expansion bus format called the Micro-Channel Bus. Unlike the original PC design, microchannel designs support intelligent interface cards, i.e., cards with microprocessors on them. Consequently, a fully equipped PS/2 supported multitasking hardware as well as multitasking operating systems such as the Operating System/2 (OS/2).

IC: Integrated circuit.

ICD: *See* **International Code Designator.**

Icon: In a Graphical User Interface (GUI) environment, an on-screen symbol for a program or data file or other computer function.

IDDD: *See* **International Direct Distance Dialing.**

IDE: *See* **Integrated Drive Electronics.**

Identifier: In database management systems, an identifier specifies information uniqueness contained in a data record.

Idle line: Synonym for inactive line.

IEC: Inter-exchange Carrier.

IEEE: *See* **Institute of Electronic and Electrical Engineers.**

IETF: *See* **Internet Engineering Task Force.**

IF/THEN/ELSE: In programming, branch control structure testing variables or data to prove if a condition is true. Depending on the answer will determine the direction of the branch in the structure.

Illegal character: An unusable character as determined by the syntax rules of command-driven programs and programming languages. For example, in a computer's Disk Operating System (DOS), a file name cannot be given to a file if the name includes an asterisk (*) or some other wildcard.

Image compression: A compression algorithm reducing a graphics file size which normally consumes much disk space.

Impact printer: A printer pressing a physical representation of a character against an inked ribbon against a page. Impact printers are noisier than most printers, but they can produce multiple copies using carbons. *See* **Dot-matrix printer and Nonimpact printer.**

Import: To load a file from one program into another program.

Impulse noise: A sudden spike on a communications circuit if the received amplitude goes beyond a prescribed level. This level can be caused by momentary impulses such as lightning or power surges.

Inactive files: Files or data no longer in use.

In-band signaling: Signaling occurring within a voice signal frequency range. This term can be contrasted with out-of-band signaling. Also, a flow control method wherein a device transmits a character (usually an XOFF) to inform a second device to hold transmission and another character (usually an XON) to resume transmission.

Increment: To increase a value. The measurement of the value increased. *See* Decrement.

Incremental backup: A hard disk backup program procedure to back up only the files changed since the last backup occurred.

Incremental update: *See* **Maintenance release.**

Indentation: Paragraph alignment, right or left, of the margins within the document. For a printer's proportional typefaces, text will not properly align. Also, very often each line must be changed individually.

Index: In database management programs, a file containing information or pointers locating records in a database. Index operations can operate more quickly than sorts or searches. In a word processing program, an index is an alphabetical listing in an appendix of words or concepts chosen by the author; page numbers are marked where the terms occur. *See* **Sort; Sort order.**

Index hole: In a floppy disk, an electro-optical hole detected by the drive to locate the first sector on the disk. *See* **Floppy disk drive; Sector.**

Industry-standard user interface: An IBM standard for on-screen computer display organization and for part of the System Application Architecture (SAA). This Common User Access (CUA) standard insists on user interface features found in a Graphical User Interface (GUI), such as dialog boxes and pull-down menus. The CUA standard is in many character-based Microsoft Disk Operating System (MS-DOS) applications.

Information bearer channel: A data transmission channel carrying the information to permit communications, such as the user data synchronizing sequences and control signals.

Information bits: In data communications, those bits generated by the data source but not used for error control.

Information processing: Synonym for data processing.

Information Resource Management: The information-related resources organized within a company. The management processes must usually oversee data communications and processing, voice communications and more.

Inheritance: In object-oriented programming, the passing of a message up through the object levels until the message is trapped by the appropriate object. In HyperTalk, the lowest-level object is a button; the highest level is the HyperCard. Inheritance is also the ability of two new programming objects to inherit the behavior of the original objects from which they were created. *See* **Object-oriented programming language.**

INIT: In a Macintosh environment, a utility program which turns on during a system start/restart.

Initialization: The synchronization of two computing devices to a known initial state or condition. *See* **Format.**

Inkjet printer: A nonimpact printer spraying ink from tiny jets.

Input: The information entered into a computer or system for processing.

Input device: Any peripheral assisting in the retrieval of data into a computer. The peripheral could be a keyboard, modem, mouse, or trackball, etc.

Input/Output (I/O) bound: The operation state of an I/O port which limits a program execution.

Input/Output (I/O) redirection: In the Disk Operating System (DOS) and in UNIX, one of two routing changes. Either the program output is rerouted to a file or device, or program input is rerouted from a file rather than from a keyboard.

Input/Output (I/O) system: A part of the computer system architecture allowing data and program instructions to pass through the Central Processing Unit (CPU).

Inquiry and transaction processing: An application wherein inquiries and transaction records are used to update one or more master files.

Inquiry/Response Communications: In a network over one exchange, the exchange process usually involving a request or inquiry for information and a response providing the answer.

Insert mode: In word processing programs, a condition in which inserted text shifts existing text to the right without writing over it. *See* **Overtype mode.**

Insertion point: In Macintosh and Windows applications, the vertical bar I-beam indicating where the text will appear when typing begins. Some point must first be clicked in order to generate an insertion point. *See* **Cursor.**

Installation program: A utility program within an application program assisting in the installation and configuration of a program.

Institute of Electronic and Electrical Engineers (IEEE): A U.S. professional organization active in creating, promoting, and supporting communication specifications and standards.

Institute of Electronic and Electrical Engineers 802 (IEEE 802): IEEE standards for physical and electrical connections in a Local Area Network (LAN).

Institute of Electronic and Electrical Engineers 802.ID (IEEE 802.1D): A media-access control-level standard for interLocal Area Network (interLAN) bridges linking IEEE 802.3, 802.4, and 802.5 networks.

Instruction: A program statement interpreted or compiled into machine language so the computer will understand and execute the statement and/or program.

Instruction cycle: The time for a Central Processing Unit (CPU) to execute one instruction and move to the next.

Instruction set: A keyword list description of all actions or operations within which a Central Processing Unit (CPU) can perform. *See* **Complex Instruction Set Computer; Reduced Instruction Set Computer.**

Integrated circuit (IC): A semiconductor circuit with more than one transistor and electronic components.

Integrated Drive Electronics (IDE) Drive: A hard disk drive for 80286, 80386, 80486 processors containing most controller circuitry within the drive. IDE drives combine Enhanced System Device Interface (ESDI) speed with Small Computer System Interface (SCSI) hard drive interface intelligence.

Integrated program: A program combining software functions, such as word processing and/or database management.

Integrated Services Digital Network (ISDN): Standards evolving for a digital public telephone network.

Integrated Video Display Terminal (IVDT): A terminal combining a VDT and a telephone.

Intel 8086: A microprocessor introduced in 1978 with a 16-bit data bus structure.

Intel 8088: A microprocessor introduced in 1978 with an external 8-bit data bus and an internal 16-bit data bus structure.

Intel 80286: A microprocessor introduced in 1984 with a 16-bit data bus structure and the ability to address up to 16 MegaBytes (MB) of Random Access Memory (RAM).

Intel 80287: Numeric coprocessor designed to work with the Intel 80286. *See* **Numeric coprocessor and Weitek coprocessor.**

Intel 80386DX: A microprocessor introduced in 1986 with an internal and external 32-bit data base structure and the ability to address up to four GigaBytes (GB) of memory depending on the Operating System (OS).

Intel 80386SX: A microprocessor introduced in 1988 with the characteristics of the Intel 80386 except that the chip has a 16-bit data bus structure for use with less expensive peripherals working in conjunction with the Intel 80286.

Intel 80387: A numeric coprocessor designed to work with the Intel 80386. *See* **Numeric coprocessor; Weitek coprocessor.**

Intel 80486DX: A microprocessor introduced in 1989 with a full 32-bit data bus structure and the ability to address 64 GigaBytes (GB) of memory.

Intel 80486SX: Introduced in 1990, the 80486DX microprocessor without the numeric processor circuitry. Choose the 8048DX if working with spreadsheet recalculations and/or statistical analysis.

Intelligent terminal: A programmable terminal. Also, a personal computer with a hard drive that operates as a stand-alone computer but that can double as a terminal using terminal emulation software.

Interactive communications (IAC): In the Macintosh System 7, a specification aiding in the creation of hot links and cold links between applications. *See* **Hot links; System 7.**

Interactive videodisk: A Computer-Assisted Instruction (CAI) technology employing a computer for access to video information stored from a read-only videodisk designed specifically for the storage and retrieval of video and still images. *See* **Computer-Assisted Instruction; Videodisk.**

Interconnect industry: That part of the communications industry making equipment attached to a telephone network and providing such equipment as decorative telephones in the home environment and private telephone systems for the business environment.

IntereXchange Carrier (IXC): Long distance carriers. Contrast with Local Exchange Carriers.

Interface: A shared boundary of interchanged signals, physical interconnection characters, and signal characteristics. Synonymous with port.

Interface Layer: The Internet suite protocol layer for single physical network transmission.

Interface standard: In hard disk drives, connection specifications for between the drive controller and drive electronics. Some personal computer interface standards include Enhanced Small Device Interfaces (ESDIs), Small Computer System Interfaces (SCSIs), and ST506. *See* **Small Computer System Interface; Seagate Technology 506/412.**

Interlacing: A video monitor display technology scans the even lines in one pass and the odd lines in another pass, thus creating an annoying flicker. Interlaced monitors are cheaper to manufacture.

Inter-LATA calls: Long distance calls between individual Local Access Transport Areas (LATAs). Inter-LATA calls are handled by an interchange carrier.

Interleave factor: On a hard disk drive, the ratio of physical disk sectors skipped to each sector actually written. Interleave factor is set by hard disk manufacturers but can be changed by internal software.

Interleaved memory: An access acceleration process for Dynamic Random Access Memory (DRAM) chips. The RAM is divided into two sections or pages with bit pairs stored in alternate banks. *See* **Random Access Memory.**

Internal command: In the Disk Operating System (DOS), a permanent and available command remaining in memory. The basic commands are included in COMMAND.COM. *See* **External command.**

Internal hard disk drive: A hard disk drive inside a computer's case. The internal drive pulls its power from the computer's power supply.

International Code Designator (ICD): A two-octet designation identifying an international organization. The registration authority for the ICD is maintained by the British Standards Institute.

International Direct Distance Dialing (IDDD): A telephone exchange service allowing a caller to contact subscribers in other countries without the help of an operator.

International Organization for Standardization (ISO): Based in Geneva, Switzerland, one of two international bodies developing data communications and networking standards and promoting global trade. ISO has developed the (Open System Interconnection) OSI model.

International Telecommunications Union (ITU): One portion of the telecommunications agency within the United Nations. The ITU provides communications procedures and practices, such as frequency allocations. The ITU was originally called the Consultative Committee for International Telephony and Telegraphy (CCITT).

International Telecommunications Union-Telecommunications Standards Section (ITU-TSS): That section of the ITU promulgating standards for various telecommunications.

Internet: Collected gateways and networks including the Advanced Research Projects Agency NETwork (ARPANET), MILnet, and National Science Foundation Network (NSFnet) and all computers connected to them whether for business or individual use. Internet employs Transmission Control Protocol/Internet Protocol (TCP/IP) protocols.

Internet Engineering Task Force (IETF): The organization providing standard coordination and specification development for Transmission Control Protocol/Internet Protocol (TCP/IP) networking.

Internet Package eXchange (IPX): Novell NetWare's built-in networking protocol for Local Area Network (LAN) communication and derived from the Xerox Network System protocol. IPX moves data between a server and/or workstation programs from different network nodes.

Internet Protocol (IP): Originally developed by the U.S. Department of Defense (DoD) for internetworking of dissimilar computers across a single network. This connectionless protocol aids in providing a best-effort delivery of datagrams across a network.

Internet Protocol (IP) address: A 32-bit address identifying networks and hosts within a network.

Internet Protocol Next Generation (IPng): Name of the Internet Engineering Task Force (IETF) efforts to define a newer Internet Protocol (IP) to handle larger IP addresses. Three newer versions were CATNIP, TUBA, and Simple Internet Protocol Plus (SIPP).

Internetworking: Communication between and among devices through varied and multiple networks.

Interoffice trunk: A direct connection (trunk) between or among central offices on the same exchange.

Interoperability: A computer process for interactivity with other computers across a network. Interoperability does not require data conversion or human intervention.

Interpreter: A translator for a high-level programming language. Interpreters do not create executable versions of programs; interpreters simultaneously translate and run a program.

Interrupt: A signal momentarily suspending a program, process, or data flow so another operation can occur. Interrupts often transfer control to an Operating System (OS) when necessary. Various interrupts may be arranged into priority levels.

Interrupt ReQuest (IRQ): A computer instruction designed to interrupt a program for an Input/Output (I/O).

Interrupt Request Lines: In the Disk Operating System (DOS) and Windows, the hardware lines through which the various peripherals get microprocessor permission to send or receive data

Intertoll trunk: A connection or trunk between tool offices within telephone exchanges.

Intranet: A private network inside a company or organization using similar software from a public Internet but for restricted and internal use.

Inverse concentrator: Equipment receiving a high-speed data stream from a computer. The concentrator then dissasembles and transmits the data stream over other slower speed circuits.

I/O: *See* **Input/Output.**

IPng: *See* **Internet Protocol Next Generation.**

IPX: *See* **Internet Package eXchange.**

IRQ: *See* **Interrupt ReQuest.**

Italics: A variation of a serif typeface slanting to the right (as in this text). Italics are commonly used for citations, book titles, etc. *See* **Roman.**

Iteration: A command or program statement repetition.

ITU: *See* **International Telecommunications Union.**

ITU-TSS: See International Telecommunications Union-Telecommunications Standards Section.

Jabber lock-up: When the transmit data time exceeds a predetermined time, usually 20 milliseconds (ms) to 150ms, the Medium Attachment Unit (MAU) automatically inhibits transmission data from reaching the medium to protect the medium from data from defective equipment.

Jack: A device to connect and arrange a circuit wire or wires for the insertion of a plug.

Jam: The collision reinforcement signal output by a repeater to all ports so all devices cease transmission.

Jam signal: A signal, consisting of 96 bits of alternating 1s and 0s, generated by a card ensuring all cards know a packet collision has occurred.

JANET: *See* **Joint Academy NETwork.**

Java Development Kit (JDK): A software development package from Sun Microsystems with the tools to write testing and debugging Java Applications and applets.

JCL: *See* **Job Control Language.**

JDK: *See* **Java Development Kit.**

Jitter: The undesirable data packet fluctuation measured against a standard clock cycle. Also, a small yet rapid amplitude phase change in an analog signal. These unwanted pulse variations shift the digital signal from its ideal temporal position.

Job: A unit of work performed by a computer without human intervention. This term is more applicable to mainframe environments in which jobs are submitted and carried out.

Job Control Language (JCL): In mainframe computing, a programming language allowing programmers to specify batch processing instructions and functions. *See* **Batch processing.**

Job queue: A series of tasks automatically and sequentially executed. The term is now used for jobs lined up in the print queue within a computer environment. The queue is often viewed via the Print Manager or by double clicking on the printer icon.

Join: In relational database management programs, a data retrieval operation constructing a new data table from data existing in two or more other data tables.

Join condition: In relational database management programs, a statement describing how two databases are joined to form a single table. *See* **Join.**

Joint Academy NETwork (JANET): A United Kingdom (UK) university network renamed to "Super-JANET."

Joint Photographic Experts Group (JPEG): The committee, under the auspices of the International Standards Organization (ISO) and the Consultative Committee for International Telephony and Telegraphy (CCITT), that developed the JPEG graphics standard defining how to compress still pictures. JPEG can achieve compression ratios of 10:1 or 20:1, superior to Graphics Interchange Format (GIF) ratios, without noticeable picture quality degradation.

Journaling: The recording of transactions against a data set. Once done, the data set is reconstructed by applying transactions in the journal against the previous version of the data set.

Joy stick: A cursor-controlling device used mostly for computer games and some computer-aided design functions.

Jughead: In the Gopher environment, a service allowing the search of all Gopherspace using key words from directory titles and not menu items. To search both directory titles and menu items, use Veronica.

Jump line: An end message in a news article showing the page on which the article is continued.

Jumper: A plastic electrical connector permitting the user to select a particular circuit board configuration. The jumper is used to aid in modem and printer configuration and more.

Jumper settings: The configuration of jumpers or adapters. Jumper settings dictate adapter interaction by determining the Interrupt ReQuest (IRQ) channel.

Justification: The alignment of text along the left or right margin, or along both margins.

JPEG: *See* **Joint Photographic Experts Group.**

JUNET: Japan UNIX NETwork.

Kanji: Character symbol set used in Japanese ideographic alphabets.

Kb: Abbreviation for Kilobit.

KB: Abbreviation for KiloByte.

Kermit: Asynchronous communications protocol on mainframe systems used for transmitting program files error-free over telephone lines. Transmission must move at a minimum speed of seven bits per byte. *See* **Communications protocol; XMODEM.**

Kernel: In an operating system, the parts of the program that do the most essential tasks, including management of the internal memory and disk input and output operations. Users access the kernel through a variety of external shells, not all of them highly user-friendly. This program runs continuously while the system is operating.

Kerning: Tightening the space between pairs of characters so that they look better when printed. Used primarily in display type; in body type used primarily with headings and titles. Some page layout programs allow for automatic kerning using a database of common problem letter pairs (for example, AV and YA). Most page layout and some word processing programs allow for manual kerning.

Kerr effect: The tendency of polarized lights reflected from a magnetized surface to shift orientation. The Kerr effect makes it possible to read and write data on magnetic optical disks.

Key: (1) The button or lever on a keyboard that activates a specified function; to "key in" is to enter characters or data from a keyboard. (2) The explanation of how plain text data has been encrypted.

Key assignments: The functions a computer program gives to specific keys. Most personal computer keyboard keys are fully programmable; however, the best programs follow accepted standards for assigning keys. For instance, on IBM PC-compatible keyboards, the F1 key is commonly used for initiating on-screen help. Programs that ignore the standards raise training costs because users cannot transfer their skills from one program to another.

Keyboard: A set of alphabetic, numeric, punctuation, symbol, and control buttons that is the most common input device for all computers. Pressing a numeric or punctuation key on the keyboard sends a coded input signal to the computer, which responds by displaying a character on-screen. *See* **Keyboard layout.**

Keyboard buffer: The location where the codes of the last keystrokes pressed on the keyboard is stored so that even if it is busy the computer can continue to accept keystrokes.

Keyboard layout: How the keyboard is organized. A PC uses the QWERTY layout that typewriters have used for a century. The more efficient

Dvorak keyboard designed in 1930 is designed so that more than two-thirds of the words can be typed using only the home row keys (For QWERTY keyboards, the figure is 32 percent). Early IBM PCs used an 83- key layout that was criticized for its odd layout and small Enter key. Toggle keys such as Scroll, Number, and Caps Locks lacked lights indicators. The next version, the AT, used a standard QWERTY key layout with toggle key indicator lights. The latest standard is an enhanced, 101-key layout, with 12 function keys above the numeric keys and a separate cursor-control keypad. The 101-key layout relocates the Ctrl key, used with other keys to give commands, from left of the A key, within easy reach of your left pinky, to the less accessible lower left. Many IBM PC-compatible computers have put the Ctrl key back where it was. The original Macintosh keyboard contained only 58 keys and had no numeric keypad or arrow keys, which were considered unnecessary because of the Mac's extensive use of the mouse. Widely criticized, this keyboard was replaced first by a 78-key keyboard with numeric keypad and arrow keys for the Macintosh Plus, and more recently by and 81-key Apple with Ctrl and Esc keys, and the 105-key Apple Extended Keyboard, which includes function keys.

Keyboard Send/Receive (KSR): A teletype transmitter and receiver with transmission capability from keyboard only.

Keyboard template: A plastic card that can be attached to the keyboard to explain which function keys do what.

Key disk: A specially encoded floppy disk that must be inserted before a software program will start so that illegal copies of the program cannot be run. Key disk protection systems are disappearing because of their complexity. *See* **Software piracy.**

Key-encrypting key: A cryptography key used to encipher and decipher other keys.

Key status indicator: An on-screen status message that appears when a toggle key on the keyboard has been activated.

Keystroke: The physical action of pressing a key down to enter a character or initiate a command.

Key system: A private telephone system, usually small.

Key variable: In a spreadsheet program, a constant such as a tax rate placed in a cell at the upper left corner and applied throughout the spreadsheet so that you need make only one change if the rate changes.

Keyword: A word in programming languages (including software command language) that describes an activity or operation so that the computer can recognize and execute it.

Kill: (1) To stop a process in mid-activity. (2) In certain UseNet newsreaders, to delete an article containing a certain word, name, or point of origin so that the article is not included in the article selector. *See* **Global kill file; Kill file.**

Kill file: In a UserNet newsreader a file holding a list of subjects or names about which the user does not want to receive information. Used to block offensive messages or messages from listed senders.

Kilobit (Kb): 1,024 bits of information.

KiloByte (KB): The basic unit of measurement for computer memory, equal to 1,024 bytes. Because the computer world uses twos, not tens, the prefix kilo hear means not 1,000 as elsewhwere but 210 = 1,024. Because one byte equals one character in personal computing, a 1KB memory can hold 1,024 characters (letters, numbers, or punctuation marks).

Kilostream: A digital network operating in the United Kingdom.

Kiosk: A publicly accessible computer system set up to allow interactive browsing. In a kiosk, the operating system is hidden; the program runs full-screen, using only a few simple tools for navigation. *See* **Kiosk mode.**

Kiosk mode: In a Web browser, a mode that zooms the program to full screen, allowing it to be used as an information navigation tool.

Kludge (also spelled Kluge): An inelegant improvised solution; often a computer system assembled with poorly matched components.

Knowbot: *See* **Agent.**

Knowledge acquisition: In expert system programming, how knowledge form experts are acquired and systematized. A major limitation of today's technology is that acquiring knowledge is slow and painstaking; the process, knowledge representation, is designed to express knowledge in terms of computer-readable rules.

Knowledge base: In an expert system, the part of the program that expresses knowledge; usually uses IF/THEN rules (for example, "if the pressure exceeds 800 pounds per square inch (PSI), then sound a warning").

Knowledge domain: In Artificial Intelligence (AI), an area of problem-solving expertise. Currently AI only works well in very narrow domains such as a single manufacturing system, repair or a designated problem, or analysis of a restricted list of securities.

Knowledge engineer: In expert system programming, a specialist who finds out what experts in a given domain know and translates this knowledge into a form usable by an expert system. *See* **Expert system; Knowledge domain.**

Knowledge representation: In expert system programming, how knowledge is encoded and stored in a knowledge base.

L-2 cache: *See* **Secondary cache.**

Landscape font: A font in which the characters are oriented vertically rather than horizontally.

LANE: *See* **Local Area Network Emulation.**

LAPD: *See* **Link Access Procedure D.**

Layer: The conceptual layer of network processes and functions as determined by the Open System Interconnection (OSI) model.

Layer entity: An active element inside a layer.

Layer function: The activity of layer entities.

Layer service: The capacities of lower layers that are provided at the boundary to the next layer up.

LE: *See* **Local Area Network Emulation.**

Leadership priority: The priority of a logical node to be elected leader of its peer group.

Learning bridge: One that automatically learns the Local Area Network (LAN) addresses of each node as it receives packets; requires little or no setup time.

Legacy hardware: Hardware you already own which may not represent the state of the art but is too expensive to replace.

LES: *See* **Local Area Network Emulation Server.**

Library manager: A middleware connection between a backup, archive, or similar application and a tape library, optical jukebox, or other automated media repository that catches the call for a file, looks up its location, and commands the media repository to retrieve it. Usually the library manager has built-in media management capabilities.

Lifecycle management (tape): Tracking how often a medium is recorded or zones are overwritten, showing the number of passes over the heads and monitoring raw error rates to prevent excess usage.

Light-Emitting Diode (LED) indicator: *See* **Drive activity indicator.**

Line interactive uninterruptible power supply (UPS): A power supply that protects against brownouts as well as power failures by monitoring current from a wall outlet to provide full operating power if the line voltage becomes inadequate.

Line mode browser: A Web browser created for text-only UNIX systems. The World Wide Web (WWW) Consortium currently maintains this browser.

Line mode terminal: Designed to communicate only one line of text at a time, like an old-fashioned teletype machine. In response to a one-line command, the terminal responds with a one-line confirmation or error message. See Network virtual terminal; Telnet.

Line noise: Interference in a telephone line caused by fluctuations in current, poor connections, lightning or other weather conditions, or cross-talk from nearby lines that may reduce the data transfer rate or introduce irrelevant characters into the data stream.

Link Access Procedure D (LAPD): Link Access Procedure D, a protocol that transfers information reliably across a Layer 1 link to support multiplexing of different connections at Layer 2.

LISTSERV: The most common commercial mailing list manager program, developed in 1986 for Because It's Time NETwork (BITNET) but now marketed by L-Soft International also for UNIX and the Windows products.

Local Area Network (LAN): A system using high-speed connections at 2 to 200 MegaBytes Per Second (MBPS) over high-performance cables to communicate among computers within a few miles of each other, allowing users to share peripherals and a massive secondary storage unit, the file server. Less appropriate than Multiuser systems for vertical applications where each node needs its own processing circuitry.

Alternative network topologies are bus, ring, and star networks, all using either baseband or broadband methods to communicate. *See* **AppleTalk; Baseband; Multiuser system; Network operating system; Novell Netware; Ring network; Star network.**

Local area network (LAN) aware program: An application program modified to function in a network environment. Licensing agreements often prohibit placing the application on a file server. Also, Network versions of programs are designed for concurrent access, create and maintain shared files, and have Logical Block Addressing (LBA) allowing hard disks to store significantly more data.

Local Area Network Emulation (LANE or LE): The services and protocols that allow Asynchronous Transfer Modes (ATMs) to be connected with LANs.

Local Area Network Emulation Configuration Server (LECS): The LECS provides the Local Area Network Emulation Server (LES) Asynchronous Transfer Mode (ATM) addresses for assigning individual clients to different emulated LANs.

Local Area Network Emulation Server (LES): The LES implements the coordination function by, for example, enabling an LECS to joint an Emulated Local Area Network (ELAN).

Local bus: High-speed technology linking the Central Processing Unit (CPU) with slots on the expansion bus, allowing signals from an adapter (video or hard disk controller) to travel more quickly by bypassing the expansion bus.

Local echo: *See* **Half-Duplex.**

Local UseNet hierarchy: UseNet newsgroups set up for local distribution only.

Log: (1) A record. (2) A feature in communications programs that record what is only the monitor for later review, thus reducing the connection fee.

Logical drives: Formatted sections of a hard drive each assigned a separate letter and treated by users as separate drives. Sometimes a drive letter is substituted for a directory; logical drives on networks result because networks usually map directories to drive letters. *See* **Partition drive; Physical drive.**

Logical network: A network as the user sees it, though it may be composed of more or less than one network. Note that though the Internet links tens of thousands of separate networks, a user sees one single global network.

Logic gate: A switch in computer chips that automatically takes certain actions if certain conditions are met, central to the computer's ability to do what is expected of it.

Login file: A batch or configuration file that starts Local Area Network (LAN) software when the work station is turned on.

Login name: How a user is identified to gain access to a network system; usually used with a password.

Login script: Instructions for dial-up access that automatically dial the service provider's number, supply the login name and password, and make the connection.

Loop network: A single path in a network between all nodes and the path configured in a closed circuit.

Loopback test: A test in which signals run from an instrument through a modem or loopback switch and back to the instrument for measurement.

Lossless compression: A technique that compresses a file by up to one-third without discarding any original data, so that the restored file is an exact replica of the original. Lossless compression is suitable for text and computer code.

Lossy compression: A technique for compressing files to as little as two percent of the original by deliberately discarding certain data, though the loss is not noticeable when the file is restored; used for graphics files, as in the Joint Photographic Experts Group (JPEG) compression technique.

Lost chain: Section of a Microsoft Disk Operating System (MS-DOS) file for which the File Allocation Table (FAT) no longer contains the information needed to reconstruct its links to other sections.

Lost cluster: Section of a file for which the File Allocation Table (FAT) no longer records its links to the rest of the file, usually occurring when the computer is turned off or the power fails while the file is being written.

Lost revenue: (1) The cost of server downtime, real or opportunity. (2) The productivity loss that occurs when users manage their own storage.

Lotus Notes: The most popular groupware application allowing shared databases and discussions, first released in 1988, provided with an application development language that allows it to be customized for a particular workgroup and makes it popular with workgroups of all sizes. Primary competition is Microsoft Exchange.

Lotus-Intel-Microsoft Expanded Memory Specification (LIM EMS): A standard that allows programs recognizing it to work with expanded memory, more than 640Kb Ram under Disk Operating System (DOS); LIM Version 4.0 was introduced in 1987, supporting up to 32 MegaBytes (MB) of expanded memory. *See* **Expanded memory; Extended memory.**

Low-level format: Also called Physical format, low-level format defines the physical location of magnetic tracks and sectors on a hard drive or diskette. *See also* **High-level format.**

Low-level programming language: A language (for example, machine or assembly language) that requires the programmer to defer to what happens in the Central Processing Unit (CPU); fast and efficient for those who have detailed knowledge of how computers work but does not take human language into account. *See also* **Assembly language; High-level programming language; Machine language.**

Low migration threshold: That point in storage pool capacity where migration or retrieval of files to or from the next storage pool must stop.

Low power microprocessor: A microprocessor that runs on 3.3 volts of electricity or less; often used in portable computers to conserve the batteries. See 0.5-micron technology; Complementary Metal-Oxide Semiconductor.

Low resolution: A visual definition in monitors and printers too low to produce well-defined characters or smooth graphic curves, resulting in a jagged effect.

Low speed circuit: Also called Subvoice-grade circuit. A telegraph and teletype circuit designed to be used at speeds from 45 to 200 bits per second (bps) that cannot handle voice transmissions.

Lurk: Read a newsgroup or mailing list without making one's presence known by posting a message.

Lycos: An automatic search engine named after a highly energetic night spider that prowls the World Wide Web (WWW) continuously. Lycos, provided by the Carnegie Mellon University Center for Machine Translation, discovers some 5,000 Web, File Transfer Protocol (FTP), and Gopher documents a day, adding them to a database now approaching five million documents. For each, Lycos indexes the title words, heads, subheads, all hyperlinks, the 100 most important words, and the words in the first 20 lines of text.

LYNX: A full-featured Web browser for UNIX computers, designed by Lou Montoulli of the University of Kansas, which displays only texts, no on-line images.

MAC: *See* **Media Access Control.**

MacBinary: A file transfer protocol for Macintosh computers making it possible to store Macintosh files on non-Macintosh computers without losing anything. Most Macintosh communications programs send and receive files in MacBinary.

Machine-dependent: Runs only on specific hardware.

Machine language: The native language of a computer's Central Processing Unit (CPU); a low-level, difficult language using only 0s and 1s as symbols. *See* **Assembly language; High-level programming language.**

Macintosh: A family of personal computers introduced by Apple Computer in 1984 characterized by a Graphical User Interface. The Mac had the first 32-bit microprocessor, the Motorola 68000 running at 7.8 MegaHertz (MHz), compared with the Intel 8088's 4.77 MHz. The original Mac monitor displayed 512 by 312 black pixels on a paper-white background, also an innovation. The Mac Application Program Interface (API) and mouse made the program much easier to learn. In 1986 the Mac virtually created desktop publishing with the release of the LaserWriter printer, which with the PageMaker layout program and high resolution outline fonts gave Apple a substantial edge in the business world in the late 1980s.

Macintosh II: A high-performance Apple personal computer introduced in 1987. The Motorola 68020 microprocessors used in the first models were soon replaced with Motorola's 68030s running at 15.67 MegaHertz (MHz).

Macintosh Classic: A high-performing entry-level Mac using a 68000 microprocessor running at 8 MHz introduced in 1990 and upgraded to the Classic II with a 68030 microprocessor in 1992.

MacPaint: The original, widely imitated, Mac computer paint program. *See* **Paint program.**

Macro: Stored commands for a repetitive task such as backing up a file to a floppy that can be activated easily with one or two keystrokes. Some programs record the original keystrokes; others allow the commands to be edited.

MacTCP: A utility program to connect Macintoshes to the Internet. Although MacTCP is included with the Apple System 7.15 Transmission Control Protocol/Internet Protocol (TCP/IP), a separate program is needed to connect via Serial Line Internet Protocol (SLIP) or Point-to-Point Protocol (PPP).

Magnetic media: Disks or tapes coated with ferrous oxide or another magnetically sensitive material used as secondary storage for data. Like iron filings on a sheet of waxed paper, these materials are reoriented when a magnetic field passes over them. The data can be arranged positively or negatively; in read operations the head senses the polarities encoded on the medium; in write operations the head emits a magnetic field that reorients the materials to correspond to the data.

Magnetic tape: Inexpensive high-capacity backup medium for storing up to 100 MegaBytes (MB) of data. Magnetic tape drives use slow sequential access techniques; they are mostly used for hard disk back-up. *See* **Sequential access.**

Magneto-Optical (MO) cartridge: A highly stable data storage device for use in MO drives. The 5 1/4 inch cartridge stores up to 1300 MegaBytes (MB); the 3 1/2 inch stores up to 230MB.

Magneto-optical (MO) drive: A device to store data that lets the user change data on an MO cartridge or disk by using the read/write head. Though slow and relatively expense, MO drives are good for storing large programs or data that is used rarely.

Magneto-Resistive (MR) head: An advanced head with separate read and write portions to increase throughput and pack racks tighter, often used in hard disks that use Partial-Response Maximum Likelihood (PRML) technology.

Mailbox: Where electronic messages are stored until the addressee can pick them up. An on-screen message lets the user know when mail is waiting.

Mailbox name: The part of an electronic mail address to the left of the @ sign that specifies the name of the recipient; often the same as the login name.

Mail bridge: A connection for exchanging electronic mail between one on-line information service or network and another.

Mail exploder: *See* **Mailing list manager.**

Mail merge: A common word processing utility that puts information from a database (for example, a mailing list) into a template letter (for example, a letter) to provide individualized documents. The word processing program is used to create the database, called the secondary file, and the main document (primary field), into which codes are typed to tell the program where to put the information from the database.

Mail program: A utility program for a specific computer to manage incoming and outgoing electronic mail. Popular mail programs are cc: Mail and Microsoft Mail.

Mail server: A program for generating responses to electronic mail by, for instance, sending back specific information or changing the user's name on a mailing list.

Mailing list: A list of users on a network who are part of a work group or should get copies of mail messages on a given topic; Internet users can subscribe to numerous mailing lists on topics as varied as creative writing or Lebanese food.

Mailing list manager: Server software for a mailing list, such as LIST-SERV or Majordomo that receives information and disseminates it to subscribers. The term is synonymous with mail exploder.

Mainframe: A multi-user computer designed to meet the information-management and accounting needs of large organizations.

Mainframe distribution frame: A frame on which both the permanent line entering a building and the subscriber line, trunk, or other cabling terminate.

Main program: The part of a program containing the master instructions, in contrast to the subroutines, procedures and functions the main program calls upon.

Main storage: *See* **Random Access Memory.**

Maintenance programming: Updating programs to add features, correct bugs, or change variables.

Maintenance release: A minor program revision; usually numbered in tenths (4.5) or hundredths (4.05). Maintenance is similar to incremental update.

Majordomo: Freeware mailing list manager for UNIX systems. *See* **LIST-SERV; Mailing list manager.**

Male connector: A computer cable device in which the pins protrude from the connector's surface.

MAN: *See* **Metropolitan Area Network.**

Managed system: An entity run by one or more management systems.

Management domain: An entity that defines the scope of naming.

Management Information Base (MIB): (1) A directory of logical names for all the information in a network. (2) The objects that can be accessed by means of a network management protocol.

Management Information System (MIS): A computer system that gives managers current information on how the organization is performing.

Manchester coding: A method of signaling to maintain bit synchronization by sending a voltage transition at the midpoint of every bit.

Manufacturing Automation Protocol (MAP): A communications program for automated manufacturing based on Open System Interconnection (OSI).

Mapping: Converting data from one format or device to another. For example, a database index converts the records from the format used for storage to a more useful format on the display screen.

Mark: One of the two possible states of a binary information element in a teleprinter circuit. *See* **Space.**

Mask: A technique for simplifying data entry by imposing a limiting pattern on a data field, as when the field for a date is set up as __/__/___.

Mass storage: *See* **Secondary storage.**

Master: Where the management agent software for Backups and Slaves is contained in a department concentrator chassis; it holds the only active image of the management agent.

Master boot record: *See* **Boot record**

Master document: A word processing document containing the commands that tell the program to print not only itself but additional documents as if they were one. *See* **Chain printing.**

Master station: The station (or node on a network) that controls other stations.

Math coprocessor: The secondary unit that frees the Central Processing Unit (CPU) from calculation-intensive tasks while speeding up spreadsheet and Computer-Aided Design (CAD). It does not noticeably improve the performance of Microsoft's Windows '95. See **Numeric coprocessor.**

Maximize: Enlarge a window to fill the screen.

Maximum Cell Rate (MaxCR): The maximum capacity of connections belonging to a given service category.

Mb: *See* **Megabyte.**

MCA: *See* **Micro Channel Architecture.**

MDI: *See* **Medium Dependent Interface**

Mean Time Between Failure (MTBF): The average length of time from the point when a component is created until its first failure, mechanical or electronic; because MTBF is calculated from laboratory tests performed under extreme conditions, the figure is not particularly useful for comparison shopping.

Mean Time To Repair (MTTR): Average time it takes to correct failures.

Measured rate service: A method of charging for local telephone calls based on their number, length, and the distance between the parties.

Mechanical mouse: A device to communicate with the Central Processing Unit (CPU) using metal rollers turned by a rubberized ball, usable in most computer environments but tending to require more frequent cleaning than an optical mouse.

Media Access Control (MAC): A sublayer in the Open System Interconnection (OSI) data link layer that controls access, control, procedures, and format for a Local Area Network (LAN), for example, Institute of Electronic and Electrical Engineers (IEEE) 802.3, 802.4 and 802.5 standards.

Media Control Interface (MCI): Microsoft Windows multimedia extensions that greatly simplify the programming of multimedia device functions such as Stop, Play and Record.

Media player: A Microsoft Windows 3.1 accessory looking like a tape player that controls multimedia devices like the Computer Disk Read Only Memory (CD-ROM) drives.

Media-sharing Local Area Network (Media-sharing LAN): A network in which cables are shared through a Media Access Control (MAC) arrangement, rather than through circuit or packet switching.

Medium Attachment Unit (MAU): A transceiver plugging into the Attachment Unit Interface (AUI) port on an Ethernet adapter to attach twisted pair, fiber-optic, and other media.

Medium Dependent Interface (MDI): The interface between the trunk cable and the Medium Attachment Unit (MAU), allowing like devices to connect through different pin-outs to avoid conflicts in receiving and transmitting packets through the same pin-out.

Meg: *See* **MegaByte.**

Megabits per second (Mbps): Million bits per second; a measure of the rate of data movement.

MegaByte (MB or Meg): One million bytes (1,048,576 bytes); a measure of memory capacity.

Megaflop: One million floating point operations per second, the mainframe or minicomputer benchmark used to rate scientific and professional workstations.

MegaHertz (MHz) One million electrical vibrations or cycles per second, a measurement for comparing computers by their clock speeds (which are now in the 133 to 150 MHz range and beyond). *See* **Clock speed; Hertz (Hz).**

Membrane keyboard: An inexpensive flat keyboard covered with a dirt-proof plastic sheet on which is printed a two-dimensional outline of the computer keys. When the user presses the plastic sheet, it engages a hidden switch. Document typing on membrane keyboards is difficult, but they are useful in locations like restaurants where users may not have clean hands.

Memory: Primary storage area on a computer, such as Random Access Memory (RAM); secondary storage refers to disk drives. *See* **Primary storage; Secondary storage.**

Memory address: A code number specifying a location in Random Access Memory (RAM). *See* **Random Access Memory.**

Memory cache: *See* **Cache memory.**

Memory check: Part of the Power-On Self-Test (POST) to verify that Random Access Memory (RAM) is functioning properly. As the computer boots up, the progress of the memory check is displayed on the screen, as is the memory address of any problem.

Memory management program: A utility program that allows a computer running the Disk Operating System (DOS) to access more memory, such as the program provided with expanded memory boards, windowing environments, and virtual memory programs that treat a portion of a hard disk as a Random Access Memory (RAM) extension. *See* **EMM386.EXE; Expanded memory emulator; Extended memory; HIMEM.SYS.**

Memory map: Allocation of segments primary storage that determines which areas of Random Access Memory (RAM) the computer can use for given purposes. An example would be the Intel 8088 microprocessor, where a portion of the potential 1 MegaByte (MB) of RAM is reserved for such functions as the keyboard buffer and display adapters, leaving 640 KiloBytes (KB) of base memory for user programs.

Memory-resident program: *See* **Terminate and Stay Resident program.**

Menu: Display that lists command choices. *See* **Pull-down menus.**

Menu bar: A bar across the top of the screen or window contains the names of pull-down menus, a basic feature in Graphical User Interfaces and industry-standard programs. *See* **Graphical User Interface; Industry standard user interface; Pull-down menu.**

Menu-driven program: A program offering the user menus for program options rather than requiring the user to memorize commands.

Merge printing: *See* **Mail merge.**

Mesh network: A configuration presenting at least two paths between any two nodes.

Message: (1) Data organized in a form that can be processed by the recipient. (2) A sequence that can be transferred as an entity.

Message Handling Service (MHS): A program for exchanging files between programs and sending files through gateways to other computers. Marketed by Novell and Action Technologies, which developed it to link electronic mail systems.

Message queue: A line of messages waiting to be processed or sent to a terminal.

Message routing: The process by which the computer chooses the appropriate path for a message.

Message switching: A technique that passes messages through intermediate points rather than directly through a dedicated path. At each node, the entire message is stored briefly before being passed on. Also called Store and forward.

Message text: The message without the header or control information.

Messaging Application Program Interface (MAPI): The Application Program Interface (API) through which Microsoft gives developers access to messaging services. MAPI Version 3.2 allows for cross-platform messaging independent of operating system and underlying hardware. MAPI can exchange messages with Vendor Independent Messaging (VIM) programs.

Metal-Oxide Semiconductor (MOS): A chip using silicon dioxide, aluminum oxide, and other oxidized metals that provide improved conductivity and insulation but are highly vulnerable to static electricity. *See* **Complementary Metal-Oxide Semiconductor and Semiconductor.**

Metal-Oxide Varistor (MOV): A device used in surge protectors to divert current over 350 volts away from the computer. *See* **Power surge.**

Metropolitan Area Network (MAN): A public speed network operating at 100 megabits per second or more that can transmit voice and data messages within a 50-mile range (80-kilometer range). The Institute of Electronic and Electrical Engineers (IEEE) are defining the standards.

MHS: *See* **Message Handling Service.**

MHz: *See* **Megahertz.**

Micro: Prefix meaning one millionth; occasionally used as an abbreviation for microcomputer.

Micro Channel Architecture (MCA): IBM's 32-bit expansion-bus architecture for its high-end PS/2 computers; not compatible with other bus architectures. Though technically advanced, MCA is not compatible with peripherals and adapter designed for the AT 16-bit expansion bus. Because of this incompatibility, manufacturers of IBM compatibles first used a 32-bit bus design called Extended Industry Standard Architecture (EISA) and then used local bus technology and the Peripheral Component Interconnect (PCI) expansion bus.

Microcode: The program instructions embedded in the microprocessor to make software easier to program. Microcode requires extra internal components, which makes chips that contain it larger and slower than those without it do. *See* **Complex Instruction Set Computer; Reduced Instruction Set Computer.**

Microcomputer: A computer with its Arithmetic Logic Unit (ALU) and control units in a single integrated circuit, the microprocessor. Since the mid-1980s the distinction between minicomputers and microcomputers has broken down as microcomputers became more powerful and were configured into networks to exchange information among users. Microcomputers can now be used as stand-alones or as part of distributed systems that allow individual users to share resources.

Microcon Network Protocol (MNP): Any of 10 protocols used by modems to correct errors and compress data. MNP1 is now obsolete. MNP2, MNP3 and MNP4 are the error-correction protocols in the V.42 international standard. MNP5 is the data-compression protocol used in most modern modems and the other five MNPs are proprietary.

Microcon Network Protocol-4 (MNP-4): A popular protocol for filtering out line noise and eliminating errors during transmission and reception of data via modem. For errors to be corrected, both sending and receiving modems must use the same protocol.

Microcon Network Protocol-5 (MNP-5): In this protocol the MNP-4 error-correcting protocol is added to a protocol for speeding modem transmissions by compressing (i.e., encoding actually) data on the sending end and decompressing it on the reception end, speeding transmission by up to 200 percent. *See* **Data-compression protocol.**

Microfine toner: A toner for laser and Liquid Crystal Shutter (LCS) printers with finer particles than standard toner, allowing them to print with sharper detail.

Micro manager: The person responsible for acquiring, modifying, and maintaining personal computers within an organization, and for training staff to use them.

Micron: A millionth of a meter (about 0.0000394 inch).

Microphone: A device for converging sounds into electrical signals that may be processed by a computer, common on Macintosh but rarer on IBM PC-compatible computers that may be used to change system sounds or add voice announcement to documents.

Microprocessor: The integrated circuit containing the Arithmetic-Logic Unit (ALU) and control units of a computer's Central Processing Unit (CPU). *See* **Intel 8086, Intel 8088, Intel 80286, Intel 80386DX, Intel**

80386SX, Intel 80486DX, Motorola 68000, Motorola 68020 and Motorola 68030.

Microsoft at Work: The Microsoft standard for computer control of such office machines as copiers, printers, fax machines, and telephones. Windows '95 contains a limited version for controlling printers and fax machines.

Microsoft Corporation: The largest software publisher in the world, maker of Microsoft Windows '95, Microsoft Word, and Microsoft Excel, among other programs. In 1982, IBM agreed to buy the operating systems for its new personal computers exclusively from Microsoft; the Microsoft Disk Operating System (MS-DOS) is still one of the company's top products. From Redmond, Washington, Microsoft commands such market share that its products, even when inferior to competing products, often become standards.

Microsoft Disk Operating System (MS-DOS): Microsoft Disk Operating System, the standard single-user system used in IBM and IBM-compatible computers, and marketed by IBM as PC DOS; the two systems are almost indistinguishable. Based on Control Program/Microcomputers (CP/M), the Operating System (OS) for 8-bit computers popular in the late 1970s, the original version was created by a small Seattle firm and sold to Microsoft, which had the contract to create an operating system for IBM personal computers. The intent was that popular CP/M business programs could be converted quickly and cheaply for the new IBM PC. The chief advantages of MS-DOS over CP/M are that it is extremely compact and does not require huge amounts of memory; some commands were improved and that the computer does not crash when a disk is removed before the system is rebooted. Version 2.0 of MS-DOS added UNIX-like directories and subdirectories with hard disks. It has limited Application Program Interface (API) capabilities and few standard routines for displaying information on screen. These are handled by individual applications, causing a jumble of incompatible user interfaces. MS-DOS requires that the user memorize commands, arguments and syntax; once this is done, the user has considerable control over the system's capabilities, setting file attributes, creating automatic batch files, and developing semi-automated backup procedures. Its worst limitation is the 640 KiloBytes (KB) Random Access Memory (RAM) barrier it imposes on IBM PC-compatible computing. When the system was devised, before the appearance of applications like Lotus 1-2-3 and Terminate and Stay Resident (TSR) programs, 640KB seemed like more than enough memory. That is no longer the case. However, MS-DOS remains the most common OS.

Microsoft Disk Operating System (MS-DOS) features

Version Number	Features
1.25	320KB floppy disk support
2.0	360 KB floppy disk support ANSI display driver CONFIG.SYS file Device Drivers File Handles Filters Hard Disk Support Hierarchical File Systems Improved Batch Program Language Input/Output Redirection International Features More File Attributes Pipes Print Spooling Volume Labels
3.0	1.2MB Floppy Disk Support Clock/Calendar Board Support File Locking Multiple Hard Disk Partitions Network Support RAB Disk
3.1	Network Drives Network File Sharing
3.2	3 1/2-inch 720KB Floppy Disk Support XCOPY Command
3.3	3 1/2-inch 1.44MB Floppy Disk Support Multiple 32MB Hard Disk Partitions
4.0	Hard Disk Partitions to 2 Gigabytes Memory Drivers MS-DOS Shell
5.0	2.88Mb Floppy Disk Support Accesses More than two Hard Disks Device Drivers in Upper Memory Directory Sorting with DIR DOS in High Memory Area (HMA) Doskey Macros Improved Hard Disk Partitions MS-DOS Editor (Full-Screen Editor) MS-DOS Qbasic (Improved BASIC) MS-DOS Shell Improved On-help help for MS-DOS Commands Undelete Command Unformat Command

Microsoft Disk Operating System (MS-DOS) QBasic: An improved programming environment notable for its on-line help, supplied with MS-DOS 5.0 and later versions.

Microsoft Disk Operating System (MS-DOS) shell: A user interface conforming to the industry standard, supplied with MS-DOS 5.0 and later issues that provides menu-driven access to most Disk Operating System (DOS) commands. Shell allows the user to copy, delete, move and rename files, back up and restore a hard disk, format disks, undelete files deleted accidentally, create and delete directories, and view and edit file attributes, virtually eliminating the need for utility packages such as PC Tools.

Microsoft Excel: A graphical spreadsheet program Microsoft Corporation developed for IBM PC-compatible computers running Microsoft Windows and for the Macintosh computer. Excel offers multiple typefaces and sizes, object-oriented graphics, shading, and color, enabling users to output charts and graphics as well as spreadsheets. Buttons on the on-screen toolbar initiate automated command sequences to guide users through various options.

Microsoft Exchange: A program for managing fax and electronic mail messages; works best with Microsoft Exchange Server but handles Microsoft Mail, Internet Mail and mail from other on-line information services.

Microsoft Internet Assistant: A free HyperText Markup Language (HTML) editor and Web browser for Microsoft Word that makes the program a What-You-See-Is-What-You-Get (WYSIWYG) HTML editor showing the results of HTML tags rather than the tags themselves. Forms capabilities are limited and early versions do not handle recent additions to HTML automatically; they could be adding manually.

Microsoft Mail: An electronic mail program primarily for Local Area Networks (LANs) with a server that distributes mail to various clients, where network users read, write, and manage mail. A Microsoft Mail Servicer allows clients exchange messages with users of Microsoft Exchange.

Microsoft mouse: A optical-mechanical mouse and its software for IBM and IBM-compatible personal computers including IBM's Personal System/1 (PS/1) and PS/2 computers that sets the standard for third-party mice; available in both serial and bus versions.

Microsoft Office Professional: A suite of application programs that adds Microsoft Access to the programs in Microsoft Office Standard.

Microsoft Office Standard: A suite of application programs that includes Microsoft Word, Microsoft Excel, Microsoft PowerPoint and Microsoft Mail.

Microsoft PowerPoint: A presentation graphics program that can import information from spreadsheets and word processors (especially Microsoft Excel and Microsoft Word) into attractive presentations, making it easier to enliven numbers and lists with color and graphic elements; the program's multimedia capabilities are limited. Video clips can only be incorporated by using Object Linking and Embedding (OLE).

Microsoft Publisher: A DeskTop Publishing (DTP) program for users who only occasionally need to design documents. Microsoft Publisher is not competitive with high-end DTP programs but for a minimum investment allows those with a minimum of design skill to generate good-looking documents.

Microsoft Windows: An Application User Interface (AUI) for the Disk Operating System (DOS) that brings to IBM computing such Macintosh-type Graphical User Interface (GUI) features as pull-down menus, multiple typefaces, desk accessories (clock, calculator, calendar, notepad), and the capability to move text and graphics from one program to another via the clipboard. All Window applications have a consistent interface. The history of Windows shows the reluctance of users and software developers to move to Operating System/2 (OS/2), the operating system that was supposed to replace MS-DOS. Originally, Windows was to be little more than a preview of OS/2's Presentation Manager. Windows ran a few applications specifically developed for it in a GUI but like MS-DOS remained tied to the 640 KiloBytes (KB) Random Access Memory (RAM) barrier. The new generation of IBM-format programs needed the Intel 80286 and 80386 microprocessors, with their 16 MegaBytes (MB) of memory. Microsoft insisted that similar protected-mode programs must be developed for the OS/2 and Presentation Manager. As there appeared other windowing systems such as DESQview (QuarterDeck Systems) that could run Microsoft Disk Operating System (MS-DOS) programs in protected mode, Microsoft released its own competing product, Windows Version 3.0, which promptly sold millions of copies. Microsoft's Windows-compatible applications Excel and Word for Windows were thus in a good position to grab a huge share of the spreadsheet and word processing markets. The leading MS-DOS spreadsheets (Lotus 1-2-3) and word processing programs (Word Perfect), whose Windows versions came out considerably later, never caught up with the Microsoft applications. The release of Windows 3.1 in 1992 offered major speed improvements, an enhanced program manager, better mouse control of MS-DOS applications, improved help screens and multi-tasking, built-in screen savers, Object Linking and Embedding (OLE) capabilities, and multimedia extensions. It clearly set the standard. Running Windows takes more computing power than running comparable MS-DOS applications. The minimal platform for Windows is an 80386SX running at 16 MegaHertz (MHz) (preferably 20 MHz or 25 MHz) at least 4MB of RAM, an 80MB hard disk drive, a 16-bit Video Graphics Array (VGA) video adapter and VGA monitor and an inkjet or laser printer that can run Window's fonts.

Microsoft Windows '95: An operating system for running Windows applications on Intel-based 80386DX, 486 and Pentium microprocessors with a completely redesigned Graphical User Interface (GUI) that is easy to learn as well as to use. It also offers longer file names, 32-bit disk and file systems, preemptive multitasking, improved problem handling, and built-in support for the Microsoft Network and the Internet. Combining 16-bit and 32-bit source code, Windows '95 is not a true 32-bit operating system (like OS/2 Warp or Microsoft's own Microsoft Windows NT); nevertheless, users appreciate not having to upgrade their applications. For corporate environments Windows '95 includes built-in network support for a variety of physical media. To simplify the installation of new hardware, Windows '95 incorporates Plug and Play capabilities for nearly automatic configuration of such accessories as sound cards and Computer Disk Read Only Memory (CD-ROM) drives.

Microsoft Windows NT: A 32-bit Operating System (OS) for high-end Pentium, Alphas, and MIPS processors that combines high performance with personal productivity applications compatibility; designed for users such as scientists and other professional technical workers whose work is processor-intensive. Windows NT is designed for use by engineers, scientists, statistics and other professional or technical workers who carry out processor-intensive tasks.

Microsoft Word: A full-featured word processing program with What-You-See-Is-What-You-Get (WYSIWYG) features for Microsoft Disk Operating System (MS-DOS) and Macintosh computers that was inspired by the Bravo on-screen formatting programs developed in the 1970s. Version 6.0 includes AutoCorrect, which automatically fixes common spelling errors; Wizards, automated helps for common applications; and support for Object Linking and Embedding (OLE). It is easy to customize by changing toolbars and menu bars as well as using Word Basic to create macros.

Microsoft Works: A simple integrated program for Macintosh computers and IBM PC compatibles that offers a word processing module with a spelling checker, a spreadsheet with business charts, a flat-file database manager, and macro-recording and telecommunications utilities, with an object-oriented drawing program in the word processing and spreadsheet modules. Each module includes the most common features but without the complexity of advanced program functions. Data can be moved around with ease and the object-oriented drawing program enhances the printed documents. Printing form letters and mailing labels or including a chart in a business report are easy. *See* **Module; Object-oriented graphic.**

Micro-to-mainframe: How personal computers are connected to mainframe or minicomputer networks.

Midsplit: A broadband cable system in which the frequencies are split into two groups, one for transmission and one for reception, thus requiring a frequency converter.

Migration: The movement from an older computer hardware platform, operating system, or software version to a newer one.

Million Instructions Per Second (MIPS): The benchmark for measuring how fast a computer executes microprocessor instructions; 0.5 MIPS equals 500,000 instructions per second. Referring usually to mainframes and supercomputers, MIPS measurements do not adequately state system throughput, a performance measure taking into account the speed of data transfer to and from memory and the speed of important peripherals such as disk drives. *See* **Benchmark; Supercomputer; Throughput.**

Millisecond (MS): One-thousandth of a second, a measure commonly used to specify the access time of hard disk drives. *See* **Access time.**

MIME: *See* **Multipurpose Internet Multimedia Extension.**

Mini-AT-size case: A horizontal case that mounts the motherboard much like the Advanced Technology-size (AT-size) case, but taking up less space. Though space-efficient, mini-AT-size cases do not always have enough expansion slots. *See* **Mini-tower case.**

Minicomputer: A multi-user computer designed for a small company or a department; currently losing ground to networking personal computers.

Minimize: In a Graphical User Interface (GUI) such as Microsoft Windows, to use either the down arrow in the upper right or the Minimize command on the control panel to shrink a window down to an icon appearing at the bottom of the screen. When a number of windows have been minimized, the Arrange Icons command on the Window menu can be used to make them easier to distinguish.

Mini-tower case: A vertical case that fits into a smaller space than a full-sized tower case, with less for disk drives and other devices than tower cases but with smaller footprints and an equal number of expansion slots. *See* **Mini-AT-size case.**

MIS: *See* **Management Information System.**

Mission-critical: An application that is so necessary to business operations that if it were not available the company would have major revenue or productivity losses.

MMF: *See* **MultiMode Fiberoptic cable.**

MNP: *See* **Microcon Network Protocol.**

MNP-4: *See* **Microcon Network Protocol-4.**

MNP-5: *See* **Microcon Network Protocol-5.**

Mobile net: A network made up in part of portable devices that transmit via unbounded media.

Modem: *See* **Modulator/demodulator.**

Moderated newsgroups: A conference on a given topic in a distributed bulletin board system such as UseNet or EchoMail, contributions to which are screened by volunteers before they are posted.. The moderator's job is not to censor but to ensure that postings adhere to the stated topic. A moderator also may rule out discussion on subtopics if postings on such subjects are likely to cause unproductive and bitter debate ("flame bait").

Moderator: A volunteer who screens the messages submitted to a UseNet newsgroup or a mailing list.

Modified Final Judgment (MFJ): The stipulation (ending a major antitrust case and opening up telephone competition) that on January 1, 1984, AT&T would divest itself of the 22 operating companies that then made up the Bell system.

Modified Frequency Modulation (MFM): Also called double density; a method of recording digital information on magnetic media by eliminating redundant or blank areas that doubles the storage available in the Frequency Modulation (FM) recording technique. Since it refers to the method used to pack data on a disk, MFM is not synonymous with such disk drive interface standards as ST-506, Small Computer System Interface (SCSI) or Enhanced Small Device Interface (ESDI). *See* **Run-Length Limited.**

168

Modula-2: A high-level programming language that allows Pascal to execute program modules independently developed in 1980 by Pascal creator Niklaus Wirth. Among its more notable features Modula-2 supports the separate compilation of program modules.

Modular jack: The RJ-11 jack, the standard receptacles for telephone cable connectors in wall sockets and on modems. Wall sockets installed before 1970 have a four-prong connector that requires an RJAIX adapter when connecting with modular jacks.

Modular programming: A programming style in which each module contains all the source code and variables needed to accomplish a single function, useful in very large programs that are otherwise difficult to maintain. Modular programming makes it much easier to find the source of program errors. It is often used in object-oriented programming languages, such as SmallTalk and HyperTalk.

Modulate: To use a baseband-input signal to control such wave characteristics as amplitude, frequency, or phase.

Modulation: The process of varying a characteristic of the carrier wave, usually amplitude, frequency, or phase, according to the value or sample of the intelligence to be transmitted.

Modulation protocol: The standards used in modems to govern the speed at which information travels over telephone lines. *See* **Consultative Committee for International Telegraphy and Telephony protocol.**

Modulation rate: The reciprocal of the shortest nominal time interval between successive significant instants of the modulated signal. If the internal is expressed in seconds, the rate is given in bands.

Modulator: The portion of the modem that converts the digital to an analog signal.

Modulator/demodulator (Modem): A device that converts digital signals generated by a computer to modulated analog signals for transmission over a telephone line, and transforms incoming analog signals to their digital equivalents. The speed at which a modem operates is measured in bits per second (bps). Most 2400 bps modems use the V.22bits protocol, while 9600 bps modems use the V.32 protocol, 14,400 bps modems use the V.32bits standard and 28,000 bps modems use the V.34. Faster modems are usually compatible with slower ones. Two common standards, Microcon Network Protocol-4 (MNP-4) and V.42, eliminate errors attributable to problems like noise in the telephone system. There are also two standards for data-compression, V.42bits and MNP-5. *See* **Auto-dial/auto-answer modem; Consultative Committee for International Telegraphy and Telephony protocol; Dirty, Echoplex; External modem; Full duplex; Half duplex; Hayes command set; Hayes compatible modem; Microcon Network Protocol-4; Microcon Network Protocol-5; Reliable link; Universal asynchronous receiver/transmitter.**

Modulator/demodulator (Modem) eliminator: A wiring device, often a simple cable, that allows two Personal Computers (PCs) within several hundred feet of each other to communicate directly through their serial ports rather than through modems.

Module: A unit or sections of a computer program that can function on its own, like the word processing module in an integrated program.

Monitor: The device with its internal support circuitry that produces an on-screen display; also known as a Video Display Unit (VDU) or, earlier, a Cathode Ray Tube (CRT). *See* **Analog monitor; Digital monitor; Enhanced graphics display; Monochrome monitor.**

Monitor program: (1) A program that records the behavior of other programs, usually to track bugs. (2) Software or hardware that observes, supervises, or controls how a system operates.

Monochrome Display Adapter (MDA): The original single-color monitor for IBM PC-compatible computers that displayed text (but not graphics) with a resolution of 720 pixels horizontally and 350 lines vertically, placing characters in a 7 x 9 matrix.

Monochrome monitor: A monitor that displays a single color against a black or white background.

Monospace: A typeface, in which the width of each character is the same, producing output that looks typed; useful for columnar material. *See* **Proportional spacing.**

Monospaced font: *See* **Monospace.**

Monster File Transfer Protocol (FTP) sites list: A highly extensive listing and description of anonymous FTP sites.

Monthly duty cycle: The number of pages a printer can print every month, which can be as low as a few hundred pages for personal laser printers and as high as 200,000 pages or more for departmental laser printers.

MOO: *See* **Multi-User Dungeon (MUD) Object Oriented.**

MOS: *See* **Metal-Oxide Semiconductor (MOS).**

Motherboard: The logic board, a circuit board that contains the computer's Central Processing Unit (CPU), microprocessor support chips, Random Access Memory (RAM), and expansion slots.

Motorola 68000: The microprocessor running at 8 MegaHertz (MHz) that powers the Macintosh Classic; it can process 32 bits internally and can address up to 32 Mb of Random Access Memory (RAM), but uses a 16-bit data bus to communicate with the rest of the computer.

Motorola 68020: A microprocessor similar to the Motorola 68000 but using a full 32-bit architecture and running at 16 MegaHertz (MHz). The 68020 powered the original Macintosh II but was then displaced by the Motorola 68030 chip.

Motorola 68030: A full 32-bit microprocessor that can run at speeds of 16 MegaHertz (MHz) to 50 MHz which is substantially higher than its predecessors and includes special features for virtual memory management; any Macintosh equipped with the 68030 chip can implement the advanced memory management features of System 7.5.

Motorola 68040: A 32-bit microprocessor that packs more circuitry, including a numeric coprocessor, into an even smaller space than its predecessors, improving performance while reducing the need for support chips; the Motorola 68040 powers Macintosh Quadra models.

Motorola 68881: The numeric coprocessor used with Motorola 68000 and 68020 microprocessors. *See* **Numeric coprocessor.**

Mount request queue: The location where requests for files are stored while the media manager checks current file storage and searches for a drive on which to place specific media.

Mouse: An input device equipped with one or more control buttons housed in a palm sized case; as it is moved about next to the keyboard, its circuits relay signals that position a cursor on screen, choose commands on menus, and perform other operations such as marking text for editing. The device was invented to make it unnecessary for a computer user to memorize numerous keyboard commands. Two types of mouse internal mechanisms are popular: The mechanical mouse moves on a rubber-coated ball; as the ball rotates, optical sensors detect the motion. The optical mouse detects reflections from a light-emitting diode; unlike the mechanical mouse, it requires a special metal pad to reflect the beam properly and cannot be moved beyond the pad. Mechanical mice must be cleaned regularly for best performance. The ball is locked in with an easily manipulated retainer ring.

Once that is unlocked, the ball can be removed, it and the rollers can be swabbed with rubbing alcohol, and any dust can be blown out. Mice are connected to computers in three ways: Most mice are connected through a special mouse port. A bus mouse connects through an adapter pressed into one of the expansion slots. A serial mouse connects through the standard serial port.

Mouse port: A small round socket in the computer, also called a PS/2 mouse port, into which the mouse cable is plugged to connect the mouse to the computer, leaving the serial port free.

MOV: *See* **Metal-Oxide Varistor.**

Moving Picture Experts Group (MPEG): A group of digital video experts sponsored by the International Standards Organization (ISO) and the International Electrotechnical Commission (IEC) that develops standards for compressed digital audio. The group's first standard, MPEG-1, compresses video to approximately 1.2 megabits per second and screen audio to a rate of approximately 250 kilobits per second.

MPEG: *See* **Moving Picture Experts Group.**

MPU 401: The standard for the design of the Musical Instrument Digital Interface (MIDI) port through which musical instruments are connected to computer soundboards; it requires that the port have its own sound-processing circuitry to relieve the load on the computer.

MR head: *See* **Magneto-Resistive head.**

MS-DOS: *See* **Microsoft Disk Operating System.**

MTBF: *See* **Mean Time Between Failure.**

MTTR: *See* **Mean Time To Repair.**

Multicast backbone (MBone): An experimental system for delivering real-time audio and video on the Internet, allowing for one-to-many and many-to-many transmissions while consuming few network resources. Mbone software is not currently installed on most computers connected to the Internet. *See* **Multicasting.**

Multicasting: The routing of a single message to two or more networked workstations.

MultiColor Graphics Array (MCGA): The video display standard for IBM's Personal System/2 (PS/2).

Multi-drop circuit: Multipoint circuit, one with several nodes connected to it.

MultiFinder: An Apple utility program to expand the Finder-the Macintosh shell-so that the Macintosh can run more than one application at a time. MultiFinder, which is also incorporated into System 7, makes the Macintosh a multiloading operating system that can perform some tasks in the background, such as printing or downloading information via telecommunications. However, MultiFinder is not a true multitasking operating system; when you activate one application, the others freeze. *See* **Context switching; System 7.**

Multilaunching: The opening of an application program on a network by more than one user at a time.

Multilevel sort: An operation that uses two or more data fields to determine how data records will be arranged; performed by identifying two or more fields as sort keys.

Multimedia extensions: Additions to an Operating System (OS) that allow multimedia software to synchronize graphics and sounds without extensive additional programming. Programmers know these extensions as "hooks," and they provide an Application Program Interface (API) for such tasks as accessing a Compact Disk Read Only Memory (CD-ROM) drive so it is not necessary to access the multimedia hardware directly by writing code. Early multimedia programs were tied to specific brands; extensions allow the use of the entire CD-ROM player supported by the system software. *See* **Application Program Interface; Media Control Interface; Microsoft Windows; QuickTime.**

Multimedia Personal Computer (MPC): The standard for multimedia hardware and software developed by the MPC Consortium (consisting of Microsoft, Phillips, Tandy, and Zenith Data Systems) and based on Micro-soft Windows 3.1, which incorporates multimedia extensions formerly packaged separately. The MPC standard relies on an IBM PS/2 or compatible hardware platform; Apple has a competing standard, QuickTime, for Macintoshes. *See* **Computer Disk Read Only Memory; QuickTime.**

Multimedia Personal Computer-2 (MPC-2): The advanced version of the MPC standard, calling for a 486SX-25 microprocessor, 8 Megabytes (Mb) of Random Access Memory (RAM), a Video Graphics Array (VGA), a monitor, and a double speed Computer Disk Read Only Memory (CD-ROM) disk drive.

Multimode: A fiber with a core approximately 50 microns or .050 millimeters in diameter used in fiber optics.

MultiMode Fiberoptic cable (MMF): Cable in which the signal or light is dispersed over multiple paths, which may be of different lengths, with pulses sometimes arriving at different times; this may limit the distance signals can travel over MMF.

Multiple Document Interface (MDI): An interface allowing a user to have more than one document or worksheet open at the same time. Rather than using MDIs, the Microsoft Windows '95 Application Program Interface (API) opts for running multiple copies of programs, each carrying a different document.

Multiple selection: Bringing together two or more noncontiguous ranges in a spreadsheet program, allowing the user to apply the same formats to or perform other operations on more than one range at a time.

Multiplex: To transmit two or more interleaved messages simultaneously on a single channel, allowing more than one computer to access the network at the same time. Multiplexing raises network cost because it requires devices to mix signals for transmission. *See* **Frequency division multiplexing; Local Area Network; Time division multiplexing.**

MUltipleXer (MUX): A device making it possible for several independent data streams to share a link.

Multipoint access: Configuration in which more than one terminal is supported by a single computer.

Multipoint line: Also called a multidrop line; a single line using a polling mechanism to link two or more devices to one computer and more than one terminal.

Multiport: *See* **Split stream operation.**

Multipurpose Internet Mail Extension (MIME): The standard for how such tools as electronic mail programs and Web browsers transfer non-text files complete with sounds, graphics, and video over the Internet. Before MIME was developed, everything transferred over the Internet had to be American Standard Code for Information Interchange (ASCII) coded. See Uudecode; Uuencode.

Multipurpose Internet Multimedia Extension (MIME) type: The code in a MIME that specifies the content type of a file. The Internet Registered Numbers Authority (IRNA) controls the naming of MIME types, which include, for example, *.mpg or *mpeg indicating an Moving Picture Experts Group (MPEG) video.

Multiscan monitor: A color monitor adjustable to a range of input frequencies for use with different display adapters. Often erroneously called multisync monitors, though Multisync is a proprietary name belonging to NEC.

Multistation Access Unit (MAU): The name IBM uses for a Token ring wiring concentrator.

Multitasking: The use of more than one computer program; not to be confused with multiple program loading, in which Random Access Memory (RAM) contains two or more programs but only one program at a time. In multitasking the foreground task responds to the keyboard while he background task continues to run without active control. Multitasking operating systems require no Terminate and Stay Resident (TSR).

Multi-User Dungeon Object Oriented (MOO): A type of Multi-User Dungeon (MUD) incorporating an object-oriented programming language participants can use to create their own personalized characters and world.

Multi-user system: Systems allowing more than one person to access programs and data at the same time from separate terminals. If the system has a single Central Processing Unit (CPU) multiple access is provided by a technique called time-sharing, which cycles access among users. Personal computers equipped with advanced microprocessors are powerful enough to serve as the nucleus of a multi-user system, which typically are equipped with the UNIX operating system. Such technical advances have helped blur the distinction between personal computers and minicomputers.

Musical Instrument Digital Interface (MIDI): A protocol for the exchange of information between computers and music synthesizers, allowing a musician using a synthesizer, a computer equipped with the necessary software, and a MIDI port to transcribe a composition into musical notation by playing the composition at the keyboard. Once the music is in a computer-based, virtually every aspect of it, such as pitch and tempo can be edited.

Musical Instrument Digital Interface (MIDI) cueing: The set of MIDI messages that determines when events other than musical notes (such as recording, playing back, or turning on lighting devices) will occur. *See* **Musical Instrument Digital Interface.**

Musical Instrument Digital Interface (MIDI) file: A file of data encoded to MIDI specifications. Microsoft Windows MIDI files are identified by the extension MID. *See* **Musical Instrument Digital Interface.**

Musical Instrument Digital Interface (MIDI) port: The port through which a musical synthesizer is connected to a personal computer.

NAK: *See* **Negative Acknowledgement.**

Name server: The computer in a Local Area Network (LAN) linked to the Internet that translates alphabetical domain names into numerical Internet protocol addresses.

Named pipes: A technique for communicating between applications operating on the same computer or network having a relatively simple Application Program Interface (API) that makes inter-application programming easy.

Nano: Prefix indicating one billionth.

Nanosecond (NS): One billionth of a second, a unit often used to indicate response time of computer chips.

National Center for Supercomputing Applications (NCSA): A research center affiliated with the University of Illinois at Urbana-Champaign specializing in scientific visualization; the place where NCSA Mosaic, a popular Web browser, was created.

National Information Infrastructure (NII): A proposed U. S. national computer network for high-speed delivery of voice, data, and video services over existing fiber-optic and coaxial cable systems, to be developed with minimal government funding by private corporations, including cable and telephone companies.

National Research and Education Network (NREN): Synonymous with the "Information Superhighway," a network that was designed to become the major state-of-the-art high-speed carrier for U.S. research and education.

National Science Foundation (NSF): An independent federal agency in the United States that seeks to promote the pubic good throughout encouraging science and engineering.

National Television Standards Committee (NTSC): The organization that sets the standards for television broadcasting in the United States and most of Central and South America. The current standard is 525-line frames displayed full frame at 30 frames per second, using two interlaced fields at about 50 frames per second to respond to the U.S. alternating current frequency of 60 Hertz (Hz).

Native address: An address that matches one of a given node's summary addresses.

Native application: A program designed to work with a particular microprocessor (binary compatible).

Native code: *See* **Machine language.**

Native file format: The default format a program uses to store data on disk, often a proprietary format that other programs cannot read. Encountering a native file format is not usually a problem because many programs can save data in several forms. *See* **American Standard Code for Information Interchange; File format; Proprietary file format.**

Natural language: A language such as Spanish, French, German, or Tamil that is used by people, as opposed to an artificial language that is used by machines. Computer scientists are working to make computers responsive to natural languages, but there is no single theoretical model of a natural language grammar system. The problem is further complicated by the lack of understanding about how natural human sentences are decoded and problems in recognizing patterns of speech.

Natural language processing: Using a computer to analyze human language.

NAU: *See* **Network Address Unit.**

NCC: *See* **Network Control Center.**

NCP: *See* **Network Control Program.**

NCSA: *See* **National Center for Supercomputing Applications.**

NDIS: *See* **Network Driver Interface Specifications.**

Near Letter Quality (NLQ): A dot matrix printing mode that produces characters that look typed. NLQ printers are typically slower than other dot-matrix printers.

Negative AcKnowledgement (NAK): Negative acknowledgment: A code letting a sender know that a character or block of data was not properly received. *See* **Acknowledgment.**

Negotiation: *See* **Handshaking.**

Nested structure: A structure in which one control is inside another. *See* **Control structure; DO/WHILE loop.**

Nested subtotal: A spreadsheet formula that adds values and is included in a larger formula that adds subtotals.

Net abuse: Any action that interferes with the rights of users on UseNet, including unwanted posting in newsgroups ("spamming"), organized forgery campaign, or creating an organized effort to derail discussion.

NETBIOS: *See* **NETwork Basic Input/Output System.**

Net lag: Delay in accessing a document on a packet-switching network, caused by delivery problems like latency.

NetManage Chameleon: A popular series of Transmission Control Protocol/Internet Protocol (TCP/IP) connectivity programs and Internet tools created by NetManage, Inc. that includes many Internet tools but lacks Local Area Network (LAN) connectivity, though it may be used for Serial Line Internet Protocol (SLIP) or Point-to-Point Protocol (PPP) connections. Internet Chameleon, the commercial version, includes the WebSurfer browser.

Netscape Commerce Server: A World Wide Web (WWW) server from Netscape Communications for UNIX and Microsoft Windows NT systems incorporating Secure Sockets Layer (SSL) Protocol security that displays an icon when a secure connection has been made indicating that any information uploaded has been protected from interception en route.

Netscape Communications Server: A World Wide Web (WWW) server from Netscape Communications for UNIX and Microsoft Windows NT systems without the security features of Netscape Commerce Server.

Netscape Navigator: A Web browser available without charge at ftp.mcom.com. Netscape Navigator often supports advanced Web sites including ones that use formats or flashing text. Faster than its main competition, NCSA Mosaic, it has an intuitive interface.

Netscape News Server: A UseNet server from Netscape Communications protected by the Secure Sockets Layer (SSL) protocol, so that when users access the newsgroup with Netscape Navigator, the posting is assured to be authentic.

NetWare: A implementation and control approach developed by Novell, Inc. to define the architecture and software modules needed for Local Area Network (LAN) operation for both IBM PC compatibles and Macintoshes; also the name of the software. It accommodates more than 90 types of Network Interface Cards (NICs) as well as 30 varieties of architecture and a number of communications protocols.

NetWare Loadable Modules (NLMs): Applications and drivers running in a server under Novell's NetWare 386 that can be loaded or unloaded without dedicated Personal Computers (PCs).

Network: A continuing communications and data exchange system connecting two or more computers that to share files and resources. A Local Area Network (LAN) as small as two or three computers may share only an expensive printer; others connect up to 100 personal computers sharing applications and files. Larger Wide Area Networks (WANs) use telephone lines or other long distance communications media to link the system. Personal computer networks also differ in how they are connected; some are linked to a central file server (star topology), others to a single backbone cable (bus topology. All Macintosh computers contain AppleTalk, a low bandwidth network protocol suitable for small networks. Larger networks can use EtherNet or IBM's token ring network. *See* **Bus network; Local Area Network; Network protocol; Network topology; Star network; Token-ring network.**

Network address unit (NAU): In Systems Network Architecture (SNA), the origin or destination of information transmitted by the path control network; it may be a logical or physical unit or a systems service control point.

Network administrator: The person who maintains a Local Area Network (LAN) and guides its users.

Network application: How a network is used, such as for data collection or inquiries and updates.

Network architecture: (1) The set of principles, including the organization of functions and the description of data formats and procedures, used in designing and implementing a telecommunications application network. (2) The set of hardware, software, and cabling standards that specify the design of a Local Area Network (LAN).

NETwork Basic Input/Output System (NETBIOS): A program included in the Microsoft Disk Operating System (MS-DOS) versions 3.1 and later for linking personal computers to a Local Area Network (LAN). NETBIOS was originally developed by IBM and Sytek; a version NETBIOS is now offered by many hardware vendors so that their products can be networked.

Network congestion: The condition that occurs when there is more traffic than a network can carry.

Network Control Center (NCC): A point from which a network is operated.

179

Network control mode: The functions of a network control program that let it direct a communications controller to perform all necessary activities.

Network Control Program (NCP): The program that operates a front-end processor or communications controller.

Network drive: A disk drive made available through a Local Area Network (LAN), rather than a drive connected directly to a single workstation.

Network Driver Interface Specifications (NDIS): The set of device driver specifications that cause a request to be submitted to the network operating system or a local action to be performed without full communications with other software functions. NDIS was co-developed by Microsoft and 3Com and allows protocol drivers to send and receive packets on a network. NDIS support both the Disk Operating System (DOS) and Operating System/2 (OS/2); it also offers protocol multiplexing.

Network File Systems (NFS): A file access utility developed by Sun Microsystems, which released it to the public as an open standard, allowing users on UNIX and Microsoft Windows NT networks to access files and directories on other computers as if it were on their own workstations.

Network Information Center (NIC): A repository of Internet-related information including File Transfer Protocols (FTPs), archives of Requests For Comments (RFCs), Internet drafts, For Your Information (FYI) papers and other documents, including handbooks on how to use the Internet. Though there are a number of NICs, the official one is the Defense Data Network NIC (DDN NIC).

Network Interface Card (NIC): A board with encoding and decoding circuitry and a receptacle for a network cable connection that, bypassing the serial ports and operating through the internal bus, allows computers to be connected at higher speeds to media for communications between stations.

Network laser printer: A laser printer, often with a large monthly duty cycle and remote management features, that can fill the printing needs of numerous users on a network.

Network layer: The layer in the Open System Interconnection (OSI) model containing the rules for routing and delivering data passed to it from the transport layer through an entire large network.

Network management: The procedures, software, and operations that keep a network operating at near maximum efficiency.

Network Management Protocol (NMP): A set of protoc ols from AT&T for exchanging information with and controlling the devices that govern such components of a network as modems and T-1 multiplexers.

Network neighborhood: A Microsoft Windows '95 desktop icon clicked to display Personal Computers (PCs) and other resources within the user's workgroup and allowing the user to access files on other machines as if they were on the user's own computer.

Network News Transport Protocol (NNTP): The standard governing the distribution of UseNet newsgroups through the Internet.

Network operating system (NOS): The file server and workstation software that integrates the hardware on a Local Area Network (LAN), usually including such features as a menu-driven interface, security restrictions, facilities for sharing printers, central storage of network applications and information, remote log-in via modem, and support for diskless workstations. The NOS maintains the connection between the workstation and the file server. The workstation software consumes huge amounts of base memory, which should be taken into account in designing the network. *See* **File server; Local Area Network; Novell NetWare; Workstation.**

Network operator: The person or program responsible for controlling all or part of a network.

Network printer: A printer accessed through a Local Area Network (LAN).

Network protocol: The standard governing a workstation's access to a computer network to prevent data collisions. *See* **Carrier Sense Multiple Access with Collision Detection; Token passing.**

Network Protocol Data Unit (NPDU): A type of packet. The Open System Interconnection (OSI) term for the block of data and control symbols transmitted by the network layer protocol.

Network redundancy: The condition of installing more links that the minimum required to provide alternative connecting paths between all stations.

Network server: *See* **File server.**

Network simulator: *See* **Workload generator.**

Network termination: The point where a virtual channel, virtual path, or virtual path/virtual channel ends at the User Network Interface (UNI).

Network topology: The relationship of stations and cable links in a network, both physical and logical; typically the configuration is a star, ring, tree, or bus, though there are hybrids of these. In centralized topologies such as star networks, a central computer controls access ensuring data security. In decentralized topologies such as bus or ring networks, each workstation can access the network and establishes connections with other workstations independently. *See* **Bus network; Ring network; Star network.**

Network Virtual Terminal (NVT): A generic standard that allows programmers to create non-specific terminal applications rather than programming for a single brand. Telnet is the Internet NVT standard. *See* **Line mode terminal.**

Neutral networks: An artificial intelligence technique copying how nerve cells are connected in the human brain. Software based on a neutral network, trained to recognize patterns, can make predictions in areas like weather forecasting and stock market analysis.

Newbie: A new UseNet who makes his or her presence known, generally by asking for information already available in a Frequently Asked Question (FAQ).

New Internet KnOwledge Systems (NIKOS): A search engine developed funded by Rockwell Network Systems and California State Polytechnic University, San Luis Obispo, NIKOS uses a spider, an automated search routine, to map and locate 90 percent of the documents on the World Wide Web (WWW).

Newsfeed: A service for downloading UseNet articles directly to a computer and uploading contributions from that computer, able to dump as much as 100 MegaBytes (MB) of UseNet articles per day; useful for large organizations running high-capacity minicomputer systems that want to set up a UseNet site accessible to numerous users.

Newsgroup: A discussion group on the World Wide Web (WWW) Bulletin Board System (BBS), such as the WELL or a distributed bulletin board system such as EchoMail or UseNet, that is devoted to a single topic. The topics can vary from Star Trek, model aviation, and books by Ayn Rand to the music of the Grateful Dead. Those reading messages posted to the group can reply directly to the author or can post replies that can be read by the whole group.

News hierarchy: One of the seven standard UseNet newsgroup organizations. A hierarchy is concerned with UseNet itself; newsgroups deal with administrative issues, new newsgroups, announcements, and UseNet software.

Newsreader: A client program that lets a user access a UseNet news server, subscribe to UseNet newsgroups, and read and respond to articles and messages posted to newsgroups. Web browsers such as Netscape Navigator usually include newsreader functions.

News server: A computer that provides access to UseNet newsgroups once the newsreader program or Web browser has provided its domain name.

NexGen Nx585: A 64-bit microprocessor advertised to be compatible with the Pentium but substantially less expensive. Available in 70 MegaHertz (MHz), 75 MHz, 84MHz and 93 MHz versions, the NexGen Nx585 uses register renaming to get around the 8-register limit that slows the Pentium, and 0.5 micron and Complementary Metal Oxide Semiconductor (CMOS) technology to reduce power consumption. Though throughput is on par with the Pentium, because the two chips are not binary compatible, the nx585 requires a special motherboard and supporting chip set.

NeXT: A UNIX-based professional workstation developed by NeXT, Inc., under Apple cofounder Steve Jobs, who also figured in the development of Macintosh. After a disappointing release in 1988, four competitively priced and well-received workstations were released in 1990. The workstations, which all drive the 68040 at 25 MegaHertz (MHz), can be equipped with high-resolution color displays. Originally aimed at the higher education market, NeXT is now targeted lower, at the professional workstation market now dominated by Sun. A significant advantage of NeXT is NeXTStep, an integrated windowing environment and application development system. NeXT computers run Berkley 4.3 UNIX, normally not user-friendly, supplemented by a Graphical User Interface that makes it unnecessary to enter UNIX commands directly. Screen displays show fonts as they will print on the system's 400-Dots Per Inch (DPI) laser printer. Programmers can also customize applications using the preprogrammed buttons, scrollers, front panels, window managers, and memory management modules in the NeXT Application Kit, which can cut program development time by as much as 75 percent compared with Macintosh or Windows applications. Though there has been a shortage of NeXt application software, two full-featured spreadsheet package for NeXT computers (Lotus Improv and Ashton Tate's PowerStep) may have started to improve the picture.

NFS: *See* **Network File Systems.**

NIC: *See* **Network Information Center; Network Interface Card.**

NII: *See* **National Information Infrastructure.**

NIKOS: *See* **New Internet KnOwledge Systems.**

NLMs: *See* **NetWare Loadable Modules.**

NLQ: *See* **Near Letter Quality.**

NMP: *See* **Network Management Protocol.**

NNTP: See Network News Transport Protocol.

Node: The point in a Local Area Network (LAN) where one or more functional units connect with each other; often applied to a workstation, though the term includes repeaters, file servers, and shared peripherals. *See* **Network topology; Workstation.**

Noise: (1) Any interference with the normal operation of a device or system. (2) Random electrical signals or variations in current, voltage, or data, whether resulting from circuit components or natural disturbances, that can cause errors in transmission. (3) A random signal of known statistical properties of amplitude, distribution, or spectral density.

Non-dedicated: A file server that is also used as a workstation.

Nondisclosure agreement: A contract stipulating that sensitive information will be kept confidential often required by software publishers of their beta testers so that data about developing products is less publicized.

Non-DOS application: A Microsoft Disk Operating System (MS-DOS) application program that does not take full advantage of Microsoft Windows' interfaces, including on-screen display of fonts and user interface conventions. Such non-Windows applications run on Windows as they would on MS-DOS. Users of Windows' Standard or 386 Enhanced modes can move from one non-Window application to another without quitting a program and in 386 Enhanced mode can multitask two or more MS-DOS applications, each in its own window. It is believed that many copies of Microsoft Windows have been bought in order for users to run MS-DOS applications. *See* **Application Program Interface; Microsoft Windows; Standard mode.**

Nonimpact printer: A printer that forms an image by spraying or fusing ink on page, such as an inkjet, laser, or thermal printer and operates more quietly than an impact printers; cannot print multiple copies by using carbon paper. *See* **Impact printer.**

Non-interlaced monitor: A monitor that can display high-resolution images without flickering or streaking because it does not use the screen refresh techniques called interlacing. *See* **Interlacing.**

Nonprocedural language: *See* **Declarative language.**

Nonvolatile memory: Memory designed to hold information after power is switched off, including Read Only Memory (ROM) and all secondary storage units such as disk drives. *See* **Random Access Memory; Volatility.**

Non-Windows application: An application that can not run on the Microsoft Windows environment.

No parity: A protocol in asynchronous communications that disables parity checking, leaving no space for the parity bit. *See* **Communications protocol; Parity bit; Parity checking.**

NOS: *See* **Network Operating System.**

Notebook computer: A portable or laptop computer weighting approximately six pounds and measuring 8 inches x 11 inches x 1 1/2 inches, fitting easily into a briefcase, and, unlike subnotebook computers, usually including a floppy disk drive.

Novell NetWare: A Network Operating System (NOS) for 80286 and 80386-based computers with the Disk Operating System (DOS) that has established a commanding lead in the Local Area Network (LAN) market thanks to an excellent reputation for reliability, software compatibility, and system features. *See* **Local Area Network; Network Operating System.**

NPDU: *See* **Network Protocol Data Unit.**

NREN: *See* **National Research and Education Network.**

NS: *See* **Nanosecond.**

NSF: *See* **National Science Foundation.**

NTSC: *See* **National Television Standards Committee.**

NuBus: The high-speed expansion bus of Macintosh II computers, which requires adapters especially designed for its 96-pin receptacles. See Expansion bus.

NUL: *See* **Null character.**

Null Character (NUL): A control character used to accomplish media-fill or time-fill that can be inserted into or removed from a sequence of characters without affecting the meaning of the sequence; can affect control of equipment or format.

Null value: A blank field in an accounting or database management program in which no value has been typed, as distinguished from a value of zero that has been entered.

Num Lock key: A toggle key used to lock the numeric keypad into a numbers-only mode and disable the cursor-movement keys on the numeric pad on IBM-PC compatible keyboards.

Number crunching: Calculations, especially of large amounts of data.

Numbering plan: A uniform numbering system in which each telephone central office connected to the nationwide dialing network has a unique designation, in which the first three of ten dialed digits constitute the area code; the next three designate the office code, and the final four indicate the station number.

Numeric coprocessor: A support chip that performs mathematical computations that use a Binary Coded Decimal (BCD) and floating point calculations at speeds up to 100 times faster than a microprocessor alone.

Numeric format: Displays values with a specified number of decimal places, ranging from 0 to 15. Lotus 1-2-3 rounds number that have more decimal places than are specified. If the number of digits exceeds the column width, asterisks appear across the cell.

Numeric keyboard: Extra keys on a keyboard that function like a ten-key calculator.

Numeric keypad: A group of keys, usually to the right of the typing area on a keyboard, for rapid touch-type entry of numerical data.

NVT: *See* **Network Virtual Terminal.**

Object: A data entity that can be manipulated as a whole, as in a document, a widget in a Graphical User Interface (GUI) environment, or a piece of stand-alone code in an object programming environment.

Object code: The machine-readable instructions in programming created from source codes by a compiler or an interpreter.

Object Linking and Embedding (OLE): A set of standards, developed by Microsoft Corporation and incorporated into Microsoft Windows and

Apple Macintosh System software, for creating dynamic automatically updated links between documents and for embedding documents created by another. With OLE, changes made in a source document can be automatically reflected in a destination document. They are linked by using the clipboard to copy the source document but then using Paste Link or Paste Special to insert the copy in the destination document, which can be created by same application or by another OLE program. Linked objects can be edited by double clicking, which starts the application that created the object, so that you can edit the source document and update the copy. Embedding actually places the source document or part of it physically into the destination file, creating a compound file containing information needed by both the server application and the client application, but the two documents are not linked. The value is that embedding places a fully editable copy of the source document into the destination document that can be modified at will without affecting the source document. Linking allows the user to maintain one authoritative version of a file that can be copied many times. Embedding allows the user to place a copy of an object in a file where it can be changed without affecting the original. Using OLE requires applications capable of serving as client and server for OLE purpose. Searching the Edit menu for a command such as Paste Link or Paste Special can check this. Most programs that can function as OLE clients also can function as servers. See **Client application; Embedded object; Server application.**

Object Linking and Embedding (OLE) client: An application that can serve as the recipient of a linked or embedded object created by a client application. See **Client application.**

Object Linking and Embedding (OLE) server: An application that can provide an object to be linked or embedded into a destination document. See **Object linking and embedding.**

Object-oriented graphic: A graphic composed of distinct elements, for example, lines, circles, ellipses, and boxes, that can be edited separately; often called vector graphics because they are stored as mathematical formulas for the vectors or directional lines that compose the image. Unlike bit-mapped graphics, which distort when resized, object-oriented graphics are resized without problems.

Object-Oriented Programming (OOP) language: A non-procedural language in which program elements are considered objects that pass messages to each other; the ultimate extension of modular programming, it is especially suited to a Graphical User Interface (GUI). In an object-oriented program, each object is self-reliant, with its own data and programming code; the object becomes part of a larger whole by incorporation into a hierarchy of layers, but the modules can stand on their own and be copied into other programs, raising the possibility of inheritance. An object can be copied or modified and then moved into a new program without having to be recreated. Objects in object-oriented programming are useful for program construction because they hide their internal complexity and can be moved in chunks into new programs-an object-oriented programming language then is highly extensible. On a GUI, a completed object can be seen on the screen as an icon to be repositioned or copied. In HyperCard, for example, when a button is pasted onto another card, the script is also copied. The one disadvantage of object-oriented languages is that they require a great deal of memory and move more slowly than other languages.

OCC: *See* **Other Common Carrier.**

Octal: A compact numbering system that uses a base (radix) of eight, starting with 0 and moving up to 7, sometimes used to represent binary numbers.

Odd parity: An error-checking protocol in asynchronous communications in which the parity bit is set to 1 if there is an odd number of 1-digits in a one-byte data item, as in the five 1s in: 01011011. If the parity bit indicates odd but the data transmitted contains an even number of 1s, the system will report a transmission error. *See* **Communications parameters; Communications protocol; Even parity; Parity checking.**

Off-hook: In analogy with telephones, a data set automatically answering on a public switched system. *See* **On-hook.**

Off-line: Either not directly connected with a computer or in command mode; a printer has two modes, off-line, in which commands are programmed, and on-line, in which it actually prints.

Off-screen formatting: *See* **Embedded formatting commands.**

Offset: The gutter, the amount of space added to the margin of a word-processed document to allow space for binding.

Onboard audio: A circuit on the motherboard simulating a soundboard by using credit Frequency Modulation (FM) synthesis techniques but usually adequate only for business audio applications. They are readily replaced in a desktop computer with a soundboard of higher quality.

1Base-5: Twisted pair cable with maximum segments up to 500 meters and transmission speeds up to 1 Megabit per second (Mbps).

100Base-X: A throughput with rates up to 100 Megabits per second (Mbps) over a hierarchical twisted-pair wiring scheme. Usually employs the Carrier Sense Multiple Access with Collision Detect (CSMA/CD) access method.

One-way communications: Communications in which information is always transferred in the same direction. One-way communications are also called Simplex.

One-way trunk: A trunk between central exchanges where traffic originates only at one end.

On-hook: Deactivated, in analogy to telephones. *See* **Off-hook.**

On-line: (1) The state of being connected with a computer (usually referring to a functional unit. (2) Connected with a distant computer, as in the successful connection with a host computer in a client server network. (3) When a file or application is available to the users of a Bulletin Board System (BBS).

On-line help: A help utility available on-screen to users of a network or an application program.

On-line information service. A for-profit firm that offers current news, stock quotes, and other information to electronic subscribers over standard telephone lines. *See* **American OnLine; CompuServe; Prodigy.**

On-screen formatting: A technique in a word processing program in which formatting commands directly affect text visible onscreen. *See* **Embedded formatting commands.**

On-the-fly data compression: A method by which data sent by modem is compressed during transmission rather than before, thereby increasing apparent transmission speed; subject to protocols such as V.42bis and Microcon Network Protocol-5 (MNP-5).

OOP: *See* **Object-Oriented Programming.**

OOPS: Object-Oriented Programming System. *See* **Object-Oriented Programming language.**

Open architecture: A network philosophy calling for standard protocols to increase the interoperability of computer systems.

Open Data link Interface (ODI): A standard interface that allows transport protocols to share a single network card.

Open Network Architecture (ONA): Standards imposed by the U.S. Federal Communication Commission (FCC) on the Bell Operating

Companies (BOCs) and AT&T to ensure that unregulated enhanced network services would be available and accessible.

Open Protocol Technology (OPT): Novell's strategy for creating NetWare software that can be supported by a wide variety of hardware manufactured by numerous vendors.

Open Software Foundation (OSF): A consortium of computer companies promoting standards and publishing specifications for programs operating on computers that run UNIX. OSF designed OSF Motif, a Graphical User Interface (GUI) for UNIX and provided much of the design inspiration for Microsoft Windows '95. OSF also inspired the OSF Distributed Computing Environment (DCE), a set of programs that enable cross-platform networks interoperability, and the OSF/1 operating system, a non-proprietary variant of UNIX. *See* **Proprietary.**

Open standard: A set of specifications describing the design or operating characteristics of a program or device that is made freely available to the technical community, contributing to rapid market growth when it encourages interoperability (the ability of a device made by one manufacturer to work with one made by another manufacturer). Its opposite is a proprietary standard pushed by a company hoping to dominate the market.

Open System Interconnection (OSI) reference model: A standard for the organization of a Local Area Network (LAN) set by the International Standards Organization (ISO) and the Institute of Electronic and Electrical Engineers (IEEE) that improves network flexibility. Also called the ISO/OSI reference model. The model separates the communication process into seven layers each insulated from one another but using and building on the services provided by those below it. Among them are the physical hardware and cabling layer, the transport layer (which carries the data), the presentation layer (how the transmitted data interacts with programs in each computer), and the application layer (the programs available to all users).

OpenView: Hewlett-Packard's network management application, server platform, and support services suite, based on HP-UX, which complies with the UNIX system.

Open wire line: A line in which the conductors are for the most part bare, uninsulated wire attached to telephone poles by ceramic, glass, or plastic insulators properly spaced to avoid short circuits.

Operating System (OS): The lower-level master-control program that manages a computer's internal functions and thus its operations, handling communication to various input-output devices and organizing stored data. The most popular operating systems for personal computers are the Microsoft Disk Operating System (MS-DOS), Operating System/2 (OS/2), Microsoft Windows '95, and the Macintosh system.

Operating System/2 (OS/2): A multitasking operating system for IBM PC and compatible computers that uses flat memory to emulate separate Disk Operating System (DOS) machines; it can run DOS, Windows, and OS/2 programs concurrently, protecting the others if one program crashes and allowing dynamic exchange of data between applications.

Operating System/2 (OS/2) Warp: An operating system from IBM that offers most of the features of Operating System/2 (OS/2) while also running Windows applications; among its features are built-in Internet connectivity.

Operating voltage: The electrical voltage, at which a microprocessor operates, usually 5 volts (an arbitrary specification picked when the transistor was invented) but sometimes 3.3 volts to save electricity (a real concern in portable computers) and reduce heat output.

Optical Character Recognition (OCR): Machine recognition of patterns such as printed or typed text so that documents scanned in can be converted into editable word processing documents.

Optical disk: A large-capacity secondary data storage medium for computers on which information is stored at extremely high density in the form of tiny pits representing binary 0s and 1s that are coded and decoded using a highly focused laser beam. Erasable optical disk drives offer more capacity than hard disks and are removable, but they are more expensive and much slower than hard disks. *See* **CD-ROM; Interactive videodisk; Write-Once Read-Many.**

Optical fiber: A communications medium composed of very fine glass or plastic fiber that conducts light waves.

Optical mouse: A mouse that as it moves shines a beam of light into a grid on a special mouse pad, which conveys the mouse's positions to the computer.

Optical resolution: A measure of the sharpness with which a scanner can digitize an image. The more Charged Coupled Devices (CCDs) a scanner contains (300 is average; 600 is very good), the better the optical resolutions. Software interpolation can improve output but is a poor substitute for high optical resolution.

Optimizing compiler: A compiler that translates source code into machine language, designed to run at maximum efficiency on a particular minicoprocessor; virtually essential when preparing programs to run on microprocessors equipped with superscalar architecture.

Original Equipment Manufacturer (OEM): The company that manufactures a given piece of hardware, unlike a Value-Added Reseller (VAR) that changes, reconfigures, or repackages hardware for sale; for example, Sony is the OEM for monitor tubes that are sold under many names, including Apple Macintosh.

Originate: To make the call rather than receive it; usually applies to contacting another computer system via modem.

OS/2: *See* **Operating System/2.**

Oscilloscope: An instrument that displays changes in a varying current or voltage.

OSI: *See* **Open System Interconnection.**

Other Common Carrier (OCC): A mode in which a modems will originate but not receive calls. *See* **Auto-answer mode.**

Outband signaling: A method of flow control in which a Recommended Standard 232 (RS232) control signal (usually Clear to Send) is lowered to tell a device to stop transmitting and raised to tell it to resume.

Outlier: A node which should be excluded from its containing peer group to improve the accuracy and simplicity of the other nodes in the group.

Out-of-band signaling: Signaling outside the frequency range allowed for a voice signal. Contrast with in-band signaling.

Output: The display or printing of the results of an application. *See* **Input.**

Outside link: A link to an outside node.

Outside node: A node participating in Personal Network-Node Interface (PNNI) routing which is not a member of a particular peer group.

Overflow: The aftereffects of what happens when a program tries to put more data in a memory area than it can hold, causing an error message.

Overhead: The information that must be added to a message in order to ensure its error-free transmission in a network. In asynchronous communications, for example, a start bit and stop bit must be added to every byte of transmitted data, adding an inefficient overhead of roughly 20 percent.

Overrun error: A serial port error in which a microprocessor sends data too fast for the Universal Asynchronous Receiver/Transmitter (UART) to handle it, causing the loss of data.

Overscan: A condition resulting when the image created on a display tube is larger than the visible portion of the display, pushing the relatively fuzzy perimeter of a Cathode Ray Tube (CRT) image to portions of the screen that are not visible. The overscan effect sometimes sends icons and text at the edges beyond the edges of the CRT.

Overtype mode: An editing mode in word processing and other programs in which new characters entered erase existing characters rather than moving them over; also called typeover mode. *See* **Insert mode.**

Overvoltage: Unusually high voltage, typically in spikes or surges greater than 130 volts from a wall unit. A high-quality surge protector can help to protect vulnerable areas of the computer from overvoltage.

Overwrite: To destroy original data by writing new data onto a magnetic disk at a point where the original data was stored.

P24T socket: A receptacle on an Intel 486 motherboard for an Intel P24T microprocessor, which can boost performance to near-Pentium levels.

PAS: The extension usually attached to the name of a file written in Pascal.

PABX: *See* **Private branch exchange.**

Pacing: A technique by which the receiving rather than the sending station controls the rate of transmission.

Package: The icon in Microsoft Windows 3.1 that represents a linked or embedded object, object file, or part of a file that has been reduced by the Object Packager utility.

Packet: A block of transmitted data of fixed size containing sending and receiving addresses, error-control information, and part of a message.

Packet Assembler/Disassembler (PAD): A hardware and software device in some PCs that allow users to access an X.25 network; installation is governed by the International Telecommunications Union (ITU) Recommendations X.3, X.28, and X.29.

Packet Data Network (PDN): A network using packet switching techniques to transmit data.

Packet filler: A traffic-control feature of a bridge that decides whether each arriving packet meets the specifications set by the network administrator and whether the bridge should forward or reject it.

Packet INternet Groper (PING): A common utility program used to determine whether a computer is connected to the Internet properly.

Packet Level Procedure (PAP): A protocol for transferring packets between an X.325DTE and an X.25 DCE. The PAP for the latter is a fully duplex, supporting data sequencing, flow control, error detection, recovery, and accountability.

Packet sequencing: The process for ensuring that packets are delivered to the receiver in the same sequence as they were transmitted.

Packet switching network: A design for a Wide Area Network (WAN) that makes no effort to establish a single electrical circuit between two computing devices; instead a message is divided into units called packets, each of which is addressed to the same destination. The packets are sped on their way by routers, though not all packets in one message necessarily follow the same routes. The receiving computer orders the packet and delivers the message. The Internet is a packet switching network. Though reliable, packet-switching networks are not suited to real-time voice and video messages. *See* **Circuit switching network.**

PAD: *See* **Packet Assembler/Disassembler.**

Page: A Random Access Memory (RAM) block of fixed size; also, in word processing and desktop publishing, the representation of a printed page. *See* **Paging memory.**

Page break: The code in word processing programs that tells the printer where to start a new page; sometimes, as in WordPerfect, inserted automatically when a page is full (soft page break), though page breaks can be forced (hard page break) where the user desires. The position of a soft page break, but not a hard page break, can change when the document is edited.

Page description language: A programming language that controls printer output no matter which type of printer is being used, transferring the burden of processing output from computer to printer and eliminating printer-dependent codes.

Paged Memory Management Unit (PMU): A chip or circuit that enables empty or virtual memory, an advanced feature that lets a computer use space on the hard disk to make more space in Random Access Memory (RAM), making it possible to run several programs simultaneously.

Page layout program: A desktop publishing program that brings together for placement on a page text and graphics from a variety of files, allowing them to be changed in size and shape to meet the demands of the page chosen by the user.

PageMaker: One of the more effective desktop publishing programs, created by Aldus Corporation for both Windows and Macintosh applications, for newsletters, brochures, reports, and books.

Page-mode RAM: A high-performance Random Access Memory (RAM) in high-end computer systems that divides memory into separate pages to allow the Central Processing Unit (CPU) to access data faster and more efficiently without wait states. Page-mode RAM is not to be confused with paging memory systems that use special circuits to extend memory storage in hard disks. *See* **Paging memory; Random Access Memory; Virtual memory; Wait state.**

Page orientation: *See* **Portrait orientation.**

Page printer: A printer, including laser, liquid crystal shutter, and light-emitting diode printers, that develop an image of the whole printed page in memory before transferring it to paper in a single operation.

Pages Per Minute (PPM): Measurement of efficiency of page printers, including inkjet and laser printers. This measurement is usually not very accurate, referring to maximum efficiency under opti-mal conditions.

Page Up/Page Down keys: The keys on IBM PC-compatible computer keyboards that move the cursor to the top of the preceding page or the previous screen (Page Up) or the top of the next page or the next screen (Page Down).

Page-white monitor: A monitor that displays black text and graphics against a white background. A page-white monitor often is preferred for word processing or desktop publishing.

Pagination: The processing of dividing a word processing document into pages for printing. *See* **Background pagination.**

Paging memory: A system in which data is located by where column and row intersect on the page (a unit of memory) rather than by physical location, allowing pages to be stored wherever space is available; used to implement virtual memory. *See also* **Paged Memory Management Unit; Random Access Memory; Virtual memory.**

Paint file format: A bit-mapped graphics file format. The MacPaint standard for Macintosh is 72 dots per inch. The Windows format, BMP, is increasingly common, as are such programs as PC Paintbrush. *See* **File format; Paint program.**

Paint program: A program that switches individual dots and pixels on and off to make up a bit-mapped screen display; the first was MacPaint for Macintosh.

Paired bar graph: A bar graph with two different category (x) axes, an excellent way to relate two data series with the same y-axis values but different x-axis ones.

Paired pie graph: A graphic containing two separate pie graphs used to show, for example, the breakdown of product sales in two different periods; often using a proportional pie graph to show the different in the size of the two totals.

Palette: (1) The colors that a computer video system can display; each screen can display 256 colors at once, though the full palette for Video Graphics Array (VGA) contains 262,144 colors. (2) The on-screen display of options in paint and draw programs, including drawing tools as well as colors.

Pan: The capacity of a multimedia synthesizer or soundboard to change left and right channel volumes to suggest that the source of the sound is moving.

Pantone Matching System (PMS): A method of describing and adjusting colors, starting from a booklet that provides a software code for each color so that output on a specially calibrated printer resembles the color in the booklet.

PAP: *See* **Packet Level Procedure.**

Paperless office: An office where the use of paper for sending messages, filling forms, and maintaining records has been reduced or eliminated. There are few paperless offices, given the absolute legal status and psychological authority of paper documents.

Parallel interface: See Parallel port.

Parallel port: A high-speed connection to peripheral devices, especially printers, for synchronous flow of data along parallel lines. IBM PC-compatible systems can be configured with three parallel ports.

Parallel printer: A printer that can connect to a computer's parallel port; easier to install and use than serial printers unless the printer must be positioned more than 10 feet from the computer.

Parallel processing: *See* **Multitasking.**

Parallel transmission: Simultaneous transmission of bits down parallel wires.

Parameter: An option that customizes the behavior of a command rather than using the default value.

Parameter Read Access Memory (RAM): A small bank of battery-powered memory that stores Macintosh hardware configuration choices after the power is turned off.

PARC: Palo Alto Research Center.

Parent directory: The directory above a given subdirectory in a tree-structured hierarchy.

Parity: A check of the total number of 1 (rather than 0) bits, with an 8th bit available to make sure that the count when transmitted is always off or always even, used to detect transmission errors.

Parity bit: An extra bit added to a data word for checking asynchronous communications and primary storage, for example, setting the parity bit option at non-parity and the data bits option at eight bits in a communications program. *See* **Parity checking.**

Parity checking: A technique for detecting errors in memory or data communication by automatic calculation of the number of bits in a one-byte data item either received or read from memory, checking whether the answer is odd or even, and comparing the answer to a previous setting. If the parity bit is incorrect, an error message is displayed.

Parity error: The data processing or transmission error reported by the computer when parity checking shows that one or more bits are incorrect.

Park: To position the read/write head of a hard drive over a designated safety zone to prevent damage in transit.

Parse: To organize a data file into logically meaningful parts, for example, columns, words, and paragraphs.

Parser: A program that breaks large groups of data into smaller groups for easier interpretation. For example, a HyperText Markup Language (HTML) identifies the parts of a document (for example, body text, headings, and bulleted lists) but does not specify how the parts are to be arranged on screen. The parser formats and organizes the parts for on-screen display.

Partition: A section of storage on a hard disk, usually set aside before the disk is formatted. Every MS-DOS hard disk has at least one DOS partition, for instance, though some versions require more. Utility programs, such as MultiDisk, make it possible to create several system partitions, which the operating system treats as if they were different disks. *See* **Directory; Subdirectory.**

Pascal: A high-level language developed by Nicklaus Wirth in the early 1970s and named after the 17th century mathematician and philosopher Blaise Pascal; widely accepted for teaching and applications development because it encourages the development of well-structured modular programs. *See* **BASIC; C; C++; FORTRAN; Modula-2.**

Passive matrix display: A Liquid Crystal Display (LCD) used in notebook computers in which a single transistor controls and entire column or row of tiny electrodes. Because they rely on ambient light passive matrix displays are cheaper than active ones but their contrast and resolution are lower.

Password: A method for limiting the access to and defining privileges for use of programs or networks to authorized users who identify themselves by a word or letters known only to them and the system administrators. Since hackers are aware that many people choose passwords based on address, birthdays, addresses, Social Security numbers, or other easily remembered words, it is best to have a password that no one else can guess.

Password aging: The feature of a computer Network Operating System (NOS) that monitors the length of time passwords are in effect; when a designated time has past, users are alerted to change passwords by a message on screen.

Password protection: A method of protecting data and networks by limiting access to users who enter recognized passwords.

Paste: The part of a text editing operation where material cut from elsewhere to the Clipboard storage area (in Windows and Macintosh systems) is inserted at the cursor, either within the same document or in another document.

Patch: A quick fix of a program added, in the form of a program statement, to correct errors or increase capabilities.

Path name: A statement in the Disk Operating System (DOS) that shows precisely where a file can be found on a hard disk; must be specified to store or retrieve a file beyond the directory in active use. Some applications have a default directory through which documents can be retrieved without a full path name.

Path statement: An entry in the AUTOEXEC.BAT file in the Disk Operating System (DOS) that lists directories where executable programs are linked.

PBX: *See* **Private Branch Exchange.**

PC: *See* **Personal Computer.**

PC-DOS: *See* **Personal Computer Disk Operating System.**

PCI slot: *See* **Peripheral Component Interconnect slot.**

PCM: *See* **Pulse Code Modulation.**

PCMCIA: *See* **Personal Computer Memory Card Interface Adapter.**

.PCX: A file extension for bit-mapped graphics originally used in the PC Paintbrush but now used generally.

PDA: *See* **Personal Digital Assistant.**

PDF: *See* **Portable Document Format.**

PDL: *See* **Page Description Language.**

PDN: *See* **Packet Data Network; Public Data Network.**

PDS: *See* **Portable Document Software; Premises Distribution System.**

Peer-to-peer communications: Resources shared by all computers in a network.

Peer-to-peer file transfer: A technique in a Local Area Network (LAN) by which each user can access files made public by other users on their work stations.

Peer-to-peer network: A Local Area Network (LAN) with no central file server, in which all users have access to the files made public on other workstations.

Peer-to-peer resource sharing: An architecture that allows any workstation to contribute resources simultaneously to the network and run other applications.

PEM: *See* **Privacy-Enhanced Mail.**

Pen-based computer: A personal computer equipped with pattern recognition circuitry so that handprinted data on a screen with a pen-like stylus is accepted as data input. The stylus can also be used to choose commands from menus.

Pentium: Microprocessors in the Intel 8086 family with clock speeds of up to 155 Mhz, using Complex Instruction-Set Computer (CISC) architecture with two pipelines and a 64-bit internal data bus.

PerfectOffice Professional: A suite of Novell application programs that adds a database management program, called Paradox, to the programs in PerfectOffice Standard.

PerfectOffice Standard: A suite of Novell application programs that includes WordPerfect, QuattroPro, Presentations, InfoCentral (a personal information manager), Envoy (desktop publishing), and GroupWise (workgroup coordination. Competes with Microsoft Standard and Lotus SmartSuite.

Pentium OverDrive: An upgrade microprocessor that plugs into the motherboard of an Intel 486DX/2 Central Processing Unit (CPU) to improve performance to Pentium levels.

Peripheral: A printer, disk drive, or other device external to a computer but connected to and controlled by the computer's Central Processing Unit (CPU).

Peripheral Component Interconnect (PCI) slot: An adapter socket in a motherboard equipped with a PCI expansion bus, faster than a Video Electronics Standards Association (VESA) local bus and IA slots; usually found on Pentium microprocessor motherboards.

PERL: *See* **Practical Extraction and Report Language.**

Permanent font: A font that when downloaded to a Hewlett Packard (HP) laser printer is held in memory there until the printer is shut off. *See* **Downloadable font; Temporary font.**

Permanent swap file: Contiguous disk sectors set aside by Microsoft Windows programs for rapid storage and retrieval of program instructions or data; used in virtual memory operations, but slower than Random Access Memory (RAM) and using more disk space. *See* **Paged Memory Management Unit; Swap file; Temporary swap file.**

Permanent Virtual Channel Connection (PVCC): An Asynchronous Transfer Mode (ATM) connection, left up and managed through the network, where switching is performed on the Virtual Path Identifier/Virtual Channel Identifier (VPI/VCI) fields of each cell.

Permanent Virtual Circuit (PVC): A logical connection between network endpoints that is installed until the network administrator redoes the network.

Permanent Virtual Path Connection (PVPC): An Asynchronous Transfer Mode (ATM) connection, left up and managed through the network, where switching is performed only on the Virtual Path Identifier (VPI) field of each cell.

Persistence: The quality of the phosphors coating the interior of a Cathode Ray Tube (CRT) display that ensures uniform brightness of the display; after a phosphor is struck by an electron beam, persistence keeps it glowing until the next beam strikes.

Personal Computer (PC): A computer designed around an Intel or Motorola processor that has its own hard drive rather than having only local storage like a work station; can be equipped with all the software and peripherals a single person needs to perform one or more tasks.

Personal Computer Disk Operating System (PC-DOS): The Disk Operating System (DOS) packaged by IBM, functionally identical to the Microsoft Disk Operating System (MS-DOS).

Personal Computer Memory Card Interface Adapter (PCMCIA): An interface standard for plug-in cards for portable computers; devices meeting the standard (for example, fax cards, modems) are theoretically interchangeable.

Personal Computer Memory Card Interface Adapter (PCMCIA) bus: An expansion bus specification allowing numerous credit-card-sized peripherals to be connected to portable computers.

Personal Computer Memory Card Interface Adapter (PCMCIA) card reader: The device allowing a portable computer to use peripherals that connect to the PCMCIA bus.

Personal Computer Memory Card Interface Adapter (PCMCIA) slot: The receptacle through which devices such as modems and network adapters are connected to a PCMCIA bus.

Personal Digital Assistant (PDA): A small hand-held computer accepting input that is hand-written on a screen with a stylus, used in such daily organizational tools as an appointment calendar, address book, notepad, and fax modem.

Personal Information Manager (PIM): A program, such as Lotus Agenda, for managing a variety of personal information, such as names and addresses, appointments, memos, and notes, optimized for a variety of views.

Personal laser printer: A laser printer with a monthly duty cycle of a few hundred pages designed to serve the printing needs of one rather than numerous persons.

PGA: *See* **Pin Grip Array.**

PgUp/PgDn keys: *See* **PageUp/PageDown keys.**

Phase modulation: Changing the phase of a signal in order to transmit digital data.

Phosphor: The electrofluorescent material coating the inside of a Cathode Ray Tube (CRT); phosphor's glow of which is energized by an electron beam repeated many times per second. *See* **Cathode Ray Tube; Raster display.**

PhotoCD: Standard popular with publishers for encoding photographs taken with 35-millimeter cameras onto multi-session PhotoCD-compatible CD-ROMs.

PhotoGrade: Apple method of enhancing the resolution of grayscale images, including photographs, when they are laser-printed.

Photorealistic: Printer output of professional photographic quality images, with well-saturated colors that blend smoothly.

Phreaking: Illegal use of knowledge of telephone technology to make long distance calls without being charged.

Physical drive: The local board and floppy drives in a network computer. The drives on other users' computers can be accessed through the network are called logical drives.

Physical layer: The lowest layer of the operating system, consisting of network wiring and cable, and the interface hardware for sending and receiving signals across the network.

Physical medium: The cabling through which data travels across a computer network. *See* **Coaxial cable; T-1; T-3.**

Physical memory: The actual Random Access Memory (RAM) chips on the system board, as contrasted to the apparent RAM (virtual memory) produced by using the hard disk as an extension of physical memory. *See* **Random Access Memory; Virtual memory.**

Physical Unit (PU): A terminal, printer, or similar device connected to the controller in an Systems Network Architecture (SNA) network.

.PIC: File extension indicating a business graphic in Lotus 1-2-3.

Pica: A typographical measure equal to 12 points, approximately 1/6 inch, used to describe horizontal and vertical dimensions of a page (points are used to describe type sizes).

Pico (p): Prefix for one trillionth (1012) of a second.

Picosecond: *See* **Pico.**

PICT: A Microsoft object-oriented graphics file format based on the Apple McDraw program that consists of separate objects that can be managed independently and stored as bit-mapped images. *See* **Bit mapped graphic; File format; Object-oriented graphic.**

Pie graph: A graph that displays data in a circle to emphasize the contribution each item makes to the whole. In presentation graphics each slice has a distinct pattern; combinations of patterns must be carefully handled to prevent distortion. Slices can be exploded from the whole for emphasis. *See* **Proportional pie graph.**

PIF: *See* **Program Information File.**

PIM: *See* **Personal Information Manager.**

Pin Grid Array (PGA): The collection of pins protruding from the bottom of a chip, allowing the microprocessor to be connected to a socket or circuit board.

Pin-compatible: Able to connect through the same socket as a chip made by another manufacturer.

Pine: A UNIX electronic mail program that has easy-to-use full screen default editors. The name is an acronym for Pine Is Not Elm, Elm being a predecessor program.

PING: *See* **Packet INternet Groper.**

Pipe: A symbol that tells a Disk Operating System (DOS) or UNIX operating system to send a command directly to another command, bypassing the screen.

Pipeline: An "assembly line" designed into microprocessors to speed the processing of instructions. The pipeline in the Intel 80486 allows it to process an instruction every clock cycle; the Pentium can process two per clock cycle because it has two pipelines, one for data and one for instructions. Superscalar architecture refers to a microprocessor with two or more pipelines.

Pipelining: A technique for sending multiple frames without waiting for each to be acknowledged and, thereby, increasing link throughput.

Pitch: The number of characters per horizontal linear inch in a monospaced font, as used in typewriters and dot matrix and daisy wheel printers. Elite pitch equal 12 Characters Per Inch (CPI), pica pitch (not to be confused with pica) is 10 CPI. *See* **Monospace; Pica; Point.**

Pixel: The smallest picture element a device can display; the element from which a displayed image is constructed. *See* **Bit-mapped graphic.**

Plain text document: A document containing only American Standard Code for Information Interchange (ASCII) text and number characters without formatting codes; often an alternative method of saving documents for telecommunications transfer.

Planar: *See* **Motherboard.**

Plasma display: Gas plasma display; technology produced by energizing an ionized gas held between two transparent panels, used with high-end laptop computers.

Platen: The cylinder in dot matrix and impact printers that guides paper through the printer, providing a hard surface for impressing the image onto the page.

Platform: *See* **Hardware platform.**

Platform independence: The capacity of a Local Area Network (LAN) to connect different makes of computer.

Plotter: A printer that uses ink pens moving over the page from one x, y coordinate to another to produce high-quality line drawings-circles, for example, are actually composed of very short, straight lines; common in computer-aided design (CAD) and presentation applications.

Plotter font: A Microsoft Windows vector font, for use with a plotter, that uses dots connected by lines to create characters.

Plug and play: An emerging standard that requires add-in hardware to carry the software to configure itself in a given way supported by Microsoft Windows '95. Plug and play makes, for instance, peripheral configuration software, jumper settings, and Dual-In-line Package (DIP) switches unnecessary.

Plug and print: A design standard developed by the Desktop Management Task Force that creates a management information file or base to improve how printers and computers communicate.

Plug compatible: *See* **Pin compatible.**

PMMU: *See* **Paged Memory Management Unit.**

PMS: *See* **Pantone Matching System.**

Pocket modem: An external modem, about the size of a package of cigarettes, used with portable computers. The pocket modem is fast losing ground to credit-card-sized Personal Computer Memory Card Interface Adapter (PCMCIA) modems.

Point: A unit of typographical measurement (72 points = 1 inch in computer programs). *See* **Pica; Pitch.**

Pointer: On-screen, a symbol, usually an arrow, showing the current position of the mouse; in database management, the record number in an index showing where the data record is physically stored.

Pointing device: The device, such as a mouse, trackball, or stylus, that displays the point of data entry on screen in a Graphical User Interface (GUI) environment.

Point Of Presence (POP): The point in a Wide-Area Network (WAN) where the local phone call provides access to the network.

Point Of Sale (POS) software: Business programs like barcode readers that automatically adjust accounting and inventory databases when merchandise is sold; include features like bar code label printing, sales tracking by employees, credit card verification, customer tracking, reorder reports, sales analysis, and links to accounting software.

Point to point: Data link directly connecting two devices.

Point-to-Point Protocol (PPP): One of two standards for dial-up telephone connection of computers to the Internet, with better data negotiation, compression, and error corrections than the other Serial Line Internet Protocol (SLIP), but costing more to transmit data and unnecessary when both sending and receiving modems can handle some of the procedures. *See* **Serial Line Internet Protocol.**

Polarity: (1) The negative or positive property of an electronic charge. (2) The total relationship between foreground and background elements in computer graphics: positive polarity is dark characters printed on a light background; negative is light characters on a dark background.

Polling: A method for controlling channel access in local area networks in which the central computer tests the lines at assigned intervals to determine whether each workstation has data to transmit; some nodes can be given greater access than others. *See* **Carrier Sense Multiple Access with Collision Detection; Token-ring network.**

Polyline: A primitive object created in a graphics program by drawing a straight line to a point and then carrying it in a different direction (as in depictions of constellations in astronomy). *See* **Graphics primitive; Object-oriented graphic.**

Polyphony: The use of a soundboard to reproduce multiple sounds together; high-end boards can emit more than 20 sounds at once.

POP: *See* **Point Of Presence; Post Office Protocol.**

Pop-up menu: A menu that appears on-screen but not in the standard menu bar location. *See* **Pull-down menu.**

Port: (1) The interface that synchronizes the flow of data between the Central Processing Unit (CPU) and devices such as mice, printers, modems, and soundboards. (2) Reprogramming an application to run on a different computer. *See* **Parallel port; Portable; Serial port.**

Port address: A number regulated by the Internet Assigned Numbers Authority (IANA) and included in the header of every Internet packet that identifies where a particular Internet application such as Gopher can be found on a computer directly connected to the Internet. *See* **Well-known port.**

Portable: Capable of working on more than one hardware platform, for example, UNIX. Most operating systems are designed for a given Central Processing Unit (CPU).

Portable computer: A computer designed for easy transportability. The first portables weighed well over 25 pounds; today, battery-powered computers can weigh less than 10 pounds. *See* **Notebook computer.**

Portable document: A document, whether containing graphics or text, that can be transferred from one computer system to another without losing its formatting. *See* **Portable document format; Portable document software.**

Portable Document Format (PDF): The file format used by documents created by Adobe Acrobat, accessible to computers of all platforms that use the Acrobat Reader software.

Portable Document Software (PDS): Programs combining a document publishing program and a file viewer to create documents that can be transferred to different computer systems without losing formatting and graphics. The publishing program creates an American Standard Code for Information Interchange (ASCII) file that can be distributed electronically through on-line services or the Internet to computers equipped with file viewers designed to run on specific computers that lets user read and view documents as originally formatted. Adobe Acrobat is the most popular PDS; others include Common Ground (No Hands Software), Replica (Farallon Computing), and Envoy (Word Perfect).

Port conflict: The error resulting when two devices try to access the same port at the same time. Though serial ports are typically dedicated to a single device, if a new sound board, say, is designed to use COMmunications port number 2 (COM 2), which is dedicated to a modem, the system must be reconfigured to eliminate the conflict. Because additional COM ports are less standardized in the Disk Operating System DOS, they are more often the source of port conflicts.

Portrait monitor: *See* **Full-page display.**

Portrait orientation: The vertical, orientation of a page of text; also the default setting for the orientation of the page to be printed.

POS: *See* **Point Of Sale.**

Post: To create or add to a data record.

POST: *See* **Power-On Self-Test.**

Postmaster: The person who configures the electronic mail manager in a network and responds to problems as they arise.

Post Office Protocol (POP): A standard that specifies how an Internet-connected computer handles electronic mail. Electronic mail programs for personal computers detect whether new mail has arrived in a user's mailbox on the service provider's computer and allows the user to read, download, reply to, print, or store it.

Postmaster: The person who configures the electronic mail manager in a network and responds to problems as they arise.

PostScript: A page description programming language from Adobe Systems, Inc., used to print high-quality text and graphics. PostScript, usually invisible and automatic, can be customized for embedding in documents to be printed. PostScript can be used with any printer that has a PostScript interpreter, from Linotronic typesetters with a resolution of 2,400 Dots Per Inch (DPI) to high-end office laser printers. Service bureaus can adapt documents from standard word processing applications to high-resolution PostScript documents.

PostScript font: An Adobe Type 1 scaleable outline font that requires a specially programmed printer or that must be downloaded before printing; it produces smooth letters that can be printed at maximum resolution and the screen font simulates the printed product. *See* **PostScript; PostScript Printer; Scaleable font; TrueType.**

PostScript Level 2: A faster version of PostScript that supports color printing and file compression.

PostScript printer: A laser printer able to process printing instructions written in PostScript, a Page Description Language (PDL) widely used in desktop publishing. More expensive than other laser printers, PostScript printers can produce special effects, including printing in subtle gradations of gray; they need at least 1Mb of Read Access Memory (RAM) to create the image for each page.

Posture: The slant of characters in a font, though the term italic is usually reserved for custom-designed serif faces.

POTS: "Plain old telephone service," for example, voice-only, dial-up telephone service; the analog communications system good for voice and slow data communication but lacking the bandwidth for high-speed digital communications.

PowerBook: One of the Macintosh notebook computers jointly manufactured by Sony and Apple starting in 1992 that features a built-in trackball so that it can be used without a mouse.

Power down: To turn off the computer's power switch, which clears everything out of Random Access Memory (RAM).

Power line filter: An electrical device that conditions the power coming into a computer by smoothing out peaks and valleys in the voltage delivered at the wall socket.

Power Macintosh: A Macintosh computer built around a Motorola Power PC microprocessor such as the Power PC 601.

Power management: A microprocessor feature that reduces electricity consumption by turning off peripherals when they are not in use, common in portable computers where energy savings equal longer battery life.

Power-On Self-Test (POST): The internal test encoded in Read Only Memory (ROM) and performed whenever a computer is started or reset. The POST program first runs a few simple operations to check the microprocessor, then checks the memory and first writes then reads various data patterns before checking with all attached peripherals. *See* **Basic Input/Output System.**

PowerPC: A Motorola Reduced Instruction Set Computer (RISC) microprocessor adopted by IBM for the RS/6000 line and by Apple for the new generation of Macintosh computers. The PowerPC is competitive with the Pentium and supports Windows NT, OS/2, and UNIX, now that the industry is committed to PowerOpen, a standard for PowerPC operating system.

Power supply: The electrical component that converts standard Alternating Current (AC) to the Direct Current (DC) used by a computer. An overloaded power supply can cause read/write errors or system crashes and was often a problem when early personal computers were upgraded. Systems with hard disks and several adapters require a power supply of at least 200 watts.

Power surge: A sudden, brief, but often substantial increase in power supply caused by turning off other appliances, lightning strikes, or the return of power after an outage. *See* **Surge.**

Power users: A expert computer user who can use advanced application features and learn new applications quickly.

PPM: *See* **Pages Per Minute.**

PPP: *See* **Point-to-Point Protocol.**

Practical Extraction and Report Language (PERL): An interpreted scripting language from UNIX created by Larry Wall for extracting information from text files and preparing summary reports. PERL has often been used to create Common Gateway Interface (CGI) scripts for outputting HyperText Markup Language (HTML) forms. *See* **HyperText Markup Language.**

Precedence: The sequence in which a program works through a formula, starting usually with exponentiation such as squaring a number, following by multiplication, division, and finally addition and subtraction.

Precision: The number of digits after the decimal used in expressing a quantity.

Pre-decode stage: A step in which a microprocessor using superscalar architecture decides which resources to use to process an instruction and, therefore, allowing the instruction to move through a pipeline.

Preemptive multitasking: A method of running more than one program in which the operating system decides which application should be given processor attention; more responsive to user commands than cooperative multitasking, in which a busy application can monopolize the computer for several minutes. Operating System/2 (OS/2) uses preemptive multitasking, as does Microsoft Windows '95 for 32-bit applications.

Premises Distribution System (PDS): Building-wide telecommunications cabling system proprietary to AT&T.

Presentation graphics program: An application that can create a variety of charts and graphs for visual appeal and ready comprehension, with facilities for adding text within as well as outside the graphics and usually a library of clip art to add pictures related to the subject matter. Presentation programs can be printed, displayed on-screen through a computer slide show, and outputted to a film recorder.

Presentation layer: The sixth layer in the Open Systems Interconnection (OSI) model, where data is formatted for the screen and incompatible file formats are translated.

Presentation Manager: A Graphical User Interface (GUI) and Application Programming Interface (API) developed by Microsoft Corporation and IBM for Operating System/2 (OS/2). An alternative to the command-line interface that is also part of OS/2, Presentation Manager features include multiple on-screen typefaces, pull-down menus, desktop accessories, and multiple on-screen windows.

Pretty print: A programming feature that makes printouts of source codes easier to understand.

PRI: *See* **Primary Rate Interface.**

Primary access: A multiplexing arrangement that uses a common line to allow numerous Integrated Services Digital Network (ISDN) basic subscribers to be connected to a digital network.

Primary cache: Memory built directly into microprocessor, like the 8Kb cache in an Intel 486 chip. Also called Internal cache or On-board cache.

Primary Rate Interface (PRI): The Integrated Services Digital Network (ISDN) specifications for the high-volume trunk connections to Private Branch Exchange (PBX) and central-office facilities or the connections linking network switches. The rate specified is a 23 BV ("bearer") channel and D ("data") channel, both operating at 54 kbps, with a combined signal-carrying capacity of 1.544 Mbps, equal to a T-1 channel.

Primary storage: The main memory directly accessible to the Central Processing Unit (CPU), containing in personal computers both Random Access Memory (RAM) and Read Only Memory (ROM).

Primitive: An interaction, independent of applications, between the user and the provider of a layer service.

Print engine: The mechanism inside a laser printer that creates an electrostatic image of a page and fuses it to the paper; print engines are differentiated by their resolution, speed, endurance, paper handling ability, and print quality. Most laser printers have a resolution of 300 Dots Per Inch (DPI); high-end printers produce up to 600 DPI. The life span of a print engine matters primarily in heavy-demand network applications; different brands vary from 180,000 to 600,000 with most lasting through 300,000 copies. Current paper trays can handle 250 pages with ease. Write-white engines generally produce darker images than write-black engines. Print speeds refer to the maximums possible, currently about 10 Pages Per Minute (PPM), but speed is slowed by graphics.

Printer: The peripheral device that transfers computer-generated text or graphics to paper. Impact printers such as daisy wheels are now obsolete for all practical purposes, having been supplanted by laser printers. Laser printers use an electrostatic technology similar to copiers to produce high-quality images quietly but at relatively high speeds on cut sheets or letterhead. Though they come with built-in fonts, most readily accept font cartridges or downloadable fonts. Dot-matrix printers press a matrix (pattern) of individual wires against a ribbon that transfers the image to paper; excellent for producing more than one copy at a time, but slower and sometimes the image is ragged. Ink jet printers form the image by spraying ink directly onto paper; the quality is good but the process, though very quiet, is slow. Thermal printers use special heat-sensitive paper and produce low-quality printing; they are used only in calculators, fax machines, and some portable computer systems.

Printer control language: The language established by a manufacturer to control its brand of printers. Some examples are the Epson command set that is the standard for dot matrix printers and the Hewlett Packard Printer Control Language for IBM-compatible laser printers. Unlike page description languages, which are true programming languages, printer control languages are usually variants of American Standard Code for Information Interchange (ASCII) control codes used to specify features such as bold or italic printing.

Printer driver: The file that tells an Operating System (OS) which printer to use. Application programs for IBM PC-compatible computers are equipped with a printer driver for each of numerous brands; the printer drivers work only with the program for which they were written. Printer drivers for Macintosh, however, are part of the operating system, allowing all programs to use the same printer.

Printer emulation: A printer's ability to operate using a standard printer control language to recognize the printer control language of a different brand.

Printer font: A font outputted to the printer rather than the screen; do not confuse with screen font. The Disk Operating System (DOS) character-based programs can only display typefaces that are built into the Read Only Memory (ROM). Microsoft Windows and Macintosh systems can accept TrueType or AdobeType Manager (Asynchronous Transfer Mode — ATM) fonts that appear as they will be printed. *See* **TrueType.**

Printer port: *See* **Parallel port; Serial port.**

Print head: The mechanism that actually gets the image onto the paper; technologies include those that use physical pressure (impact printers) or heat (thermal); spray ink (ink jet), or are electrostatic (laser).

Print queue: The order of files waiting to be printed that print spooler software feeds to the printer while the computer performs other tasks.

Print Screen (PrtSc): The key on IBM-PC-compatible keyboards that tells the computer to print an image of what is displayed on the screen.

Print server: A personal computer accessible to workstations in a Local Area Network (LAN) that uses print spooler software to establish a print queue, store files, and send them out in order to a designated printer. *See* **Local Area Network; Print queue; Print spooler.**

Print spooler: A program that stores files for printing, establishing a print queue and sending the files in order to a designated printer. *See* **Background printing; Print server.**

Privacy-Enhanced Mail (PEM): An Internet standard using public key encryption techniques to make sure that only the person to whom a message is directed can read it.

Private Asynchronous Transfer Mode (ATM) address: The 20-byte address that identifies the termination point of an ATM connection.

Private automatic branch exchange: *See* **Private Branch Exchange.**

Private Branch Exchange (PBX): Telephone switching equipment for a single customer that allows a large number of telephones to access the telephone company network through a small number of lines.

Procedural language: A language, such as Pascal or BASIC, that requires the programmer to specify exactly what the computer must do to get a given task done.

Process color: One of the four primary colors — cyan, magenta, yellow, or black — that can be mixed to get other colors. *See* **CMYK; Color model; Spot color.**

Processing: What the Central Processing Unit (CPU) does to execute program instructions.

Processor upgrade: (1) A chip that improves the performance of a microprocessor either by complementing or replacing it. (2) The act of installing the chip.

Prodigy: An Internet Service Provider who provides the program one needs for connection to the Internet, an easy setup program, and a local service number. Similar to CompuServe and America Online.

Professional workstation: A personal computer such as those manufactured by NeXT, Inc., or Sun Microsystems designed for professional applications like architecture, technical drawing, or circuit design, with speedy, powerful processing, ample memory, and high-quality screen resolution, typically using the UNIX operating system.

Program: Instructions written in a language that the computer can understand and which direct the computer to act in a given way.

Program generator

Also called software. Some programs written in high-level programming languages such as BASIC that use symbols and sequences resembling English must be converted into machine language by an assembler, interpreter, or compiler before they can be used. The three types of programs are: (1) system software which computers require to function effectively; (2) utility programs which supplement the system software in virus detection and data compression, etc.; and (3) application programs which the computer uses to perform a specific work, such as data or word processing or design.

Program generator: A program allowing non-programmers to describe an application for which the program creates the code. In data base management, a program generator can be used to specify the graphic output format.

Program Information File (PIF): A configuration file telling Windows how to run Disk Operating System (DOS) programs. Though Windows can run applications that lack PIF files, they create a generic default. *See* **Microsoft Windows.**

Program item: The icon representing a Microsoft Windows application.

Programmable: Capable of accepting a variety of instructions according to the user's needs.

Programmable Read Only Memory (PROM): A Read Only Memory (ROM) chip electronically programmed by the manufacturer, typically with configuration information, for a particular computer.

Programmer: The person who designs, codes, tests, trouble-shoots, and documents a computer program; sometimes educated in computer science but not necessarily.

Programmer's switch: A plastic accessory for early Macintosh computers that made it possible to reset hardware, access built-in troubleshooting, and restart the system after a crash without subjecting it to a start-up power surge. The switch is no longer necessary, since current models allow these operations to be performed from the keyboard.

Programming: The act of creating instructions to tell a microprocessor what must be done. This ranges from design (the decisions about what the program should do), through coding (using a programming language to express the logic in computer-readable form); testing and debugging (to discover and eliminate flaws), and documentation (writing a manual that explains how to use the program). Programming with an event-driven language such as HyperTalk (Macintosh) or Visual BASIC (Windows) is a good way to start, embedding a few lines of code in a window or button on-screen and thus picking up the basic concepts of programming, including variables and control structures. A well-structured high-level language such as QuickBASIC or Pascal makes it possible to create complete programs that run without errors. It is important to avoid excessive use of the GOTO command, which creates poorly organized programs ("spaghetti code"). *See* **C; C++; Event-driven environment; HyperTalk; Object-oriented programming language; Pascal; QuickBASIC; Spaghetti code; Well-structured programming language.**

PROgramming in LOGic (PROLOG): A language used in artificial intelligence programming, particularly for expert systems at the research system level. It provides tools that allow the programmer to state knowledge about the world as well as rules from which conclusions can be drawn.

Programming language: An artificial language with a fixed vocabulary and set of rules (syntax) used to create instructions for computers (programs). Most programs use a text editor or word processing program to create source code, which is then translated into the machine language computers can actually work with. High-level programming languages such as BASIC, C, or Pascal use keywords and syntax that crudely resemble natural language and therefore run more slowly than low-level languages. Low-level programming languages, including assembly language, are highly efficient to run but are harder to create because they require detailed understanding of the capabilities of a given microprocessor and system. Programming languages can also be described as procedural, in which the programmer spells out the procedure a computer must follow to reach a given goal, or declarative (non-procedural), in which the language defines a set of facts and relationships from which given results can be chosen. *See* **BASIC; C; C++; COBOL; Compiler; FORTRAN; Expert system; Object code; Object-oriented programming language; Pascal; Source Code.**

Program overlay: The portion of a program called into memory from the hard disk only as required.

Project management program: Software that tracks the individual components of an entire job

PROLOG: *See* **PROgramming in LOGic.**

PROM: *See* **Programmable Read Only Memory.**

Prompt: A symbol or phrase displayed on the screen to indicate that the computer is ready to accept input.

Propagation delay: The interval between when a signal enters a channel and when it is received; unimportant in a Local Area Network (LAN), but very important in satellite communications.

Property: An item of information such as the start-up direction or password associated with a program in Microsoft Windows and the Microsoft Disk Operating System (MS-DOS) shell. *See* **Microsoft Windows; Microsoft Disk Operating System Shell.**

Property sheet: The location in Microsoft Windows '95 where all the properties of an embedded object are recorded; set by right clicking on the object.

Proportional spacing: The allocation to a character of width proportional to shape, so that wide characters (for example, m) are given more space than narrow (for example, j). *See* **Kerning; Monospace.**

Proprietary: (1) Created for use only with specific equipment. (2) Privately owned, based on technology or specifications that the owner will not make public, in order to keep others from copying a product or program without an explicit license.

Proprietary file format: The file format a manufacturer creates for storing data produced by its programs, for example, Lotus spreadsheets are stored as .WKS format; usually unreadable by applications created by other manufacturers. Many WordPerfect versions, for instance, cannot read Word documents, but conversion utilities ("filters") are part of more sophisticated programs to allow access to files created in other programs.

Proprietary protocol: A set of rules adopted by a single manufacturer but not industry-wide or internationally, allowing only items of equipment made by a single manufacturer to be used together. *See, for example,* **V.32bis.**

Protocol: The formal rules governing the logic, formatting, and timing of an information exchange between layers.

Protocol analyzer: A device for decoding a bit stream into characters representing the format and information context of a transmission protocol.

Protocol control information: The information that corresponding entities exchange in a lower-layer connection to coordinate their operations.

Protocol suite: A set of standards that together define the architecture of a network; the Internet is based on the collection of more than 100 standards designed to work together known as the Transmission Control Protocol/Internet Protocol (TCP/IP) protocol suite.

Prototype: A demonstration version of a program or device; often called a beta version. The prototype of a program is usually a mockup of the user interface without much support code; a hardware prototype usually has lots of wires and components that in production would be replaced by circuit boards and integrated circuits.

PrtSc: *See* **Print Screen.**

PS/2 mouse: A mouse whose connector fits into a dedicated mouse port and, thus, is one that does not require a separate serial port.

Pseudocode: An algorithm expressed in English before being coded into a programming language. *See* **Algorithm.**

PSTN: *See* **Public Switched Telephone Network.**

PU: *See* **Physical Unit.**

Public Data Network (PDN): A Wide Area Network (WAN) through which organizations and individuals access long distance data communication services, in the U.S. based usually on the x.25 and Transmission Control Protocol/Internet Protocol (TCP/IP) protocols.

Public domain software: Software that has not been copyrighted and can therefore be used without permission and without paying a fee. *See* **Freeware; Shareware.**

Public key cryptography: A method of encryption that has two keys, the public one used for encryption and the private one used for decryption, with the result that the receiver does not have to receive the key in a separate transmission.

Public Switched Telephone Network (PSTN): With a total of 300 million connections, probably the largest network using circuit switching.

Pull-down menu: A list of command options that is displayed when a command name on the menu bar is clicked; the pointer is used to choose a command. The name comes from the Macintosh version, which stays on screen only if the mouse button is held down; in Windows the menu stays after the mouse is clicked.

Pull quote: A quotation extracted in desktop publishing from a news item or article and printed in large type elsewhere on the page.

Pulse Code Modulation (PCM): A technique used in multimedia applications to sample sounds digitally by transforming an incoming analog into a noise-free digital signal; often used for digitizing voice signals when 64 Kbps bandwidth is available.

Purge: To remove information no longer wanted in a computer system.

Pushbutton: A large button to initiate action in a dialog box, which usually offers an OK option to initiate action and a Cancel option.

PVC: *See* **Permanent Virtual Circuit.**

PVCC: *See* **Permanent Virtual Channel Connection.**

PVPC: *See* **Permanent Virtual Path Connection.**

QAM: *See* **Quadrature Amplitude Modulation.**

QBasic: *See* **Microsoft Disk Operating System (MS-DOS) QBasic.**

QBE: *See* **Query By Example.**

QIC: *See* **Quarter-Inch Cartridge.**

QOS: *See* **Quality Of Service.**

Quad density: *See* **High density.**

Quad issue processor: A microprocessor with a two-pipeline superscalar architecture that can accept four instructions at once.

Quadbit: A group of four bits which in 16-phase modulation is encoded as one of 16 separate carrier phase shifts. *See* **Dibit; Tribit.**

Quadra: A series of Macintosh professional workstations powered by Motorola's 68040 microprocessor. *See* **Motorola 68040.**

Quadrature Amplitude Modulation (QAM): A combination of phase and amplitude modulation with relatively low signaling rates used in modems to encode data very fast.

Quadrature modulation: *See* **Quadrature Amplitude Modulation.**

Quad-speed drive (4x): A Computer Disk Read Only Memory (CD-ROM) disk drive that can transfer data at 600Kb per second, functioning about 40 percent faster than double-speed drives (access time cannot be reduced as easily as data transfer rates are increased). There are now 32x drives.

Quality Of Service (QOS): A measure of network effectiveness based on a number of factors, including transit delay, cost, and the likelihood of packets being lost, duplicated, or damaged.

Quantization: Allocation of a value to a subrange or interval of the range of values of a variable.

QuarkXPress: A highly regarded Quark, Inc., page layout program for Macintosh computers that can handle documents of unlimited length and has some word processing functions.

Quarter-inch cartridge: (1) A tape standard for the backup process. (2) A popular backup cartridge that uses 1/4-inch-wide magnetic tape.

Quattro Pro for Windows: A three-dimensional spreadsheet program from Borland International that uses a notebook of separate spreadsheet pages that can be named separately; formulas link values from one page to another; its graphic capabilities are comparable to those of presentation programs.

Query: A search question that tells the program what kind of data to retrieve from a database, thereby eliminating unnecessary data; a question that sets the criteria the computer can use to reach the data desired. *See* **Data independence; Declarative language; Query language; Structured Query Language.**

Query By Example (QBE): A query technique used in certain IBM data management programs that prompts the user to type search criteria into a template similar to the data record. No special language is needed to frame the query. When a search is begun, the first screen lists all the data fields for every data record; the information entered restricts the search to the criteria specified.

Query language: A programming language designed for retrieving information from a database. *See, for example,* **Structured Query Language (SQL).** A good query language, although necessarily somewhat rigid, approximates a natural language, as in:

> SELECT title
> FROM videos
> WHERE CATEGORY = Western
> AND RATING = PG
> OR RATING = PG13.

See **Query; Query By Example.**

Question mark: A wild-card symbol (?) indicating a single character at a specific location, unlike an asterisk (*) which can indicate several characters. In AB?DE, for example, only file names or character strings that have five characters, starting with AB and ending with DE, would be selected.

Queue: A line or list of items waiting to be processed. *See* **Job queue; Print queue.**

Queuing: The process of placing items into a queue.

QuickBASIC: A high performance compiler for programs written in Beginner's All-purpose Symbolic Instruction Code (BASIC) that allows for the creation of programs with a full set of control structures, enabling programmers to omit line numbers. QuickBASIC is useful in creating commercial software because QuickBASIC programs operate much faster than interpreted programs. *See* **Beginner's All-purpose Symbolic Instruction Code; Compiler; Control structure.**

QuickDraw: The object-oriented graphics and text-display technology stored in the Read Only Memory (ROM) of Macintoshes, allowing programmers to quickly create on-screen windows, dialog boxes, menus, and shapes and achieve a consistent look.

Quicken: A complete checkbook management program for home and small business use developed by Intuit for both PCs and Macintosh computers that does not require accounting knowledge and produces a wide variety of reports.

QuickTime: A multimedia extension to Macintosh software that synchronizes animated or video sequences with high-quality sound.

Quit: Exit a program by storing all your work properly.

QWERTY: The standard keyboard layout for both typewriters and computers named for the sequence of the six left-most keys on the top letter row. Alternative keyboard layouts (for example, Dvorak) place the most used letters on the home row to increase typing speed.

Radio button: One of the round option buttons that appear in dialog boxes in a Graphical User Interface (GUI); only one may be chosen, unlike check boxes that allow multiple selections. *See* **Graphical User Interface.**

Radio Frequency (RF): A generic term for the technology in cable television and broadband networks that transmits via electromagnetic wave forms usually in the MegaHertz (MHz) range.

Radio Frequency Interference (RFI): Radio noise generated by computer and other electronic and electromechanical devices in operation that in excess can severely degrade radio and television reception and when generated elsewhere can cause screen flickering and even data loss if computers are not properly shielded. *See* **Federal Communications Commission certification.**

Radio paging: The broadcast of a radio signal, activating a small portable receiver carried by the person to whom the signal is directed.

Ragged-left alignment: Alignment of lines of text so that the right margin is even, but the left is also common. Also called "flush right."

Ragged-right alignment: Alignment of lines of text so that the left margin is even, but the right is not. Also called "flush left."

RAID: *See* **Redundant Array of Inexpensive Disks.**

RAM: *See* **Random Access Memory.**

RAMDAC: *See* **Random Access Memory Digital-to-Analog Converter.**

RAMDRIVE.SYS The configuration provided with the Microsoft Disk Operating System (MS-DOS) that treats part of random access memory as if it were a disk drive; where as in Windows there is plenty of memory, RAMDRIVE.SYS can be used to store temporary (.TMP) files to improve speed. To do this, add the following command to CONFIG.SYS:

DEVICE =C:\WINDOWS\RAMDRIVE.SYS

Once the WINDOWS directory contains this CONFIG.SYS file, add the following command to AUTOEXEC.BAT:

SET TEMP=D:

If the computer has more than one hard disk, or the single hard disk has more than one partition, give the drive a letter other than D, such as E or F.

Random access: A technique allowing the computer to access stored information directly, without having to go through intermediate locations (sequential access). Because the information is not stored randomly, a better term might be direct access; a useful analogy is a Compact Disk (CD) compared with a cassette tape (sequential access). *See* **Random Access Memory; Sequential access.**

Random Access Memory (RAM): Read-write memory, the work area where operating system, program, and data files are stored while the power is on. Data files to be retrieved or updated later must be saved to a secondary storage area.

Random Access Memory (RAM) cache: A section of RAM that acts as a buffer between the Central Processing Unit (CPU) and the disk drives. The RAM cache stores and programs instructions an application needs often for quick access from RAM and speeding operations by accepting data to be written to disk as fast as the CPU can send it, which is much faster than the disk drive can function. *See* **Central Processing Unit; Disk cache; Random Access Memory.**

Random Access Memory (RAM) disk: An area of RAM configured to emulate a disk drive for quicker access to data stored there. As a virtual disk drive, it operates much faster than a real disk drive, improving performance, but risking the disappearance of data that has not been saved to a real disk when the power is turned off. *See* **Configuration file; Device driver; Expanded memory; Extended memory; Random access memory.**

Random7-Access Memory Digital-to-Analog Converter (RAMDAC): The chip in a video adapter that converts the digital signals for each of the three primary colors into a single analog signal for display, using on-board Random Access Memory (RAM) to store the digital signals before conversion.

Range: A cell or a rectangular group of contiguous cells in a spreadsheet program on which a single operation, for example, formatting, can be performed, including part of a column, part of a row, or a block covering several columns and several rows.

Range expression: An expression that describes a range in a spreadsheet program by defining the upper left and lower right cells, written, for example, in Lotus 1-2-3 by typing the beginning cell address, with periods, and the ending cell address.

Range format: A numeric or label alignment format in a spreadsheet program that applies only to a range, over-riding the global format. *See* **Global format; Numeric format; Range.**

Range name: A set of cells in a spreadsheet program to which a distinctive name is attached.

Raster: The horizontal pattern of lines consisting of dots that can be illuminated individually forming the image on a computer or television screen.

Raster display: The technology used in television sets and computer monitors in which a highly focused electron beam zigzags line by line from top to bottom down the screen's raster pattern, scanning the screen dozens of times per second. *See* **Raster graphics; Vector graphics.**

Raster font: *See* **Bit-mapped font.**

Raster graphics: The display of images using a bit map, a collection of small separate dots (also called Bit-mapped graphics). Resolution is limited by the capabilities of the display or printer.

Rate center: A geographic location specified by telephone companies for applying inter-exchange mileage rates.

Rate Increase Factor (RIF): The amount by which cell transmission increases when a Resource Management (RM) cell is received.

Raw data: Data that has not yet been arranged, edited, or otherwise processed into a form for easy retrieval and analysis.

RBOC: *See* **Regional Bell Operating Company.**

RDBMS: *See* **Relational Database Management System.**

Read: Retrieve data or instructions from a hard or floppy disk for placement into Random Access Memory (RAM).

Read cache: A cache segment for saving information from the disk drives that is likely to be requested soon by the system; only if the information is not in read cache will the system go into the disk.

README file: A text file included on the installation disk of an application containing last-minute information not included in the documentation.

Read only: Data that can be displayed or manipulated but not deleted; if displayed and modified, it must be saved under another name. *See* **File attribute; Read/write.**

Read-only attribute: The attribute sorted with a file entry in a Microsoft Windows '95 and Operating System/2 (OS/2) directory that tells whether or not the file can be changed or deleted; when the attribute is on, the file can be displayed but not modified or erased.

Read Only Memory (ROM): Memory containing data programmed in before it was placed in the computer that cannot be rewritten or changed.

Read/write: The capability of a storage device to record data (write) and play it back (read).

Read/write file: In the Microsoft Disk Operating System (MS-DOS), Microsoft Windows '95, and Operating System/2 (OS/2), a file whose file attribute is set to allow it to be modified or deleted.

Real enough time: Response time fast enough to meet the needs of a given application.

Real mode: An Intel operating mode that gives one program at a time a defined area of Random Access Memory (RAM) and direct access to peripherals.

Real time: The immediate processing of time-dependent input, such as point-of-sale transactions or computer-assisted instruction.

Real-time clock: A battery-powered clock built into a computer that keeps track of the time of day even when the power is off (not to be confused with the system clock that governs microprocessor cycles).

Reboot: Restart a computer, often necessary after a crash to re-initialize the Random Access Memory (RAM); usually generated from the keyboard or a reset button, but after severe crashes, the computer may have to be turned off and back on. *See* **Programmer's switch.**

Rec: One of the seven UseNet newsgroup hierarchies in UseNet, containing groups by recreational interests, including movies, comics, science fiction, audio systems, sports cars, aviation, collections and music of all kinds, brewing, cooking, board games, humor, and numerous individual sports.

Recalculation method: The way a spreadsheet program recalculates cell values after cell contents are changed. *See* **Recalculation order.**

Recalculation order: The sequence in which spreadsheet calculations are performed when new values, labels, or formulas are entered. Options recalculations by column or row, and natural recalculation.

Receive-Only (RO): A one-way device such as a printer plotter or graphics display that cannot send data.

Receive-Only (RO) device: A teletypewriter without a keyboard, used where no input to the computer is necessary.

Recommended Standard 232 (RS-232 or RS232C): (1) The electrical, mechanical, and procedural standard interface developed by the Electronic Industries Association (EIA) for communications among computers, printers, and modems. (2) The mechanical and electrical specification for asynchronous transmission between Data Terminal Equipment (DTE) and Data Communication Equipment (DCE); external peripherals such as modems are attached to personal computers through an RS-232-compatible serial port. *See* **Modem; Printer; Scanner.**

Recommended Standard 336 (RS-336): A specification for the interface between a modem (Data Communication Equipment or DCE) and a terminal or computer (Data Terminal Equipment or DTE) that, unlike RS 232-C, allows for automatic dialing of calls via modem.

Recommended Standard 422/422A (RS-422 and RS-422A): An Electronics Industries Association (EIA) standard governing the asynchronous transmission of computer data at speeds of up to 920 Kilobits per second (Kbps), used as the serial port standard for Macintosh computers.

Recommended Standard 423A (RS-423A): The electrical standard for unbalanced interchange circuits between a Data Terminal Equipment (DTE) and Data Communication Equipment (DCE).

Recommended Standard 448 (RS-448): A specification for the interface between a modem (Data Communication Equipment or DCE) and a terminal or computer (Data Terminal Equipment or DTE) that overcomes some of the problems associated with the RSS 232-C interface specifications.

Recommended Standard 449 (RS-449): An Electronic Industries Association (EIA) mechanical and procedural standard for transmissions between a Data Terminal Equipment (DTE) and a Data Communication Equipment (DCE) that interfaces to an analog circuit-switched network, applying to binary, serial, or asynchronous systems.

Record: *See* **Data record.**

Record locking: A feature that prevents other users from accessing or writing to a record in a file the first user is accessing.

Record-oriented database management program: A program that displays data records in response to queries, unlike a table-oriented database management program, in which all data query operations result in tables. *See* **Data retrieval; Database Management System; Structured Query Language.**

Record printer: An on-screen status message showing the number of the data record now visible (or where the cursor is positioned).

Recover: Bring a computer system back to a stable operating state or restore erased or lost data; necessary after a system or user error, such as trying to write data to a drive where there is no disk. *See* **Undelete utility.**

Recoverable error: An error that does not cause a program or system crash or the irretrievable loss of data.

Recursion: Program instructions used to implement searches or perform repetitive calculations by causing a module or subroutine to call itself.

Recycle bin: A Microsoft Windows '95 on-screen icon where deleted files are stored and from which they can be restored as well as discarded permanently.

Red Book: Standard 10149 from the International Standards Organization (ISO), describing how music is to be recorded on Computer Disk-Digital Audio (CD-DA) disks. Other CD standards are identified by other colors, including orange, yellow, and green.

Red-Green-Blue (RGB) monitor: A color digital monitor that accepts separate inputs for red, green, and blue, producing much better resolution than composite color monitors.

Redirection: *See* **Input/Output redirection.**

Redirection operation: A Microsoft Disk Operating System (MS-DOS) symbol for routing a command from or to a device other than the keyboard and monitor, such as a file or a printer. *See* **Input /Output redirection.**

Redirector: A software module loaded into network workstations to capture requests for file sharing and equipment sharing and route them through the network for action.

Redlining: A display attribute such as reverse video or double underlining that highlights text different users have added to a document so that other users can see easily what has been added or deleted.

Reduced Instruction Set Computer (RISC): A Central Processing Unit (CPU) in which the computer's processing speed is increased by reducing the number of instructions to the microprocessor to the bare minimum; RISC processors optimize the most common instructions for the fastest possible execution. RISC processors usually run 50 to 75 percent faster than Complex Instruction Set Computers (CISCs) and are cheaper to design and debug.

Redundancy: The portion of information in a message that can be eliminated without loss of clarity.

Redundant Array of Inexpensive Disks (RAID): A system backup method, common on network servers, using software working with several hard drives to assure data redundancy and security.

Redundant Array of Inexpensive Disks (RAID) level 0: A RAID scheme that uses data stripping to improve disk performance but does not protect against data loss due to drive failure.

Redundant Array of Inexpensive Disks (RAID) level 1: A RAID version using two hard disks with identical contents. Because RAID Level 1 does not employ data stripping, it offers no speed advantage.

Redundant Array of Inexpensive Disks (RAID) Level 2: One of the more popular RAID versions, using data stripping over as many as a dozen hard disks, several of which have copies of the same data so that they can catch and fix errors in outgoing data streams.

Redundant Array of Inexpensive Disks (RAID) Level 3: A RAID version similar to RAID level 2, but not able to correct the errors it catches.

Redundant Array of Inexpensive Disks (RAID) level 4: A RAID version that copies sectors across various hard disks and uses one drive to check for, but not correct, outgoing errors.

Redundant Array of Inexpensive Disks (RAID) level 5: The most common RAID version distributes both sectors and sector-checking functions across the entire array.

Redundant Array of Inexpensive Disks (RAID) level 5.3: A RAID version that uses data stripping on two separate RAIDs of level 3, which are both fast and fault-tolerant.

Redundant Array of Inexpensive Disks (RAID) level 6: A RAID version that retains data even if two hard disks fail; similar to level 5 but distributing two copies of the error-checking data across the array rather than one; RAID 6 is very good at data reading but not at data writing.

Reed relay: A switch the contacts of which open or close in response to an electrical current.

Re-engineering: Redesigning how work is done and programming computers to enhance the new work process.

Reference model: The Open System Interconnection (OSI) classification scheme for communication among computers.

Reflective Liquid-Crystal Display (LCD): A type of LCD that relies on ambient light for readability. The reflective LCD is usually unsuitable for use outdoors, where sunlight may drown out the image.

Reformat: (1) To repeat a formatting operation on a floppy or hard disk. (2) To change the arrangement of text elements on a page.

Refresh: Repeat a transmission to keep it from fading either partially or completely. Monitor signals are constantly refreshed, as are the signals sent to Random Access Memory (RAM) chips.

Refresh rate: *See* **Vertical refresh rate.**

Regional Bell Operating Company (RBOC): The regional telephone companies ("Baby Bells") created in 1982 when the telephone monopoly held by AT&T was broken up.

Regional center: A control center (also known as a class 1 office) which connects sectional centers of telephone systems. Pairs of U.S. regional centers each have a direct circuit group connecting them.

Register: The location where a microprocessor stores values and external memory addresses while performing logical and arithmetic operations on them; more registers allow a microprocessor to handle more information.

Registered Jack (RJ11/RJ-45): Common 8-pin modular telephone connectors. RJ0-11 is used in most voice connections, RJ-45 for data transmission over twisted-pair telephone wire.

Registered Jack (RJ12): A 6-pin modular jack.

Registered Jack (RJ21): A 50-pin Telco connector.

Register renaming: A method for enabling software designed for x86 microprocessors, which can recognize only 8-bit registers, to work on more advanced microprocessors with superscalar architecture and 32-bit or more registers. A microprocessor capable of register renaming can address the actual number of registers available, and will divert information sent to a register that is in use to one that is not.

Registration: The mechanism by which client servers give their addresses to the Local Area Network (LAN) emulation server.

Registry: A Microsoft Windows '95 program allowing the user to choose options for configuration and applications to set them; it replaces confusing text-based *.INI files used with Windows 3.1 applications.

REL: Release message.

Relational Database Management System (RDBMS): An application that comes with all the programs, programming tools, and documentation necessary to create, install, and maintain custom databases, and which stores data in two-dimensional data tables; the program can work with two or more tables through links established by a common column or field. Edgar Codd introduced the term 'database management' in 1970 to refer to storage and retrieval of data in tables that define the relationship between the items listed in rows (data records) and columns (data fields). Although there are few relational database programs that treat all data as tables, most of those that store data as records, like dBASE, can be treated as if it were a true relational program.

Relational operator: A symbol used to describe the relationship between two numeric values, often used to specify search criteria in query language and used in spreadsheet programs to return the number 1 if the expression is true and if it is false. In @ IF formulas, relational operators can be used to test data, displaying different values, depending on the results of the test. Many programs use the following conventions to express relationship operators:

= equal to
< less than
> greater than
<= less than or equal to
>= greater than or equal to
<> not equal to

Relative cell addressing: A formula's cell reference that the spreadsheet program adjusts when a formula is copied from one cell to another cell or range of cells. When a formula such as "=SUM(C6:C8)" is typed in cell C10, the spreadsheet program records a code that means: "Add all the values in the cells C6 through C8." The message (equation) is preserved when the formula is copied to other desired cells, and the values in those cells are then summed correctly.

Relative transmission level: The ratio, expressed in decibels, of the test-tone power at one point to the test-tone power at a point elsewhere in the system chosen as a reference point. The level at the transmitting switchboard is often taken as the zero level reference point.

RELative Uniform Resource Locator (RELURL): One of the two basic Uniform Recovery Identifiers (URIs). The RELURL is a string of characters that gives the name of a resource file (such as merlot.html) but not its type or exact location; Web browsers and other pairers will assume the resource can be found in the same directory as the RELURL. *See* **Uniform Resource Locator.**

Relay center: A message center, the central point where message switching takes place.

Relaying: The function by which one layer receives data from another and passes it on.

Relay rack: A rack 19 inches wide used for mounting cabling hubs.

Release number: The number, usually a decimal, that identifies a program version that is only incrementally improved, rather than a major revision, which is numbered with an integer: Version 5.1 would be the second release of Version 5. Not all software publishers use this numbering scheme, and not all versions numbered in integers are in fact greatly improved. *See* **Version.**

Relevance feedback: A search feature in a Wide Area Information Servers (WAIS) that allows the user to select a highly relevant document for the search software to use subsequently as a model for finding additional relevant documents. Clicking a check box next to a document that contains relevant information provides relevance feedback.

Reliability: The capability of computer hardware or software to perform consistently as the user expects, without failures or erratic behavior. *See* **Mean Time Between Failure.**

Reliable connection: *See* **Reliable link.**

Reliable link: An error-free connection through the telephone system between two modems that both use error-correction protocols.

RELURL: *See* **RELative Uniform Resource Locator.**

Remark: Explanatory text in a batch file, macro, or source code that the computer ignores when it executes the commands. Remarks make it possible for programmers other than the original to produce code that can be evaluated, changed, and improved.

Remote: A link-attached terminal.

Remote control program: A utility program that links two personal computers so that one can be used to control the operation of the second. Such popular remote control programs as Carbon Copy Plus are being used to train users to perform tasks at the office while working from home, to install and demonstrate software on clients' computers, and to provide technical support by logging on to the remote computer to diagnose problems.

Remote File Service (RFS): A distributed-file system network protocol developed by AT&T and adopted as part of UNIX V that allows one computer to use files and peripherals of another as if they were local.

Remote Job Entry (RJE): A method of submitting work in batch format to IBM mainframes still widely used although superseded by the 3270 system.

Remote management: A feature of networked laser printers that transmit information about toner level, paper supply, and mechanical problems to the printer administrator.

Remote Network Monitoring Probe (RNMP): A device designed to help perform management on a network segment.

Remote Procedure Call (RPC): Software tool developed by a consortium of manufacturers for developers who create distributed applications that automatically generates code for both client and server.

Remote system: The computer or network to which a non-on-site computer (remote terminal) is connected by a telephone line and modem.

Remote terminal: *See* **Terminal.**

Remote vaulting: Software that can manage remote data either over phone lines or by direct connection with other sites as if the remote data were local.

Remote workstation: A computer used to dial into a Local Area Network (LAN) but not connected to it constantly.

Removable mass storage: A high-capacity secondary storage medium that can be removed from the drive for safekeeping. Though a high-density floppy disk qualifies as a removable mass storage medium, the term usually is reserved for a Bernoulli box or cartridge-based tape backup systems with huge amounts of storage capacity.

Removable storage media: Storage media such as magnetic disks or tapes that can be removed from the drive from safekeeping. *See* **Removable mass storage.**

Rendering: The conversion of an outline drawing into a full graphic image.

Repagination: A formatting operation in which pages are renumbered to reflect editing changes to a document, such as insertions or deletions. Though most programs repaginate automatically and reflect changes on screen, some do not.

Repeater: The component of a communications system that maintains a signal across a network by amplifying or regenerating it to compensate for signal attenuation over time and distance.

Repeating field: An error of database design that compromises data integrity by requiring that the same item be repeatedly retyped, thus increasing the possibility of error. *See* **Database design; Data integrity; Data redundancy; Relational database management system.**

Repeating label: A character provided by a label prefix that causes the character to be repeated across the cell in a spreadsheet program. For example, Lotus 1-2-3- uses \ as a signal to repeat, so \- would produce a line of hyphens across the cell. Repeating hyphens can be used to create a single line, repeating equal signs to create a double line.

Repeat key: A key that keeps entering the same character as long as it is held down.

Repetitive Strain Injury (RSI): An occupational illness caused by constant repetition of hand and arm movements that can inflame or kill nerves in the hands, arms, shoulders, or neck. A Cumulative Trauma Disorder (CTD), RSI results when tendons and ligaments are strained by constant motion. Common among meat packers, musicians, and certain workers on assembly lines, RSI is increasing among journalists and other white-collar workers who use computer keyboards for long periods of time. One form of RSI, Carpal Tunnel Syndrome (CTS), often afflicts supermarket cashiers who repeatedly drag items over scanners. Symptoms include burning, tingling, or numbness in the hands and loss of muscle control and dexterity. RSI injuries are believed to cost U.S. corporations $27 billion per year in medical bills and lost workdays. Realigning chair heights and other aspects of a workstation or desk to eliminate unnecessary extension or flexing of the wrist can help prevent RSI, as can good posture, frequent breaks, and varying activities throughout the day.

Replace: A text processing utility that searches for a string and then substitutes a different string for it; should be used only in the mode that requests confirmation for each replacement to avoid incorrect substitutions. Accuracy can be improved by specifying case matching and whole-word options, so that a word will be substituted only when the string exists independently or with certain capitalization and not when it appears as part of another word.

Replaceable parameter: The symbol in a batch file, consisting of a percent sign and a number from 1 through 9, that the Microsoft Disk Operating System (MS-DOS) replaces with information chosen by the user. For instance, if a batch file, PRINTNOW.BAT, contains the statement COPY%!PRN, and the command PRINTNOW LETTER.DOC is entered, MS-DOS replaces the %1 symbol with LETTER.DOC and sends it to the printer. *See* **Batch file.**

Report: Printed database output, usually formatted with page numbers and headings, and including calculated fields showing subtotals, totals, averages, and other figures.

Report Program Generator (RPG): A language developed by IBM allowing a novice programmer to generate reports from a database by describing the desired printed format, for which the language generates the necessary codes.

Request For Comments (RFC): An Internet system, currently controlled by the Internet Architecture Board (IAB), that has become the chief method of promulgating standards (although not all RFCs apply to new standards); RFCs, now totaling more than 1,000 are accessible from Network Information Centers.

Request For Discussion (RFD): The period, usually two or three weeks, in which users negotiate the particulars of new newsgroups.

Request For Proposal (RFP): A letter or document asking vendors how a (communications) problem can be addressed, to which vendors usually respond with a proposed solution and estimated prices.

Request For Quotation (RFQ): *See* **Request For Proposal.**

Request Unit or Response Unit (RU): A message during a session that asks or answers a question.

Research network: A Wide Area Network, for example, National Science Foundation NETwork (NSFNET) or Advanced Research Projects Agency NETwork (ARPANET), federally developed and funded to support research in areas of national interest.

ResEdit: A free utility program that allows Macintosh users to edit and copy to other programs features such as menus, icons, cursor shapes and dialog boxes. Every Macintosh file has both a data fork and a resource fork that contains program resources such as dialog boxes, sounds, icons, menus, and graphic images. ResEdit makes it possible to customize the program by editing the resource fork or copying resources to other programs, though it is recommended that this be done with a backup copy of a program to avoid corrupting the original program.

Reserved memory: *See* **Upper memory area.**

Reserved word: A word, also called a keyword, that has a fixed function in an operating system or programming language and cannot be used for any other purpose, including naming files or variables. *See* **Keyword.**

Reset button: A button, usually mounted on the front panel of a computer, or a key combination (Ctrl-Alt-Del in Disk Operating System [DOS] machines) that makes it possible to restart the computer after a crash without turning off the electricity. *See* **Hardware reset; Programmer's switch; Warm boot.**

Resident font: A font that remains in the printer's memory whether or not it is turned on.

Resident program: *See* **Terminate and Stay Resident program.**

Resolution: A measurement of the sharpness of an image, expressed in pixels for monitors and dots per inch for printers. Because a Color Graphics Adapter (CGA) monitor displays fewer lines than a Video Graphics Array (VGA) monitor, its resolution is lower and its images appear more jagged. Resolutions of common video adapters for IBM PCs and compatibles are:

Adapter	Resolution (pixel x lines)
Monochrome Display Adapter (MDA)	720 x 350
Color Graphics Adapter (CGA)	640 x 200
Enhanced Graphics Adapter (EGA)	640 x 350
MultiColor Graphics Array (MCGA)	640 x 480
Video Graphics Array (VGA)	640 x 480
Super VGA (extended VGA)	800 x 600
Extended Graphics Array (XGA)	1,024 x 768

Macintoshes with 9" screens display 512 pixels by 342 lines; those with 12" or 13" monitors display 640 by 480. For printers, the higher the number of Dots Per Inch (DPI), the sharper the resolution. Low-quality dot-matrix printers print approximately 125 DPI, laser printers 300 DPI, and professional typesetting machinery at 1,200 or more DPI.

Resolution enhancement technology: A Hewlett Packard (HP) method for smoothing curves in laser printing output by inserting small dots in 20 percent increments between larger ones to increase effective resolution.

Resource Management (RM): The management of critical resources such as buffer space and bandwidth within a network.

Resource management (RM) cell: The control cell or resource management cell, which conveys information about the state of the network, such as present or potential congestion and bandwidth availability.

Response: The answer to an inquiry.

Response time: The time a computer needs to react to a request, a measure that more fairly states system performance than access time. *See* **Access time.**

Retrieval: The set of procedures for finding, summarizing, organizing, displaying, or printing information in a useful form.

Reverse channel: A method of synchronizing or controlling simultaneous communications from receiver to transmitter over half-duplex data transmission systems, usually used only to transmit control information because it is much slower than the primary channel; also used to arrange turnaround so that one modem can start transmitting when the other stops.

Reverse engineering: The common though ethically dubious practice of taking apart a computer chip or application to find out how it works in order to duplicate or imitate its functions. Some chips have been copied outright in clear violation of U.S. and international law by firms outside North America. But Advanced Micro Devices (AMD) used reverse engineering to discover how the Intel 80386 microprocessor worked and used the information in a logical simulation not to copy but to design a microprocessor that duplicates the 83086's performance without duplicating its circuitry. *See* **Am386; Intel 80386DX; Intel 80386SX.**

Reverse Polish Notation (RPN): Also called Polish notation. A way of describing mathematical operations that makes calculation easier for computers; compilers often convert arithmetic expressions into RPN. In RPN, the expression "a b +" adds the variables a and b, and would be written as "a + b" in standard notation.

Reverse video: A method of highlighting text on monochrome monitors to show normally dark characters as bright characters on a dark background or normally bright characters as dark characters on a bright background. *See* **Highlighting.**

Rewrite: Overwrite.

RF: *See* **Radio Frequency.**

RFC: *See* **Request For Comments.**

RFD: *See* **Request For Discussion.**

RFI: *See* **Radio Frequency Interference.**

RFP: *See* **Request For Proposal.**

RFQ: *See* **Request For Quotation.**

RFS: *See* **Remote File Service.**

RGB monitor

RGB monitor: *See* Red-Green-Blue monitor.

Rich Text Format (RTF): A Microsoft text formatting standard that enables a word processing program to create a file containing all the document's formatting instructions without using any special codes, so that formatting is retained in RTF-encoded documents transmitted by modem or read by another RTF-compatible word processing program.

RIF: *See* Rate Increase Factor.

Right justification: Alignment of text along the right margin to make it look like professionally printed text, not always effective when a printer is incapable of proportional spacing; most artists advise leaving the right margin ragged.

Ring: (1) A connection method in networks that routes messages through each station in turn, usually by means of a protocol that allows a station to put a message on the network acknowledging receipt of a special bit pattern. (2) A path between network nodes that forms a complete circle, with each node connected to two adjacent nodes. (3) The signal made by a telephone to indicate an incoming call. (4) The negative battery side of a telecommunications line.

Ringback tone: The audible signal that a message is coming through to the recipient.

Ring network: A topology in which workstations, peripherals, and file servers are connected by a closed loop cable, and each workstation sends messages to all other workstations. Ring networks can cover larger physical areas than bus networks, which lack the repeaters in each node that amplify and send signals along to the next node, which has its own address and checks the ring constantly for its own messages. Although the failure of one node can disrupt the whole network, fault-tolerance schemes allow the network to function even after the failure or one or more nodes. The actual physical layout may resemble not a ring but a star or multiple stars; the ring refers to the electronic connections. *See* **File server; Local Area Network; Network topology; Node.**

Ripple-through effect: The sudden appearance of ERR (error) values throughout the cells of a spreadsheet after a change breaks the link among formulas. Once a spreadsheet change corrupts a formula so that it is judged ERR or NA (Not Available value), all the formulas that depend on the corrupted formula will display the same message; once the problem is repaired in the base formula, all the other formulas will also be corrected.

RISC: *See* **Reduced Instruction Set Computer.**

River: Accidental patterns of white space between words caused by being in full justification mode that encourage the eye to leave the text and follow the flow down through three or more lines. When properly formatted, a page should be perceived as an overall shade of gray without interruption from white spaces (rivers), bad work breaks, poor character spacing, or uneven line spacing.

RJ: *See* **Registered Jack.**

RJE: *See* **Remote Job Entry.**

RLL: *See* **Run Length Limited.**

RM: *See* **Resource Management.**

RNMP: *See* **Remote Network Monitoring Probe.**

RO: *See* **Read Only; Receive-Only.**

Roll call polling: The most common type of polling system, in which one station on a line is designated as the master and the others are slaves.

ROM: *See* **Read Only Memory.**

Roman: (1) An upright serif typeface of medium weight. (2) A proofreading notation that characters should not be typographically emphasized. *See* **Serif; Weight.**

Root directory: The top-level directory that the Microsoft Disk Operating System (MS-DOS) creates when a computer disk is formatted. *See* **Directory; Parent directory; Subdirectory.**

Root name: The first, mandatory, part of a Disk Operating System (DOS) file name, no more than eight characters long. *See* **Extension; File name.**

Rotary dial: The dialing method used in a switched system that creates a series of pulses to identify the called station. *See* **Dual-tone multiple frequency.**

Rotated type: Text that is at an angle to its normal horizontal position on a page; graphics programs such as CorelDRAW! make it possible for the type to be edited even after it has been rotated.

Rotation tool: The on-screen command option, represented by an icon, that allows users of desktop publishing or graphics programs to rotate type from its normal horizontal position.

Rot-13: A simple encryption technique common in UseNet newsgroups that offsets each character by 13 places (so that, for example, an "a" would become an "n"), used for any message that may ruin a game (by providing the solution) or offend a reader (such as erotic poetry). A reader, who decides to decrypt the message, rather than the author, thus bears the responsibility for any discomfort the message may cause. *See* **Spoiler.**

Roughs: The preliminary page layout a desktop publisher creates, using sketches rather than finished work to represent page design ideas; also called thumbnails.

Router: The node that determines how best to transfer a message from one station to another, based on the address provided by the sending station. Unlike a bridge, the router services packets or frames containing certain protocols and can handle multiple protocol stacks simultaneously. Routers can connect networks that use different topologies and protocols.

Route server: The device that runs one or more network layer routing protocols and provides forwarding descriptions to clients.

Row: (1) A horizontal block of cells, the width of a spreadsheet, usually numbered from the top down. (2) A record in a database.

Row-wise calculation: An order that calculates all the values in row 1 of a spreadsheet program before moving to row 2 and beyond. When a spreadsheet does not offer natural recalculation, the row-wise process in which rows are summed and totals are forwarded is recommended over column-wise recalculations, which may result in errors. *See* **Recalculation order.**

RPG: *See* **Report Program Generator.**

RPN: *See* **Reverse Polish Notation.**

RSI: *See* **Repetitive Strain Injury.**

RS-232/RS232C: *See* **Recommended Standard 232.**

RS 336: *See* **Recommended Standard 336.**

RS 422/422A: *See* **Recommended Standard 422/422A.**

RS 423A: *See* **Recommended Standard 423A.**

RS 448: *See* **Recommended Standard 448.**

RS 449: *See* **Recommended Standard 449.**

RTF: *See* **Rich Text Format.**

RU: *See* **Request Unit; Response Unit.**

Rule: Term used in graphics and desktop publishing programs for a thin black line at any angle.

Ruler: An on-screen bar that allows desktop publishers to measure the page horizontally, showing the current margins, tab stops, and paragraph indents; on-screen symbols in Windows and Macintosh programs can be manipulated by the mouse to change margins and indents.

Run: Execute a program.

Run-length code: A code used to compress long binary bit strings containing much repetitious data.

Run-Length Limited (RLL): A method of storing information on a hard disk that increases the amount of data that can be stored by at least 50 percent (compared with double density techniques) as a result of translating the data into a format that can be written more compactly. RLL requires that complex electronics be added to the storage device, making Advanced Run-Length Limited (RLL) drives more expensive than Modified Frequency Modulation (MFM) drives. *See* **Advanced Run-Length Limited; Modified Frequency Modulation.**

Run-time version: A commercial version of a program created for another environment that operates in a stand-alone mode for those users who may lack the interpreter or windowing environment. For example, before Windows was common, Aldus Pagemaker came with a run-time version of Windows that loaded every time the program was used, i.e., enough of Windows to run the program properly but not technically "Windows." *See* **Interpreter; Windowing environment.**

RW: *See* **Read/Write.**

S register: Modem component that provides alternatives to the IBM Advanced Technology (AT) command set, such as the number of rings to wait before responding to a call or the time to wait for connection to the carrier.

SA: *See* **Source Address.**

SAA: *See* **Systems Applications Architecture.**

Safe format: A method of formatting disks so that the data on them can be recovered if necessary.

Sans serif: A typeface that has no ornamental straight or curved lines across the ends of the main strokes of a character (serifs), for example, Helvetica and Arial.

SAP: *See* **Service Access Point.**

SASE: *See* **Specific Application Service Element.**

SASI: *See* **Shugart Associates Standard Interface.**

SATAN: *See* **Security Administrator Tool for Analyzing Networks.**

Satellite: A terminal or worksheet linked to a host computer.

Satellite carrier: A company that sells communications services that travel by space satellites orbiting the earth.

Satellite microwave radio: Radio waves used in unbounded media that transmit via space satellites over very long distances.

Save: To command the computer to transfer data from Random Access Memory (RAM), where it can be erased, to a protected storage area such as a disk drive.

Scalable font: A font, either screen or printer, the size of which can be changed within a specific range without noticeable distortion, for example, PostScript and TrueType fonts. Most scalable fonts are created using outline font technologies, but such other technologies as stroke fonts, which form characters from a matrix of lines, are sometimes used. *See* **Bit-mapped fonts.**

Scalar architecture: A microprocessor design which has only one pipeline. *See* **Superscalar architecture.**

Scale-up problem: A technical problem that develops when a network expands far beyond its projected maximum size.

Scaling: The adjustment of the y-axis (values) that a presentation program chooses to emphasize differences in the data; manual adjustment is often more satisfactory than the programmed scale.

Scanner: A peripheral device that digitizes artwork, photographs, and sometimes text for storage as a file that can be imported into word processing and page layout programs. Whether the images produced by scanning are dithered, which looks roughly like a photographic halftone, or Tagged Image File Format (TIFF), which is slightly better, they remain inferior to professional half-toning. *See* **Bit-mapped graphic.**

Scanning pass: The trip a scanner's Charge-Coupled Device (CCD) makes over material being scanned. Single-pass scanners are more popular than triple-pass scanners but not always faster.

Scan rate: *See* **Vertical refresh rate.**

Scatter diagram: A graphic that plots data items as points on numeric axes; showing how numeric data cluster.

Scatter plot: *See* **Scatter diagram.**

Scientific notation: The expression of very large or very small numbers as powers of 10, such as 7.24' 10 23 . Spreadsheet programs usually express scientific notations with the symbol E, which stands for the exponent, as in the following example: 7.24E23.

Scissoring: A technique for editing images by cropping them to the size of a frame placed over the image.

Scrambler: An encryption device that makes a voice unintelligible to those without a descrambler, thus foiling attempts at wiretapping.

Scrapbook: A Macintosh Desk Accessory (DA) that holds frequently used images, such as a company logo, for quick insertion as required.

Screen: An illuminated display.

Screen blanking: A method for saving electricity, far inferior to Display Power Management Signaling (DPMS), in which monitors go blank after they recognize a screen-saver utility has begun to operate.

Screen capture: A copy of a screen display saved as a text or graphics file on disk, usually in Tagged Image File Format (TIFF), like many of the illustrations in this book.

Screen dump: A printout of a screen display. *See* **Print Screen.**

Screen element: A component of an image displayed in Microsoft Windows '95, such as a border, dialog box, push-button, or scroll box.

Screen flicker: *See* **Flicker.**

Screen font: A bit-mapped font designed to look like the printer font on a medium-resolution monitor. While laser printers can produce a resolution of 300 Dots Per Inch (DPI) or more, only the most expense video displays can show typefaces that precisely, though Adobe Type Manager (ATM) and True Type do reasonably well.

Screen memory: *See* **Video memory.**

Screen pitch: The distance by which phosphors on a Triniton-type display are separated; the pitch should be 0.31 millimeters (mm) or less. *See* **Slot pitch.**

Screen saver: A utility program used to prolong the life of a monitor by changing the screen display to a variable pattern or graphic background while the computer is not in use. A display that remains in place too long "burns" into the screen phosphors, causing a permanent ghost image; not required with green PC monitors, which automatically go blank when not in use.

Script: A set of instructions, like a macro, that tells a program how to perform a given procedure, such as logging on to an electronic mail system. Some programs allow a user to write scripts with a limited programming language; others write the script automatically by recording keystrokes and command choices as the procedure is performed. *See* **HyperTalk; Scripting language.**

Scripting: The process of creating a brief program (a "handle") to trap messages as they are initiated for an object in an object-oriented programming language such as HyperTalk. *See* **Inheritance.**

Scripting language: A simple programming language that allows computer users to automate certain tasks, for example, HyperTalk, for the Macintosh HyperCard application, and Practical Extraction and Report Language (PERL), for writing Common Gateway Interface (CGI) scripts for World Wide Web (WWW) forms processing.

Scroll: To move a window horizontally or vertically in order to change its position over a document or worksheet.

Scroll arrow: An arrow (pointing up, down, left or right) at the end of a scroll bar that can be clicked in a Graphical User Interface (GUI) to scroll the screen in the desired direction.

Scroll bar/scroll box: Long, thin, rectangles on the right and bottom borders of the window of a Graphical User Interface (GUI) with arrows at each end that can be clicked to scroll a document slowly in the direction required, and a box that can be dragged for faster scrolling.

Scroll Lock key: A toggle key on IBM-PC compatible keyboards that switches the cursors movement keys between two modes determined by the particular program being used.

SCSI, SCSI-2, SCSI-3: *See* **Small Computer System Interface.**

SDLC: *See* **Synchronous Data-Link Control.**

SDU: *See* **Service Data Unit.**

SE: *See* **Switching Element.**

Seagate Technology 506/412 (ST-506/ST-412): A hard disk interface using Modified Frequency Modulation (MFM) and Run-Length Limited (RLL) standards, once common on IBM and IBM-compatible computers but now virtually unavailable; slower and cheaper than drives that use more recent interface standards. *See* **Enhanced System Device Interface; Integrated Drive Electronic Drive; Small Computer System Interface.**

Search and replace: *See* **Replace.**

Search engine: Any program that locates information in a database, usually a service that locates information on the Internet by typing one or more key words. These bring up a list of documents or files containing these words in their titles, descriptions, or text. Most Internet search engines can access World Wide Web (WWW) documents; some also access Gopher menus and File Transfer Protocol (FTP) file archives. Search engine databases are compiled using an automated routine called a spider, forms filled out by Web authors, or a search of other databases. *See* **Lycos; WebCrawler; World Wide Web.**

Secondary cache: Memory placed on the motherboard rather than inside a microprocessor, creating dramatic improvements in system performance. Secondary cache memory, also called L2 cache memory, ranges from slow, inexpensive direct-map cache to fast, expensive four-way set-associative cache. Write-back secondary cache memory is preferable to write-through. *See* **Full-associative cache.**

Secondary storage: A storage medium such as a magnetic disk, magnetic tape, or optical disk that stores program instructions and data even after the power is turned off. Also called auxiliary storage. *See* **Primary storage.**

Second-person virtual reality: A Virtual Reality (VR) system that presents the user with a high-definition video screen and cockpit controls, as in a flight simulator program, rather than bringing the user into a computer-generated world through goggles and gloves.

Sector: A segment of a concentric track encoded on a floppy or hard disk in a low-level format, usually containing 512 bytes of information in IBM PC-compatible computing. *See* **Cluster.**

Sector interface factor: *See* **Interleave factor.**

Secure HyperText Transport Protocol (Secure HTTP): An extension of the World Wide Web (WWW) Hyper Text Transport Protocol (HTTP) used to keep commercial transactions secure on the Web by verifying the customers (authentication) and by encrypting sensitive information (for example, credit-card numbers) so that it cannot be intercepted while en route. Secure HTTP was created by Enterprise Integration Technology (EIT) and the National Center for Supercomputer Applications (NCSA); Terisa Systems developed the commercial applications. Netscape's Secure Sockets Layer (SSL) protocol is a competing and incompatible technology, but in 1995, Netscape made a substantial investment in Terisa Systems in order to integrate Secure HTTP and SSL into a single protocol that will work with any security-capable browsers.

Secure Socket Layer (SSL): An Internet Security standard incorporated into Netscape Navigator and Netscape Commerce Server software; unlike Hyper Text Transport Protocol (Secure HTTP), SSL is it works with all the Internet tools, not just the World Wide Web (WWW).

Security: The protection of data to prevent unauthorized users from using it.

Security Administrator Tool for Analyzing Networks (SATAN): A program that assesses the security status of a computer or a Local Area Network (LAN) by checking whether the configuration of Internet-related software could render the system vulnerable to a cracker. Unfortunately, the program can be used by crackers as well as system administrators, especially since its authors, Dan Framer and Wietse Vernema, offered it generally through the Internet.

Security features: Those features of a program that allow only those authorized to access certain files and data, including password control and operator privileges.

Seek: To locate specific regions of a disk drive and position the read/write head to access it.

Seek time: The time it takes the read/write head to reach the correct location on a secondary storage device. *See* **Access time.**

Segmented memory architecture: A method of addressing memory in 16-bit operating systems like Intel 80386 and later microprocessors that do not take full advantage of the 32-bit architecture of the 386 and larger microprocessors. Since the Microsoft Disk Operating System (MS-DOS) and Windows 3.1 must use 16-bit memory addresses, only 64 KiloByte (KB) address locations can be uniquely identified; segmented memory architecture divides the memory into 64 KB segments. However, accessing the memory requires a heavy segment identifying code as well as the memory code. The memory address in a 32-bit operating system such as Microsoft Windows '95 or Operating System/2 (OS/2), on the other hand, can uniquely identify up to 4 GigaBytes (GB) of memory locations without segmentation.

Seize: To gain control of a line so as to allow transmission of data. *See* **Bid.**

Select: To highlight part of a document of any length on which an operation is to be performed, or choose an item in a list box or check box to toggle on or off.

Selection: (1) The part of a document highlighted for formatting or editing purposes. (2) A branch or conditional control structure in programming. (3) The retrieval of database records by using a query. *See* **Branch control structure.**

Selective backup: A function through which the backup programs chooses which files will be backed up systematically.

Self-powered speaker: An auxiliary speaker that uses power from outside the computer, such as a battery, to strengthen an audio signal from a sound board.

Semantic net: A set of connections among the ideas in a hypertext document. A hypertext document is created from "chunks" or units of meaning in a document; hyperlinks exploit every possible connection between the base document and others in the series of linked documents that constitute the semantic net.

Semiconductor: A material such as a silicon or germanium that is not as efficient a conductor of electricity as the copper and insulating materials, used to create wafers or chips of varying resistance for manufacturing electronic devices such as microprocessors, memory, and other computer circuits. *See* **Integrated circuit.**

Semipermanent connection: A connection established by a service order or a network administrator's decision.

Send statement: A statement in a Serial Line Internet Protocol (SLIP) or Point-to-Point Protocol (PPP) that tells the dialer program to send certain characters; send statements are matched with expect statements, which tell the program to wait until the server computer send certain characters to the receiving computer.

Sensor glove: An interface worn on the hand that enables the user to manipulate objects in a Virtual Reality (VR) environment. *See* **Head-mounted display.**

Sequence control structure: The fundamental control structure, one of three that govern the order in which program statements are executed, that tells the computer to execute program statements in the order in which they were written; the default install programming language, loops and branch control structures can be used to alter the sequence.

Sequenced Packet Exchange (SPX): An enhanced set of commands implemented on top of Novell's Internet Packet eXchange (IPX) to create a true transport-layer interface, providing more functions, including guaranteed packet delivery.

Sequence Number (SN): A four-octet Resource Management cell field as defined in International Telecommunications Union-Telecommunications (ITU-T) Recommendation I.371.

Sequence Number (SN) cell: The Sequence Number cell sent periodically on each link of an Asynchronous Transfer Mode Inverse Multiplexing (AIMUX) to show how many cells have been transmitted since the previous SN cell, used to verify the sequence when reassembled.

Sequential access: An information retrieval technique such as a cassette tape in which the computer must move through a sequence of stored items to reach the desired data, operating much more slowly than random-access media like hard disk drives.

Serial: The sequential performance of two or more activities in a single device, or processing of parts of a whole, for example, bits of a character or characters of a word, using the same facilities for successive parts. *See* **Multi-tasking parallel port; Serial port.**

Serial communication: A type of electronic communication that requires data bits to be sent one after the other (as opposed to parallel communication), as in transmissions sent from modems over telephone lines. *See* **Serial port.**

Serial Line Internet Protocol (SLIP): The standard (one of two) for how a workstation or personal computer (PC) can dial up a link to the Internet that defines the transport of data packets through an asynchronous telephone line, allowing computers not part of a Local Area Network (LAN) to be fully connected to the Internet. The other standard is Point-to-Point Protocol (PPP). SLIP is preferable to shell access (a dial-up, text-only account on a UNIX computer) because users, no matter what Internet tools they have chosen (for example, a graphical Web browser), can run more than one Internet application at a time and download data directly.

Serial mouse: A mouse designed to connect directly to a computer serial port. *See* **Bus mode.**

Serial port: A port that, by transmitting one bit at a time, facilitates asynchronous communications between the computer and, for example, serial printers, modems, and other computers. It not only transmits and receives asynchronous data it also negotiates with the receiving device to make sure that transmissions are received without loss of data, through hardware or software handshaking. *See* **Asynchronous communication; Modem; Recommended Standard 232C; Universal Asynchronous Receiver/Transmitter.**

Serial printer: A printer designed to connect to a computer through a serial port.

Serial transmission: A method transferring information by ending the bits that compose a character one at a time in sequence.

Serif: The ornamental cross strokes across the ends of the main strokes of a typeset character.

Server: (1) A computer with a large power supply and cabinet capacity. (2) A computer that makes printer or communication services available to other network stations. *See* **File server; Print server; Web server.**

Server application: The program that creates a source document in Object-Linking-Embedding (OLE); from the source document, an object can be linked or embedded in one or more destination documents.

Server-based application: A version of a program stored on a network file server that can be accessed by more than one user at a time. *See* **Client-based application.**

Server Message Block (SMB): A network protocol developed by Microsoft and adopted by many other vendors that allows one computer to use the files and peripherals of another as if it were local.

Service Access Point (SAP): An address through which a higher adjacent layer can gain access to an Open System Interconnection (OSI) address.

Service bureau: A business that provides access to the Internet or some other Wide Area Network (WAN), whether for-profit companies or publicly subsidized.

Service Data Unit (SDU): A unit of interface information that is remains the same from one end of a layer connection to the other.

Service level agreement: Performance objectives between which the user and the provider of a service have reached consensus.

Serving central office: A telephone subscriber's local Class 5 central office.

Servo-controlled DC motor: An inexpensive electronic motor used to run the spindle of a hard disk that, unlike synchronous motors, can operate at any speed the designer chooses because its rotation speed is independent of the frequency of the incoming current.

Servo-voice coil actuator: A closed-loop head actuator, the most popular in modern hard disks, uses electromagnets to pull the read/write head against tension created by a spring.

Session: The temporary logical connection between two addressable units in a network that results when a terminal in a network communicates with the server or mainframe; hardware configuration and gateway software limit the number that can run simultaneously in a Local Area Network (LAN).

Session layer: The fifth layer of the Open System Interconnection (OSI) model, which sets up the rules for how individual nodes on a network communicate with each other, used for many purposes, including determining who transmits when during half-duplex communications.

Session Protocol Data Unit (SPDU): The logical block of data and control symbols transmitted by the session layer protocol.

Set: The category of UseNet newsgroups devoted to topics in the sciences from astronomy through biology, engineering, geology, mathematics, and psychology to statistics and zoology.

Set associative: A design used in the fastest Random Access Memory (RAM) caches and in the internal caches of 486 and Pentium chips that divides each cache into two to eight sets or areas from which stored data is distributed in bits sequentially to each set. Because data from each set is usually read sequentially, a set just used can prepare to be read or written to again while data from the next set is being used. The design allows the microprocessor to complete an instruction in one clock cycle. A four-way set associative cache is the best compromise between cost and performance.

Setup parameters: System information encoded in the Basic Input/Output System (BIOS), including the geometry of the hard disk, how much Random Access Memory (RAM) is in the computer, and what keyboard can be used; governed by the setup program, which can be used to change it.

Setup program: A program recorded in the Basic Input/Output Systems (BIOS) that can be used to change the setup options when a given key combination (usually shown on-screen) is pressed as the computer boots up.

Setup string: A series of characters that a program sends to a printer instructing it to operate in a certain mode.

Setup switches: Dual In-line Package (DIP) switches for setting options in older modems, such as whether to answer incoming calls, succeeded in modern modems by the communications program.

SFT: *See* **System Fault Tolerance.**

SGML: *See* **Standard Generalized Markup Language.**

Shadowing: Copying data from Read Only Memory (ROM) into Random Access Memory (RAM) so that the microprocessor can access them more quickly. *See* **Shadow RAM.**

Shadow mask: A metal screen just inside the display of a cathode ray tube, aligned with the electron guns and the phosphors, that prevents electronic beams from striking phosphors that glow in the wrong color, so that, for example, the red electron guns strike only red phosphors.

Shadow RAM: Part of the Random Access Memory (RAM) between 640 KiloBytes (KB) and 1 MegaByte (MB) set aside in 386 and 486 computers for programs ordinarily retrieved from Read Only Memory (ROM), thus improving performance.

Shannon's law: The theoretical maximum bit-rate capacity for transmissions on a noisy analog channel.

Shareware: Copyrighted programs made available at no charge on a trial basis; users who adopt a program are expected to pay a fee to its author. *See* **Public domain software.**

Sheet-fed scanner: A flatbed scanner that automatically loads a series of documents for scanning. A sheet-fed scanner is especially useful for Optical Character Recognition (OCR).

Shell: An easy-to-use interface between the user and an operating system that substitutes menus for command lines.

Shell account: An inexpensive but indirect and limited Internet dialup access that uses a communications program to access another computer, usually a UNIX computer, to get text-only access to the second computer's operating system (its shell), from which its Internet tools, such as the text-only Web browser Lynx, can be run. Its major disadvantage is that any data downloaded goes to a separate storage area on the service provider's computer, and the holder of the shell account must then quit the Internet application to download the data again. Using the Serial-Line Internet Protocol (SLIP) or Point-to-Point Protocol (PPP) can help overcome the text-only and two-step downloading problems, as can applications such as SlipKnot that disguise the shell.

Shielded speaker: An auxiliary speaker used to protect the monitor and other computer components from the magnetic field that generates sound, which can distort displays and erase data.

Shielded Twisted Pair (STP): Twisted pair cable protected by a metallic or foil shielding.

Shielding: A metallic sheath on the center conductor of a cable, as in coaxial cable.

Shift key: The key used to enter uppercase letters or punctuation marks.

Shift+Click: A maneuver accomplished by holding down the Shift key while the mouse is clicked to extend a selection (which selection depends on the program).

Shortcut key: A key combination that provides one-stroke access to a menu command or dialog box option, bypassing any intermediate menus. *See* **Hot key.**

Shortkey: A Microsoft Windows '95 icon created by the user to speed access to a program; it appears on the desktop where it can be started by double clicking.

Shugart Associates Standard Interface (SASI): A standard developed early in the 1980s for connecting hard disks to personal computers, evolving later into the Small Computer System Interface (SCSI) standard.

Side-by-side columns: Unequal blocks of text positioned in parallel on a page, so that the first block is always positioned next to the second one, often called parallel columns; not formatted as newspaper columns, in which there is no relationship between paragraphs in one column and those in another. *See* **Table column.**

Sidetone: The residue of signal fed back from a telephone mouthpiece to its own receiver.

SIG: *See* **Special Interest Group.**

Signal splitting device: A network device that splits a signal for delivery to multiple destinations.

Signal-to-noise (S/N) ratio: The ratio between meaningful UseNet content and ranting, flaming, and other noise. The S/N ratio was originally an electrical engineering term for the ratio of information to background noise in an electronic circuit). Moderated newsgroups ensure a high signal-to-noise ratio.

Signal transformation: The modification of one or more characteristics of a signal, such as its shape or timing.

Signature: In electronic mail and UseNet newsgroups, the file of three or four lines that contains the sender's name, organization, address, e-mail address and perhaps telephone numbers, usually added automatically by most systems at the end of each message sent. Long signatures are considered bad manners. *See* **American Standard Code for Information Interchange.**

Silicon chip: *See* **Chip.**

Silicon Valley: The area in the Santa Clara Valley of California that is believed to have the largest concentration of high-technology businesses in the world.

SIM: *See* **Society for Information Management.**

SIMM: *See* **Single In-line Memory Module.**

Simple Internet Protocol Plus (SIPP): Switched Multi-megabit Data Services (SMDS) interface protocol, one of three Internet Protocol ng (IPng or Internet Protocol Next Generation) candidates.

Simple list text chart: A presentation text chart in which each item has equal emphasis since they are listed in no particular order.

Simple Mail Transfer Protocol (SMTP): A U.S. Department of Defense (DOD) standard for electronic mail systems (Military Standard 1781 or MIL-STD-1781) that have both host and user selections. User software is often included in Transmission Control Protocol/Internet Protocol (TCP/IP) PC packages; host software is available for exchanging SMTP mail with mail from proprietary systems.

Simple Network Management Protocol (SNMP): A standard for managing hardware devices connected to a network, approved for UNIX use, that lets administrators know, for example, when a printer has a paper jam or is low on toner; may be replaced by the Microsoft at Work or the Desktop Management Interface (DMI) standard.

Simplex: Transmission where the signal travels only in one direction.

Simplex circuit: A one-way circuit.

Simplex transmission: A channel that allows transmission only in for one direction.

Simulation: The creation of a model of an item in order to investigate its properties by observing its behavior.

Simultaneous transmission: Transmission of data in one direction while data is being received from the other direction.

Sine wave: A single-frequency analog signal the amplitude and phase of which are constant.

Single address message: A message to be delivered to only one destination.

Single density: An early method, now rare, of recording digital data using Frequency Modulation (FM) on single-density disks, which use large-grained magnetic particles. The storage capacity of these disks being low, 90 KiloBytes (KB) per disk, they have been superseded by double-density disks with finer-grained partitions and the even finer-grained high density disks. *See* **Modified frequency modulation.**

Single In-Line Memory Module (SIMM): A plug-in unit containing all the chips required to increase Random Access Memory (RAM) by 256 KiloBytes (KB), 1 MegaByte (MB) or 2MB.

Single In-line Package (SIP): A set of Random Access Memory (RAM) chips encased in hard plastic and attached to the motherboard with pins, replaced in modern computers by single in-line memory units.

Single mode: Optical fiber with a glass or plastic core about five microns (.005 millimeters) in diameter.

Single-pass scanner: Any scanner, but especially a color scanner, that "reads" a document in one procedure. Single-pass color scanners collect data about all three primary colors on a single trip, but are not necessarily faster than triple-pass scanners.

Single-sided disk: A floppy disk of which only one side can be used for read/write operations. *See* **Single density.**

Sink: A telecommunications receiver.

SIP: *See* **Single In-line Package.**

SIPP: *See* **Simple Internet Protocol Plus.**

Site license: An agreement with a software publisher that allows a buyer, such as a Local Area Network (LAN), to copy specified software for internal use. Usually, the number of copies is limited. The cost per copy is thus much less than buying individual licenses for each network user.

Skip factor: A formula that specifies how many data items a graphics presentation program should skip when it labels a chart or graph used when the category axis has too many headings.

Slave: The second of two hard disks connected to an Integrated Drive Electronics (IDE) adapter. The first, master, disk decodes instructions from the host adapter before sending them to the slave.

Slave station: A data station that can transmit only to a master or control station when that station requests transmission.

Slide show: A list of charts and graphs displayed one after another.

SLIP: *See* **Serial Line Internet Protocol.**

Slot: *See* **Expansion slot.**

Slot pitch: The distance between wires in the aperture grille of a Triniton monitor; an important Trinitron specification but not as important as screen pitch.

Slow mail: The U.S. Postal Service. This term is not as popular as snail mail. *See* **Snail mail.**

Slow-scan video: The process wherein still images are transmitted at speed to suggest motion.

SLPP/PPP: The abbreviations for the two types of direct dialup access to the Internet. *See* **Serial Line Internet Protocol; Shell account; Point-to-Point Protocol.**

Slug: A code inserted to generate page numbers when a document is printed.

Small Computer System Interface (SCSI): A complete expansion bus interface that accepts such devices as a hard disk, Compact Disk Read Only Memory (CD-ROM), disk drivers, printers, or scanners. The most common is the SCSI hard disk, which contains most of the controller circuitry, leaving the SCSI interface free for other peripherals; it is possible to daisy chain as many as seven SCSI devices to a single SCSI port. The current version (SCSI-2) reduces conflicts among daisy-chained devices by using a common command set, but a new version (SCSI-3) is in the works that will increase the number of devices that can be chained to 16. *See* **Enhanced System Device Interface; Seagate Technology.**

SmallTalk: A high-level programming language and environment that treats computations as reusable objects that send messages to one another, encouraging the programmer to define objects in terms relevant to the intended applications. SmallTalk inspired HyperTalk, the command language of HyperCard, an application provided with every Macintosh produced since 1987.

Smart machine: Any electronic device using microprocessors that allow it either to move to alternative operating sequences as conditions require, repeat operations until a condition is fulfilled, or execute a series of instructions more than once.

Smart terminal: A network terminal with its own processing circuitry that cannot be programmed but has a memory that can be loaded with information from a host computer and can run programs from the host.

SMDS: *See* **Switched Multi-Megabit Data Services.**

Smiley: *See* **Emoticon.**

SMISS: *See* **Society for Information Management; Society for Management of Information Systems.**

SMTP: *See* **Simple Mail Transfer Protocol.**

SN: *See* **Sequence Number; SubNetwork Connection.**

SNA: *See* **Systems Network Architecture.**

SNADS: *See* **Systems Network Architecture Distribution Services.**

Snail mail: The U.S. Postal Service and its conventionally delivered mail.

Snap-on pointing device: A pointing device that snaps on to the side of the case of a portable computer without using a serial port or mouse port cable.

Snapshot: *See* **Print screen.**

SN cell: *See* **Sequence Number cell.**

Sneakernet: A method of moving data in which a person physically carries a data-laden floppy disk or tape from one computer to another, usually across an office but occasionally by air or across a continent.

SNMP: *See* **Simple Network Management Protocol.**

SNOBOL: *See* **String-Oriented Symbolic Language.**

Snow: *See* **Video noise.**

.SOC: One of the standard UseNet newsgroup hierarchies, dealing with social issues, social groups, and world cultures.

Society for Information Management (SIM): A professional society for information-systems executives managing multiple branch locations, formerly called the Society for Management of Information Systems (SMISS).

Society for Management of Information Systems (SMISS): *See* **Society for Information Management.**

Socket: An Internet address that combines an Internet Protocol (IP) address (the four-part numerical Internet address for a particular computer) and a port number (for a particular Internet application, such as Gopher or the World Wide Web [WWW]). *See* **Well-known port.**

Soft: Temporary and changeable, as opposed to hard (permanently wired, physically fixed or inflexible). Soft is a term used as in a page break inserted by a word processing program that moves within the document if text is added or deleted, unlike a hard page break inserted by the user that remains in place no matter what changes are made in the text.

Soft cell boundary: A feature of spreadsheet cells that allows labels to be entered that are no longer than the cell's width if the adjacent cells are not occupied.

Soft font: *See* **Downloadable font.**

Soft hyphen: An optional hyphen, one that takes effect only if the word wraps to the next line, to improve kerning. *See* **Hard hyphen.**

Soft page break: A page break inserted by a word processing program as the text fills a page to normal length; it may move up or down if text, margins, page size, or fonts are changed. *See* **Forced page break.**

Soft return: A line inserted by a word processing program to maintain set margins; it may change if margins or text is changed. *See* **Hard page; Word wrap.**

Soft-sectored disk: A disk that contains no fixed magnetic patterns of tracks or sectors until these are created during formatting.

Soft start: *See* **Warm boot.**

Software: System utility or application programs expressed in a machine language. *See* **Firmware; Hardware.**

Software cache: A large area of Random Access Memory (RAM) set aside by programs like SMARTDRV.EXE to store frequently accessed data and program instructions, thus speeding up data-base management and other disk-intensive applications.

Software command language: A high-leveling programming language that can be used with programs that do their own saving and retrieving of information, maintaining data structures, controlling interfaces, and so on, to create simple but powerful custom programs. Software command languages, from word processing and spreadsheet programs to a full-fledged language like dBASE, may include control structures that perform functions like iteration and logical branching.

Software compatibility: The ability of a computer system to run specific software; the fact that two computers use the same microprocessor has no relevance.

Software engineering: The applied science of improving and optimizing the production of software.

Software error control: A protocol that resides partly or entirely in a communications program rather than in the modem hardware, making modems cheaper but supported by few communications programs and putting extra strain on the computer.

Software handshaking: A method of controlling data flow through the exchange of special codes so that a modem does not send more than the modem with which it is communicating can handle.

Software license: A legal agreement included when commercial programs are sold that specifies the rights and obligations of the buyer and limits the liability of the seller, the software publisher.

Software package: A ready-to-run program delivered to the user complete with all necessary utility programs and documentation. *See* **Application software.**

Software piracy: The unauthorized duplication of copyrighted software without the permission of the publisher.

Software program: An application program. Although redundant, the term is common. *See* **Application software; Software.**

Software protection: *See* **Copy protection.**

SOH: *See* **Start-Of-Heading Character.**

SONET: *See* **Synchronous Optical NETwork.**

Sort: An operation common to most programs that arranges data into a specified ascending or descending order, usually alphabetical or numerical, using, for example, list commands in word processing programs, or commands that sort the contents of the cells in a range in spreadsheet programs. The sort process is not to be confused with database management index operations, which sort the index rather than the records to which it refers. *See* **Data integrity; Sort order.**

Sort key: The data fields that determine how the sort operation will arrange records, a column or row in a spreadsheet program, a word or a word position in a word-processing program.

Sort order: The collating sequence in which a sort program arranges data, usually the standard order of American Standard Code for Information Interchange (ASCII) characters. *See* **American Standard Code for Information Interchange sort order; Dictionary sort; Sort.**

Soundboard: An adapter that allows an IBM PC-compatible personal computer to reproduce sound digitally, allowing for multimedia applications and making it more competitive with Macintosh computers.

Sound card: *See* **Soundboard.**

Sound Recorder: A Microsoft Windows '95 accessory, for use with a Multimedia Personal Computer (MPC) compatible sound board with recording capabilities including a microphone, that turns a computer into a digital tape recorder, saving recordings in .WAV files that can be accessed by other MPC-compatible programs.

Source: The record, file, document, or disk from which information is taken or moved. *See* **Destination.**

Source Address (SA): The address from which data including messages originates.

Source code: The typed instructions in high-level programming language created before a program is translated into machine language instructions for the computer to execute.

Source document: A document that contains Dynamic Data Exchange (DDE) or Object Linking and Embedding (OLE) data linked to its copies in other documents called destination documents.

Source file: The Microsoft Disk Operating System (MS-DOS) file from which data or program instructions are copied. *See* **Destination file.**

Source route: Parameters in the Asynchronous Transfer Mode (ATM) Traffic Descriptor used during set-up to provide the connection traffic characteristics that the source requests.

Source worksheet: A Microsoft Excel worksheet containing cell or range changes in which are linked or embedded in one or more dependent worksheets.

SPA (Systems and Procedures Association): *See* **Association for Systems Management.**

Space: (1) The signal condition equaling a binary 0, one of the two possible states of a binary information element. (2) The open circuit or no-current state of a teleprinter line. *See* **Mark.**

Spaghetti code: A program that uses too many GOTO statements, making it almost impossible to read and debug; the poor organization results from failure to use a programming language such as C, Pascal, or QuickBASIC that offers a full set of control structures. *See* **Structured programming.**

Spamming: Posting an irrelevant message to dozens or even hundreds of inappropriate UseNet newsgroups, or posting the same message too often to the same newsgroup. The source of spamming is a Monty Python lyric: "Spam, spam, spam, spam, spam, spam, spam, spam, lovely spam, wonderful spam..." Spamming is not to be confused with Velveeta; usually spamming articles are cross-posted to an excessive number of newsgroups. Spam is bad because posting messages separately drains more disk space and network bandwidth; news reading software needs only one copy of a cross-posted message. *See* **Cancelmoose and Cancelbot.**

Spanning Tree Algorithm (STA): A technique based on an Institute of Electronic and Electrical Engineers (IEEE 802.1) standard that eliminates logical loops in a bridged network by letting a bridge use only the most efficient of multiple paths and reconfiguring the network when a path fails.

Spanning Tree Explorer (STE): A bridging frame that uses the Spanning Tree Algorithm (STA) to choose a route.

SPDU: *See* **Session Protocol Data Unit.**

SPEC: *See* **Standard Performance Evaluation Corporation.**

Special Interest Group (SIG): A network or organization of members who share a common interest, such as literary genres with such groups for mystery, science fiction, hobbies, or sports. *See* **User group.**

Specific Application Service Element (SASE): An aspect of the International Standards Organization (ISO) application layer that provides defined user services, for example, File Transfer, Access and Management (FTAM).

Specific polling: A technique that sends characters to a device to find out whether the device is ready to enter data.

Speculative execution: The explanation for how instructions entering a microprocessor with superscalar architecture are analyzed to route the instructions most efficiently through the pipelines. This type of execution, thus, enhances throughput.

Speech synthesis: Computer audio output that resembles human speech often used by the visually impaired.

Spell checker: A common feature of word processing programs that compares each word in a document against a file of correctly spelled words and asks the user whether a mismatch should be replaced by another word.

Spider: A program that prowls the Internet to locate new public resources such as World Wide Web (WWW) documents, files available in public File Transfer Protocol (FTP) archives, and Gopher documents and add them to databases Internet users can search themselves; also called wanderers or robots.

Spike: *See* **Surge.**

Spindle: The axle on which a disk turns, turned by a spindle motor; permanently attached at the center of hard disk plates, but not permanently attached to floppy disks.

Spindle motor: A synchronous or a servo-controlled Direct Current (DC) motor that turns hard and floppy disks, on whenever the computer is on for hard disks but only when data is being written to a floppy disk.

Split bar: A bar on a Graphical User Interface (GUI) that can be dragged to split a computer window horizontally or vertically.

Split screen: A technique that divides a screen into two or more windows, often used in word processing programs to allow reference to one document while another is being worked on; also facilitates cut-and-paste editing.

Split stream operation: A modem feature that combines several slower data streams whose total speed does not exceed the capacity of the circuitry, into a faster one for transmission, splitting them apart when they reach their destination.

Spoiler: A message posted to a UseNet newsgroup giving the ending of a novel, movie, or television program or the solution to a computer or video game; netiquette requires that such messages be encrypted so that only those who choose to do so can read them.

Spooler: A common operating system utility program that routes print commands to a file on disk or in Random Access Memory (RAM), sending them to the printer when the Central Processing Unit (CPU) is not handling the user's continuing work with the program.

Spot color: A method of printing color in which each color is the text and considered as a separate layer. The printer then prints each color with a separate pass.

Spreadsheet: *See* **Worksheet**.

Spreadsheet program: A program that simulates an accountant's worksheet on-screen, allowing the user to embed hidden formulas that perform calculations on the visible data; these programs often include graphics and presentation capabilities.

Sputtering: A method of coating the hard disk substrate with thin-film magnetic media, also called link plating, that uses heat and the attraction of particles with opposite charges to produce an even coating.

SQL: *See* **Structured Query Language**.

Squelch: To suspend or cancel a user's right to access a network, usually after the user has repeatedly violated the agreed terms for using the network.

SSL: *See* **Secure Socket Layer**.

SS7: Signal System 7, a set of protocols drawn from narrowband telephony used to set-up, manage, and eliminate connections and exchange other information.

ST-506/ST-412: *See* **Seagate Technology.**

Stack: (1) A data structure in which the first items inserted are the last ones removed, unlike control structure programs that use the Last In First Out (LIFO) structure; allows the computer to back up to what it was doing before it jumped to a procedure. (2) In HyperCard, a file with one or more cards that share a common background.

Stacked column chart: *See* **Stacked column graph.**

Stacked column graph: A graph that displays two or more data series on top of one another.

STACKS: An area set aside in Microsoft Disk Operating System (MS-DOS) to store information about a current task when an interrupt instruction has been issued, so that the original task can be resumed when the interrupt has been processed. For application programs that require stacks, the STACKS command should be used in CONFIG.SYS to specify the size and number of stacks to be set aside.

Staggering windows: *See* **Cascading window.**

Stand-alone computer: A system that can meet all the computer needs of an individual user, incorporating just the software needed for that user's daily tasks. *See* **Multi-user system; Professional workstation.**

Standard: The rules or specifications which together define the architecture of a hardware device program or operating system. *See* **Open standard.**

Standard Generalized Markup Language (SGML): The language used to describe other tag-based structural document languages.

Standard mode: A Microsoft Windows operating mode that can take advantage of extended memory in 80286 and higher computers but cannot access all the technical capabilities of 80386 and higher microprocessors. Though faster than 386 Enhanced mode, standard mode is not effective with Disk Operating System (DOS) applications, which take over the screen and virtual memory, preventing multi-tasking.

Standard newsgroup hierarchy: The categories that every UseNet site is expected to carry if there is enough storage; it includes comp.*, misc.*, news.*, rec.*, sci.*, soc.* and talk*; users vote on the creation of newsgroups within the standard newsgroup hierarchies. *See* **Call For Votes.**

Standard parallel port: A port that transfers data in one direction only at about 200Kb per second, used to connect early computers to peripherals such as printers but since replaced by bi-directional parallel ports such as the Enhanced Parallel Port (EPP) and the Extended Capabilities Port (ECP).

Standard Performance Evaluation Corporation (SPEC): A consortium of companies working to establish fair benchmarks for evaluating computers that has so far produced the CINT92 test (a type of C INTeger computation) for measuring integer calculations and the CFP92 (a type of Computer Floating Point benchmark) test for floating point computations.

Standby server: A server that is takes over on manual command when the primary server is disabled by a power outage.

Standby UPS: An inexpensive Uninterruptible Power Supply (UPS) protecting against complete power failure but not against reduction in line voltage (brownouts). *See* **Surge protector.**

Star: *See* **Star network.**

StarLAN: An AT&T networking system using Client/Server Micro Applications (CSMA) protocols on twisted-pair telephone wire; StarLAN is a subset of the Institute of Electronic and Electrical Engineers (IEEE) 802.3 standard.

Star network: A network with a physical layout that resembles a star, with a central processor or wiring concentrator around which the nodes are arranged and to which they connect directly; wiring costs are considerably higher for star than for other networks a separate cable links each workstation to the central processor.

Star topology: *See* **Star network.**

Start bit: A space signal consisting of a single data bit used in asynchronous transmission to let the receiving computer know that a byte of data will follow. *See* **Asynchronous communication; Stop bit.**

Starting point: A World Wide Web (WWW) document that contains useful starting points for Web navigation, such as introductions to the Internet and to the Web, subject trees, or search engines.

Start-Of-Heading Character (SOH): The first character of a message heading used as a transmission control character.

Start signal: (1) A signal which tells a receiving mechanism to get ready to receive data or perform a function. (2) A start bit.

Startup disk: A disk, often a hard disk, containing portions of the operating system, used to boot up a computer. If the startup disk is on a floppy disk, then it characteristically called a boot disk or system disk.

Startup screen: The display shown at the beginning of a program, usually containing the program name and version and often a distinctive program logo.

State link: A World Wide Web (WWW) hyperlink to a document that is no longer there, having been erased or moved; also called a Black hole.

Statement: An expression in a high-level programming language used to generate machine language instructions when the program is interpreted or compiled.

State-of-the-art: The highest level of technical or technological achievement.

Statical multiplexer: A multiplexer that uses the down time of devices connected to it to carry data from active devices.

Static object: A document or portion of a document pasted into a destination document that is not changed when changes are made to the source document; desired changes must be copied again or made in the destination document. *See* **Embedding object; Object Linking and Embedding.**

Static Random Access Memory (SRAM): A chip that holds its contents without constant refreshing from the Central Processing Unit (CPU), much faster but also significantly more expensive than Dynamic Random Access Memory (DRAM) chips, often used for RAM caches. *See* **Cache memory.**

Static routing table: A routing table defined before a network becomes operational; can be updated.

Station: *See* **Workstation.**

Station features: Features of a telephone system that can be activated by users.

Statistical software: Application programs that make it easier to conduct statistical measurements.

Status line: The line on a display screen that lets the user know what is being done with a program, including information such as the name of the file being worked on, the cursor location, and the name of any toggle keys, such as Caps Lock, that are active.

STC: The System Time Clock, which is the master clock in any Moving Picture Experts Group 2 (MPEG-2) system.

STE: *See* **Spanning Tree Explorer; Synchronous Optical NETwork Section Terminating Equipment.**

Stem: The main vertical stroke of a typographical character.

Step-by-step switch: A switch that is synchronized with a pulse device, such as a rotary telephone dial, so that successive selector switches carry the connections forward until the desired line is reached.

Stepper motor: A motor, part of the head actuator mechanism in disk drives, that makes a precise fraction of a turn in response to each electrical impulse.

Stickup initial: An enlarged letter at the beginning of a paragraph that rises above the top of the first line.

STM: *See* **Synchronous Transfer Module.**

Stop bit: A single data bit used in asynchronous transmission to signal to the receiver the end of a transmission. *See* **Asynchronous communication; Start bit.**

Stop-and-wait: A technique of controlling flow on a link by holding the next frame for transmission until an acknowledgment of the previous frame is received.

Storage: The retention of program instructions and data within the computer so that it can be used at will for processing. *See* **Primary storage; Secondary storage.**

Storage device: Any optical or magnetic device that can hold information within a computer. *See* **Secondary storage.**

Storage pool: A collection of storage volumes, which may be on-line, near-line, or off-line.

Storage server: A network application that provides centralized storage for multiple workgroups and runs storage management applications for the network.

Store and forward: A communications application in which messages are stored at an intermediate point until the receiver can retrieve them.

Store-and-forward network: A Wide Area Network (WAN) based on telephone systems in which each computer in the network stores messages received during the day and then at night, when telephone rates are low, uploads the messages to a central distribution site and downloads from it messages from the other network computers. This technology is the basis of a UNIX network called the UNIX-to-UNIX Copy Program (UUCP) and of FidoNet which is one of several WANs that link a computer's Bulletin Board System (BBS).

Stored program concept: The theory underlying all modern computers that programs as well as data should be stored in memory.

Storefront: A World Wide Web (WWW) document through which a commercial enterprise creates a presence on the Web, often offering free information or downloadable software but not usually displaying the entire offerings of the firm. Increasingly, as security on the Web improves, storefronts can accept credit card payments as well as orders. *See* **Secure HTTP; Secure Sockets Layer.**

STP: *See* **Shielded Twisted Pair.**

Streaming tape drive: A secondary storage device that uses continuous tape packaged in a cartridge.

Streams: Architecture introduced with UNIX System V. Release 3.2, and adopted in a number of other applications, that allows for flexible, layered communications paths between programs and device drivers.

Stress test: An alpha test procedure for measuring how a program will behave under heavy demand.

Strikeout: A font attribute, also called strike-through, where text is struck through with a hyphen (This text has strikeout formatting), often used to mark text to be deleted from, say, an official document so that it is clear how the changes will affect the sense. *See* **Overtype mode; Redlining.**

String: A series of alphanumeric characters.

String formula: A spreadsheet formula that performs a string operation, such as changing a label from lower case to upper case.

String operation: A computation performed on alphanumeric characters.

String-Oriented Symbolic Language (SNOBOL): A high-level programming language for text-processing applications that has strong text-pattern-matching capabilities; useful for generating indexes or concordance to literary works, and text reformatting, but generates difficult source code. *See* **Beginner's All-purpose Symbolic Instruction Code; FORmula TRANslator.**

Strobe: An electrical pulse used to solicit the transfer of information.

Stroke weight: The width of the lines—light, medium, or bold—that compose a character.

Strowger switch: A step-by-step switch named after its inventor, Almon B. Strowger.

Structured programming: A set of quality standards that make programs longer but more readable and easier to maintain.

Structured Query Language (SQL): A concise IBM query language (only 30 commands) structured like English, widely used in database management applications for mainframes and minicomputers. Four basic commands (SELECT, UPDATE, DELETE, and INSERT) correspond to four basic functions of data manipulation (retrieval, modification, deletion, and insertion). Answers to a query are displayed in a table consisting of columns (data fields) and rows (data records).

STS-1: *See* **Synchronous Transport Signal-1.**

Style: A defining font characteristic, such as double underlining or italic.

Style sheet: A library of styles often used for a certain type of document such as a regular report that can be saved together.

Stylus: An instrument used to select menu options on a monitor or draw line art on a graphics tablet.

Subdirectory: The subdivision of an Microsoft Disk Operating System (MS-DOS) or UNIX directory, containing files and additional subdirectories. Formatting a hard disk creates a root direction that can contain information for only 512 files; to add more, it is necessary to create subdirectories, ending up with a hierarchy of directories in which programs and files can be grouped, usually by subject, and subdivided in up to nine levels.

Subject drift: The tendency of the subjects of follow-up articles in UseNet groups to become less and less relevant to the contents of the original article, a consequence of software that carries over only a one-line description of the original article into follow-up articles.

Subject selector: A UseNet program mode in which a list of articles is alphabetized by subject and shows the exact relationships among articles. The subject selector behaves differently from a threaded newsreader. *See also* **Thread selector.**

Subject tree: A guide to the World Wide Web (WWW) that organizes sites by subject, many of which have subcategories (for example, sports); the finest level of the tree offers hyperlinks to particular Web documents. *See* **ElNet Galaxy; Virtual Library; Yahoo.**

Submenu: A menu offering further choices that may appear when certain commands are selected from pull-down menus.

Subnetting: Using several data paths to reduce traffic on a network and avoid problems if a single path should fail; usually configured as a dedicated Ethernet subnetwork between two systems based on two Network Interface Cards (NICs).

Subnetwork: A network connected by a bridge or router to a more powerful network.

Subnetwork Connection (SNC): An entity that passes Asynchronous Transfer Mode (ATM) cells without adding overhead.

Subroutine: A portion of a program that is set aside so that the common function it performs can be used by more than one aspect of the program, for example, writing disk to disk. In BASIC programs, subroutines are referenced by GOSUB statements.

Subscript: A character printed slightly below the typing line. *See* **Superscript.**

Substitution code: An encryption technique that replaces data with other symbols.

Subvoice-grade circuit: A bandwidth circuit that is narrower than a voice-grade circuit, often a sub-channel on a voice-grade line.

Suitcase: A Macintosh icon containing a screen font or desk accessory not installed in the System Folder.

Supercomputer: A computer designed to execute complex calculations at the highest possible speed, used for modeling complex dynamic systems such as weather or the national economy.

SuperDrive: A now standard 3 1/2" floppy disk drive that can read all Macintosh formats (400Kb, 800Kb and 1.4Mb) with the help of Apple's

Apple File Exchange software. The SuperDrive can also format disks in the Disk Operating System (DOS) format, and read and write up to 720Kb and 1.44Mb DOS disks, making it possible to move data files easily between IBM PC and Macintosh systems.

SuperPaint: An illustration program from Silicon Beach Software combining MacPaint's bit-mapped graphics and MacDraw object-oriented graphics in independent but superimposed layers, one in the foreground, one in the background.

Superscalar architecture: A microprocessor design with multiple pipelines. *See* **Scalar architecture.**

Superscript: A character printed slightly above the typing line, for example, a^2. *See also* **Subscript.**

Superserver: A high-capacity server that is equipped with fault-tolerant storage.

Super VGA: An enhancement of the Video Graphics Array (VGA) display standard for IBM personal computers that can display at least 800 pixels horizontally and 600 lines vertically, and up to 1,024 pixels by 768 lines with 16 or 256 colors; it can use as much as 1Mb of video memory.

Support: *See* **Technical support.**

Surge: A momentary increase in the amount of voltage delivered through a power line, sometimes capable of destroying computer data and circuits.

Surge protector: An inexpensive electrical device that prevents high-voltage surges from damaging a computer. *See* **Power line filter.**

SVID: *See* **System V Interface Definition.**

Swap file: A file used to store instructions and data that do not fit in random access memory (RAM). *See* **Permanent swap file; Temporary swap file; Virtual memory.**

Swash: Ornamental italic characters with elaborate flourishes that sweep over or under adjacent characters.

Switch: An addition to an Microsoft Disk Operating System (MS-DOS) command that affects how the command works; its symbol is a forward slash, followed by a letter (for example, /p or /a).

Switched connection: A mode of operating a data link by dialing to connect to switching facilities.

Switched line: A telecommunications line in which the connection is set up by dialing.

Switched Multi-Megabit Data Services (SMDS): A service used to link a Local Area Network (LAN), Metropolitan Area Network (MAN), and Wide Area Network (WAN) for data exchange without connections.

Switched Virtual Circuit (SVC): A connection set up by signaling, with the user defining the endpoints when the connection is made.

Switchhook: A switch on a telephone set, operated by removal or replacement of a handset or other receiver on its support.

Switching center: A location where numerous circuits terminate, making it possible to interconnect or transfer data between circuits.

Switching Element (SE): The device or network node that performs Asynchronous Transfer Mode (ATM) switching operations.

Switching system: A set of systems that appear to be a single switch for Private Network Node Interface (PNNI) routing.

Symbol: The graphic representation of an idea, such as a letter, word, icon, or number.

Symbolic coding: The expression of an algorithm in symbols, used by all modern programming languages.

Symmetric connection: A connection where the specified band-width value is the same for both directions.

Symphony: *See* **Integrated program.**

Sync character: A character transmitted to synchronize clocks in the receiving station with those in the transmitting station.

Synchronous: A method of communicating blocks of data, introduced by initial sync characters and a common clock signal, with no stop or start bits.

Synchronous communications: Very-high speed transmission over circuits, in which the transfer is synchronized by electronic clock signals, used internally in computers and in high-speed mainframe systems.

Synchronous Data-Link Control (SDLC): IBM code-independent link-control protocol that is transparent to the bit pattern being handled; a single format is used for both data and control information.

Synchronous line control: The operating procedure and signals that control telecommunications lines.

Synchronous Optical NETwork (SONET): An American National Standards Institute (ANSI) standard, a variation of the Synchronous Digital Hierarchy (SDH) International standard, accepted in the United States and Canada for transmissions over optical fiber.

Synchronous Optical NETwork Section Terminating Equipment (STE): Equipment used in a Wide Area Network (WAN) to end the links between transmitter and repeater, repeater and repeater, or repeater and receiver.

Synchronous Transfer Module (STM): The basic module defined by Consultative Committee for International Telephony and Telegraphy/International Telecommunications Union module T (CCITT/ITU-T) for a synchronous multiplexing hierarchy, operating at a rate of 155.52 MBPS.

Synchronous Transfer Module n (STM-n): Standards for optical fiber transmission achieved by multiplexing a given number ("n" equaling the integer) of STM-1 frames.

Synchronous Transfer Module nc (STM-nc): Standards for optical fiber transmission achieved by multiplexing a given number ("n" equaling the integer) of STM-1 frames, but with the information fields treated as a single concatenated ("c") payload.

Synchronous Transfer Module 1 (STM-1): The Synchronous Digital Hierarchy (SDH) standard for transmitting over OC-3 optical fiber at 155.52 MBPS (the same rate as STS-3).

Synchronous transmission: A mode in which synchronization is established for transmitting a block of data, with both sending and receiving stations operating at virtually the same frequency.

Synchronous Transport Signal-1 (STS-1): The Synchronous Optical Network (SONET) standard for OC-1 optical fiber transmissions, 51.84 MBPS. The number may change according to the number of frames multiplexed; when the information fields are treated as a single concatenated payload, a "c" is added.

Syntax: All the rules that specify how a computer is instructed so that instructions are processed correctly.

SYSOP: *See* **SYStem OPerator.**

System: The operating system for Apple Macintosh computers.

System date: The calendar date maintained by a computer system.

System disk: The disk, usually the hard disk that holds the operating system and all the files needed to start the computer.

System Fault Tolerance (SFT): The ability of a computer to recover from or avoid a system crash.

System features: Features of a telephone system available to all users, which may be automatically activated.

System file: A program or data file holding the information used by the operating system rather than application programs.

System folder: The Macintosh desktop folder that holds the System and Finder Files which constitute the operating system, plus all the desk accessories, INITs, Control panel DEVice (CDEV), screen fonts, downloadable printer fonts, and printer drivers that may be used during an operating session. Because the Finder consults only the System Folder when searching for a file, applications configuration files, dictionaries, and other files must also be placed in this folder. *See* **Blessed folder; Control panel DEVice; Downloadable font; Finder; INIT; Printer; Screen font.**

SYStem OPerator (SYSOP): System operator, the person who runs a bulletin board.

System prompt: The indicator that lets users know that the operating system is available for such maintenance tasks as formatting disks and loading programs, in the Disk Operating System (DOS) a letter designating the disk drive, followed by a greater-than symbol, for example, C>. The system prompt can be customized. *See* **Command-line operating system.**

System software: All the software used to operate and maintain a computer system.

System time: The time of day maintained by the computer system.

System unit: The case that houses the computer's circuitry and in some systems a monitor; sometimes inaccurately called the Central Processing Unit (CPU), which rather refers only to the microprocessors and memory (usually housed on the motherboard) but not peripherals, such as disk drives.

System V Interface Definition (SVID): The standard for UNIX operating systems established by AT&T Bell laboratories. *See* **Berkeley UNIX; UNIX.**

System 7: The 1991 version of the Macintosh operating system software, containing improvements to Finder (the program and file-management system), true multitasking (rather than multiple program loading), program launching from menus, true virtual memory (with 68030 microprocessors), outline (scalable) fonts, network file sharing without the need for a file server, external database access, and hot links across applications to update copied data. System 7 requires a minimum of 2Mb of Random Access Memory (RAM), but 4Mb is optimal.

Systems analyst: A person who sets specifications, calculates feasibility and costs, and implements a business system.

Systems and Procedures Association (SPA): *See* **Association for Systems Management (ASM).**

Systems Applications Architecture (SAA): The standards for communications among different types of IBM computers.

Systems Network Architecture (SNA): A seven-layer communications architecture developed by IBM.

Systems Network Architecture Distribution Services (SNADS): An IBM protocol for distributing electronic mail through a network using Systems Network Architecture.

T-1: A 1.544 megabit-per-second long distance circuit, for voice or data transmission, usually divided into 24 64-kilobit channels.

T1E1: The American National Standards Institute (ANSI) Network Interfaces subcommittee.

T1M1: The American National Standards Institute (ANSI) Inter-Network Operations, Administration, and Maintenance subcommittee.

T1Q1: The American National Standards Institute (ANSI) Performance Standards subcommittee.

T1S1: The American National Standards Institute (ANSI) Services, Architecture, and Signaling subcommittee.

T-3: A very high bandwidth leased telephone line equivalent to 3 T-1 lines that can transfer 44.7 Megabits per second (Mbps) of computer data. *See* **T1.**

TA: *See* **Terminal Adapter.**

Tab-delimited file: A file, usually according to the American Standard Code for Information Interchange (ASCII), in which tab keystrokes separate data items. *See* **ASCII file; Comma delimited file.**

Tab key: A key used to move the cursor a fixed number of spaces previously specified in a tab stop.

Table: (1) A spreadsheet of columns and rows with mathematical capabilities created in word processing or spreadsheet programs usually with a table utility. Tables are sometimes created during a mail merge operation. (2) A relational database management storage and display structure in which data items are linked in rows corresponding to the data records and columns corresponding to data fields.

Table column: Unequal blocks of text positioned on a page so that the first block is always next to the second one; also called parallel columns with block protect.

Table of Authorities: The table of legal citations that a word processing program generates from references marked in a document.

Table utility: A word processing utility that creates a spreadsheet-like matrix of rows and columns into which text can be neatly inserted, making it easier to build tables.

Table-oriented data base management program: A program that responds to queries with data tables rather than records. *See* **Data retrieval; Record-oriented database management program; Structured Query Language.**

Tab stop: Where the cursor stops after the Tab key is pressed, usually set by default every 1/2 inch, but capable of being redefined; most programs also allow for flush-right, centered, and decimal tab stops in addition to the default flush-left tab stops.

Tactile feedback: Information gained through the sense of touch, typically applied to how a typist feels keys on a keyboard but also applied to mouse, joystick, and virtual reality design.

Tag: An Hyper Text Markup Language (HTML) code identifying elements of a document, e.g., a list, so that a Web browser can tell how to display it, delimited by angle brackets.

Tagged Image File Format (TIFF): (1) The Microsoft Disk Operating System (MS-DOS) filename extension usually attached to a file containing graphics in TIFF, often scanned photographic images. (2) A bit-mapped graphics format for scanned images, simulating gray-scale shading, with resolutions of up to 300 Dots Per Inch (DPI).

Talk: One of the seven standard UseNet newsgroup hierarchies, containing groups discussing controversial topics, often with considerable acrimony.

TAM: *See* **Telecommunications Access Method.**

Tandy Corporation: A Texas manufacturer of electronic products generally sold through its own Radio Shack franchises.

Tap: A connector to a cable that does not block signals moving down the cable.

Tape: A narrow strip of thin plastic, coated with a magnetically sensitive recording medium that is widely used as a backup medium primarily with mainframes and minicomputers. Thanks to price drops, tape is being increasingly used with personal computers. *See* **Backup procedure; Backup utility; Quarter-Inch cartridge; Random access; Sequential access; Tape drive.**

Tape backup unit: A device that reads and writes data on a magnetically-sensitive tape in order to backup the data on hard disks and store data that is important but rarely used, thus freeing space on the hard drive; the backup unit of choice for personal computers is the Quarter Inch Cartridge (QIC).

Tape drive: A secondary storage magnetic-tape medium commonly used for backup purposes. The most popular drives for backing up personal computers are Quarter Inch Cartridges (QIC); the other options, 8-mm VCR cartridge drives s and 4-mm digital audio tape (DAT) drives, are much more expensive. Mainframes and minicomputers often back up with nine-track tape heels and cartridges in a half-inch tape drive. *See* **Tape backup unit.**

Tariff: The published rates and rules for services provided by a common communications carrier, approved by regulatory agencies and operating as a contract between the carrier and the customer.

TASI: *See* **Time Assignment Speech Interpolation.**

Taskbar: A Microsoft Windows '95 application launcher and task switcher that appears at the bottom of the screen when a program is launched from the Start Menu; the user clicks buttons on the task bar to change programs.

Task button: A button that appears on the Microsoft Windows '95 taskbar when an applications program is launched; the user clicks the button to switch to the application.

TB: *See* **Transparent Bridging.**

TCAM: *See* **Telecommunications Access Method.**

T-Carrier: A family of high-speed, digital transmission systems named according to their capacity.

TCM: *See* **Trellis-code modulation.**

TCO: *See* **Tjanstemanneks Centralorganization.**

T-connector: A piece of linear bus hardware shaped like a T that connects two pieces of Ethernet cable to a network interface card.

TCP: *See* **Transmission Control Protocol.**

TCP/IP: *See* **Transmission Control Protocol/Internet Protocol.**

TDF: *See* **Transitional Data Flow.**

TDM: *See* **Time Division Multiplexer; Time Division Multiplexing.**

TE1: *See* **Terminal Equipment 1.**

TE2: *See* **Terminal Equipment 2.**

Technical and Office Protocol (TOP): An implementation of Open Systems Interconnection (OSI) standards using Ethernet specifications, developed by Boeing and others for use in office and engineering environments.

Technical support: Technical advice provided by a manufacturer to registered users of hardware or software.

Telecommunications: The transmission of information whether expressed by voice or computer signals, via the telephone systems.

Telecommunications Access Method (TAM or TCAM): IBM software that controls communications lines.

Telecommuting: Performing work at home on a computer that is linked to the office through telephone lines.

Telediagnosis: Analyzing and resolving a problem by telephone from a remote location.

Telegraph: A system that uses interruption or change in polarity of direct current to transmit signals.

Telegraph-grade circuit: A circuit on which teletypewriter equipment can transmit, normally using DC signaling at a maximum speed of 75 baud.

Telenet: (1) A commercial Wide Area Network (WAN) with thousands of local numbers through which users can log on to commercial on-line information services, e.g., Dialog Information Services and CompuServe. (2) A DEC VT-100 terminal emulation protocol. Usually, Telnet is a utility in a Transmission Control Protocol/Internet Protocol (TCP/IP) package though many companies allow for other emulators; Telnet allows users to log on to another computer linked to the Internet, in effect creating a network virtual terminal and is often used to enable communications with a Bulletin Board System (BBS) and mainframes through hyperlinks.

Telephony: Transmission of sounds, including speech.

Teleprinter: Equipment used in telegraph system services.

Teletex: A messaging technology, The logical successor to Teletypewriter Exchange Service (TWX) and Telex, that provides automatic, error-free transmission at speeds 48 times greater than Telex.

Teletype (TTY) display: A transmission method in which characters are sent one by one to the video display, which fills, line by line, as characters are received, scrolling up to accommodate new characters; the Disk Operating System (DOS) uses a teletype display for accepting commands and displaying messages. *See* **Character-mapped display.**

Teletypewriter: A slow terminal with a keyboard for input and a printer for receiving output.

Teletypewriter Exchange Service (TWX): Service provided by Western Union in which teletypewriter stations using both the Baudot and American Standard Code for Information Interchange (ASCII) coded machines are connected to a central office for exchange of information throughout the U.S. and Canada.

Telex: An international messaging service marketed in the U.S. by Western Union.

Telex network: An international public messaging service based on slow teletypewriter equipment and Baudot code, provided in the U.S. by Western Union.

TELNET: A virtual terminal protocol from the U.S. Department of Defense that interfaces terminal devices and terminal-oriented processes (MIL-STD-1782).

Template: A document or worksheet containing text, formats, or formulas for creating standardized documents; templates often include letterheads and logos.

Temporary font: A font that stays in the memory of a printer only until the printer is reset.

Temporary swap file: A Microsoft Windows file created for program instructions or data in the 386 Enhanced mode that will not fit in Random Access Memory (RAM); consumes less disk space than a permanent swap file but operates less efficiently.

10Base-2: The transmission medium based on the Institute of Electronic and Electrical Engineers (IEEE) 802.3 standard with rates up to 10 Megabits per second (Mbps) and distances up to 185 meters. Also called Cheapernet, Thin coax, Thin EtherNet, or Thinnet.

10Base-5: The transmission medium based on the Institute of Electronic and Electrical Engineers (IEEE) 802.3 standard with rates up to 10 Megabits per second (Mbps) and distances up to 500 meters. Also called Thick coax, Thick EtherNet, or Thicknet.

10Base-FL: A fiber optic standard for up to 2,000 meters of fiber optic cable (multimode duplex) for point-to-point links. Also called IEEE 802.3 Fiber Optic Ethernet.

10Base-T: The transmission medium based on the Institute of Electronic and Electrical Engineers (IEEE) 802.3 standard with rates up 10 Megabits per second (Mbps) and distances up to 100 meters though shorter distances are more typical. Usually employs Registered Jack 45 (RJ45) connectors along with Unshielded Twisted Pair (UTP) cable.

Tensioning wire: A very thin wire across an aperture grille, perpendicular to the other wires to keep them steady, which sometimes casts a shadow on the display (most visibly in solid white images).

Ter: Latin for "third," used as a suffix to denote the third version of a Consultative Committee on International Telephony and Telegraphy (CCITT) modem standard.

Tera: Prefix for one trillion (10 12).

Terabyte: A unit for measuring memory equal to approximately 1 trillion bytes (actually 1,099,511,627,776 bytes), 1,000 gigabytes, or 1 million megabytes. *See* **GigaByte; KiloByte.**

Terminal: (1) A device, usually equipped with a keyboard and a monitor, that can send and receive information over a link. (2) Any point in a system or network at which data can be entered or received. A terminal, which has its own processing circuitry, is considered a smart terminal; a terminal which can only interact with a distant server is considered a dumb terminal.

Terminal Adapter (TA): A device used to connect equipment that does not have an Integrated Services Digital Network (ISDN) interface to the digital network, functionally equivalent to a modem and usually plugging into the expansion bus. *See* **Terminal emulation.**

Terminal component: A separately addressable port for input or output, e.g., the display components of a keyboard display device.

Terminal emulation: The use of software to enable a personal computer or terminal to duplicate the screen attributes of a specific terminal for data communications purposes.

Terminal Equipment 1 (TE1): A device complying with the Integrated Services Digital Network (ISDN) network interface that can be connected directly to the digital network.

Terminal Equipment 2 (TE2): A device not complying with the Integrated Services Digital Network (ISDN) network interface that must be connected to the digital network through a Terminal Adapter (TA).

Terminal mode: A state in which the computer on which a communications program is running becomes a remote terminal for another computer to which it is linked by modem.

Terminate and Stay Resident (TSR) Program: An accessory or utility program designed to remain in Random Access Memory (RAM) for quick activation even when other programs are also in memory.

Terminator: A resistor, a hardware device used at each end of an Ethernet cable to prevent signals from reflecting back, usually grounded at one end.

Test driver: A program to test another program, often as part of an alpha text.

Test Management Protocol (TMP): A protocol used in coordinating a particular test suite.

Test message: A message posted to see whether newsreader software and UseNet connections are working.

Test tone: A tone used to locate trouble or adjust circuits.

Texas Instrument Graphics Architecture (TIGA): A high-resolution graphics standard for IBM PC-compatible personal computers, offering 1,024 pixels horizontally and 786 lines vertically with 256 simultaneous colors. *See* **Super VGA.**

Text: Data composed of standard American Standard Code for Information Interchange (ASCII) characters only, with no formatting codes.

Text chart: A slide, transparency, or handout containing text, such as a bulleted series of lines. *See* **Bullet list chart; Simple list text chart.**

Text editor: A program to alter the sequence of words and numbers, but lacking the features of full-fledged word processing program; used for creating basic text documents and writing source code.

Text file: A file containing only standard American Standard Code for Information Interchange (ASCII) characters, with no control codes or extended characters.

Text mode: Also known as character mode. Text mode is an operating mode of IBM PC-compatibles in which the images displayed are constructed from the built-in American Standard Code for Information Interchange (ASCII) 256-character set. The character set includes several graphics characters, allowing display of boxes, lines, and a few other graphics images, and text in bold and reverse. Text mode is much faster than its opposite. *See* **Graphics mode.**

TFT: *See* **Thin-Film Transistor.**

TFTP: *See* **Trivial File Transfer Protocol.**

Thermal dye sublimation printer: An expensive color printer that can generate photo-realistic output; dyes on a special ribbon are transferred to a coated paper by a highly focused heat source, producing excellent color saturation, but at a cost of three dollars per page or more in additional to the hardware cost.

Thermal fusion printer: A printer, usually portable, that transfers dye from a ribbon onto plain paper.

Thermal printer: A non-impact printer, quiet and fast, that moves heated styluses over specially treated paper (which unfortunately has a waxy feel and a somewhat unpleasant smell).

Thermal wax-transfer printer: A printer, less expensive than a dye-sublimation printer, that uses heat to deposit wax-based dyes in a dense pattern on the page, producing excellent saturation and an image that is nearly photo-realistic.

Thick Ethernet: A cabling system in which transceivers are connected to each other by stiff large-diameter cable and to nodes through flexible multi-wire cable.

Thin Ethernet: A cabling system using thin, flexible coaxial cable to connect each node to the next.

Thin-film magnetic medium: A recording medium made up of thin layers of special metal alloys plated and sputtered on hard disk substrates to achieve disk substrates higher densities and increased coercivities than media based on metal-oxide bits.

Third-Party Call Control (TPCC): A function by which a party not involved in the data flow can set up and manage a connection.

Third-party vendor: A firm that markets an accessory to computer equipment made by a different firm.

3174: A new version of the 3274 terminal cluster controller.

32-bit The number of bits used by the Operating System (OS) to complete an operation. The number of bits is based on the microprocessor designed to work in concert with the OS.

3270: The generic name for the family of inter-operable IBM system components - terminals, printers, and terminal cluster controllers - that can be used to communicate with a mainframe by means of the Systems Network Architecture (SNA) or bisync protocols. All of these components have four-digit names some of which begin with the digits 327.

3274/3276: The most commonly used cluster controller. This device links as many as thirty-two 3270 type terminals and printers to a mainframe front-end processor.

3278: The most commonly used terminal in the 3270 family. It features a monochrome display and offers a limited graphics sets.

3279: A color terminal that is part of the 3270 family.

3287: A current series of printers in the 3270 equipment family.

3705: A common-front end processor, typically used to link several 3274s and 3276s to a mainframe.

3725: A common front-end processor, intended for linking groups of cluster controllers to a mainframe.

3745: A new communications controller that combines the functions of a cluster controller and a front end processor. The 3745 can interface simultaneously with as many as 8 Token-ring networks, 512 terminals or printers and sixteen 1.544 Megabits per second (Mbps) communications lines.

Thread: (1) A chain of UseNet postings on a single subject, accessed usually by a command that lets the user jump over unrelated messages. (2) A program segment that can operate independently, sometimes simultaneously, with other segments, with the operating system allocating the processor's attention, so that, e.g., a file can be downloaded in the background without tying up other applications (a process known as Preemptive multitasking). *See* **Cooperative multitasking.**

Thread selector: A UseNet program mode in which articles are sorted by threads.

Threaded newsreader: A UseNet program that groups articles by topic, indicating where a given article stands in the chain of discussion. *See* **Thread selector.**

3+Open: A family of 3Com products for Local Area Network (LAN) Manager file / print servers that includes connectivity, messaging, and network management services.

Three-dimensional graph: A chart using three axes to show information for more than one data series: width (x-axis), height (y-axis), and depth (z-axis). In Microsoft Excel, the y-axis is called the value axis, the x-axis is the category axis, and the z-axis is the series axis.

Three-dimensional spreadsheet: A program that can create a file containing stacked pages, each a separate worksheet.

Three-gun tube: A color Cathode Ray Tube (CRT) with separate electron guns for each of the primary colors on the display. (One-gun tubes really have three guns, assembled into a single unit; monochrome monitors have a single gun.)

Throughput: The productivity of a computer or network as measured by its capability to send data through all components of the system, a more meaningful indication than benchmark speeds for executing computation-intensive algorithms; slow Random Access Memory (RAM) chips or hard disk or lack of cache memory can reduce throughput.

Thumbnail: On the World Wide Web, a small version of the full image. If the user clicks on the thumbnail, the image will fill the computer screen.

Thunking: The process by which 32-bit operating systems like Microsoft Windows '95 or Operating System/2 (OS/2) communicate with 16-bit applications, slowing computer systems noticeably.

TIC: *See* **Token-Ring Interface Coupler.**

Tie link: *See* **Tie trunk.**

Tie trunk: A telephone line connecting two branch exchanges.

TIFF: *See* **Tagged Image File Format.**

TIGA: *See* **Texas Instruments Graphics Architecture.**

Tiled windows: A Graphical User Interface (GUI) display mode in which all windows occupy an equal portion of screen space, being resized automatically as additional windows are opened. *See* **Cascading window.**

Time Assignment Speech Interpolation (TASI): A method of multiplexing telephone calls by assigning another call to the channel during the natural pauses in human speech.

Time-bomb: A program, either independent or built into a larger program, that waits until a pre-determined date and time to actuate a disruption.

Timed backup: A program feature that saves work automatically at a pre-set interval.

Time Division Multiplexer (TDM): A device that allows two or more independent data channels to be transmitted on a single high-speed circuit by interleaving data from each channel by time.

Time Division Multiplexing (TDM): A technique that divides the capacity of a Local Area Network (LAN) circuit into time slots, some as small as a microsecond, each used by a different signal. *See* **Frequency Division Multiplexing.**

Time out: An interruption created when a computer tries to access a non-responsive device or a remote computer, freezing the keyboard; after trying for a predetermined time, the computer gives up, releasing the keyboard and returning control to the user.

Time-sharing: The use of computer resources from one common source by a number of users, each apparently operating independently; as usage increases, system response time may decline.

Timeslips III: A time-tracking and billing program marketed by Timeslips Corporation for professionals like accountants and lawyers who charge by the hour.

Tin: A UseNet threaded newsreader program developed by Iain Lee for UNIX computers that is easier to use than other UNIX newsreaders.

T-Interface: A basic interface using four copper wires.

Tip: The connector attached to the positive end of the plug used to connect circuits in a manual switchboard or patch panel. Contrast this term with Ring.

Title bar: A bar across the top of a Graphical User Interface (GUI) window, such as Operating System/2 (OS/2), that shows the name of the document being used.

Tjanstemanneks Centralorganization (TCO): The Swedish Confederation of Professional Employees. A Swedish white collar labor union which has established the most stringent regulations in the world for electromagnetic radiation from monitors; few TCO-certified monitors are available in the United States.

TLV: *See* **Type/Length/Value.**

TMP: *See* **Test Management Protocol.**

TNS: *See* **Transit Network Selection.**

Toggle: To switch back and forth between two modes or states, e.g., to use the Caps Lock key on the IBM PC-compatible keyboard to type continuous capitals without using the Shift key.

Token: A control frame with a special bit field, giving permission for the recipient terminal to transmit over the network.

Token passing: An IBM access protocol architecture in which stations relay packets in a logical ring configuration, described in the Institute of Electrical and Electronic Engineers (IEEE) 802.5 standards. A node sends information across the network by obtaining a token, converts it into a data frame containing a network message, and receives information by monitoring the network top path for tokens containing its address. Token passing prevents data collisions resulting when two devices begin transmitting at the same time. *See* **Carrier Sense Multiple Access with Collision Detection; Contention; Local Area Network; Polling.**

Token-passing bus: A Local Area Network (LAN) technology that uses a token for controlling access over a bus, e.g., Institute of Electrical and Electronics Engineers (IEEE) 802.4 standard.

Token Ring: A Local Area Network (LAN) technology that circulates a special message (the token) among network nodes, giving them permission to transmit, e.g., Institute of Electrical and Electronics Engineers (IEEE) 802.5 standard.

Token-Ring Interface Coupler (TIC or TRI): An IBM device for attaching a controller or processor directly to a token-ring network, optional in several IBM terminal cluster controllers and front-end processors.

Token-Ring network: A Local Area Network (LAN) architecture from IBM that combines token passing with ring topology, using as its hub a multi-station access unit wired with twisted-pair cable configured like a star but actually a decentralized ring network of up to 255 workstations.

Toll: A charge based on time and distance for a connection in a public switched system beyond an exchange boundary.

Toll calls: Calls to units outside the originating service area.

Toll office: The Class 4 office where channels and toll circuits terminate, usually one to a city except in larger cities that require several toll offices.

Toll trunk: A communications circuit between telephone company toll offices.

Tone dialing: *See* **Dual-Tone Multiple Frequency.**

Toner: The dry ink applied to electrostatically charged drums in laser printers and photocopying machines to fuse the image to the paper using a heating element. The toner cartridge in laser printers contains the toner the printer uses to fuse to a page to produce the image.

Tone signaling: Messages sent by sending tones over a circuit.

Toolbar: A bar across the top of a Microsoft or Macintosh window containing icons on pushbuttons that represent commonly used command, called in other applications speedbars, SmartIcons, power bars, or buttonbars.

Toolbox: A set of programs for developing software. Also called a tool kit.

Toolkit: *See* **Toolbox.**

TOP: *See* **Technical and Office Protocol.**

Top-down programming: A method of program design in which the process begins with a "mission statement" for the program (in English), broken into subcategories each of which describes an anticipated function and corresponds to a program module that can be coded independently. The design works best with structured languages such as Pascal or Modula-2 and object-oriented languages like C++.

Topology: (1) The process in which a network's circuits are configured. (2) A map of the network showing how wires or cables are laid out (physical) or how messages flow (electrical or logical).

Topology aggregation: Compression of topology information for reading at the level below.

Topology attribute: A link or a node.

Topology constraint: A constraint controlled by either a link or a node.

Topology database: The database that describes the entire domain as seen by a node.

TOPS: A program for Local Area Networks (LANs) that allows Macintosh and PC users to share files in AppleTalk or Ethernet networks; because each user has access to public files located on all other network workstations, every node becomes potentially a file server.

Torn tape message systems: A teletypewriter-based system in which paper tape was torn off one teletypewriter and read into another.

Touch screen: *See* **Touch-sensitive display.**

Touch-sensitive display: A display consisting of a pressure-sensitive panel in front of the screen on which options are selected by pressing, used generally for public-access information purposes in museums, supermarkets, airports, and kiosks.

Tower case: A system case designed to be positioned vertically on the floor rather than horizontally on a desk, offering more room for accessories than desktop case and greater flexibility in monitor positioning but less convenient if floppy disks and CD-ROMs must be changed often.

TP-4: *See* **Transport Protocol 4.**

TPCC: *See* **Third-Party Call Control.**

TPI: *See* **Tracks Per Inch.**

TP-MIC: *See* **Twisted-Pair Media Interface Connector.**

Track: One of many concentric rings encoded on a floppy or hard disk during low-level formatting that defines distinct areas of data storage. *See* **Sector.**

Trackball: An input device embedded in the keyboard or a case near the keyboard to replace the mouse, moving the pointer on-screen as its ball is rotated by the thumb or finger; often built into portable or notebook computers since unlike a mouse it does not need a clean flat surface. *See* **Snap-on pointing device.**

Track buffering: A design feature in which the entire contents of a hard disk track are read into a memory area, whether or not it has all been requested by the hard disk controller and host adapter; eliminates the need for interleaving. All modern hard disks and most Enhanced Small Device Interface (EDSI) drives are track-buffered.

Trackpad: A device controlling the mouse pointer that is moved by sliding a finger around on a touch-sensitive surface, tapping the surface or pressing a button to click.

Tracks Per Inch (TPI): A measurement of the data-storage density of magnetic disks; Disk Operating System (DOS) double-density 5 1/4 inch floppy disks are formatted with 48 tpi, high-density 5 1/4 inch disks with 96 tpi, and high-density 3 1/2 inch disks with 135 tpi.

Track-to-track Seektime: How long it takes to move the read/write head from one track to the next, less important than access time in comparing disk drives.

Tractor feed: A paper-feed mechanism common in dot-matrix printers in which continuous paper moves through the printer on a sprocket wheel which sprocket fits into pre-punched holes on the left and right edges of the paper; the printer pages must then be separated from each other and the sprocket holes.

Traffic: The messages travelling over a network.

Traffic management: Control of data traffic to avoid congestion, using such functions as feedback and usage parameter control.

Traffic shaping: A mechanism that alters the characteristics of a stream of cells to improve efficiency or to make sure it conforms to what is needed at a later interface.

Trail: An entity that transfers information from a client between points in a server layer network, monitoring it at the termination points.

Trailer: Any part of a message that follows the text.

Transactional application: A program on a Local Area Network (LAN) a program that creates and maintains a master record of all network transactions, such as filling out invoices, for use in restoring files after a system crash.

Transaction processing systems: Systems running prewritten programs to perform repetitive business transactions.

Transaction Tracking System (TTS): A log of all NetWare file activity.

Transceiver: (1) A terminal that can transmit and accept messages. (2) A modem in a wireless Wide Area Network (WAN) that can transmit and accept data via radio. *See* **Personal Digital Assistant.**

Transfer rate: The number of bytes of data that can be transferred per second from disk the microprocessor, limited by how fast the disk rotates and the density of the data on the disk although caching information can reduce such hardware limitations. *See* **Access time; Hardware cache; Small Computer System Interface.**

Transfer Rate of Information Bits (TRIB): A measure for comparing the efficiency of one protocol over another.

Transfer syntax: The format of data during transmission.

Transient: *See* **Power surge.**

Transient error: An error that occurs once or occasionally at unpredictable intervals.

Transistor-Transistor Logic (TTL) monitor: An obsolete monochrome monitor accepting digital signals that works only with Hercules and Monochrome Display Adapter (MDA) video adapters; replaced by monitors meeting Video Graphics Array (VGA) and Super VGA standards.

Transit delay: The period between the times when the first bit and the last bit of a packet cross-designated boundaries.

Transit Network Selection (TNS): A signal that identifies a public carrier with which to make a connection.

Transition: Moving from one state to another.

Transitional Data Flow (TDF): Transmission of data across national borders.

Translate: Convert a file from one format to another or a program from one programming language to another.

Transmission code: A code for sending information over telephone lines.

Transmission control: The layer in the Systems Network Architecture (SNA) that manages communications.

Transmission control character: Any character used to control or facilitate transmission of data between Data Terminal Equipment (DTE), initiating such operations as addressing, polling, delimiting and blocking messages, and checking for transmission errors.

Transmission Control Protocol (TCP): A specification for software that bundles and unbundles data into packets, manages network transmission of packets, and checks for errors.

Transmission Control Protocol/Internet Protocol (TCP/IP): A set of communications standards created by the U.S. Department of Defense (DOD) in the 19701 that has now become an accepted way to connect different types of computers in networks because the standards now support so many programs. Occasionally called Transfer Control Protocol/Internet Protocol.

Transmit: To send information electronically.

Transparency: A clear piece of acetate on which information can be written or printed (by laser, ink jet, or copier, though different materials may be required) for display by overhead projection.

Transparency adapter: An attachment that lets scanners scan slides and transparencies.

Transparent: A computer operation or entity that is invisible to those using it (e.g., the formatting codes a program inserts in the document that are not present on the screen).

Transparent Bridging (TB): An Internet Engineering Task Force (IETF) standard using a Spanning Tree Algorithm where the behavior of the bridge is transparent to the traffic.

Transport connection: A communications path that is a virtual circuit between users.

Transport layer: The fourth layer of the seven layers in the Open Systems Interconnection (OSI) model, above the network, data-link, and physical layers. The transport layer is responsible for the integrity and quality of data transmission. Its primary function is error detection and error correction.

Transport Protocol 4 (TP-4): An Open Systems Interconnection (OSI) Layer-4 protocol created by the National Bureau of Standards.

Transport stream: A stream consisting of 188 byte packets that can hold multiple programs, one of two types produced by the Motion Picture Experts Group 2 (MPEG-2) Systems layer.

Transpose: Change the order of characters, words, or sentences, often in response to commands included in a word processing program.

Transposition: An encryption technique that reorders the symbols in a message.

Trapping: *See* **Error trapping.**

Tree and Tabular Combined Notation (TTCN): The international standard or specifying abstract test suites.

Tree structure: A way of organizing information into a hierarchy with a root and branches, much like a genealogy chart. *See* **Directory; Subdirectory.**

Trellis-code modulation (TCM): A group coding modulation technique used by high speed modems in which one or more redundant bits are added to each group used to generate a signal change, resulting in a lowering of the error rate and data transfer rates of 9,600 bits per second (bps) or faster.

TRIB: *See* **Transfer Rate of Information Bits.**

Tribit: A group of three bits; in eight-phase modulation, each possible tribit is encoded as one of eight carrier phase shifts. Contrast this term with Dibit and Quadbit.

Trinitron: A Cathode Ray Tube (CRT) design that uses an aperture grill rather than a shadow mask to ensure that electrons hit the proper pixels on the display. An invention of Sony, uniformly bright, unlike other designs that are less bright around the edges, but tensioning wires may sometimes cast shadows.

Triple-pass scanner: A color scanner that gathers data about a different primary color on each of three scanning passes; not necessarily slower than single pass scanners, but may wear out more quickly.

Trivial File Transfer Protocol (TFTP): A simplified version of the File Transfer Protocol (FTP), associated with the Transmission Control Protocol/Internet Protocol (TCP/IP) family, that does not provide password protection or a user directory.

Trojan horse: A program that appears to performs a valid function but contains hidden instructions that damage the system.

Trolling: Posting a UseNet message containing a obvious exaggeration or factual error to trick another user into posting an article pointing out the error.

Troubleshooting: Determining why a system or a device is not working efficiently.

Trouble ticket: An online record or a paper form that documents the diagnosis of a problem and any correction attempts.

True BASIC: A well-structured version of the BASIC programming language developed by its originators, John Kemeny and Thomas Kurtz, in response to criticism of earlier versions, used to teach the principles of structured programming but not often used for professional programming, since it is interpreted rather than compiled.

TrueType: A cost-effective alternative to PostScript font technology included with Apple Computer's System 7 and Microsoft Windows '95 that brings the same scalable fonts to both screen and printers of Macintosh and Windows system without the need for an add-on utility program.

Trumpet Winsock: A common shareware program written by Peter Tattam compatible with the Winsock specification that provides Transmission Control Protocol/Internet Protocol (TCP/IP) support for early Microsoft Windows system; it includes a dialer utility.

Truncate: Cut off part of a number or character string.

Truncation error: A rounding error occurring when part of a number is not stored because it exceeds the amount of memory set aside for number storage. *See* **Floating point calculation.**

Trunk: (1) A telephone channel between two central offices, or a telephone switching device used to link subscribers. (2) A multi-line circuit used to connect switching or distribution centers.

Trunk group: Trunks between two switching centers, message distribution points, or both that use the same terminal equipment.

TSR: *See* **Terminate and Stay Resident Program.**

TTCN: *See* **Tree and Tabular Combined Notation.**

TTL: *See* **Transistor-Transistor Logic monitor.**

TTS: *See* **Transaction Tracking System.**

Tuning: The process of adjusting a system to improve performance.

Turbo Pascal: A high performance compiler developed by Borland International in 1984 for Pascal that comes with a full-screen text editor and creates executable programs (object code); now one of the most popular compilers ever written, thanks to its relatively low cost, Turbo Pascal is used mainly in hobby and academic environments.

Turnaround time: The actual time required to reverse the direction of transmission on a half-duplex circuit, typically 200 milliseconds but affected by line propagation effects, modem timings, and computer reaction.

Turnkey system: A computer system developed for a specific application and delivered with all the application programs and peripherals need for it to run immediately.

Tutorial: A form of instruction that teaches students in a step-by-step process how to apply a program to a specific task.

Tweak: To adjust a program or system slightly to improve performance.

Twisted pair: Cable comprised of two insulated copper wires braided together at six turns per inch to provide self-shielding by randomizing interference from other circuits.

Twisted-pair Ethernet: An Ethernet network that runs over inexpensive twisted-pair wiring. *See* **IEEE, 10Base T.**

Twisted-Pair Media Interface Connector (TP-MIC): The jack on the equipment that receives the twisted pair plug.

Two-way set-associative cache: A secondary cache memory design that is faster than direct-map cache and not as expensive as the faster four-way set-associative cache.

Two-wire circuit: A metallic circuit formed by two conductors insulated from each other that can be used as a one-way transmission, half-duplex, or duplex path.

TWX: *See* **Teletypewriter Exchange Service.**

.TXT: The extension usually attached to a file containing American Standard Code for Information Interchange (ASCII) data.

Typeface: The distinctive design of a set of characters and numerals. Many laser printers have numerous typefaces already available in Read Only Memory (ROM) and will accept download of hundreds more. *See* **Font; Font family.**

Type/Length/Value (TLV): A flexible method of coding parameters within a frame: type = parameter type; length = value length of the parameter; value = actual value of the parameter.

Typeover: *See* **Overtype.**

Typeover mode: *See* **Overtype mode.**

Typesetting: The production of camera-ready copy on a high-end imagesetter such as a Linotronic or Varityper, producing an image far superior to the 1200 Dots Per Inch (DPI) output available from current office-quality laser printers. *See* **Resolution.**

Type size: The size of a font, measured in points (approximately 1/72 inch) from the top of the tallest ascender to the bottom of the longest descender. *See* **Pitch.**

Type 1 font: A Post-Script-compatible font that incorporates Adobe Systems' font-scaling technology for better legibility at low resolutions and small type sizes. *See* **PostScript font.**

Type 3 cable: An unshielded twisted-pair wire meeting IBM specifications for use in four-megabit per second token-ring networks.

Typography: (1) The arrangement of printed matter. (2) The design of attractive and readable typefaces.

UA: *See* **User Agent.**

UAE: *See* **Unrecoverable Application Error.**

UART: *See* **Universal Asynchronous Receiver/Transmitter.**

UDP: *See* **User Datagram Protocol.**

U Interface: A standard interface between two copper wires.

ULSI: *See* **Ultra-Large Scale Integration.**

Ultra-Large Scale Integration (ULSI): The fabrication of a chip containing more than one million transistors.

UME: *See* **User Network Interface Management Entity.**

Unassigned cells: Cells identified by a Virtual Path Identifier and Virtual Channel Identifier.

Unbalanced: An interchange circuit where transmit and receive voltages are measured in relation to a common return path.

Unbounded media: A communications path in which the signal is not confirmed by an electrical cable, optical fiber, or other physical medium.

Undelete utility: A program that can restore a file path accidentally erased from disk as long as no other data is written to the disk after the erasure.

Undo: A command that restores program and data to the stage they were in just before the previous command or action, thus canceling the effects of giving the wrong command.

Unformat utility: A program that can restore data on an inadvertently formatted disk; if a safe-format technique was used, data is restored quickly; if not, data can be recovered with the Microsoft Disk Operating System (MS-DOS) 5.0 MIRROR utility or certain utility programs such as PC Tools. *See* **Safe format.**

Unformatted text file: *See* **Plain text document.**

Unicasting: The operation by which a source interface transmits a single Packet Data Unit (PDU) to a single destination.

Unified Network Management Architecture (UNMA): AT&T company-specific architecture conforming to the Common Management Interface Protocol (CMIP) of the International Organization for Standardization (ISO).

Uniform Resource Locator (URL): A string of characters precisely identifying the type and location of an Internet resource, one of two basic kinds of Universal Resource Identifiers (URIs) and the standard way to find a resource. *See* **RELative uniform resource locator.**

Uninterruptible Power Supply (UPS): A battery that can supply continuous power to a computer system if the power fails; it charges while the computer is on and if the power fails provides power for about ten minutes, allowing the user to shut down the computer properly to preserve crucial data.

Universal Asynchronous Receiver/Transmitter (UART): An integrated circuit found on the motherboard of most computers that transforms the parallel data stream operating within the computer it to the serial data stream used in asynchronous communications, although serial communication will also require a serial port and modem. *See* **Asynchronous communications; Modem; Motherboard; Serial port.**

UNIX: An operating system written at Bell Laboratories in the 1970s in highly portable programming language C for a wide variety of computers from mainframes to personal computers, supporting multitasking and ideally suited to multiuser applications. UNIX is a comprehensive and efficient programming environment based on the philosophy that each software tool should perform only one function and all tools should be part of the operating system; applications programs can take advantage of the software tools to accomplish functions, thus keeping applications programs manageable. Data is communicated from one software tool to another by a highly flexible pipe, a user command that couples the output of one command to the output of another, allowing the user to control virtually every aspect of the operating environment and create commands for situations not anticipated when the operating system was developed. With more than 200 commands, inadequate error messages, and a cryptic command syntax, however, UNIX is not easy for occasional users to cope with. New UNIX shells like NeXTStep, a shell for the NeXT workstation, that is as easy to use and as versatile as the Macintosh Finder, may solve this problem. NeXT Steps has an Application Program Interface (API) that handles virtually all screen routines. NeXT step can be made available for 80386 and 80486 computers. Another common UNIX shell is X Windows, which is currently being developed in academic computing centers. (UNIX is rare on personal computers.) With the release of System V, AT&T established a set of UNIX standards called System V Interface Definition (SVID) toward which most UNIX systems are now migrating, especially now that major corporate purchasers are requiring this standard. IBM adopted the SVID standard for its own version of UNIX. *See* **Input/output redirection; NeXT; Pipe; Shell; System V Interface Definition; X Window.**

UNIX-to-UNIX Copy Program (UUCP): A standard utility for exchanging information between two UNIX nodes, allowing UNIX users to exchange files, electronic mail, and UseNet articles via long-distance telephone uploads and downloads.

UNMA: *See* **Unified Network Management Architecture.**

Unmoderated newsgroups: In a distributed Bulletin Board System (BBS), for example, EchoMail (FidoNet) or Usenet (Internet), an unmoderated newsgroup is a topical discussion group in which postings are reviewed before distribution. Though sometimes engagingly spontaneous, insensitive postings may cause flame wars. *See* **Moderated newsgroups; Newsgroup.**

Unordered list: A list created in HyperText Markup Language (HTML) with <UL> ... </UL> stages; often seems to be bulleted.

Unplanned outage: An event in which users cannot access the servers because of, for example, a power outage, disk drive failure, or software bug.

Unrecoverable Application Error (UAE): A crash resulting after one Microsoft Windows program invades another program's memory space and wipes out part of its code; common in Windows 3.0 but much rarer in subsequent versions.

Unsubscribe: Remove a UseNet newsgroup from your subscription list so that it does not appear on the list of those you are actively following or remove your name from a mailing list.

UNZIP: To expand (decompress) a file that has been saved via a compression utility.

UPC: *See* **Usage Parameter Control.**

Update: A fundamental database management manipulation that adds, deletes, or modifies records to bring the data up to date.

Upgrade: Buy a new version of a program or a more powerful computer or peripheral.

Upload: Transmit a file by telecommunications to another computer user or a bulletin board.

Upper memory area: In a Microsoft Disk Operating System (MS-DOS) environment, the memory between the 640 KiloBytes (KB) limit of conventional memory and 1 MegaByte (MB), some of which in the original PC system design was reserved for system uses, but most of which is available for programs. The upper memory area is configurable by memory management programs and MS-DOS 5.0 for system utilities and application programs. *See* **Conventional memory; HIMEM.SYS; Microsoft Windows.**

UPS: *See* **Uninterruptible Power Supply.**

Uptime: The period when the system can respond to client requests, as opposed to downtime.

Upward compatibility: Software that functions without modification on more powerful versions of a computer system.

URL: *See* **Uniform Resource Locator.**

Usage Parameter Control (UPC): The set of actions a network takes to control traffic.

UseNet: The news distribution and bulletin board channel of the Unix-to-Unix Control Program (UUCP), the international Wide Area Network (WAN) that links UNIX computers. *See* **Wide Area Network.**

UseNet Frequently Asked Questions(FAQs) by Newsgroup: A document that lists all FAQs for all UseNet newsgroups.

UseNet Info Center launch pad: Where links to information about UseNet and its newsgroups are to be found.

UseNet site: A computer system with huge amounts of disk storage, one of about 120,000 that receives news feeds and enables multiple users to participate in UseNet.

User: *See* **End user.**

User Agent (UA): The Open System Interconnection (OSI) term for a client program that runs on the user's machine and helps it to contact a server, often used to refer to electronic mail clients such as Eudora or Pegasus Mail.

User Datagram Protocol (UDP): A Transmission Control Protocol/Internet Protocol (TCP/IP) normally bundled with an Internet Protocol (IP)-layer software that describes how messages received reach application programs within the destination computer.

User default: The program operating preferences that a user defines.

User-defined: Selected or chosen by the user.

User-friendly: A program or computer system designed so that those who lack extensive computer experience or training can use it with relative ease. Among the common elements of user-friendly programs are: (1) menus instead of keyboard commands; (2) on-screen help at the touch of a key; (3) logical program functions mapped to the keyboard following established conventions; (4) understandable error messages providing solutions; (5) transparent intermediate and advanced features; (6) methods for preventing inadvertent data destruction; and (7) simple, clear tutorials and documentation.

User group: A voluntary association of users of a specific computer or program who meet regularly to discuss problems, exchange tips and techniques, hear presentations by computer experts, and obtain public domain software and shareware.

User interface: All the features of a program or computer that govern how people interact with it. *See* **Graphical User Interface.**

User-Network Interface (UNI): The Asynchronous Transfer Mode (ATM) Forum standard for connecting users with a local switch.

User Network Interface (UNI) Management Entity (UME): The software in the devices on a User-Network Interface circuit that handles the management interface with an Asynchronous Transfer Mode (ATM) network.

Utility program: A program used to maintain and improve the efficiency of a computer system, which may but is not necessarily included in the operating system. The Microsoft Disk Operating System (MS-DOS) includes utilities such as BACKUP and RESTORE, but many MS-DOS users buy additional utilities such as virus detectors and vaccines, file compression and defragmentation utilities, and shells that DOS may not provide. *See* **Shell.**

UUCP: *See* **UNIX-to-UNIX Copy Program.**

Uudecode: A UNIX utility program for reading a uuencoded American Standard Code for Information Interchange (ASCII) file, restoring the original binary file (such as a program or graphic), needed to decode the binary files posted to UseNet and often built into UseNet newsreaders.

Uuencode: A UNIX utility program often built into UseNet newsreaders and other systems that transforms a binary file such as a program or graphics into coded American Standard Code for Information Interchange (ASCII) text for Internet transfer or posting to a UseNet newsgroup; the file is restored at the receiving end by a uudecode utility.

V.17: An International Telecommunications Union (ITU-T) standard for transmitting and receiving faxes at speeds up to 14,400 bits per second (bps).

V.21: An International Telecommunications Union (ITU-T) standard for transmitting and receiving data at 300 bits per second (bps) that conflicts with the Bell 103 standard once common in North America.

V.22: An International Telecommunications Union (ITU-T) standard for transmitting and receiving data at speeds up to 1,200 bits per second (bps) that conflicts with the Bell 212A standard once common in North America.

V.22bis: An International Telecommunications Union (ITU-T) standard for transmitting and receiving data at 2,400 bits per second (bps); though modems meeting the standard can deal with slower data transfer rates, they are being made obsolete by V.32 bis standard modems at competitive prices.

V.24: A Consultative Committee for International Telephony and Telegraphy (CCITT) specification. V.24 is virtually identical to RS232C, for the interface between modems (Data Communications Equipment or DCE) and a terminal or computer (Data Terminal Equipment or DTE).

V.27ter: An International Telecommunications Union (ITU-T) standard for equipment transmitting and receiving fax information at 4,800 bits per second (bps). Modems meeting the standard can handle transfers as slow as 2,400 bps.

V.29: An International Telecommunications Union (ITU-T) standard for equipment transmitting and receiving fax information at 9,600 bits per second (bps). Modems meeting the standard can handle transfers down to 7,200 bps if line noise requires.

V.32: An International Telecommunications Union (ITU-T) standard for modems transmitting and receiving data at 9,600 bits per second (bps), at which speed they use Trellis-Code Modulation (TCM); modems meeting the standard v.32 standard can handle transfers as slow as 4,800 bits per second (bps), but without TCM.

V.32 bis: An International Telecommunications Union (ITU-T) standard for modems transmitting and receiving data at 14,400 bits per second (bps); modems meeting the standard are popular and can also transfer data at 12,000 bps, 9,600 bps, 7,200 bps, and 4,800 bps as needed.

V.32 turbo: A proprietary standard developed by AT&T for modems transmitting and receiving data at 19,200 bits per second (bps) that can fall back to the rates supported by the v.32 bis standard; V.32 turbo is not an International Telecommunications Union (ITU-T) standard and has been replaced by V.32.

V.34: An International Telecommunications Union (ITU-T) standard for modems transmitting and receiving data at 28,800 bits per second (bps) that supports adjustment to changing line conditions for data transfer at maximum possible speeds.

V.42: An International Telecommunications Union (ITU-T) standard designed to correct the effects of line noise. Modems, meeting the standard, check to make sure each piece of data transmitted arrives and retransmit those that do not. The default error-correction method they use is the Link Access Protocol for Modems (LAPM) as Microcon Network Protocol-4 (MNP-4) is available if needed.

V.42 bis: An International Telecommunications Union (ITU-T) standard that increases the throughput of modems with on-the-fly compression that reduces the amount of data that has to be transmitted.

V.FAST Class (V.FC): A proprietary standard used by modem manufacturers before V.34 was adopted; V.FC modems can be upgraded to the V.34 standard.

V.FC: *See* **V.Fast Class (V.FC).**

Vaccine: A program, also called an immunizing program, which protects against viruses by adding a small code to files that sound an alert when a virus tries to operate within the file.

Validation: A more positive description for testing or debugging a program, for example, proving that a program does its job.

Value: A numeric cell entry in a spreadsheet program. A constant is a value typed directly into a cell; a second kind of value is produced by a formula placed into a cell and can cause problems when a constant is typed over it. *See* **Cell protection.**

Value-added carrier: A carrier offering enhanced communications services, the enhancement usually consisting of computation as well as basic communications service.

Value-Added Network (VAN): A private packet-switched network whose services are sold to the public. *See* **Packet Data Network.**

Value-Added Reseller (VAR): A business that repackages and improves hardware manufactured by a different business; VARs typically add better documentation, integrated packaging, and new finishes.

VAN: *See* **Value-Added Network.**

Vanilla: Plain, with no advanced features, as in "It's a plain vanilla 486".

Vaporware: A program heavily marketed while still under development, which may in fact never be published.

VAR: See Value-Added Reseller.

Variable: A named area in memory that stores a value or a string.

Variable Bit Rate (VBR): A service category defined by the Asynchronous Transfer Mode (ATM) Forum that supports variable traffic with average and peak parameters.

VBA: *See* **Visual Basic for Application.**

VBR: *See* **Variable Bit Rate.**

VC: *See* **Virtual Circuit.**

VCC: *See* **Virtual Channel Connection.**

VCI: *See* **Virtual Channel Identifier.**

VCL: *See* **Virtual Channel Link.**

VCO: *See* **Voltage Controlled Oscillator.**

VDT: Video Display Terminal. *See* **Monitor.**

VDU: Video Display Unit. *See* **Monitor.**

Vector graphics: *See* **Object-oriented graphics.**

Vector-to-raster conversion program: A utility program attached to many illustration programs, including CorelDraw that translates object-oriented (vector) into bit-mapped (raster) graphic images. *See* **Object-oriented graphics.**

Vendor: A seller or supplier.

Vendor-Independent Messaging (VIM): An Application Program Interface (API) allowing different electronic mail programs to exchange mail. The consortium of developers that created VIM did not include Microsoft Corporation, which uses the Messaging Application Program Interface (MAPI) and exchanges mail with VIM programs through a VIM-to-MAPI Dynamic Link Library (DLL) file.

Ventura Publisher: A page layout program (for IBM PC-compatible computers) that is particularly effective for long documents. *See* **PageMaker.**

Verify: To determine the accuracy and thoroughness of a computer operation.

Veronica: A search service that scans Gopher directory titles and resources and generates from it a new Gopher menu on a given topic. *See* **Jughead.**

Version: A specific release of a software or hardware product. The higher the number, the more recent the release.

Verso: The left, even-numbered, page of a two-page spread.

Vertical application: An application program created for a tightly defined market, such as a single profession or a specific type of retail store, usually offering complete management from scheduling and billing through inventory and purchasing.

Vertical centering: Automatic centering of data vertically on the page, usually requiring a separate command, as in the WordPerfect Center Top to Bottom command.

Vertical flat: A design used in Trinitron and other monitors that reduces image distortion with a display curved like a cylinder rather than a sphere as in most Cathode Ray Tubes (CRTs). *See* **Flat-square monitor; Flat-tension mask monitor.**

Vertical frequency: *See* **Vertical refresh rate.**

Vertical justification: The use of feathering (adding vertical space) to align newspaper columns so they all end evenly at the bottom margin. The feature inserts white space between frame borders and text, between paragraphs, and between lines.

Vertical market program: An application designed for a specific career or profession, such as real estate, law, or architecture, for example, a time, expense, and billing program for a small law office. *See* **Timeslips III; Vertical application.**

Vertical Redundancy Check (VRC): A parity check performed on each character as data is received.

Vertical refresh rate: The frequency, measured in Hertz (Hz), at which the electron guns of a Cathode Ray Tube (CRT) move from the top of the display to the bottom. The vertical refresh rate determines whether a display seems to flicker, for example, at a resolution of 1,280 pixels by 1,024 lines, a refresh rate of at least 72 Hertz (Hz) is necessary.

Vertical retrace: The process by which the yoke directs the electron beam in a Cathode Ray Tube (CRT) from the end of a vertical scan to the beginning of the text, causing blanking; adapters must allow time for vertical retrace in preparing video signals.

Very High-Level Language (VHL): A declarative language, usually proprietary, used to solve a particular kind of problem, for example, in spreadsheet and database management programs for generating reports.

Very Large-Scale Integration (VLSI): Manufacture of semiconductor chips that include more than 100,000 and up to 1 million transistors each.

VESA: *See* **Video standard; Video Electronics Standards Association.**

VHL: *See* **Very High-Level Language.**

Vi: A text editor that is the default editor on many UNIX systems and famously difficult to learn; UNIX users often prefer applications that have built-in text editors. *See* **Emac.**

Video accelerator: *See* **Graphics accelerator board.**

Video adapter: The adapter that generates the output required to display text and graphics on a monitor, which must be compatible with the adapter; most current computer models have Super Video Graphics Array (VGA) video adapters and monitors. *See* **Color Graphics Adapter; Enhanced Graphics Adapter; IBM 8514/A display adapter; Monochrome Display Adapter; MultiColor Graphics Array.**

Video amplifier: The monitor circuit that amplifies the signal from a video adapter to a level high enough to drive the electron gun; monochrome monitors have one video amplifier, and color monitors have three.

Video capture camera: A device that records data in the form of digitized images saved as files that, with the right software, can later be retrieved to allow the images to be run on monitors as movies or in multimedia presentations.

Video card: *See* **Graphics accelerator board.**

Video controller: A microprocessor on the video adapter that reads data in display memory, organizes it into a continuous stream, and sends it to the monitor.

Video disk: An optical disk used to store still pictures or television pictures and sound for playback via a videodisk player on a standard television monitor. *See* **Interactive videodisk**.

Video Display Terminal (VDT): *See* **Monitor**.

Video Display Terminal (VDT) Radiation: Electromagnetic waves radiated by a video display terminal. *See* **Cathode Ray Tube; Extremely Low Frequency emission**.

Video Display Unit (VDU): *See* **Monitor**.

Video driver: A program that tells other programs how to work with a particular video adapter and monitor, often with user-accessible controls for resolution, refresh rate, and color.

Video Electronics Standards Association (VESA) bus: *See* **Local bus**.

Video Electronics Standards Association (VESA) local bus (VL-Bus): A local bus, designed to work with the Intel 486 and compete with proprietary local buses, commonly used to connect video and network adapters to the expansion bus.

Video Electronics Standards Association (VESA) local bus slot: A socket for adapters on expansion buses that is compatible with the VESA local bus standard. This enables 32-bit communications between microprocessor and adapter and is common in versions of the 486-class microprocessor, though likely to be replaced by the more flexible Peripheral Component Interconnect (PCI) slots over the next several years.

Video memory: A set of memory chips to which the Central Processing Unit (CPU) writes display information and from which the video controller reads it before sending it to the monitor, often using Dynamic Random Access Memory (DRAM) chips though the more expensive Video Random Access Memory (VRAM) chips are faster.

Video monitor: *See* **Monitor**.

Video noise: Random dots on a display, also called "snow". Video noise is rarely a problem currently, but noticeable with Color Graphics Array (CGA) video adapters and monitors.

Video RAM (VRAM): Dynamic Random Access Memory (DRAM) chips designed to maximize the performance of video adapters; dual-ported VRAM allows simultaneous reading and writing of data. *See* **Random Access Memory; Video adapter**.

Video signal compression: Reduction of the number of bits required to carry a digitized video signal while maintaining quality.

Video standard: A standard defined by an industry group for screen resolution, color, and other aspects of displays that allows software developers to know how their programs will appear on screen. *See* **Extended Graphic Array; MultiColor Graphics Array; Super VGA.**

Videotex: An application which allows a computer to store text and images in digital form and transmit them to remote terminals.

Video text: Transmission of news headlines, stock quotes, movie reviews, and other data through a cable television system. *See* **On-line information service.**

View: The on-screen display of information in a database that meets the criteria specified in a query. Most database management programs can save views; the best update them whenever the records are changed.

VIM: *See* **Vendor-Independent Messaging.**

VINES: *See* **Virtual Networking Software.**

Virtual: On-screen representation of an entity or object that does not exist.

Virtual 8086 mode: A mode available with 80386 and higher microprocessors in which the chip simulates an almost unlimited number of Intel 8086 machines.

Virtual Channel Connection (VCC): The unidirectional virtual channel links between two endpoints in an Asynchronous Transfer Mode (ATM) network.

Virtual Channel Identifier (VCI): The number defined by a 16-bit field in the header that identifies the channel over which a cell will travel.

Virtual Channel Link (VCL): The method by which Asynchronous Transfer Mode (ATM) cells travel between the point where an identifier is assigned and the point where it is removed.

Virtual channel switch: The element in a network that connects virtual channel links, ending virtual path connections and translating identifier values.

Virtual circuit: A temporary connection between two points created by software and packet switching that appears to be available as a dedicated circuit, and can be maintained indefinitely or used at will.

Virtual circuit model: A network model that provides connection-oriented service.

Virtual community: A group of people who share an mutual interest and communicate via electronic mail and newsgroups.

Virtual corporation: A business with geographically scattered units but effectively linked by a Wide Area Network (WAN) such as the Internet.

Virtual device: Simulation of a computer device or peripheral that does not exist nearby. A Local Area Network (LAN) workstation may appear to have a high-capacity hard disk that is in fact on the file server to which it is linked.

Virtual Device Driver (VxD): A Microsoft Windows '95 32-bit program that manages a resource such as a sound card or printer and runs in the processor's protected mode so it is less likely to crash the system by creating conflict with other applications. The abbreviation VxD covers Virtual Printer Devices (VPD), Virtual Display Devices (VDD), and Virtual Timing Devices (VTD) among others.

Virtual Library: A subject tree on the World Wide Web (WWW) in which volunteers maintain the tree devoted to a specific subject; much of the information in the Virtual Library is academically-oriented. *See* **Subject tree.**

Virtual Local Area Network (VLAN): Workstations connected to a device that can define membership in a Local Area Network (LAN).

Virtual machine: A computer that acts as if it were several computers. It does this through an on-screen simulation of a separate computer that runs programs independently. A virtual machine can exist in a computer with special processing circuitry and a large Random Access Memory (RAM), as in the Intel 80386DX and 80386SX microprocessor, which can run two or more virtual Microsoft Disk Operating System (MS-DOS) machines, which can run programs concurrently in their own 640 KiloBytes (KB) memory space. 80386 and higher microprocessors create a protected memory space allowing virtual machines to run their own programs and access the keyboard, printer, and other devices without conflicts.

Virtual memory: A method of extending the apparent size of Random Access Memory (RAM) by using part of the hard disk; many applications, like Microsoft Word, routinely use the disk instead of memory to store some data or program instructions. *See* **Virtual memory management.**

Virtual memory management: The management of virtual memory operations at the operating system rather than the application level.

Virtual Networking Software (VINES): A UNIX-based network operating system from Banyan Systems.

Virtual Path (VP): A unidirectional logical group of virtual connections.

Virtual Path Connection (VPC): The collection of unidirectional virtual path links between two or more switches in Asynchronous Transfer Mode (ATM) network.

Virtual Path Identifier (VPI): An eight-bit field in a header showing the path the cell should take.

Virtual Path Link (VPL): Unidirectional method of moving Asynchronous Transfer Mode (ATM) cells from the point where the identifier is assigned to the point where it is removed.

Virtual path switch: The element in a network that connects virtual path links and translates virtual path identifiers.

Virtual Path Terminator (VPT): The system that separates the channels on a virtual path for processing.

Virtual Reality (VR): An illusory computer-generated world which the user navigates at will, typically by wearing a Head-Mounted Display (HMD) that displays a stereoscopic image and a sensor glove for manipulating "objects" in the virtual environment; VR's greatest commercial potential is in the entertainment area, but other applications are highly likely. *See* **Cyberspace; Sensor glove.**

Virtual Reality Modeling Language (VRML): A "tag" language for formatting web pages to support three-dimensional graphics and interactive navigation.

Virtual Redundancy Check (VRC): The parity check performed on each character as data is received.

Virtual Scheduling (VS): A method of checking the conformance of an arriving cell by checking the actual arrival time of a cell against a theoretical time set by assuming that the source will send equally spaced cells.

Virtual Shareware Library (VSL): A popular World Wide Web (WWW) page offering a search interface for several File Transfer Protocol (FTP) software archives.

Virtual Telecommunications Access Method (VTAM): The IBM standard for software that runs on the mainframe and works with Network Control Programs to establish communications between the host and cluster controllers.

Virus: A sabotage or prank program that attaches itself to other programs to carry out unwanted and sometimes damaging operations ranging from surprise screen messages, changes in system software performance to erasure of the entire hard disk. Common sources of viruses are executable programs downloaded from a public Bulletin Board System (BBS), obtained from mail-order vendors of public domain or shareware programs, or pirated copies of commercial programs. Programs should first be downloaded to floppy disks and not hard disks. Virus-checking software is recommended for all applications, especially memory resident virus checking programs that check every file that is copied into the computer. *See* **Vaccine.**

Virus protection: A feature that screens data for computer viruses, cures them, and then tells the system administration what has been done.

Visual Basic for Application (VBA): A version of the Visual Basic programming language included with Microsoft Windows '95 applications, also called Visual Basic Programming Systems, Application Edition, which can be used to create everything from simple macros to custom applications. *See* **Event-driven program.**

VLAN: *See* **Virtual Local Area Network.**

VL-Bus: *See* **Video Electronics Standards Association local bus.**

VLSI: *See* **Very Large-Scale Integration.**

Voice actuation: Computer processing of spoken commands. *See* **Voice recognition.**

Voice-band: The 300 Hertz (Hz) to 3300 Hz band used on telephone equipment to transmit voice as well as data.

Voice-capable modem: A modem that can distinguish between and route fax transmissions, data transmissions, and voice telephone calls, often used as voice mail systems for small offices.

Voice channel: A transmission path usually limited to the bandwidth of the human voice.

Voice compression: Reduction of the number of bits required to carry a digitized voice signal while maintaining essential speech characteristics.

Voice-grade: A switched or leased telephone circuit that can carry analog signals and speech.

Voice grade circuit: A circuit suitable for carrying speech, digital or analog data, or facsimile; with a frequency range of 300 Hertz (Hz) to 3300 Hz, voice grade circuits can transmit at up to 19,000 Bits Per Second (BPS).

Voice mail: A communications system in which voice messages are transformed into digital form for storage on a network until the person called accesses it for playback; also called Voice store and forward. *See* **Voice messaging.**

Voice messaging: A computer system on which people can leave voice messages for others, the sound equivalent of electronic mail; it provides a mailbox in which the voice messages are digitized and stored. *See* **Voice mail.**

Voice recognition: Computer transformation of human speech into digitized text or instructions.

Voice store and forward: *See* **Voice mail.**

Voice synthesis: Audible rather than readable output of computer-based text; virtually any computer can be equipped to read American Standard Code for Information Interchange (ASCII) text aloud virtually error-free, allowing blind people increased access to written works. *See* **Voice recognition.**

Volatility: A computer's susceptibility to interruptions in power that can destroy all the data in Random Access Memory (RAM).

Voltage Controlled Oscillator (VCO): An oscillator whose clock frequency varies with the magnitude of the voltage presented at its input.

Volume label: The name, no longer than 11 characters, that is assigned to an Microsoft-Disk Operating System (MS-DOS) disk when it is formatted and is thereafter displayed on the first line of a directory.

von Neumann bottleneck: The limitation on processing speed imposed by computer architectures linking a single microprocessor with memory, named for mathematician John von Neumann, who discovered that a program spends more time retrieving data than processing it. One solution is parallel processing, but current programming does not deal well with parallel processing. The Pentium microprocessor solution is to incorporate separate caches for data and instructions. *See* **Stored program concept.**

VP: *See* **Virtual Path.**

VPC: *See* **Virtual Path Connection.**

VPI: *See* **Virtual Path Identifier.**

VPL: *See* **Virtual Path Link.**

VPT: *See* **Virtual Path Terminator.**

VR: *See* **Virtual Reality.**

VRC: *See* **Virtual Redundancy Check.**

VRML: *See* **Virtual Reality Modeling Language.**

VS: *See* **Virtual Scheduling.**

VSL: *See* **Virtual Shareware Library.**

VTAM: *See* **Virtual Telecommunications Access Method.**

Vulcan nerve pinch: A poorly conceived keyboard command that requires the user to contort the hands in an uncomfortable way.

VxD: *See* **Virtual Device Driver.**

W3: *See* **World Wide Web.**

WAIS: *See* **Wide Area Information Server.**

Wait state: A microprocessor clock cycle in which nothing occurs and programmed so that components, such as Random Access Memory (RAM), can catch up with the Central Processing Unit (CPU). The number of wait states depends on the relative speed of the processor compared to the memory; zero wait state machines have cache memory, interleaved memory, page-mode RAM, or static RAM chips.

WAN: *See* **Wide Area Network.**

Warm boot: A system restart performed by pressing a special key combination (often CTRL+ALT+DEL) or the reset button while the system is on; in a cold boot, the power is turned completely off and then back on. A warm boot puts less strain on the system. *See* **Programmer's switch.**

Warm link: In Object Linking and Embedding (OLE) and Dynamic Data Exchange (DDE), a dynamic link updated only in response to the update link command; warm links are available in Lotus 1-2-3 (Release 2.2 and higher) and in Quattro Pro (Version 1.0 and higher). *See* **Hot link.**

.WAV: A Microsoft-IBM sound file format specifying monaural and stereo 8-bit and 16-bit storage that is part of the Microsoft Windows '95 accessories for storing wave sounds.

Waveform sound: A type of digitized audio information that has high fidelity, especially when recorded with 16-bit resolutions but requires huge amounts of storage. For example, one minute recorded with Microsoft Windows '95 .WAV format uses 27 MegaBytes (MB) of memory.

Wave sound: A digitized recording of an actual sound which is one of the two sounds that can be captured in computer-readable files; as many as 5 MegaBytes (MB) of storage may be required to store a four-minute popular tune. Popular Internet wave file formats are *.AIFF and Moving Picture Experts Group (*.MPEG) sounds. *See* **.WAV.**

Wave table synthesis: A method of reproducing music in a sound board based on pre-recorded samples of orchestral instruments showing how particular notes played on those instruments should sound; wavetable synthesis is far superior to Frequency Modulation (FM) synthesis. *See* **Frequency Modulation synthesis.**

Web: Related documents that together make up a hypertext presentation on the World Wide Web (WWW) or some other hypertext system. Though documents need not be stored on the same computer system, they are interlinked, usually by means of internal navigation buttons.

WebAuthor: A HyperText Markup Language (HTML) editor created for Microsoft Word by Quarterdeck Systems that makes Word into a What-You-See-Is-What-You-Get (WYSIWYG) editor, with the user seeing the results of HTML tags rather than the tags themselves; it has excellent forms capabilities.

Web browser: A program, text-only or graphical, which is run on an Internet-connected computer with access to the World Wide Web (WWW).

WebCrawler: A search engine for locating World Wide Web (WWW) documents; based at the University of Washington and supported by DealerNet, Starwave Corporation, and Satchel Sports, it uses a spider (an automated search routine) to index all the words in the documents it finds. Though slow (it contains only about 300,000 documents), it is unusually accurate because its indexing is so complete.

Web server: A World Wide Web (WWW) program that processes requests for information framed in HyperText Transport Protocol (HTTP); Web servers have been developed for most computing systems, from UNIX to Macintosh. *See* **HyperText Transport Protocol Daemon; Netscape Commerce Server; Netscape communications server.**

Web site: A computer system which runs a Web server and is configured to publish documents on the Web.

Weight: The lightness or darkness of a typeface or the gradations of light to dark within a font; common gradations are extra light, light, semi-light, regular, medium, semibold, extra bold, bold, and ultrabold. *See* **Book weights.**

Weitek coprocessors: Numeric coprocessors created for computers that use Intel 80386 or 80486 microprocessors; faster than the Intel 80387 and 80487xsx, they are popular for Computer-Aided Design (CAD) applications; programs often have to be modified to use Weitek coprocessors.

Welcome page: A document accessible through the World Wide Web (WWW) that is the point of entry to related documents. The Welcome page is also known as the Home page.

Well-structured programming language: A language that encourages programmers to create programs that are easy to read, debug, and update, often using separate modules, each of which accomplishes a single function.

Well-known port: An Internet port address that is permanently linked with an application by the Internet Assigned Numbers Authority (IANA), allowing Transmission Control Protocol/Internet Protocol (TCP/IP) software to direct incoming data to that application. Because IANA fixes port numbers for such common Internet applications as Telnet, File Transfer Protocol (FTP), and the World Wide Web (WWW), the port numbers can be accessed by the domain name alone without a port address.

What-if analysis: The use of changes to key variables in spreadsheet programs to analyze how such changes will effect other computations and to give users a way to compare the effects of different strategies.

What-You-See-Is-What-You-Get (WYSIWYG): A design philosophy for word processing programs in which formatting commands allow the screen to show the user how the printed text will appear. *See* **Embedded formatting command.**

Whipuptitude: The effectiveness of a programming language in creating quick and easy solutions, for example, Practical Extraction and Report Language (PERL) has a much greater whipuptitude than the C language.

White noise: *See* **Background noise.**

White pages: A computer version of a telephone book set up by corporations, universities, and other organizations to help people find phone numbers and electronic mail addresses. The white pages are often accessible through the Internet. *See* **X.500; Whois server.**

White space: A portion of the page in which no print appears. White space is used to balance the printed areas and improve readability.

White-write technique: *See* **Print engine.**

Whois: (1) A UNIX utility, run by a Whois server, users employ to locate an electronic mail address, often the telephone number, and sometimes information about other users who have an account on the same computer system. (2) A command that displays a list of all users logged on to a Novell network.

Whois server: An Internet program that responds to requests for electronic mail addresses by searching a database of account holders. *See* **Whois.**

Whole Internet Catalog: On the World Wide Web (WWW), a subject tree that has hyperlinks to Web documents containing arts and entertainment, business and finance, computers, education, government, health and medicine, and a number of other topics. The book publisher O'Reilly & Associates maintains the Whole Internet Catalog. *See* Subject tree.

Wide Area Information Server (WAIS): A program or UNIX-based system linked to the Internet through which users can search worldwide archives for resources based on keywords; WAIS is considered to be not highly satisfactory as a search tool because the list of documents generated tends to contain many false drops (irrelevant documents).

Wide Area Network (WAN): A network using high-speed long-distance common-carrier circuits or satellites to cover a large geographic area. *See* **ARPANET; Internet.**

Wideband: A channel or transmission medium that can pass more frequencies than a standard 3-KiloHertz (KHz) voice channel.

Wideband circuit: A high-speed circuit that can carry data at speeds greater than voice-grade circuits.

Wideband modem: A modem which is capable of operating at over 9,600 bits per second (bps).

Widow: A formatting flaw in which the last line of a paragraph appears alone at the top of a new page or column; widows are controllable or preventable in most word processing and page layout programs.

Wild card: A character, often an asterisk and a question mark that stands for another character that may appear in the same place. For instance:

Wild card	Stands for
REP*.DOC	REPORT1.DOC
REPOS.DOC	REPORT2.DOC
REPORT?.DOC	REPORT1.DOC
REPORT2.DOC	

WIN32: The 32-bit Windows Application Program Interface (API), used in programs that run only on Microsoft Windows '95 and Microsoft Windows NT.

Win32s: A Microsoft freeware utility that upgrades Microsoft Windows 3.1 and Microsoft Windows for Workgroups 3.11 to run 32-bit applications.

Winchester drive: *See* **Hard disk drive.**

Window: (1) A range of frame numbers that it is legal to transmit or receive. (2) The on-screen rectangle containing a view of a document, worksheet, database, or drawing or application program. Though in most programs, only one window is displayed, a windowing environment makes it possible to run two or more applications concurrently, each in its own window. *See* **Application Program Interface; Graphical User Interface; Microsoft Windows '95.**

Window menu: The Microsoft Windows '95 synonym for a control menu.

Windowing environment: An Application Program Interface (API) that provides Graphical User Interface (GUI) features, such as windows and pull-down menus. *See* **Graphical User Interface; Microsoft Windows.**

Windows '95: *See* **Microsoft Windows '95.**

Windows accelerator: *See* **Graphics accelerator board.**

Windows application: An application that can run only within the Microsoft Windows environment. *See* **Non-Windows application.**

Windows Explorer: The Microsoft Windows '95 program that replaces the Windows 3.1 File Manager.

Windows Metafile Format (WMF): A file format, readable by Microsoft Windows '95 applications, that supports object-oriented graphics.

Windows printer: *See* **Graphical Device Interface.**

Winsock: Windows Socket. An open standard specifying how a Dynamic Link Library (DLL) should be written to provide Transmission Control Protocol/Internet Protocol (TCP/IP) support for Microsoft Windows '95 systems.

Winstone: A test developed by the Ziff-Davis Publishing PC Labs that simulates real-world conditions to test all aspects of system performance, making the computer execute scripts in more than a dozen popular applications.

WinVN: A public domain UseNet threaded newsreader for Windows versions through Microsoft Windows '95, developed by Mark Riordan and now supported by programmers at the NASA Kennedy Space Center.

Wireless WAN: *See* **Wireless wide area network.**

Wireless wide area network (Wireless WAN): A radio network for computers in a few large metropolitan areas equipped with transceivers that receive (or in two-way systems send and receive) electronic mail messages, news broadcasts and files; future satellite-based systems may make the network more generally available.

Wiring closet: A room containing the connections for all networked devices in a given area.

Wiring hub: A cabinet, usually in a wiring closet, which holds the connection modules for various kinds of cabling. A cabinet carries electronic circuits that retime and repeat the signals on the cable and sometimes a microprocessor board to report on network activity.

Wizard: An interactive and much-imitated help utility, such as a Setup Wizard, developed by Microsoft for its Windows application; the wizard guides a user through each step of a multi-step operation, explaining options as it goes.

WMF: An extension indicating that the file contains a graphic saved in Windows Metafile Format. *See* **Windows Metafile Format.**

Word: Information composed of characters, bits, or bytes treated as an entity that can be stored in one location; word processing programs define a word to include the space at the end of the group of characters.

WordPad: A Microsoft Windows '95 word processing program that can directly read files created by Microsoft Word and Microsoft Write, replacing the Notepad and Write accessories included with Windows 3.1.

WordPerfect: A full-featured word processing application created by Novell and now published by Corel that is in virtually a draw with Microsoft Word for best word processing program.

Word processing: The most popular computer application, which uses the computer system to create, edit, proofread, format, and print documents.

Word processing program: An application program that transforms a computer into a tool for word processing, such as Lotus Word Pro, Microsoft Word, and WordPerfect. A word processing program offers such advanced features as search-and-replace and grammar checks as well as spell-checking and the ability to display font choices; current software can also handle some desktop publishing operations. *See* **What-You-See-Is-What-You-Get.**

WordStar: A word processing program developed by MicroPro International (now WordStar International) for Control Program for Microprocessors (CP/M), Disk Operating System (DOS), and Windows systems that originated the term What-You-See-Is-What-You-Get (WYSIWYG), though many functions still use embedded commands. Good touch-typists prefer WordStar because almost all commands can be given with the fingers on the home positions.

Word wrap: A text-editing application feature that carries a word down to the beginning of the next line if its length would otherwise take it beyond the right margin.

Workaround: A quick fix that bypasses a bug rather than eliminating it, useful when time is short or programmers are in short supply.

Workbook: A collection of related worksheets kept in a single spreadsheet file, making it easy to hot-link worksheets.

Workgroup: A small group of employees, usually in a large business, working together on an assigned project, whose productivity is believed to be enhanced by linkage in a Local Area Network (LAN) to improve communication through, for example, electronic mail, group editing options, and access to a common database.

Workload generator: Software that creates transactions or other work to test a computer or network.

Worksheet: The matrix of rows and columns imitating the ledger sheet used in accounting into which headings, values, and formulas are entered in a spreadsheet program; also called the spreadsheet.

Worksheet window: A portion of the worksheet cells (visible on a computer screen) out of the maximum number of cells of an electronic spreadsheet of up to 8,192 rows and 256 columns.

Workstation: A desktop computer that is an access point to a Local Area Network and runs application programs. *See* **File server; Personal computer; Professional workstation.**

World Wide Web (WWW; W3): A global hypertext system accessed by the Internet and navigated by clicking hyperlinks from one document to the next, with the actual location of the document immaterial. Created in 1989 at the European Laboratory for Particle Physics (CERN) in Switzerland to simplify travel on the Internet, the Web relies upon the HyperText Transport Protocol (HTTP), which specifies how an application can locate and acquire resources (such as documents, sound, or graphic) stored on another computer on the Internet. Working with Web browsers, users click on emphasized words or phrases and HTTP finds and downloads the desired document. Most Web documents are created using the easy HyperText Markup Language (HTML), though that may soon be supplanted by automated tools. *See* **Secure HTTP; Secure Socket Layer; Web browser.**

Worm: A virus that seeks out all the data in memory or on a disk in order to alter it, perhaps by changing certain characters to numbers or replacing bytes of stored memory. Though some programs may still run, the data is no longer valid.

WORM: *See* **Write-Once, Read-Many.**

Wrap-around type: Type arranged to surround a graphic, used sparingly because it can be hard to read.

Write: (1) The operation in which the Central Processing Unit (CPU) records information in Random Access Memory (RAM) or a secondary storage medium such as a disk drives. (2) Storing information on a disk.

Write-back cache: The type of cache memory that stores information both written in memory and read from memory, considered superior to write-through cache.

Write-black engine: *See* **Print engine.**

Write cache: A cache segment where data is accumulated before being written to the drive, because a single large write-operation is considered more efficient than several smaller transfers.

Write-head: *See* **Read/write head.**

Write-Once, Read-Many (WORM): An optical disk drive with storage capacities of up to 1 TeraByte (TB) that becomes a read-only storage medium once data is written to the drive. A WORM is capable of storing huge amounts of information and the recommended technology for organizations that need to publish large internal databases internally, though being superseded by fully read/write-capable optical disk drives. *See* **Compact Disk-Read Only Memory; Erasable optical disk drive.**

Write precompensation: The increase by the hard disk of the magnetic file with which the read/write head records data near the spindle, where data must be closely packed; the cylinder that starts the process is included in the disk geometry.

Write-protect: Modify a file or disk to prevent editing or erasure of data.

Write-protect notch: A small notch in the protective jacket of a 5-1/4-inch floppy disk that when covered protects the data from erasure or over-writing by the disk drive.

Write-protect tab: A tab in the upper left corner of a 3 1/2-inch floppy disk; when the tab is open, the disk is write-protected.

Write-through cache: Cache memory for memory read but not memory write operations, which are cached in the much slower Random Access Memory (RAM); considered inferior to write-back caches.

Write-white engine: *See* **Print engine.**

WRT: With respect to.

WWW: *See* **World Wide Web.**

WYSIWYG: *See* **What-You-See-Is-What-You-Get.**

X.21: A Consultative Committee on International Telephony and Telegraphy (CCITT) electrical, mechanical, and procedural standard for physical access to circuit-switched digital networks.

X.21bis: A specification for interface between Data Terminal Equipment (DTE) and any analog telephone network that is for all practical purposes identical to Recommended Standard 232C (RS232C) and V.24.

X.25: A Consultative Committee on International Telephony and Telegraphy (CCITT) standard for computer access to and data handling in a packet switched network.

X86: The Intel microprocessor architecture that is binary compatible with Microsoft Disk Operating System (MS-DOS) and Microsoft Windows '95 programs.

X.400: A Consultative Committee on International Telephony and Telegraphy (CCITT) international electronic mail system designation.

X.400 Message Handling Service (MHS): A Consultative Committee on International Telephony and Telegraphy (CCITT) electronic mail protocol.

X.500: The Consultative Committee on International Telephony and Telegraphy (CCITT) directory standard that cooordinates file directories of different systems.

X-axis: The horizontal axis, usually the categories axis, in a graph. *See* **X-axis; Y-axis; Z-axis.**

Xbase: A generic term for any programming environment driven by Ashton-Tate's original dBASE pProgramming language, such as Arago, Clipper, or FoxPro.

XCFN: *See* **External function.**

XCMD: *See* **External function.**

XENIX: A Microsoft-developed Operating System (OS) meeting the UNIX System V Interface Definition (SVID) that runs on IBM PC-compatible computers.

Xerox Network Services (XNS): A multilayer protocol system by Xerox, adopted at least in part by other vendors that allows one workstation on a network to use files and peripherals of another as if they were local.

XGA: *See* **Extended Graphics Array.**

X-height: The height of lowercase letters in any font, measured from the baseline up to avoid size distortions that might be caused by very long or very short ascenders and descenders.

XMODEM: A half-duplex file transfer protocol that transmits only one file at a time.

Xmodem protocol: As asynchronous protocol primarily used for transfer of data files between microcomputers.

XNS: *See* **Xerox Network Services.**

X/Open: A consortium of computer industry vendors preparing specifications for a UNIX-based open system platform.

X Window: A windowing system that allows graphics produced on one networked workstation to be displayed on another.

Y-axis: The vertical axis n a business graph, usually the value axis, which is normally vertical. *See* **Bar Graph; Column graph; X-axis; Z-axis.**

Yahoo: A popular World Wide Web (WWW) subject tree created by David Filo and Jerry Yang of Stanford University that performs over 10 million searches a week and includes some 35,000 documents.

Yellow Book: An International Standards Organization (ISO) standard for how data is encoded on Computer Disk Read Only Memory disks (CD-ROMs), including Compact Disk-eXtended Architecture (CD-XA) specifications.

Yellow Magenta Cyan and blacK: Printer's abbreviation for Yellow, Magenta, Cyan and blacK. *See* **Color separation.**

YMODEM: A half-duplex File Transfer Protocol (FTP) that can move multiple files in 1,024-byte blocks, performing a Cyclic Redundancy Check (CRC) on each frame.

YMODEM-g: A File Transfer Protocol (FTP) that delegates error-checking to protocols encoded on modern hardware such as V.42 and

Microcon Network Protocol-4 (MNP-4); YMODEM-g is best suited to high-speed modems with little line noise.

Yoke: The collection of electromagnets positioned around the outside of a Cathode Ray Tube (CRT), controlled by the monitor circuitry and video adapter, and that directs emissions from the electron guns to the proper pixels on the display.

Zap: Erase or delete.

Zapf dingbats: Decorative symbols created by German typeface designer Herman Zapf.

Z-axis: The dimension of depth in a three-dimensional graph. *See* **Three-dimensional graph; X-axis; Y-axis.**

ZCAV: *See* **Zoned Constant Angular Velocity.**

Zero Insertion Force (ZIF) package: A socket to facilitate removal and installation of large chips, including microprocessors; a lever on the side of the ZIF package releases the pins around a chip to be removed and clamps them back around the new chip.

Zero Insertion Force (ZIF) socket: *See* **Zero Insertion Force package.**

Zero-slot LAN: A Local Area Network (LAN) that operates through the computer serial port rather than a network interface card (NIC). Because the Zero-slot LANs are slower, they are most suited to network applications that need only occasional access to a peripheral (for example, a plotter) that is not used much. *See* **Network Interface Card; Serial port.**

Zero wait state computer: An IBM PC-compatible computer with memory optimized by cache memory, interleaved memory, page mode Random Access Memory (RAM) or static RAM chips so that there is no pause in the microprocessor for the memory to catch up with processing. *See* **Cache memory; Interleaved memory; Page-mode RAM; Static Random Access Memory; Wait state.**

.ZIP: The extension of a file generated by the file compressor utility PKZIP.

ZMODEM: A fast full-duplex asynchronous File Transfer Protocol (FTP), included in most communications applications, that supports the transfer of multiple files virtually error-free, and continues an interrupted transmission at the point of interruption.

Zone: A subgroup of computers in a Local Area Network (LAN) that is named and can be treated separately by the network administrator.

Zone-bit recording: The Seagate Technologies name for a Multiple Zone Recording.

Zoom: Enlarge a window to fill the screen.

Zoom box: A box, usually on the window border, that can be clicked with the mouse to change the window from normal to full size and back. *See* **Graphical User Interface.**

APPENDIX

APPENDIX A
DATA COMUNICATION SOURCES

U.S. CARRIERS
Aliant Communications (formerly Lincoln Tel)
Americom Long Distance
Ameritech
AT&T
ATU Telecommunications
Bell Atlantic
Bell Atlantic Pennsylvania
BellSouth
Cincinnati Bell Inc.
Frontier Corporation
GTE
LCI International
LDDS
Pacific Bell
MCI
Nynex
Pacific Telesis Group
SBC Communications Inc.
Sprint
Sprint /United Telephone of Florida
U S West

MAJOR NETWORK PROVIDERS
Ameritech (U.S. Carrier)
Illinois, Indiana, Michigan, Ohio and Wisconsin
30 South Wacker, Floor 34
Chicago, IL 60606
411 or 555-1212—National Directory Assistance
1-800/EASY-FIND (1-800/327-9346)—Ameritech information
1-800/221-0994 or *611 [from cellular phones]—Customer service
1-800/EASY-FIND (1-800/327-9346)—Custom Business products and
  services information
1-800/TEAM-DATA (1-800/832-6328)
Information Industry Services:
1-800/924-3666—Network providers
1-800/242-3225—Information providers
1-800/879-5222—Local exchange carrier service center
New Media, Inc.:
1-800/848-CAST—At Your Service Center [for cable customers]
Web: http://www.ameritech.com/

MAJOR NETWORK PROVIDERS, con't.
Ardis
Two-way wireless data network, covering the top 400 metropolitan areas
of the U.S., Puerto Rico, and the Virgin Islands
The ARDIS Company
300 Knightsbridge Pkwy
Lincolnshire, IL 60069
Web: http://www.ardis.com/

AT&T (U.S. Carrier)
Web: http://www.att.com/services/

Bell Atlantic (U.S. Carrier)
Web: http://www.bell-atl.com/

BellSouth (U.S. Carrier)
Web: http://www.bellsouth.com/
Alabama, Florida, Georgia, Kentucky, Louisiana, Mississippi North
Carolina, South Carolina, Tennessee
Web:http://www.bellsouthcorp.com/t2geninq.html

MCI (U.S. Carrier)
Web: http://www.mci.com/

NetworkMCI
Web: http://www.mci.com/networkmci/indexview.html

Nortel (Northern Telecom)
Enterprise; Public Carrier; Wireless; Broadband
Web: http://www.nortel.com/

Nortel
2221 Lakeside Boulevard
Richardson, Texas 75082-4399
1-800-4NORTEL

Nortel (Northern Telecom)
4001 E. Chapel Hill-Nelson Hwy.
Research Triangle Park, North Carolina 27709
1-800-4NORTEL

Nynex/Bell Atlantic (U.S. Carrier)
Northeastern United States
largest wireless provider on the East Coast
Nynex Corporation
1095 Avenue of the Americas
New York, NY 10036
1-212-395-2121
Products and Services
Web: http://www.nynex.com/products/products.html
Web: http://www.nynex.com/

Pacific Telesis
Pacific Bell (U.S. Carrier)
Corporate Headquarters
140 New Montgomery Street
San Francisco, CA 94105
1-800-303-3000
Web: http://www.pacbell.com/ot

Pacific Bell Network Integration
6379 Clark Avenue
Dublin, CA 94568
510-803-6000
info@pbni.com

Pacific Bell Interactive Media
35 North Lake Avenue, Suite 300
Pasadena, CA 91101
888-428-4263

Pacific Bell Internet Services
303 Second Street, Suite 650 N.
San Francisco, CA 94107
1-800-708-4638

Pacific Bell Mobile Services
4420 Rosewood Dr., Bldg. 2, 4th Fl.
Pleasanton, CA 94588
510-227-3000

Sprint (U.S. Carrier)
SONET, High-speed ATM, IP Services
Web: http://www.sprintbiz.com/

Skytel
Talking, Faxing pagers
Web: http://www.skytel.com/

SBC Communications Inc. (U.S. Carrier)
175 E. Houston, Suite 520
San Antonio, TX 78299-2933

Southwest Bell
Arkansas, Kansas, Missouri, Oklahoma and Texas, Pacific Bell, Cellular
One, Nevada Bell
Web: http://www.sbc.com/

Tadiran Telecommunications
Voice and data switching products including wired and wireless CPE, CO
and transmission systems, digital cross-connects, pair gain and wireless
local loop products, electronic surveillance, EW and DEW systems.
5733 Myerlake Circle
Clearwater, FL 34620
Phone: 813-523-0000
Fax: 813-523-0010

MAJOR INTERNET SERVICE PROVIDERS (ISPS)

America Online (AOL)
Corporate Communications, Cor-porate Development, Finance, Human
Resources, Legal
22000 AOL Way
Dulles, VA 20166
Fax: 703/265-2409
e-mail: psyberman@aol.com
Web: http://www.aol.com/

Compuserve World Headquarters
5000 Arlington Centre Blvd.
P.O.Box 20212
Columbus, OH 43220
Web: http://world.compuserve.com/

Prodigy
Web: http://www.prodigy.com/
e-mail: prodigy@prodigy.net

Sprynet
Spry, Compuserve Internet Division
3535 128th Avenue SE
Bellevue WA 98006
Web: http://www.sprynet.com/

HELPFUL URLS

Software Guide Product Directory
Web: http://www.softwareguide.com/

The Broadband Telephony Buyers Guide
Web: http://www.broadband-guide.com/

**The Telecommunications Library sponsored by WWorldCom
Marketing Research Group**
Web: http://www.wcom.com/ library.html

AT&T Toll-Free Internet Directory
Web: http://att.net/dir800/

CONFERENCES & EXPOSITIONS

The International Communications Association
e-mail: intlcoma@onramp.net

The International Communications Conference
e-mail: prabhu@ee.uta.edu

The International Engineering Consortium
e-mail: info@iec.org

Interop
Web: http://www.interop.com

Conferences & Expositions, con't.
SuperComm—sponsored by the TIA Telecommunications Industry
Association
Web: http://www.super-comm.com

ATM Year
Web: http://www.tticom.com

NetWorld and Interop
Web: http://www.sbexpos.com

NGN
Web: http://www.bcr.com

ORGANIZATIONS
Electronic Frontier Foundation (EFF)
A non-profit civil liberties organization working in the public interest
to protect privacy, free expression, and access to public resources and
information online, as well as to promote responsibility in new media
Web: http://www.eff.org/

The InterNIC
Domain name registration and Internet Protocol (IP) network number
assignment
Web: http://ds.internic.net/ds-home.html

Multimedia Communications Forum
Web: http://www.mmcf.org/

Telecommunications Industry Association
Web: http://www.industry.net/tia

Standards Organizations
ATM Forum Offices
The objective of accelerating the use of Asynchronous Transfer Mode (ATM)
products and services through a rapid convergence of interoperability
specifications
World Headquarters
2570 West El Camino Real, Suite 304
Mountain View, CA 94040-1313
Phone: +1-415-949-6700
Fax: +1-415-949-6705

American National Standards Institute(ANSI)
Administrator and coordinator of the United States private sector voluntary
standardization system since 1918
General Information: 212-642-4900
Web: http://www.ansi.org
The ANSI Catalog contains a searchable database of over 11,000 ANSI stan-
dards
Web: http://www.ansi.org.cat_top. html

STANDARDS ORGANIZATIONS, con't.
CDPD Forum
Cellular Data Packet
Web: http://www.cdpd.org

Committee T1
Web: http://www.t1.org

Federal Communications Commission
Web: http://www/fcc.gov

Intellsat
3400 International Drive NW
Washington, DC 20008-3098
Telephone: +1 202.944.6800
Web: http://www.intelsat.int

International Standards Organization
Central Secretariat Address
For general information and questions on ISO:
1, rue de Varemb
Case postale 56
CH-1211 Geneve 20
Switzerland
Phone: + 41 22 749 01 11
Fax: + 41 22 733 34 30
Telex: 41 22 05 iso ch
Telegram: isorganiz
e-mail: INTERNET: central@iso.ch
Web: http://www.iso.ch

International Telecommunica-tion Union ITU (formerly CCITT)
Web: http://info.itu.ch/

National Committee for Information Technology Standards
NCITS Secretariat, Information Technology Industry (ITI) Council
1250 Eye St. NW, Suite 200
Washington, DC 20005
Telephone 202-737-8888; Fax 202-638-4922;
e-mail: NCITS@itic.nw.dc.us
Web: http://www.x3.org/

AIIM Association for Information & Image Management
Web: http://www.aiim.org

Information Infrastructure Standards Panel
Web: http://www.ansi.org.iisp.iisphome.html

National Telecommunications and Information Administration
Web: http://www.ntia.doc.gov

ACCREDITED STANDARDS COMMITTEE X12
Accredited Standards Committee X3
AES
American National Standards Institute (ANSI)
ARI
ASME
ASQC
ATM Forum
Communications Standards Review
Defense Standardization Program
Data Interchange Standards Association (DISA)
Department of Energy (DOE)
Electronic Data Interchange Standards
Institute of Electrical and Electronic Engineers (IEEE)
National Fire Protection Association (NFPA)
National Institute of Standards and Technology (NIST)
National Standards Systems Network
Optical Society of America
SPIE
T1
The Home Automation Team (Home Automation)
The Institution of Electrical Engineers (IEE)
Under Secretary of Defense (Acquistion & Technology)
Under Secretary of Defense (Acquistion & Technology)
Underwriters Laboratories
VITA

DATA COMMUNICATIONS REFERENCE
The International PGP Home Page
Web: http://www.ifi.uio.no/pgp/

The WorldWideWeb Acronym and Abbreviation Server
Web: http://www.ucc.ie/info/net/ acronyms/index.html

Technical Event Calendar sponsored by CMP Media Inc. and Knowledgeweb Inc.
Web: http://www.techweb.com/calendar/

Common Internet File Formats
Web: http://www.matisse.net/files/ formats.html

NETWORK RESOURCES
Association of Online professionals
For individuals who plan, manage and maintain remote-access, computer-based communication systems
Web: http://www.aop.org/

NETWORK RESOURCES, con't.
Network Management Forum (NMF)
1201 Mt. Kemble Avenue
Morristown, NJ 07960
Phone: +1 201-425-1900
Fax: +1 201-425-1515
e-mail: info-request@nmf.org.

ONLINE TECHNOLOGY NEWS SOURCES
News.Com Tech News First
Web: http://www.news.com/

iWorld Internet News and Resources
Web: http://www.iworld.com/

LEGAL/TECHNOLOGY ISSUES
American Bar Association On-Line
Web: http://www.abanet.org/

American Communication Association
Web: http://cavern.uark.edu/comminfo/www/ACA.html

DIGITAL COMMERCE
Digicash
licensed payment technology products
Web: http://www.digicash.com/

Network Payment Mechanisms and Digital Cash
Web: http://ganges.cs.tcd.ie/ mepeirce/project.html

Commercenet
Web: http://www.commerce.net/

GOVERNMENT AGENCIES
United States National Information Infrastructure (NII)
Virtual Library
Web: http://nii.nist.gov

Information Infrastructure Task Force (IITF)
Web: http://iitf.doc.gov/

U.S. Department of Commerce (DOC)
International Trade Administration
Microelectronics Sector Info-Page
Office of Microelectronics, Medical Equipment and Instrumentation
(OMMI)
Washington, D.C. 20230
EC/EDI: Electric Commerce/ Electronic Data Interchange at NAFTAnet
Web: http://www.nafta.net/ ecedi.htm

GOVERNMENT AGENCIES, con't.

U.S. Department of Energy's Computer Incident Advisory Capability
Web: http://ciac.llnl.gov/

High Performance Computing and Communications Program
Web: http://www.hpcc.gov

National Communications System (NCS)
Web: http://164.117.147.223

National Institute of Standards and Technology
Web: http://www.nist.gov

INTERNET ORGANIZATIONS

The Internet Engineering Task Force (IETF)
Web: http://www.ieff.cnri.reston. va.us/

The Internet Society (ISOC)
Web: http://www.isoc.org

INTERNIC - Internet Networking Information Center WWW
Web: http://www.internic.net

NSF's Internet Backbone
Web: http://www.isu.edu/departments/comcom/internet/backbone.html

INTERNET INTEREST GROUPS (NEWSGROUPS)

comp.arch: Computer architecture
comp.arch.storage: Storage system issues, both hardware and software
comp.arch.storage: Frequently Asked Questions
comp.client-server: Topics relating to client/server technology
comp.compression.research: Data compression research
comp.database: Database and data management issues and theory
comp.databases.object: Object-oriented database management systems
comp.dcom.cabling: Cabling
comp.dcom.cell-relay: Relays
comp.dcom.htmame-relay: Relays
comp.dcom.isdn: ISDN information
comp.dcom.lans.ethernet: Discussions of the Ethernet/IEEE 802.3
protocols
comp.dcom.lans.fddi: Discussions of the FDDI protocol suite
comp.dcom.lans.misc: Local area network (LAN) hardware and software
comp.dcom.lans.token-ring: Installation and usage of token ring networks
comp.dcom.modems: Data communications hardware and software
comp.dcom.net-management: Net-work management
comp.dcom.servers: Selecting and operating data communications
servers
comp.dcom.telecom: Telecom-munications information

INTERNET INTEREST GROUPS (NEWSGROUPS), con't.

comp.dcom.telecom.tech: Telecommunications information
comp.groupware: Hardware software for facilitating group interaction
comp.infosystems: Any discussion about information systems
comp.ivideodisc: Interactive video discs information
comp.multimedia: Multimedia technology
comp.os.research: Operating systems and related areas
comp.periphs: Peripheral devices
comp.periphs.printers: Information on printers
comp.periphs.scsi: Discussion of SCSI-based peripheral devices
comp.security.misc: Security issues of computers and networks
comp.sys.novell: Discussion of Novell Netware products
comp.unix.misc: General discussions regarding UNIX
comp.virus: Computer viruses security

TRADE ASSOCIATIONS

Computing
Association of Personal Computer User Groups (APCUG)
International, platform-independent, nonprofit corporation devoted to
helping user groups throughout the world
Web: http://www.apcug.org/

ACM Special Interest Group on Computer Graphics (SIGGRAPH)
Web: http://www.siggraph.org/

Data Communications
Electronic Industries Association (EIA)
2500 Wilson Boulevard
Arlington, VA 22201
Web: http://www.eia.org
Electronic Information Group@eia.org

Fibre Channel Association
Web: http://www.Amdahl.com/ext/CARP/FCA/FCA.html

Network
Optical Storage Technology Association
Web: http://www.osta.org/

Quarter-Inch Cartridge Drive Standards, Inc.
Web: http://www.qic.org/

Software
International Association of Open Systems Professionals
Web: http://www.uniforum.org/

Video Electronics Standards Association
Web: http://www.vesa.org/

Telecommunications
Alliance for Telecommunications Industry Solutions
1200 G Street, NW, Suite 500
Washington, DC 20005
Phone: 202/628-6380
Fax: 202/393-5453

Cellular Telecommunications Industry Association (CTIA)
Web: http://www.wow-com.com

Telecommunications Reseller's Association
1155 Connecticut Ave. NW, Suite 401
Washington, DC 20036
202- 835-9898
Contact: Ernest B. Kelley

SONET Forum
Alliance for Telecommunications Industry Solutions (ATIS)
1200 G Street, NW, Suite 500
Washington, DC 20005
Phone: 202-628-6380
Fax: 202-393-5453

Telecommunications—Misc:
National Association of Regulatory Utility Commissioners
National Cable Television Institute (NCTI)
National Exchange Carrier Association
Personal Communications Industry Association
Society of Cable Telecommunication Engineers
Telecommunications Industry Association
Telecommunications Resellers Association
United States Telephone Association

PUBLICATIONS
General Computer Interest
Byte: Web: http://www.byte.com/
Datamation: Web: http://www. datamation.com/
InfoWorld: Web: http://www. infoworld.com/
Information Week: Web: http:// techweb.cmp.com/iw/625/
PC Magazine: Web: http://www. pcmag.com/

Data Communications
Data Communications: Web: http:// www.data.com/
d:comm: Web: http://www.d-comm.com/

Hardware
Tape/Disc Business: Web: http://www.kipinet.com/tdb/

PUBLICATIONS, con't.
Networking
Communications News Web: http://www.comnews.com/
Communications System Design: Web: http://www.csdmag.com/
Communications Week: Web: http://techweb.cmp.com/ cw/cwi/
Digital Age On Demand: Web: http://www.cardinal.com/digitalage/
LAN Magazine: Web: http://www. lanmag.com/
LAN Times: Web: http://www. wcmh.com/lantimes/index.html
Mid-range Computing: Web: http:// www.midrangecomputing.com/
Network Computing: Web: http:// techweb.cmp.com/nc/docs/
Open Computing: Web: http:// www.wcmh.com/oc/index.html
Plug -In Datamation: Web: http://www.datamation.com/
Sys Admin: Web: http://www. samag.com/

New Media
Interactive Age: Web: http://techweb.cmp.com/ia/iad_web_/
Interactive Week: Web: http://www. hyperstand.com/
New Media: Web: http://www. hyperstand.com/
Web Week: Web: http://www.webweek.com/

Software
Oracle Magazine: Web: http:// www.oramag.com/
Unixworld Online: Web: http:// www.wcmh.com/uworld/
Windows NT Magazine: Web: http://www.winntmag.com/

Telecommunications
Broadband Systems and Design: Web: http://www.broadbandmag.com/
Discount Long distance Digest: Web: http://www.thedigest.com/
Messaging Magazine: Web: http://www.ema.org/html/pubs/messmag.htm
Telecommunications Online: Web: http://www.telecoms-mag.com/tcs. html/
Via Satellite Online: Web: http:// www.phillips.com/ViaOnline/
Wireless Design & Development: Web: http://www.wirelessdesignmag.com/
Wireless Week Online: Web: http://www.wirelessweek.com/

OUTLINES
Internet/Intranet/Messaging
EDI, Electronic Messaging
Wide Area Networking
Bridges/Routers, ATM/Broadband, CSU/DSU, Frame Relay,
T1/T3, Modems, Telecommuting, Remote Access, Muxes
Local Area Networking (LAN)
Ethernet, FDDI, Host Access, Synchronization, Token Ring, Servers
Network Management
Help Desk, Security, Disaster Recovery
Call Handling
Call Accounting, Call Center Management, CTI, Voice, PBX/ACD
Wireless
Cellular, Wireless LANs and PBXs, Radio, Paging, Microwave,

Satellite, PCS, CDPD
Conferencing
Videoconferencing, Teleconferencing
Telephony/Services
Digital Subscriber Loop, ISDN, Carrier Services, Centrex
Equipment/Cabling/Facilities Telephones, Test
Equipment, Power/UPS, Fax, Fiber Optics

Network Connectivity
Bridges, Routers, Repeaters, Switches
Cables, Converters, Transceivers
Gateways
Hubs/Concentrators
ARCNET, ATM, Ethernet, FDDI, LocalTalk, Token Ring
Network Adapter Cards
ARCNET, ATM, Ethernet, FDDI, LocalTalk, Token Ring
Terminal Emulation
Wireless LAN
WAN Connectivity
Multiplexors
WAN Links

Network Operating Systems (NOSs)
PC Based
UNIX Based

Network Management
Inventory
License Management
Network Management Applications
Software Distribution
Systems Management

Network Applications
Electronic Mail
Conferencing
Document Management
Groupware
Scheduling
Browsers
Fax
Modem Applications

Utilities
Help Desk
Network Planning
Security
Virus Protection

OUTLINES, con't.
Network Test Equipment
Protocol Analyzers
Cable Testers

Other Networking Hardware
Power Protection (UPS Systems)
Power Line Conditioners
Network Printers
Modems

INFORMATION INFRASTRUCTURE GLOSSARY

AHG:	Ad Hoc Group
AIM:	Association for Interactive Media
ANSI:	American National Standards Institute
API:	Application Program Interface
APII:	Asia-Pacific Information Infrastructure
ASC:	Accredited Standards Committee
ASCII:	American Standard Code for Information Interchange
ASC X9:	Accredited Standards Committee X9 - Financial Services
ASC X12:	Accredited Standards Committee X12 - Electronic Data Interchange
AIIM:	Association for Information and Image Management International
ATIS:	Alliance for Telecommunications Industry Solutions
ATM:	Asynchronous transfer mode
ATM-F:	The Asynchronous Transfer Mode Forum
CITA:	Center on Information Technology Accomodation
CNRI:	The Corporation for National Research Initiatives
CSPP:	Computer Systems Policy Project
DARPA:	Defense Advanced Research Projects Agency
DAVIC:	Digital Audio Visual Council
DISA:	Data Interchange Standards Association - the secretariat for ASC X12
DISA:	Defense Information Systems Agency
EC:	European Commission
ECMA:	ECMA, formerly European Computer Manufacturer's Association
EDI:	Electronic Data Interchange
EFF:	Electronic Frontier Foundation
EIA:	Electronic Industries Association
EII:	European Information Infrastructure
EMA:	Electronic Messaging Association

EPIC:	European Programme on Information Infrastructure Co-ordination Group
EPII:	European Project on Information Infrastructure (of ETSI)
EPIISG:	European Project on Information Infrastructure Starter Group (of ETSI)
ETSI:	European Telecommunications Standards Institute
EU:	European Union
EWOS:	European Workshop for Open Systems
FCC:	Federal Communications Commission
G7:	Group of Seven (Canada, France, Germany, Italy, Japan, UK, and USA)
GII:	Global Information Infrastructure
GIIC:	Global Information Infrastructure Commission
GIP:	Global Inventory Project
GIS:	Global Information Society; Geographic Information Systems
HDTV:	High Definition Television
HFES:	Human Factors and Ergonomics Society
HLSG:	European High Level Strategy Group
ICT:	Information and Communication Technologies
ICTSB:	Information and Communications Technology Standards Board (Europe)
IEC:	International Electrotechnical Commission
IEEE:	The Institute of Electrical and Electronics Engineers, Inc.
IETF:	Internet Engineering Task Force
IIP:	The Information Infrastructure Project, Harvard University
IISP:	Information Infrastructure Standards Panel
IITF:	Information Infrastructure Task Force
IMA:	Interactive Multimedia Association
IPR:	Intellectual Property Right
IS:	Information System
ISDN:	Integrated Services Digital Network
ISO:	International Organization for Standardization; International Standards Organization
ISOC:	Internet Society
ISPO:	Information Society Project Office - European Commission
IT:	Information Technology
ITI:	Information Technology Industry Council

Information Infrastructure Glossary, con't.

ITS:	Intelligent Transportation System
ITTF:	Information Technology Task Force (of ISO/IEC)
ITU:	International Telecommunications Union
ITU-R:	International Telecommunications Union - Radiocommunication Sector
ITU-T:	International Telecommunications Union - Telecommunication Standardization Sector
JEF:	Japan Economic Foundation
JEIDA:	Japan Electronics Industry Development Association
JRG-GII:	Joint Rapporteurs Group - GII (of ITU-T)
JTC1:	Joint Technical Committee 1 - Information Technology (of ISO/IEC)
KIITF:	Korea Information Infrastructure Task Force
MITI:	Ministry of International Trade and Industry (Japan)
MPEG:	Motion Pictures Expert Group
MPT:	Ministry of Posts and Telecommunications (Japan)
MRI:	Medical Records Institute
NAB:	National Association of Broadcasters
NCITS:	National Committee for Information Technology Standardization (formerly ASC X3 - Information Technology)
NCB:	National Computer Board (Singapore)
NCTA:	National Cable Television Association
NEMA:	National Electrical Manufacturers Association
NII:	National Information Infrastructure
NIIAC:	National Information Infrastructure Advisory Council (USA)
NIIIP:	National Industrial Information Infrastructure Protocols Consortium
NIIT:	National Information Infrastructure Testbed
NISO:	National Information Standards Organization
NIST:	National Institute of Standards & Technology (USA)
NITF:	National Information Technology Forum (South Africa)
NIUF:	North American ISDN Users Forum
NSA:	National Security Agency (USA)
NTIA:	National Telecommunications and Information Administration (USA)
NRIC:	Network Reliability and Interoperability Council
OAM&P:	Operations, Administration, Maintenance and Provisioning
OII:	The Open Information Interchange (OII) Initiative
OMG:	Object Management Group

PAS:	Publicly Available Specification
PASC:	Portable Application Standards Committee (of IEEE)
POTS:	"Plain Old" Telephone Services
QOS:	Quality of Service
SC:	Subcommittee
SCTE:	Society of Telecommunications Engineers, Inc.
SDO:	Standards Development Organization
SG:	Study Group
SMPTE:	Society of Motion Picture & Television Engineers
SRC6:	Sixth Strategic Review Committee (of ETSI)
SSDO:	Standards and Specifications Development Organizations
SWG-GII:	Special Working Group - GII (of ISO/IEC JTC1)
T1:	Committee T1 Telecommunications
TC:	Technical Committee
TIA:	Telecommunications Industry Association
TSACC:	Telecommunications Standards Advisory Council of Canada
TTC:	Telecommunications Technology Committee (of Japan)
USPTO:	United States Patent and Trademark Office
W3C:	World Wide Web Consortium
W3O:	World Wide Web Organization
WGIH:	Working Group on Information Highway (of TSACC)
X/Open:	X/Open Company Ltd.
XIWT:	Cross Industry Working Team

APPENDIX B
UNITED STATES GOVERNMENT INFORMATION
TECHNOLOGY AGENCIES

Center on Information Technology Accommodation (CITA):
Member of the National Information Infrastructure (NII) Task Force
charged with assuring that the NII will be accessible to disabled users.
Web: http://www.gsa.gov/coca/cocamain.htm

CITA:
See Center on Information Technology Accommodation.

**Committee on Applications and Technology/Health Information
Applications Working Group:**
National Information Infrastructure Task Force (NIITF) workgroup in
charge of coordinating the development of the NII as it affects the field
of health care.
Web: http://nii.nist.gov/cat/hia/hia.html

**Committee on Applications and Technology/Technology Policy
Working Group:**
National Information Infrastructure Task Force (NIITF) work group in
charge of addressing interoperability issues raised by the new telecom-
munications and information services.
Web: http://nii.nist.gov/cat/tp/tp.html

DARPA:
See Defense Advanced Research Projects Agency.

Defense Advanced Research Projects Agency (DARPA):
Research and development arm of the Department of Defense (DoD).
Web: http://www.arpa.mil/

Defense Information Systems Agency (DISA):
Agency responsible for information technology as it affects the
Department of Defense (DoD).
Web: http://www.disa.mil/

DISA:
See Defense Information Systems Agency.

FCC:
See U.S. Federal Communications Commission.

GITS:
See Government Information Technology Services Working Group.

Government Information Technology Services Working Group (GITS):
Group in charge of improving the way information technology is used
in federal agencies.
Web: http://nii.nist.gov/cat/gits/gits.html

HPCC:
See National Coordinating Office for High Performance Computing and Communications.

IITF:
See President's Information Infrastructure Task Force.

Institute for Telecommunication Sciences (ITS):
The research and engineering branch of the National Telecommunications and Information Administration (NTIA).
Web: http://www.its.bldrdoc.gov/its.html

ITS:
See Institute for Telecommunication Sciences.

National Coordinating Office for High Performance Computing and Communications (HPCC):
National organization conducting research into high-speed networks.
Web: http://www.hpcc.gov/

National Exchange Carrier Association (NECA):
Administrative organization working under the direction of the Federal Communications Commission (FCC) that is concerned with telecommunications access charges, rates and tariffs.
Web: http://www.neca.org/

National Industrial Information Infrastructure Protocols Consortium (NIIIP):
Develops open industry software protocols to assure interoperability among a variety of systems.
Web: http://www.niiip.org/

National Information Infrastructure Task Force (NIITF), Committee on Applications and Technology:
Committee overseeing the government's efforts to promote the use of information technology in the public and private sector.
Web: http://nii.nist.gov/cat/cat.html

National Information Infrastructure Task Force (NIITF), Information Policy Committee:
Executive branch-level policy group on information technology.
Web: http://www.iitf.nist.gov/ipc/ipc.html

National Information Infrastructure Task Force (NIITF), Security Issues Forum:
Executive branch-level group in charge of coordinating policies regarding information security across the several branches of the Information Infrastructure Task Force (IITF).
Web: http://www.iitf.nist.gov/sif/sif.html

National Information Infrastructure Task Force (NIITF), Telecommunications Policy Committee:
Executive branch-level telecommunications policy group.
Web: http://www.iitf.nist.gov/tpc/tpc.html

National Science and Technology Council (NTSC):
President's council in charge of coordinating science, space and technology policies across the federal government.
Web: http://www.whitehouse.gov/wh/eop/ostp/nstc/html/nstc_home.html

National Technology Transfer Center (NTTC):
Government organization overseeing the transfer of federally funded research into practical and commercial technology.
Web: http://iridium.nttc.edu/

National Telecommunications and Information Administration (NTIA):
Primary Executive Branch agency responsible for domestic and international telecommunications and information technology issues as they affect the needs of the citizen and enhance the competitiveness of U.S. industry. It sponsors the National Information Infrastructure (NII), and the Institute for Telecommunication Sciences (ITS).
Web: http://www.ntia.doc.gov/

NECA:
See National Exchange Carrier Association.

NIIIP:
See National Industrial Information Infrastructure Protocols Consortium.

NIITF:
See National Information Infrastructure Task Force.

NTIA:
See National Telecommunications and Information Administration.

NTSC:
See National Science and Technology Council.

NTTC:
See National Technology Transfer Center.

Office of Spectrum Management (OSM):
NTIA office responsible for managing the Federal Government's use of the radio frequency spectrum.
Web: http://www.ntia.doc.gov/osmhome/osmhome.html

OSM:
See Office of Spectrum Management.

OSTP:
See White House Office of Science and Technology Policy.

Office of Telecommunications and Information Applications (OTIA):
Agency in charge of assisting state and local governments, and other organizations that provide public services (e.g., schools, health care providers, libraries), to use telecommunications and information technology.
Web: http://www.ntia.doc.gov/otiahome/otiahome.html

Office of Telecommunications, U.S. Department of Commerce (DOC):
DOC agency promoting the growth and competitiveness of the U.S.
telecommunications industry.
Web: http://www.ita.doc.gov/industry/tai/telecom/telecom.html

OTIA:
See Office of Telecommunications and Information Applications.

President's Information Infrastructure Task Force (IITF):
A collection of agencies acting as the primary policy body in charge of
overseeing and coordinating the creation of a comprehensive information infrastructure in the United States.
Web: http://iitf.doc.gov/

SPSG:
See System Performance Standards Group.

System Performance Standards Group (SPSG):
Government organization measuring performance in audio, video, data,
and multimedia telecommunications systems and services.
Web: http://ntia.its.bldrdoc.gov/n3/index.htm

U.S. Federal Communication Commission (FCC):
High-level organization managing interstate and international commu-
nications and telecommunications policy.
Web: http://www.fcc.gov/

White House Office of Science and Technology Policy (OSTP):
Presidential advisory group.
Web: http://www.whitehouse.gov/ostp.html

APPENDIX C
INTERNATIONAL TELECOMMUNICATION CARRIERS

Africa-Africa ONE (Africa Optical NEtwork)
http://www.att.com/africaone/

Argentina-Telecom Argentina http://www.telecom.com.ar/

Argentina-Telefonica de Argentina http://www.telefonica.com.ar/

Argentina-Telintar S.A. http://www.telintar.com.ar/

Australia-Telstra Corporation http://www.telstra.com.au/

Bahrain-Batelco http://wwww.batelco.com.bh/

Belgium-Belgacom http://www.belgacom.be/

Brazil-Embratel http://www.embratel.net.br/

Brazil-Telebras (Telecomuniçaõıes Brasileiras S. A.)
http://www.sede.telebras.gov.br/

Canada-Bell Canada http://www.bell.ca/

Canada-Newtel Communications (New Brunswick) http://www.newtel.com/

Canada-Sprint Canada http://www.sprintcanada.com/

Canada-Stentor http://www.stentor.ca/

Canada-TELUS Corporation http://www.telus.com/

Canada-Teleglobe Canada http://www.teleglobe.ca/

Canada-Telesat Canada http://www.telesat.ca/

Canada-Telus Corporation http://www.telus.com/

Canada-Whistler Telephone Company Ltd. http://www.whistler.net/

Chile-Telefònica del Sur S.A. http://www.telsur.cl/

China-SinoAmerican Telecom http://www.sinoamtel.com/

China-ShangHai Post & Telecommunication Administration
http://www.sta.net.cn/

Colombia-Telecom Colombia http://www.telecom.net.co/

Czech Republic-SPT Telecom a.s. http://www.spt.cz/

Denmark-Tele Danmark http://www.teledanmark.dk/

Estonia-Estonian Telecom http://www.telecom.ee/

Finland-Helsinki Telephone Company http://www.hpy.fi/

Finland-OPOY (Oulun Puhelin Oy) http://www.opoy.fi/

Finland-PH Net http://www.php.fi/

Finland-Tampere Telephone Company http://www.tpo.fi/

Finland-Telecom Finland http://www.inet.fi/

Finland-Turku Telephone Company http://www.ttl.fi/

France-France Télécom http://www.francetelecom.fr/

Germany-Deutsche Telekom AG http://www.dtag.de/

Greece-OTE http://www.gsc.net/

Greece-Telestet http://www.telestet.gr/

Hongkong-Hongkong Telecom http://www.hkt.net/

Hungary-DataNet Tàvközlési Kft. http://www.datanet.hu/

Hungary-MATAV (Hungarian Telecommunication Company) http://www.matav.hu/

Iceland-Post and Telecom reg http://www.simi.is/

Indonesia-Indosat http://www.indosat.net.id/

Indonesia-Telkom Indonesia (Indonesia Telecom Company) ????

International-Cable & Wireless plc (Asia, Caribbean, North America, Europe) http://www.cxplc.com/

International-Concert (MCI and British Telecom) http://www.concert.com/

International-Global One (France Telecom, Deutsche Telekom, Sprint) http://www.global-one.com/

International-SITA (Societe Internationale de Telecommunications Aeronautiques) http://www.sita.int/sita/

International-WorldPartners (AT&T, KDD of Japan, Singapore Telecom) http://www.worldpartners.com/

Ireland-Telecom Eireann http://www.telecom.ie/

Israel-Bezeq http://www.bezeq.co.il/

Italy-Telecom Italia http://www.telecomitalia.interbusiness.it/

Japan-IDC (International Digital Communications) http://www.idc.co.jp/

Japan-ITJ (International Telecoms Japan) http://www.itj.com/

Japan-KDD (Kokusai Denshin Denwa Co., Ltd.) http://www.kdd.co.jp/

Japan-Nippon Telegraph and Telephone Corporation (NTT) http://www.ntt.co.jp/

Korea-Korea Telecom http://ktweb.kotel.co.kr/

Luxemburg-P&T Luxembourg http://www.pt.lu/

Malaysia-Telekom Malaysia http://www.telekom.com.my/

Mexico-Alestra http://www.alestra.com.mx/

Mexico-Avantel http://www.avantel.com.mx/

Mexico-France Telecom Mexico http://www.francetelecom.com.mx/

Mexico-Telmex (Teléfonos de México S.A.) http://www.telmex.com.mx/

Netherlands-EnerTel http://www.enertel.nl/

Netherlands-PTT Telecom http://www.ptt-telecom.nl/

Netherlands-Telfort http://www.telfort.com/

New Zealand-BellSouth New Zealand http://www.bellsouth.co.nz/

New Zealand-Clear Communications Ltd. http://www.clear.co.nz/

New Zealand-Telecom New Zealand http://www.telecom.co.nz/

Norway-Telenor International http://www.telenor.no/

Peru-Telefònica del Perù http://www.unired.net.pe/

Phillipines-Philippine Long Distance Telephone Company http://www.pldt.com.ph/

Poland-Netia Telekom S.A. http://www.netia.pl/

Poland-Telecom Poland http://www.bielsko.tpsa.pl/

Portugal-Portugal Telecom http://www.telecom.pt/

Portugal-Telepac http://www.telepac.pt/

Romania-Radiotel http://www.radiotel.ro/

Russia-Belcom-Russian PTT http://www.belcom.net/

Russia- Sprint Russia http://www.rosprint.ru/

Russia-Rostelecom http://rostelecom.msu.ru/

Russia-Sovam Teleport http://www.sovam.com/

Russia-VimpelCom Group http://www.vimpelcom.ru/

Singapore Telecom http://www.singtel.com/

South Africa-Telkom SA Ltd http://www.telkom.co.za/

South Korea-Korea Mobile Telecom http://www.kmt.co.kr/

Spain-Airtel http://www.airtel.es/

Spain-Telefonica de Espana http://www.telefonica.es/

Sri Lanka-Sri Lanka Telecom Ltd. http://www.slt.lk/index.html

Sweden-Tele2 http://www.tele2.se/

Sweden-Telia AB http://www.west.telia.se/

Switzerland-PlusNet http://www.plusnet.ch/

Switzerland-Swiss Telecom PTT http://www.vptt.ch/

Thailand- TOT (Telephone Organization of Thailand)
http://www.tot.or.th/

Thailand-CAT (Communications Authority of Thailand)
http://www.cat.or.th/

UK-BT (British Telecom) http://www.bt.com/

UK-British Sky Broadcasting http://www.sky.co.uk/

UK-Bell Cablemedia http://www.netcom.co.uk/bcm/

UK-CableTel UK http://www.cabletel.co.uk/

UK-Cambridge Cable Group of Companies http://www.camcable.co.uk/

UK-Cellnet http://http://cellnet.chc.co.uk/

UK-Energis http://www.energis.co.uk/

UK-Mercury Communications http://www.mercury.co.uk/

UK-NYNEX Cable http://www.nynex.co.uk/

UK-Talkland http://www.talkland.co.uk/

UK-Telewest Communications http://www.telewest.co.uk/

UK-Vodafone Group http://www.vodafone.co.uk/

USA-AT&T
http://www.att.com/

USA-AirData McCaw Cellular Communications

USA-AirTouch Communications

USA-Aliant Communications http://www.aliant.com/

USA-AllCom http://www.allcom.com/

USA-Alltel http://www.alltel.com/

USA-Americatel Corp. http://www.americatel.net/

USA-Ameritech http://www.ameritech.com/

USA-Bell Atlantic http://www.bell-atl.com/

USA-BellSouth http://www.bellsouth.com/

USA-Bellcore http://www.bellcore.com/

USA-CGX Telcom http://www.cgxtelecom.com/

USA-Cellular One http://www.cellularone.com/

USA-ECI (Excel Communications, Inc.) http://www.exceltel.com/

USA-GTE Corporation http://www.exceltel.com/

USA-Infonet http://www.infonet.com/

USA-LCI International, Inc. http://www.lci.com/

USA-LDDS WorldCom http://www.wcom.com/

USA-MCI, Inc. http://www.mci.com/

USA-NYNE

APPENDIX D
INTERNATIONAL DATA COMMUNICATIONS AND
NETWORK HARDWARE COMPANIES

3Com Corporation (USA)
Global data networking products and services.
Corporate Headquarters:
5400 Bayfront Plaza
Santa Clara, CA 95052-8145
USA
Phone: 1-408-764-5000 or 1-800-NET-3COM, Fax: 1-408-764-5001
Web: http://www.3com.com/

AT&T (USA)
Global telecommunications solutions, especially long distance, wireless,
DirectTV home entertainment, Submarine systems, and Universal card
services.
Corporate Headquarters:
32 Avenue of the Americas
New York, NY 10013-2412
USA
Phone: 1-212-387-5400
Web: http://www.att.com/

Adaptec, Inc. (USA)
Global data networking solutions.
Corporate Headquarters:
691 South Milpitas Boulevard
Milpitas, CA 95035
USA
Phone: 1-408-945-8600, Fax: 1-408-262-2533
Web: http://www.adaptec.com/

Alcatel N.V. (France)
Global systems integration in the telecommunications field, especially
Cabling, Satellites, and Submarine cable communications systems.
Corporate Headquarters:
33 Rue Emeriau 75015
Paris, France
Phone: +33 1 40585135, Fax: +33 1 40585912
Web: http://www.alcatel.com/

Apple Computer, Inc. (USA)
Macintosh computers and networking solutions.
Corporate Headquarters:
1 Infinite Loop
Cupertino, CA 95014-2084
USA
Phone: 1-408-996-1010, Fax: 1-408-996-0275 or 1-800-776-2333
Web: http://www.apple.com/

Ascom Systec Ltd. (Switzerland)
Global data networking solutions with specialization in
Telecommunications, Enterprise networks, and Service automation
equipment.
Corporate Headquarters:
Gewerbepark
5506 Mägenwil
Switzerland
Phone: ++41 62 889 52 11, Fax: ++41 62 889 59 90
Web: http://www.ascom.ch/

BICC Group (UK)
Global engineering and telecommunications infrastructure solutions,
especially Cabling and Multimedia networking.
Corporate Headquarters:
Devonshire House
Mayfair Place
London W1X 6AQ
UK
Phone: 44 (0) 171 629 6622, Fax: 44 (0) 171 409 0070
Web: http://www.hhdc.bicc.com/

BT (British Telecommunications) (UK)
Global telecommunications solutions.
Corporate Headquarters:
81, Newgate Street
London EC1A 7A5
United Kingdom
Phone: +44 171 3565000, Fax: +44 171 3565520
Web: http://www.bt.co.uk/

Bay Networks, Inc. (USA)
Open standards-based internetworking solutions; especially switching,
access, Internet Protocol (IP) services, and network management.
Corporate Headquarters:
4401 Great America Parkway
Santa Clara, CA 95052
USA
Phone: 1-408-988-2400, Fax: 1-408-988-5525
Web: http://www.baynetworks.com/

Bell Atlantic Corp.
Advanced telecommunications solutions in wireless, Integrated
Standard Digital Network (ISDN), and interactive multimedia.
Corporate Headquarters:
1717 Arch Street
Philadelphia, PA 19103
USA
Phone: 1-215-963-6000
Web: http://www.bell-atl.com/

Bosch Telecom GmbH (Germany)
Optical networking, Cable TV (CATV) transmission and distribution,
Integrated Standard Digital Network (ISDN) access, and DS3 protection
switching products and services.
Corporate Headquarters:
KleyerstraBe 94
Hessen, Frankfurt 60326
Germany
Phone: +49 69 7505 4117, Fax: +49 69 7505 7569
Web: http://193.175.164.66/careernet/bosch-telecom/

Bull France (France)
Enterprise infrastructure products and services.
Direction Générale
68, route de Versailles
BP 434, 78434 Louveciennes
France
Phone: 01 39 66 60 60, Fax: 01 39 66 60 62
Web: http://www.bull.com/

CWI Cable And Wireless Plc (UK)
Mobile communications devices.
Corporate Headquarters:
124 Theobalds Road
London, WC1X 8RX
United Kingdom
Phone: +44 171 315 4000, Fax: +44 171 315 5000
Web: http://www.cwi.net/

Cabletron Systems (USA)
Local Area Network/Wide Area Network (LAN/WAN) Asynchronous
Transfer Mode (ATM) switching solutions and Virtual Local Area
Networks (VLANs).
Corporate Headquarters:
35 Industrial Way
Rochester, NH 03866
USA
Phone: 1-603-332-9400
Web: http://www.cabletron.com/

Cisco Systems, Inc. (USA)
Local Area Network/Wide Area Network (LAN/WAN) switches, Routers, and Asynchronous Transfer Mode (ATM) devices.
Corporate Headquarters:
170 West Tasman Drive
San Jose, CA 95134-1706
USA
Phone: 1-408-526-4000 or 1-800-553-6387, Fax: 1-408-526-4100
e-mail: cs-rep@cisco.com
Web: http://www.cisco.com/

Compaq Computer Corporation (USA)
Servers and microcomputer equipment.
Corporate Headquarters:
20555 SH 249
Houston, TX 77070-2698
USA
Phone: 1-281-370-0670, Fax: 1-281-514-1740
e-mail: http://www.compaq.com/support/contacting/index.html
Web: http://www.compaq.com/

Corning Incorporated (USA)
Optical fiber and photonics technology products, especially High-Definition TV (HDTV), and Flat panel displays.
Corporate Headquarters:
717 5th Ave New York, NY 10022-8101
USA
Phone: 1-212-752-1100
Web: http://www.corning.com/

Data General Corporation (USA)
Network servers.
Corporate Headquarters:
4400 Computer Drive
Westboro, MA 01580
USA
Phone: 1-508-898-7600, Fax: 1-508-366-1319
Web: http://www.dg.com/

Digital Equipment Corporation (USA)
Servers, Workstations, Mid-range systems, and Integrated switching solutions.
Corporate Headquarters:
146 Main Street
Maynard, MA 01754
USA
Phone: 1-508-493 5111, Fax: 1-508-493-8780
e-mail Directory: http://www.digital.com/info/email.html
Web: http://www.digital.com/

Dynatech Corporation (USA)
Global communications equipment company.
Corporate Headquarters:
3 New England Executive Park
Burlington, MA 01803
USA
Phone: 1-617-272-6100
e-mail: corpcommunications@dytc.com
Web: http://www.dynatech.com/

Elonex plc (UK)
Microcomputer equipment.
Corporate Headquarters:
2 Apsley Way
London
NW2 7LF
United Kingdom
Phone: 0181 452 4444, Fax: 0181 452 6422
Web: http://www.elonex.co.uk/

Ericsson (Sweden)
Global data networking solutions, especially Mobile systems.
Corporate Headquarters:
Telefonaktiebolaget LM Ericsson
Telefonplan
S-126 25 Stockholm
Sweden
Phone: 46 8 719 00 00
Web: http://www.ericsson.se/

Fujitsu Japan
Global data networking solutions.
Corporate Headquarters:
6-1 Marunouchi, 1-chome
Chiyoda-ku, Tokyo
Japan
Phone: 044 866 1716, Fax: 044 861 7875
Web: http://www.fujitsu.com/

GTE Corporation (USA)
Global data networking solutions.
Corporate Headquarters:
One Stamford Forum
Stamford, CT 06904
USA
Phone: 1-203-965-2000
Web: http://www.gte.com/

General Instrument (USA)
Analog and digital cable TV systems, Satellite systems, and High-speed
data systems.
Corporate Headquarters:
P.O. Box 879
3642 Hwy. 70 East
Claremont, NC 28610
USA
Phone: 1-800-982-1708, Fax: 1-704-459-5099
Web: http://www.gi.com/

Groupe Bull (France)
Servers, Infrastructure software, and Enterprise network equipment.
Regional Headquarters:
300 Concord Rd
Billerica, MA 01821-4199
USA
Phone: 1-508-294-6000
Fax: 1-508-294-5164
Web: http://www.bull.com/

Hewlett-Packard Company (USA)
Switching hardware, Print servers, and Multi-vendor networking solutions.
Corporate Headquarters:
3000 Hanover Street
Palo Alto, California 94304
USA
Phone: 1-415-857-1501
Web: http://www.hp.com/

Hitachi Telecom Technologies, Ltd. (Japan)
Asynchronous Transfer Mode (ATM) access and switch modules,
Synchronous Optical NETwork (SONET) transmission, Private Branch
eXchange (PBX), and Video conferencing equipment.
Corporate Headquarters::
6 Kanda-Surugadai 4-chome
Chiyoda-ku, Tokyo 101-10
Japan
Phone: +81 03 3258 1111, Fax: +81 03 3258 5497
Web: http://www.hitachi.co.jp/index.html

IBM Corporation
Networking and internetworking solutions.
Corporate Headquarters:
Old Orchard Road
Armonk, NY 10504
Phone: 1-914-765-7777
E-mail: askibm@info.ibm.com
Web: http://www.ibm.com/

Intel (USA)
Semiconductors and communications products.
Corporate Headquarters:
2200 Mission College Blvd.
Santa Clara, CA 95052-8119
USA
Phone: 1-408-987-8080, Fax: 1-408-765-1821
Web: http://www.intel.com/

Italtel (Italy)
Data communications solutions in wide band access systems, mobile
radio, optical networks, and multimedia.
Via A. di Tocqueville 13
20154 Milan
Italy
Phone: ++39.2 4388.1
Web: http://www.italtel.it/

JRC (Japan Radio Co. Ltd.) (Japan)
Wireless telecommunications equipment with a specialty in marine
systems.
Corporate Headquarters:
Akasaka Twin Tower (Main)
17-22, Akasaka 2-chome
Minato-ku, Tokyo
Japan
Phone: +81-3 3584 8836
Web: http://www.jrc.co.jp/

Lexmark International, Inc. (USA)
IBM-affiliated manufacturer of network printing solutions.
Corporate Headquarters:
740 New Circle Road, NW
Lexington, Kentucky 40511
USA
Phone: 1-606-232-7541, Fax: 1-606-232-2403
Web: http://www.lexmark.com/

Lockheed Martin Corporation (USA)
High technology information systems, especially air and space commu-
nications, and secure systems.
Corporate Headquarters:
6801 Rockledge Drive
Bethesda, Maryland 20817
USA
Phone: 1-301-897-6000, Fax: 1-301-897-6252
Web: http://www.lmco.com/

Lucent Technologies
Advanced telecommunications equipment.
Corporate Headquarters:
600 Mountain Avenue
Murray Hill, New Jersey 07974
USA
Phone: 1-888-458-2368
Web: http://www.lucent.com/

Madge Networks (UK)
Asynchronous Transfer Mode (ATM) switching products.
Corporate Headquarters:
Knaves Beech Business Park
High Wycombe
Bucks HP10 9QZ
United Kingdom
Phone: +44 1628 858000, Fax: +44 1628 858011
Web: http://www.madge.com/

Matsushita Electric Industrial Co., Ltd. (Japan)
Cellular phones, Fax machines, CD-ROMs, Barcoders, and Digital video
devices.
Corporate Headquarters:
1-2 Shiba-Koen 1 chome
Minato-ku
Tokyo 105
Japan
Phone: +81 3 5460 2881, Fax: +81 3 5460 2880
Web: http://www.panasonic.co.jp/

Mitsubishi Corporation (Japan)
Electronic commerce, Multimedia, Intelligent computers,
Semiconductors, Video display, and satellite communications products.
Corporate Headquarters:
6-3, Marunouchi 2-chome
Chiyoda-ku, Tokyo 100-86
Japan
Phone: +81 3 3210 2121, Fax: +81 3 3210 9350
Web: http://www.mitsubishi.co.jp/

Motorola Inc. (USA)
Cellular and mobile networks, Satellite communications systems,
Microcomputers, Multimedia, Messaging, and Semiconductor products.
Corporate Headquarters:
1303 East Algonquin Road
Schaumburg, IL 60196 USA
USA
Phone: 1-847-576-5000
Web: http://www.mot.com/

NEC Corporation (Japan)
Fiber optic and carrier products, Satellite products, and Microwave
radios communications products.
Corporate Headquarters:
7-1, Shiba 5-chome
Minato-ku, Tokyo 108-01
Japan
Phone: +81 3 34541111 / 3798 6595, Fax: +81 3 3798 1510 / 1519
Web: http://www.nec.com/

Newbridge Networks Corporation (Canada)
Virtual Local Area Networks (VLANs), Asynchronous Transfer Mode (ATM)
switching products, Frame relays, and Broadband technology products.
Corporate Headquarters:
600 March Road
Kanata, Ontario
Canada K2K 2E6
Phone: 613 591 3600, Fax: 1 613 591 3680
Web: http://www.newbridge.com/

Nippon Telegraph and Telephone Corp. (Japan)
Telephone and communications equipment.
Regional Headquarters:
800 El Camino Real West, Suite 103
Mountain View, CA 94040
USA
Phone: 1-415-940-1414, Fax: 1-415-940-1375
http://www.nttca.com/

Nokia Group (Finland)
Communications devices, Cellular networks, Satellite receivers,
Multimedia terminals, and Telecommunications switching and trans-
mission equipment.
Nokia Corporate Communications
Keilalahdentie 4, FIN-02150 Espoo
P.O. Box 226, FIN-00045 Nokia Group
Finland
Phone: +358 9 180 71, Fax: +358 9 656 388
Web: http://www.nokia.com/

Nortel Northern Telecom Limited (Canada)
Enterprise networks, Wireless communications networks, and Carrier
networks equipment.
Corporate Headquarters:
8200 Dixie Road
Suite 100
Brampton, Ontario
L6T 5P6 Canada
Phone: 1 905 863 0000
Web: http://www.nortel.com/

Octel Communications Corporation (USA)
Networked messaging products using fax and voice transmission technology.
Corporate Headquarters:
1001 Murphy Ranch Road
Milpitas, CA 95035
USA
Phone: 1-408-324-2000
Web: http://www.octelcom/

The Olivetti Group (Italy)
Telecommunications and information technology products, especially satellite, wireless, and multimedia communications equipment.
Corporate Headquarters:
Ing. C. Olivetti & C. S.p.A.
77 Via Jervis
10015 Ivrea (TO), Italy
Phone: +39 125 5200
Web: http://www.olivetti.com/

Philips International B.V. (Netherlands)
Interactive media, Wireless communications, Satellite broadcasting, Laser-optics, Web TV, and Semiconductors.
Building EEC-200
P.O. Box 80020
5600 PB Eindhoven
The Netherlands
Phone: +31 40 27 91111
Web: http://www.philips.com/

Racal Electronics Plc (UK)
Global data communications solutions, Defense electronics, and Industrial services.
Corporate Headquarters:
Western Road
Bracknell, Berkshire
RG12 1RG
United Kingdom
Phone: +44 1344 481222, Fax: +44 1344 54119
Web: http://www.racal.com/

Rockwell International Corporation (USA)
Communications semiconductors, Switching systems, Global positioning systems, and Wireless data technology products.
Corporate Headquarters:
2201 Seal Beach Boulevard
Seal Beach, CA 90740-8250
USA
Phone: 1-310-797-3311, Fax: 1-310-797-5828
Web: http://www.rockwell.com/

Sagem Sat Networks and Telecommunications (France)
Integrated Standard Digital Network (ISDN) telecommunications products.
SAT Division Réseaux et Télécommunications
11 rue Watt, B.P. 370
75626 PARIS Cedex 13
France
Phone: +33 1 55 75 75 75, Fax: +33 1 55 75 33 18
Web: http://www.atlantis.sagem.com/

Samsung Electronics Co., Ltd.(Korea)
Multimedia, Telecommunications, and Semiconductor products along
with Asynchronous Transfer Mode (ATM) switches, Fiber optic transmitters, CDMA switching systems, and Internet TV.
San 14, NongSeo-ri
Kiheung-eup, YongIn-gun
Kyungki-Do
South Korea
Phone: +82 331 280 9240, Fax: +82 331 280 9208
Web: http://www.sec.samsung.co.kr/index.html

Scientific Atlanta (USA)
Broadband networks, Interactive cable networks, and Satellite networks.
Corporate Headquarters:
One Technology Parkway
Norcross, GA 30092
USA
Phone: 1-404-903-4000
Web: http://www.sa.com/

Siemens Nixdorf Information Systems (Germany)
Global data networking solutions.
Corporate Headquarters:
Otto-Hahn-Ring 6
D-81730 Munich
Germany
Phone: +49 89 636 01, Fax: +49 89 636 52
Web: http://www.sni.de/public/sni.htm

Silicon Graphics, Inc. (USA)
High performance servers, Workstations, and Microprocessors.
Corporate Headquarters:
2011 N. Shoreline Blvd.
Mountain View, CA 94043
USA
Phone: 1-800-800-7441
Web: http://www.sgi.com/

Sony Electronics Inc. (Japan)
Audio-visual electronics, Multimedia computers, and Semiconductors.
Regional Headquarters:
3300 Zanker Rd.
San Jose, CA 95134
USA
Phone: 1-408-432-1600, Fax: 1-408-943-0740
Web: http://www.sony.com/

Sun Microsystems, Inc.(USA)
Enterprise servers, Java development, and Solaris Operating environment.
Corporate Headquarters:
2550 Garcia Ave.
Mountain View, CA 94043-1100
USA
Phone: 1-415-336-5337, Fax: 1-415-969-9131
e-mail: info@sun.com
Web: http://www.sun.com/

Texas Instruments (USA)
Digital signal processors, Semiconductors, Calculators, and Digital light processing equipment.
Corporate Headquarters:
13510 North Central Expressway
Dallas, TX 75265
USA
Phone: 1-214-995-2011, Fax: 1-214-995-4360
Web: http://www.ti.com/

Thomson-CSF/Division R G S (France)
Communications networks and equipment, Semiconductors, and Aerospace and avionics equipment.
66, rue du Fosse Blanc
BP 156
F-92231 Gennevilliers Cedex
France
Phone: +33 1 46 132000, Fax: +33 1 46 132163
Web: http://tccweb.thomson-csf.fr/

Toshiba America, Inc. (Japan)
Portable computers and communications devices.
Corporate Headquarters:
1251 Avenue of the Americas, 41st Floor
New York, NY 10020
USA
Phone: 1-212-596-0600, Fax: 1-212-593-3875
Web: http://www.toshiba.com/

US Robotics (USA)
Modems and other communications devices.
Corporate Headquarters:
8100 N. McCormick Blvd.
Skokie, IL 60076-2999
USA
Phone: 1-847-982-5030, Fax: 1-847-933-5800
Web: http://www.usr.com/

VideoLogic Limited (UK)
Advanced solutions for multimedia graphics.
Corporate Headquarters:
Home Park Estate
Kings Langley, Hertfordshire WD4 8LZ
United Kingdom
Phone: +44 1923 260511, Fax: +44 1923 268969
Web: http:/www.videologic.com/

Vodafone Group plc.(UK)
Mobile communications products.
Corporate Headquarters:
The Courtyard
2-4 London Road
Newbury, Berkshire, RG14 1JX
United Kingdom
Web: http://www.vodafone.co.uk/

APPENDIX E
INTERNATIONAL DATA COMMUNICATIONS AND
NETWORK SOFTWARE COMPANIES

Alcatel Data Networks
Network management software.
32, avenue Kléber
92707 Colombes
France
Phone: +33-1-46-52-10-10
Web: http://www.alcatel.com/

American Management Systems, Inc.
Telecommunications network management software.
4050 Legato Road
Fairfax, VA 22033
USA
Phone: 1-703-267-8000, Fax: 1-703-267-5111
Web: http://www.amsinc.com/

Apple Computer Inc.
Macintosh networking software.
1 Infinite Loop
Cupertino, CA 95014-2084
USA
Phone: 1-408-996-1010 or 1-800-776-2333
Fax: 1-408-996-0275
Web: http://www.apple.com/

Banyan Systems Inc.
Enterprise networking software.
120 Flanders Road
P.O. Box 5013
Westboro, MA 01581
USA
Phone: 1-508-898-1000 or 1-800-222-6926
Fax: 1-508-898-1755
Web: http://www.banyan.com/

Bellcore
Telecommunications network management software.
8 Corporate Place
Piscataway, NJ 08854-4156
USA
Phone: 1-908-699-2000
Fax: 1-908-336-2559
Web: http://www.bellcore.com/

Boston Technology, Inc.
Network-based messaging software.
100 Quannapowitt Parkway
Wakefield, MA 01880
USA
Phone: 1-617-246-9000, Fax: 1-617-246-4510
Web: http://www.bostontechnology.com/

CheckPoint Software Technologies, Ltd.
Network security software.
3A Jabotinsky St. 24th Floor
Ramat Gan, 52520
Israel
Phone: +972 3 613 1833, Fax: +972 3 575 9256
e-mail: info@checkpoint.com
Web: http://www.checkpoint.com/

Cincinnati Bell Information Systems, Inc.
Billing software for the communications industry.
600 Vine Street
Cincinnati, OH 45202
USA
Phone: 1-513-784-5900, Fax: 1-513-241-4826
Web: http://www.cbis.com/

Computer Associates International, Inc.
Database tools and development tools.
One Computer Associates Plaza
Islandia, NY 11788-7000
USA
Phone: 1-516-342-5224, Fax: 1-516-342-5734
e-mail cainfo@cai.com
Web: http://www.cai.com/

Cyco Group
Enterprise document management software.
Handelskade 49
2288 BA Rijswijk
The Netherlands
Phone: +31 70 395 4179, Fax: +31 70 319 1344
e-mail: info@cyco.nl
Web: http://www.cyco.nl/

Denkart NV
Fax, Telex, Year 2000 software.
Molenweg 107
B-2830 Willebroek
Belgium
Phone: +32 (3) 866 0022, Fax: +32 (3) 866 0301
e-mail: info@denkart.be
Web: http://www.denkart.be/

Digital Equipment Corporation
Internetworking software and Networking software.
146 Main Street
Maynard, MA 01754
USA
Phone: 1-508-493-5111, Fax: 1-508-493-8780
e-mail Directory: http://www.digital.com/info/email.html
Web: http://www.digital.com/

Documentum Inc.
Enterprise document management software.
4683 Chabot Drive, Suite 102
Pleasanton, CA 94566
USA
Phone: 1-510-463-6800, Fax: 1-510-463-6850
Web: http://www.documentum.com/

Elonex Software Solutions
e-mail and fax software.
577 Airport Blvd.
Suite 180
Burlingame, CA 94010
USA
Phone: 1-800-481-1130 or 1-415-373-2500, Fax: 1-415-373-2525
Web: http://www.elonex.com/

Ex Machina, Inc.
Wireless messaging software.
11 East 26th St. 16th Floor
New York, NY 10010-1402
USA
Phone: 1-212-843-0000 or 1-800-238-4738, Fax: 1-212-843-0029
Web: http://exmachina.com/

Farallon Communications, Inc.
Macintosh internetworking software.
2470 Mariner Square Loop
Alameda, CA 94501-1010
USA
Phone: 1-510-814-5000, Fax: 1-510-814-5020
Web: http://www.farallon.com/

Fujitsu Software Corporation
Collaborative workflow software.
3055 Orchard Drive
San Jose, CA 95134
USA
Phone: 1-408-432-1300, Fax: 1-408-456-7821
e-mail: teamware@fsc.fujitsu.com
Web: http://www.fujitsu.com/

FutureSoft Engineering, Inc.
Multi-platform communications software.
12012 Wickchester Lane, Suite 600
Houston, Texas 77079
USA
Phone: 1-281-496-9400
Fax: 1-281-496-1090
e-mail: info@futuresoft.com
Web: http://www/futuresoft.com/

Hewlett-Packard Company
e-mail, Internetworking software, and Wireless communications.
3000 Hanover Street
Palo Alto, California 94304
USA
Phone: 1-415-857-1501 or 1-800-752-0900
Web: http://www.hp.com/

IBM Corporation
Communications, Development tools, Internetworking software, and
Operating systems.
Old Orchard Road
Armonk, NY 10504
USA
Phone: 1-914-765-7777
or 1-800-IBM-3333
International Phone: 1-520-574-4600
Canada Phone: 1-800-426-4968
e-mail: askibm@info.ibm.com
Web: http://www.ibm.com/

Infonet Software Solutions Inc.
e-mail, Fax, Internetwork management, Messaging, and Voice software.
4400 Dominion Street, Suite 210
Burnaby, British Columbia V5G 4G3
Canada
Phone: 604 436 2922
Fax: 604 436 3192
Web: http://www.info.net/iss/

Information Advantage, Inc.
Data warehousing software and Decision support software.
7401 Metro Boulevard
Minneapolis, MN 55439
USA
Phone: 1-612-820-0702
Fax: 1-612-820-0712
Web: http://www.infoadvan.com/

Information View
Data warehousing software.
10 Carlson Road
Rochester, NY 14610
USA
Phone: 1-716-654-7799, Fax: 1-716-654-6233
e-mail: infoview@informationview.com
Web: http://www.informationview.com/

Informix Software, Inc.
Data internetworking, Database server, and Database warehousing software.
4100 Bohannon Drive
Menlo Park, CA 94025
USA
Phone: 1-415-926-6300
Web: http://www.informix.com/

IPPOLIS Worldwide Multimedia Telematics
Interactive networking solutions.
151, Avenue Gallieni
Bagnolet - Paris, France 93177
Phone: +33 1 48 97 44 44, Fax: +33 1 48 97 43 00
Web: http://www.ippolis.fr/ippolis/htdocs/

Kenan Systems Corporation
Billing software for the communications industry: Cable TV (CATV), Internet, and Online Wireless services.
One Main Street
Cambridge, MA 02142
USA
Phone: 1-617-225-2224, Fax: 1-617-225-2220
Web: http://www.kenan.com/

Kurzweil Applied Intelligence, Inc.
Voice recognition systems.
411 Waverley Oaks Road, Suite 330
Waltham, Massachusetts 02154
USA
Phone: 1-617-893-5151, Fax: 1-617-893-6525
e-mail: Info@kurzweil.com
Web: http://www.kurzweil.com/

Lotus Development Corporation
e-mail software and Internetwork groupware.
55 Cambridge Parkway
Cambridge, MA 02142
USA
Phone: 1-617-577-8500
Web: http://www2.lotus.com/

Lucent Technologies Inc.
Network performance optimization software, Synchronous Optical
NETwork (SONET) management, and Wireless telecommunications
management.
600 Mountain Avenue
Murray Hill, New Jersey 07974
USA
Phone: 1-888-458-2368
Web: http://www.lucent.com/

McAfee Associates, Inc.
Anti-virus software.
2710 Walsh Ave., Suite 200
Santa Clara, CA 95051-0963
USA
Phone: 1-408-988-3832
Fax: 1-408-970-9727
Web: http://mcafee.com/

Micro Focus, Inc. US
Programming development tools and utilities (Cobol).
2465 E. Bayshore Rd., Ste. 200
Palo Alto, CA 94303
USA
Phone: 1-415-856-4161
Fax: 1-415-855-9218
Web: http://www.mfltd.co.uk/

Microsoft Corporation
Applications, Communications, Data management, Development, and
Internetworking software.
One Microsoft Way
Redmond, WA 98052-6399
USA
Phone: 1-206-882-8080 or 1-800-426-9400
Microsoft Network: 1-800-325-1233
Microsoft Developers Network: 1-800-759-5474
Fax: 1-206-936-7329
Web: http://www.microsoft.com/

Netscape Communications Corporation
Internet and Intranet software standards and solutions.
501 E. Middlefield Rd.
Mountain View, CA 94043
USA
Phone: 1-415-254-1900
Fax: 1-415-528-4124
Web: http://home.netscape.com/

Northern Telecom (Nortel)
Internetworking software and Networking software.
200 Athens Way, Northern Telecom Plaza
Nashville, TN 37228
USA
Phone: 1-615-734-4000, Fax: 1-615-734-5189
Web: http://www.nortel.com/

Novavox AG
Telephony application generator software and Voice recognition.
Technoparkstrasse 1
8005 Zürich, Switzerland
Phone: +41 1 445 7575, Fax: +41 1 445 7576
Web: http://www.novavox.com/

Novell, Inc.
Cross-platform software solutions for Internet, Intranets, Local Area
Networks (LANs), Networking management, Networking messaging, and
Wide Area Networks (WANs).
1555 North Technology Way
Orem, UT 84097
USA
Phone: 1-801-222-6000 or 1-800-453-1267, Fax: 1-800-668-5329
Web: http://www.novell.com/

OpenPlus International, Inc.
Open architecture entrerprise sales software.
4521 Professional Circle
Virginia Beach, VA 23455-6454
USA
Phone: 1-757-499-1900, Fax: 1-757-499-7645
Web: http://www.openplus.com/

Oracle Corporation
Enterprise information management software including Development
tools, Internetworking, Multimedia database, and Server software.
500 Oracle Parkway
Redwood Shores, CA 94065
USA
Phone: 1-415-506-7000, Fax: 1-415-506-7200
Web: http://www.oracle.com/

PeopleSoft, Inc.
Enterprise business applications.
1331 N. California Boulevard
Suite 400
Walnut Creek, CA 94596-4502
USA
Phone: 1-510-946-9460, Fax: 1-510-975-0888
e-mail: info@peoplesoft.com
Web: http://www.peoplesoft.com/

Philips Electronics N.V.
Multimedia software and Speech recognition.
80, rue des 2 Gares
Brussels, Belgium B-1070
Phone: +32 2 525 60 40, Fax: +32 2 525 60 70
Web: http://www.philips.com/

Platinum Technology, Inc.
Database management, Data warehousing software, and Systems management.
1815 South Meyers Road
Oakbrook Terrace, IL 60181-5241
USA
Phone: 1-800-442-6861 or 1-630-620-5000, Fax: 1-630-691-0718
Web: http://www.platinum.com/

Qualcomm, Inc.
e-mail software and Wireless telecommunications.
6455 Lusk Boulevard
San Diego, CA 92121-2779
USA
Phone: 1-619-587-1121, Fax: 1-619-658-2100
Web: http://www.qualcomm.com/

SAP (Systems Applications and Products in Data Processing)
Enterprise business application software.
300 Stevens Drive
International Court Three
Philadelphia, PA 19113
USA
Phone: 1-610-521-4500, Fax: 1-610-521-6290
Web: http://www.sap.com/

SAS Institute Inc.
Communications, Data warehousing, and Decision support software.
SAS Campus Drive
Cary, NC 27513-2414
USA
Phone: 1-919-677-8000, Fax: 1-919-677-8123
e-mail: software@sas.sas.com
Web: http://www.sas.com/

Santa Cruz Operation Inc.
Client-integration software, Communications and networking, and UNIX-based program development.
400 Encinal Street, P.O. Box 1900
Santa Cruz, California, 95061-1900
USA
Phone: 1-408-425-7222, Fax: 1-408-458-4227
Web: http://www.sco.com/

Siemens Rolm Communications, Inc.
Networking and Telecommunications software.
4900 Old Ironsides Dr., PO Box 58075
Santa Clara, CA 95052-8075
USA
Phone: 1-408-492-2000, Fax: 1-408-492-3430
Web: http://www.siemensrolm.com/

Silicon Graphics, Inc.
Broadband multimedia, Computer animation, Data warehousing,
Scientific visualization, and Web authoring software.
2011 N. Shoreline Blvd.
Mountain View, CA 94043
Phone: 1-415-960-1980 or 1-800-800-7441, Fax: 1-415-961-0595
Web: http://www.sgi.com/

Singapore Telecom International
Cellular network management, Customer billing software, and Paging.
Halton House
20-23 Holborn
London ECIN 2JD
UK
Phone: 0171 404 8877, Fax: 0171 404 8127
Web: http://www.commerceasia.com/sti-ss/

Sun Microsystems, Inc.
Distributed object management, Internet programming tools, and
Network file system management software.
2550 Garcia Ave.
Mountain View, CA 94043-1100
USA
Phone: 1-415-786-8070
Web: http://www.sun.com/

Sybase, Inc.
Data warehousing, Database software, Development tools, and Internet.
6475 Christie Avenue
Emeryville, CA 94608
USA
Phone: 1-510-922-3500, Fax: 1-510-922-3210
Web: http://www.sybase.com/

TCSI Corporation
Wireless communications software.
1080 Marina Village Parkway
Alameda, CA 94501
USA
Phone: 1-510-749-8500, Fax: 1-510-749-8700
Web: http://www.tcs.com/

Technology Applications Group, Inc.
Internetworking management software for the communications industry.
1350 Elbridge Payne Rd.
Suite 207
Chesterfield, Mo. 63017
USA
Phone: 1-314-530-1981, Fax: 1-314-530-1788
Web: http://www.techapp.com/

Telecorps Telecommunications Products
Call center management software.
2000 E. Oakley Park Road, Suite 101
Walled Lake, MI 48390-1501
USA
Phone: 1-810-960-1000 or 1-800-634-1012, Fax: 1-810-960-1085
Web: http://telecorpproducts.com/

Toshiba America, Inc.
Networking and internetworking software.
1251 Sixth Avenue
New York, NY 10020
USA
Phone: 1-212-596-0600, Fax: 1-714-583-3645
Web: http://www.toshiba.com/

Vocaltec Ltd.
Internet telephone and teleconferencing software.
35 Industrial Pkwy.
Northvale, NJ 07647
Phone: 201-768-9400, Fax: 201-768-8893
e-mail: info@vocaltec.com
Web: http://www.vocaltec.com/

APPENDIX F
INTERNATIONAL DATA COMMUNICATIONS ORGANIZATIONS

All sites in English unless otherwise noted.

RESEARCH
AMIC Asian Mass Communication Research and Information Centre (Singapore)
Government-sponsored research and development center dedicated to the growth of mass communication in the Asia Pacific region.
Web: http://www.irdu.nus.sg/amic/

ANRTT Association Nationale de Recherche sur les Technologies de Télécommunications (France)
Research organization advocating and promoting open systems (in French).
Web: http://excalibur.inp-fc.fr/anrtt/

CESNET Czech Educational and Scientific Network (Czech Republic)
Academic research network of the Czech Republic.
Web: http://www.cesnet.cz/

CIRCIT Centre for International Research on Communication and Information Technologies (Australia)
Research center studying the role of information technology in society.
Web: http://teloz.latrobe.edu.au/circit/

CLEI Centro Latinoamericano de Estudios en Inform·tica (Chile)
Organization coordinating the efforts of Latin American universities researching informatics (in Spanish)
Web: http://dcc.ing.puc.cl/~dfuller/clei.html

CLPP Central Laboratory for Parallel Processing (Bulgaria)
The Bulgarian Academy of Sciences' computer science and communications research center.
Web: http://www.acad.bg/

CNRI Corporation for National Research Initiatives (USA)
Group working with the government and academia to develop infrastructure technologies that promote universal network access.
Web: http://www.cnri.reston.va.us/

CRA Computing Research Association (North America)
Represents and promotes the computing research community throughout North America.
Web: http://cra.org/

CRC Communications Research Centre Canada (Canada)
Canadian government's body in charge of developing the Canadian communications infrastructure.
Web: http://www.crc.doc.ca/

CRL Communications Research Laboratory (Japan)
Government institution responsible for the study of telecommunications technologies, radio science, and radio applications in Japan.
Web: http://www.crl.go.jp/

CSIR (South Africa)
Africa's largest scientific and technological research organization.
Web: http://www.csir.co.za/

CSIRO Commonwealth Scientific and Industrial Research Organisation (Australia)
Australia's largest government-sponsored scientific research agency.
Web: http://commsun.its.csiro.au/

CWC Centre for Wireless Communications (Singapore)
Industry research and development center creating strategic and globally competitive applications in wireless communications.
Web: http://www.cwc.nus.sg/

Center for Advanced Computing Research at California Institute of Technology (USA)
Research group promoting excellence in the field of high-performance scientific computing.
Web: http://www.ccsf.caltech.edu/

Centre for Communications Systems Research (UK)
Cambridge University information systems research center.
Web: http://www.ccsr.cam.ac.uk/

DFN-Verein (Deutsches Forschungsnetz) (Germany)
German national academic and scientific research network (in German).
Web: http://www.dfn.de/

Dante (EuropaNET European research Internet)(European Union)
Organizes support for, and focuses on developing, high-quality international network services and infrastructure for the European research community.
Web: http://www.dante.org.uk/

ERCIM European Research Consortium for Informatics and Mathematics (European Union)
Organization guiding and promoting collaborative effort within the European informatics research community.
Web: http://www-ercim.inria.fr/

RESEARCH, con't.

ERNET Education and Research Network, The (India)
Initiative to develop an academic research computer network in India.
Web: http://www.doe.ernet.in/

ETRI Electronics and Telecommunications Research Institute (South Korea)
Government sponsored research institute charged with handling international standards and interoperability issues
Web: http://pec.etri.re.kr/

FTK Forschungsinstitut für Telekommunikation (Research Institute for Telecommunications) (Germany)
Pursues applied research and development in telecommunications with an emphasis on developing practical products and services.
Web: http://www-ftk.fernuni-hagen.de/welcome.html

GMD - Forschungszentrum Informationstechnik GmbH (Germany)
German national research center for informatics, communication, and media.
Web: http://www.gmd.de/GMDHome.html

IBICT Instituto Brasileiro de Informação em Ciência e Tecnologia (Brazil)
Government research institute promoting the use of information technology in the Brazilian academic community.
Web: http://www.ibict.br/~ibict/

ICSI International Computer Science Institute (USA)
Organization promoting international computer technology research.
Web: http://www.icsi.berkeley.edu/

IHPCDB Institute For High-Performance Computing And Data Bases (Russia)
Ministry of Science and Technical Policy-sponsored scientific research institute.
Web: http://www.csa.ru/Inst/

IIS Institute of Informatics Systems (Russia)
The Russian Academy of Sciences' informatics research center.
Web: http://www.iis.nsk.su/

INRIA Institut National de Recherche en Informatique et en Automatique (France)
The French Ministry of Industry's body in charge of computer science research and technology transfer.
Web: http://www.inria.fr/

IPPI Institute for Information Transmission Problems (Russia)
Organization supporting high-level research in information theory and artificial intelligence.
Web: http://www.ippi.ras.ru/

IRE Institute of Radio Engineering and Electronics (Russia)
The Russian Academy of Sciences' institute for applied research in the
development of radio engineering, electronics, and physics.
Web: http://www.cplire.ru/

IREX International Research and Exchanges Board (USA and Russia)
Organization promoting information exchange between the countries of
the former Soviet Union and the United States.
Web: http://www.irex.org/

ISDN-Research Commission, of North Rhine-Westphalia (Germany)
Body initiating technical pilot projects to integrate ISDN into the
German information infrastructure.
Web: http://www-kommsys.fernuni-hagen.de/eng/isdn-fk/isdn-fk.html

ISS Institute of Systems Science (Singapore)
National University of Singapore's information technology research
institute.
Web: http://www.iss.nus.sg/

ITRI Industrial Technology Research Institute (Taiwan)
Organ of the Ministry of Economic Affairs concerned with applied
research and development as it affects the expansion of Taiwan's high-
tech industries.
Web: http://www.itri.org.tw/

**Interactive Graphics Systems Group at Darmstadt University
(Germany)**
Promotes the growth of the European computer graphics industry by
the efforts of three organizations working together to develop practical
applications: Interactive Graphics Systems Group (GRIS), Insitut
Graphische Datenverarbeitung (IGD), and Computer Graphics Center
(ZGDV).
Web: http://www.igd.fhg.de/

MMCF Multimedia Communications Forum (USA)
International research and development organization composed of pro-
fessionals working with networked multimedia.
Web: http://www.mmcf.org/

**? MTA SZTAKI Computer and Automation Research Institute
(Hungary)**
The research and development arm of the Hungarian Academy of
Sciences.
Web: http://www.sztaki.hu/sztaki/

NLANR National Laboratory for Applied Network Research (USA)
A collaborative effort of several major academic supercomputer centers
performing network infrastructure research. Funded by the NSF
(National Science Foundation).
Web: http://www.nlanr.net/

RESEARCH, con't.

NTHP The Network Technology Group at GMD FOKUS (Germany)
Group concentrating on the improvement and validation of advanced networks and internetworks.
Web: http://www.fokus.gmd.de/nthp/

National Center for High-performance Computing (Taiwan)
Government-sponsored scientific research agency (in Chinese).
Web: http://www.nchc.gov.tw/

RELARN Russian ELectronic Academic and Research Network (Russia)
Network of educational bodies promoting the interaction of international academic and scientific communities (in Russian).
Web: http://www.ripn.net/

STI-NET Scientific and Technical Information Network of China (China)
Government sponsored academic information network.
Web: http://www.sti.ac.cn/

ThaiSarn Thai Social, Scientific, Academic and Research Network
The academic research network of Thailand.
Web: http://www.nectec.or.th/bureaux/nectec/ThaiSarn.book/

USJTMC US.-Japan Technology Management Center at Stanford University
Group conducting advanced research into the Japanese approach to technology management.
Web: http://fuji.stanford.edu/

TRADE ORGANIZATIONS

AIMIA Australian Interactive Multimedia Industry Association (Australia)
Represents the Australian interactive multimedia in its efforts to become internationally competitive.
Web: http://www.aimia.com.au/

AOEMA Asia-Oceania Electronic Messaging Association (Japan)
Promotes the development of electronic messaging in the Asia-Oceania region.
Web: http://www.iijnet.or.jp/fmmc/indexe.html

BSA Business Software Alliance (USA)
Trade group promoting strong intellectual property protection of software.
Web: http://www.bsa.org/

CEMA Consumer Electronics Manufacturers Association (USA)
Trade organization representing a wide variety of electronics products.
Web: http://www.cemacity.org/

CIAJ Communication Industries Association of Japan
Industry trade group promoting Japanese telecommunications
equip,emt manufacturers.
Web: http://inetsrv.ciaj.or.jp/

CWTA Canadian Wireless Telecommunications Association (Canada)
Trade organization representing the Canadian wireless telecommunications industry.
Web: http://www.cwta.ca/

Communications Industry Association of Japan
Telecommunications industry trade group.
Web: http://www.ciaj.or.jp/

ECA Electronic Commerce Association (UK)
Forum and advisory group for organizations implementing electronic
commerce technologies.
Web: http://www.eca.org.uk/

ECC Electronic Commerce Canada (Canada)
Forum composed of public and private sector interests that studies the
issues driving the growth of electronic commerce.
Web: http://www.ecc.ca/

ECIS European Committee for Interoperable Systems (European Union)
International advocacy group promoting open systems and fair competition in the information technology industry.
Web: http://www.eunet.be/rent-a-page/ecis/ecis.htm

EIA Electronic Industries Association (USA)
Trade association of U.S. electronics manufacturers.
Web: http://www.eia.org/

EMA Electronic Messaging Association (USA)
Trade association promoting the development of secure global electronic commerce.
Web: http://www.ema.org/

Enterprise Computer Telephony Forum
An industry organization promoting the CTI (Computer Telephony
Integration) market.
Web: http://www.ectf.org/

FIA Fibreoptic Industry Association (UK)
International association promoting the global fiber optics industry.
Web: http://www.fibreoptic.org.uk/

**HKAASCT Hong Kong Association for the Advancement of Science
and Technology, The (Hong Kong)**
Promotes scientific and technological exchanges between Hong Kong
and other countries with particular reference to products manufactured in Hong Kong.
Web: http://www.hkaast.org.hk/

TRADE ORGANIZATIONS, con't.

I*M Information Market Europe (European Union)
A European Union-sponsored initiative that provides information about European markets to multimedia content and electronic information services.
Web: http://www2.echo.lu/

IDATE Institut De l'Audiovisuel et des Télécommunications en Europe (France)
A consultancy and research group specializing in the integration of the telecommunications and audio-visual industries.
Web: http://www.idate.fr/accueil/

IDSA Interactive Digital Software Association (USA)
The association for interactive entertainment software publishers.
Web: http://www.mha.com/e3/idsa/idsa.html

IMTC International Multimedia Teleconferencing Consortium (USA)
An international organization of multimedia teleconferencing businesses that promotes open systems.
Web: http://www.imtc.org/

INMARSAT International Maritime Satellite Organization (UK)
An international consortium of 79 countries that supports worldwide mobile satellite communications capability.
Web: http://www.inmarsat.org/inmarsat/

INTELSAT International Telecommunications Satellite Organization (USA)
The world's largest commercial satellite communications services provider.
Web: http://www.intelsat.int/

IrDA Infrared Data Association (USA)
Trade association advocating interoperable infrared data interconnection standards.
Web: http://www.irda.org/

ISA Interactive Services Association (USA)
Association promoting the use of consumer-oriented interactive services world-wide.
Web: http://www.isa.net/

ITAA Information Technology Association of America (USA)
Trade association representing the U.S. information technology industry.
Web: http://www.itaa.org/

ITIC Information Technology Industry Council (USA)
Trade association shaping policies to promote free and open competition in the information technology industry.
Web: http://www.itic.org/

MDG Multimedia Development Group (USA)
Marketing and business development trade association serving interactive media companies worldwide.
Web: http://www.mdg.org/

MMTA MultiMedia Telecommunications Association
Trade association devoted to promoting the convergence of the computer and telecommunications industries.
Web: http://www.mmta.org/

OMG Object Management Group (USA)
Trade organization promoting the use of object technology in the development of distributed computing systems.
Web: http://www.omg.org/

OSTA Optical Storage Technology Association (USA)
International organization promoting the use of writable optical technology for data storage.
Web: http://www.osta.org/

Open Group, The (USA)
An organization created by the merger of X/Open and the Open Software Foundation that advocates open systems specifications.
Web: http://www.opengroup.org/

PCIA Personal Communications Industry Association (USA)
International trade organization for those in the wireless communications industry.
Web: http://www.pcia.com/

QIC Quarter-Inch Cartridge Drive Standards, Inc. (USA)
International trade association promoting the use of quarter-inch tape technology and products.
Web: http://www.qic.org/

SGML Open Consortium (USA)
Organization promoting SGML (Standard Generalized Markup Language) as the universal method of transporting documents over the Internet.
Web: http://www.sgmlopen.org/

SIA Satellite Industry Association (USA)
Trade organization for the satellite communications industry.
Web: http://www.sia.org/

SPA Software Publishers Association (USA)
Trade group representing software publishers and issues of software piracy.
Web: http://www.spa.org/

STPI Software Technology Parks of India (India)
Government resource center for the export of Indian software.
Web: http://www.stph.net/

TRADE ORGANIZATIONS, con't.

Stentor Alliance of Canada's Telephone Companies, The
An alliance of Canada's largest telephone companies working together
to ensure uniformity of products, services, and prices.
Web: http://www.stentor.ca/

TCIF Telecommunications Industry Forum (USA)
International organization representing telecommunications carriers,
manufacturers and suppliers.
Web: http://www.bellcore.com/tcif.html

TIA Telecommunications Industry Association (USA)
Trade organization for the communications and information technology
industry.
Web: http://www.industry.net/tia

USTA United States Telephone Association (USA)
Forum for the local exchange carrier industry.
Web: http://www.usta.org/

VESA Video Electronics Standards Association (USA)
Trade organization developing open standards in the video electronics
industry.
Web: http://www.vesa.org/

WCC Wireless Opportunities Coalition (USA)
Industry group promoting the expansion of wireless telecommunica-
tions products and services.
Web: http://wireless.policy.net/wireless/wireless.html

PROFESSIONAL ORGANIZATIONS

AAIM Association for Applied Interactive Multimedia (USA)
Professional group for interactive multimedia developers.
Web: http://www.aiim.org/

AEA American Electronics Association (USA)
One of the oldest and largest electronics trade associations in the
United States.
Web: http://www.aeanet.org/

AIP Associazione Informatici Professionisti (Italy)
Association of Italian information technology professionals (in Italian).
Web: http://www.a-i-p.it/

AIS Association for Information Systems (USA)
A global forum for academicians specializing in information systems.
Web: http://www.pitt.edu/~ais/

AOP Association of Online professionals (USA)
Professional association for those who work in the on-line industry.
Web: http://www.aop.org/

APIIQ Association professionnelle des informaticiens et informaticiennes du Quebec (Canada)
Association for information technology professionals in Quebec (in French).
Web: http://www.crim.ca/apiiq/

ATI Asociacion de Tecnicos de Informatica (Spain)
Association of Spanish information technology professionals.
Web: http://www.ati.es/

BIMA British Interactive Multimedia Association (UK)
The foremost organization for multimedia professionals in Britain.
Web: http://www.bima.co.uk/

CGDA Computer Game Developers' Association (USA)
A professional society for those in the interactive entertainment, educational software, and multimedia industry.
Web: http://www.cgda.org/

CTIA Cellular Telecommunications Industry Association (USA)
Professional organization for those working in the wireless telecommunications business.
Web: http://www.wow-com.com/

EG Eurographics Association (European Union)
Association for computer graphics industry professionals, researchers, developers, and educators.
Web: http://www.eg.org/

FOA Fiber Optic Association (USA)
International society for those working with fiber optics.
Web: http://world.std.com/~foa

ICA International Communications Association (USA)
Professional association for those in the data, voice, and video telecommunications equipment industry.
Web: http://icanet.com/

ICCA Independent Computer Consultants Association (USA)
National professional association of both hardware and software consultants.
Web: http://www.icca.org/index.html

IEE Institution of Electrical Engineers, The (UK)
Global organization of professional electrical, manufacturing, and information engineers.
Web: http://www.iee.org.uk/

IEEE Institute of Electrical and Electronics Engineers (USA)
The world's largest technical professional society. It is dedicated to advancing the theory and practice of electronics in computer engineering and computer science.
Web: http://www.ieee.org/

PROFESSIONAL ORGANIZATIONS, con't.

IEICE Institute of Electronics, Information and Communication Engineers (Japan)
Communications forum for professionals in the fields of electronics, information, and communications.
Web: http://ieice.ieice.or.jp/

IICS International Interactive Communications Society (USA)
International professional organization for those who work on the Internet or in multimedia.
Web: http://www.iics.org

IMA Interactive Multimedia Association (USA)
Professional association for multimedia professionals. (Formerly IVIA, Interactive Video Industry Association.)
Web: http://www.ima.org/

IMAT Interactive Multimedia Arts and Technologies Association (Canada)
Canada's largest multimedia professional's organization.
Web: http://www.goodmedia.com/imat/

INTERACTA Associazione Italiana della Comunicazione Interattiva. (Italy)
Organization for multimedia professionals (in Italian).
Web: http://www.uni.net/interacta/

ITCA International Teleconferencing Association (USA)
Association and forum for teleconferencing, and distance education technology professionals.
Web: http://www.itca.org/

ITS International Telecommunications Society (USA)
Professional association for those working in the field of telecommunications policy and economic decision analysis.
Web: http://itp-www.colorado.edu/~its/

NMAA National Multimedia Association of America (USA)
Professional forum for those working in multimedia.
Web: http://www.nmaa.org/

SIPA Silicon Valley Indian Professionals Association (USA)
Networking and advocacy group for Indian technology professionals living in the US.
Web: http://www.sipa.org/

SSPI Society Of Satellite Professionals International (USA)
International association of professionals in the satellite communications industry.
Web: http://www.sspi.org/

STC Society for Technical Communication (USA)
Major international professional organization promoting excellence in the field of technical communications.
Web: http://www.stc.org/

TSA Telecommunication Society of Australia (Australia)
National society of telecommunications professionals.
Web: http://www.tsa.org.au/

TSANet Technical Support Alliance Network (USA)
Association of technical support professionals.
Web: http://www.sanet.org/

USENIX UNIX Professional and Technical Association
Association for professionals in the field of advanced computing systems.
Web: http://www.usenix.org/

Uniforum International Association of Open Systems Professionals
Professional forum advocating open systems.
Web: http://www.uniforum.org/

GOVERNMENT ORGANIZATIONS
AIST Agency of Industrial Science and Technology (Japan)
Ministry of International Trade and Industry (MITI) agency which oversees all research and development laboratories.
Web: http://www.aist.go.jp/

APT Asia Pacific Telecommunity (Thailand)
UN-sponsored policy study group promoting the development of a telecommunications infrastructure in the Asia-Pacific region.
Web: http://www.inet.co.th/org/apt/

AUSTEL Australian Telecommunications Authority
Government group supervising fair competition in the Australian telecommunications industry.
Web: http://www.austel.gov.au/

BETECH Bernische Genossenschaft f,r Technologievermittlung (Berne Association for Technology Transfer)(Switzerland)
Oversees the transfer of government-funded technology research into practical applications (in German).
Web: http://www.thenet.ch/betech/

Bundesministerium für Post und Telekommunikation (Germany)
Government ministry that oversees postal communication, and telecommunications infrastructure (in German).
Web: http://www.bundesregierung.de/inland/ministerien/post.html

CANARIE Canadian Network for the Advancement of Research, Industry and Education (Canada)
Government and private industry alliance leading the development of the Information Superhighway in Canada.
Web: http://www.canarie.ca/

CANET Institute of Computer Application (China)
Government technology policy group (in Chinese).
Web: http://www.canet.cn/

GOVERNMENT ORGANIZATIONS, con't.

CAT Communications Authority of Thailand
Government office responsible for managing postal and telecommunication services in Thailand.
Web: http://rochana.cat.or.th/cat/

CAZ Communications Authority Of Zambia
Government agency in charge of developing the Zambian Information Infrastructure (ZII).
Web: http://www.zamnet.zm/zamnet/comms/caz/caz.html

CCTA Central Computer and Telecommunications Agency (UK)
Government policy and advisory agency representing the UK on international information systems issues.
Web: http://www.open.gov.uk/ccta/

CEIC Information Center of Ministry of Electronics Industry (China)
Ministry clearinghouse for electronics industry policy, marketing, and trade information.
Web: http://www.ceic.go.cn/

CINTEL Centro de Investigaciòn de las Telecomunicaciones (Colombia)
Agency of the Ministry of Communications concerned with developing the Colombian information infrastructure (in Spanish).
Web: http://www.colciencias.gov.co./cintel/

CNIT Center of the New Information Processing Technologies (Russia)
Novosibirsk State University division working on the development of the Russian information infrastructure.
Web: http://www.cnit.nsk.su/english/

Colciencias - Instituto Colombiano para el Desarrollo de la Ciencia y la Tecnología (Colombia)
National agency in charge of the development and promotion of the technological sector (in Spanish).
Web: http://www.colciencias.gov.co/

CONACYT Consejo Nacional de Ciencia y Tecnología (Mexico)
Government agency regulating science and technology policy (in Spanish).
Web: http://info.main.conacyt.mx/

CONCYT Consejo Nacional de Ciencia y Tecnología (Guatemala)
Government policy and regulatory agency (in Spanish).
Web: http://www.concyt.gob.gt/

CONICYT Consejo Nacional de Investigaciones Científicas y Tecnològicas (Venezuela)
Government agency overseeing scientific and technology activity in Venezuela (in Spanish).
Web: http://www.conicit.ve/

CRT Comisiòn de Regulaciòn de Telecomunicaciones (Colombia)
Colombia's national telecommunications regulatory agency.
Web: http://www.crt.gov.co/

CRTC Canadian Radio-Television and Telecommunications Commission
Regulatory agency for Canada's broadcasting and telecommunications
systems industry.
Web: http://www.crtc.gc.ca/

CTO Commonwealth Telecommunications Organisation (UK)
Agency coordinating the efforts of industry and government to promote
the growth of the telecommunications industry in Commonwealth
countries.
Web: http://www.cto.int/

**DG XIII Telecommunications, Information Market and Exploitation of
Research (European Union)**
European Commission directorate handling telecommunications and
postal service issues.
Web: http://europa.eu.int/en/comm/dg13/13home.htm

ECHO European Commission Host Organisation (European Union)
European Union-sponsored organization promoting the business bene-
fits of using electronic information services.
Web: http://www2.echo.lu/echo/en/menuecho.html

ENEA Ente per le Nuove tecnologie, l'Energia e l'Ambiente (Italy)
Italian national agency in charge of managing new technology research
and development.
Web: http://www.sede.enea.it/

ERO European Radiocommunications Office (European Union)
Regulatory agency concerned with frequency management and the reg-
ulation of the radio industry. The clearinghouse for information from
the Radiocommunications Committee (ERC).
Web: http://www.ero.dk/

ETO European Telecommunications Office (European Union)
A central clearinghouse for the rapid dissemination of new data servic-
es to members of the European Community.
Web: http://eto.dk/

**ETSI European Telecommunications Standardization Institute
(European Union)**
European Council organization in charge of establishing standards for
telecommunications, broadcasting and office information technology.
Web: http://www.etsi.fr/

EWOS European Workshop for Open Systems (European Union)
Organization developing solutions for the Global Information
Infrastructure while representing the specific economic interests of the
European Community.
Web: http://www.ewos.be/

Forf·s (Ireland)
Irish government's technology/science policy advisory board (in Gaelic).
Web: http://www.ucd.ie/gsb/business_info/forfas.html

GOVERNMENT ORGANIZATIONS, con't.

GIIC Global Information Infrastructure Commission (USA)
Independent, industry-based policy group charged with creating new
solutions to advance the growth of a global information infrastructure.
Web: http://www.gii.org/

ISPO Information Society Project Office (European Union)
Supports and promotes the development of a European information
society in accordance with the goals stipulated by the European
Commission's Information Society Project initiative.
Web: http://www.ispo.cec.be/

Infostruktura (Lithuania)
Ministry of Communications initiative to create an information infra-
structure in Lithuania.
Web: http://www.is.lt/english/

Institute for Posts And Telecommunications Policy (Japan)
Policy advisory group to the Ministry of Posts and Telecommunications
(MPT).
Web: http://www.iptp.go.jp/

**KINITI Korea Institute of Industry & Technology Information (South
Korea)**
Government sponsored organization to establish a nation-wide infor-
mation system.
Web: http://www.kiniti.re.kr/

MPT Ministry of Posts and Telecommunications (Japan)
Oversees postal communication, telecommunications, and broadcasting
infrastructure (in Japanese).
Web: http://www.mpt.go.jp/

**Ministère délégué à la poste, aux télécommunications et ‡ l'espace
(France)**
French minstry that oversees telecommunications and information
technologies.
Web: http://www.telecom.gouv.fr/

Ministério das Comuniçaõies (Brazil)
Office that establishes services and tariffs for the Brazilian telecommu-
nications industry (in Portuguese).
Web: http://www.mc.gov.br/

Ministerio del Transporte y Telecomunicaciones (Chile)
Chilean government's telecommunications regulatory agency (in
Spanish).
Web: http://www.presidencia.cl/presidencia/ministerios/transporte.html

Ministry of Communications (Israel)
Government agency responsible for setting telecommunications policy and goals, and encouraging communications industry research.
Web: http://www.israel-mfa.gov.il/gov/commun.html

NCB National Computer Board (Singapore)
The government-sponsored board responsible for information technology development in Singapore.
Web: http://www.ncb.gov.sg/

NCST National Center for Software Technology (India)
Government agency in charge of research and development, training, and industry support.
Web: http://www.ncst.ernet.in/

NECTEC National Electronics and Computer Technology Center (Thailand)
Government agency studying information management and policy.
Web: http://ish.nectec.or.th/

NIC National Informatics Centre (India)
Develops and implements computer-based information systems for the Ministries and Departments of the Central Government.
Web: http://www.nic.in/

NITC National Information Technology Committee (Thailand)
Government organization in charge of implementing an information infrastructure in Thailand.
Web: http://www.nitc.go.th/

NSTB National Science & Technology Board (Singapore)
High-level agency of the Ministry of Trade and Industry (MTI) working in collaboration with the public sector to establish Singapore as a world class center in selected fields of science and technology.
Web:nstb.gov.sg/

OFCOM Office federal de la communication (Switzerland)
Telecommunication regulatory agency of Switzerland.
Web: http://www.admin.ch/bakom/

OFTA Office of the Telecommunications Authority (Hongkong)
Government agency responsible for regulating the telecommunications industry in Hong Kong.
Web: http://www.ofta.gov.hk/

OFTEL Office of Telecommunications (UK)
Industry watchdog and advocacy group headed by the Director General of Telecommunications.
Web: http://www.oftel.gov.uk/

GOVERNMENT ORGANIZATIONS. con't.

ONPT L'Office National des Postes et Télécommunications (Morocco)
Oversees postal communication, and telecommunications infrastructure in Morocco.
Web: http://www.onpt.net.ma/welcome.htm

Radiocommunicatons Agency (UK)
Executive Agency of the UK's Department of Trade and Industry responsible for the allocation, maintenance and supervision of the British radio spectrum.
Web: http://www.open.gov.uk/radiocom/rahome.htm

Secretaria de Communicaciones y Transportes (Mexico)
Mexican government's telecommunications regulatory agency (in Spanish).
Web: www.sct.gob.mx/

Swiss Telecom (Switzerland)
Government organization overseeing the development of telecommunications (formerly, PTT).
Web: http://www.telecom.ch/

TAC Telehallintokeskus (Finland)
Ministry of Communications agency responsible for the administration of the nation's radio, telecommunications, and postal services.
Web: http://www.thk.fi/

TAO Telecommunications Advancement Organization of Japan, The
Government agency in charge of telecommunication and broadcasting satellites.
Web: http://www.shiba.tao.or.jp/

TAS Telecommunication Authority of Singapore (Singapore)
Government regulatory agency in charge of telecommunications and postal services.
Web: http://tas.gov.sg/

TDP Technology Development Program (Egypt)
Government of Egypt's initiative to develop a high technology sector.
Web: http://www.its.egnet.net/tdp/

INTEREST GROUPS

ACIS American Committee for Interoperable Systems (USA)
National advocacy group for systems using open standards.
Web: http://www.sun.com/acis/

ACM Association for Computing Machinery, The (USA)
Major American organization advancing the art, science, engineering, and application of information technology.
Web: http://www.acm.org/

ADSL (Asymmetric Digital Subscriber Line) Forum (USA)
Industry forum for the exchange of technical and marketing information regarding the use of ADSL technology.
Web: http://www.adsl.com/

AIDAT African Internet Development Action Team (South Africa)
A non-profit organization dedicated to developing the Internet in Africa.
Web: http://www.africa.com/pages/aidat/

ANUIT Associazione Nazionale Utenti Italiani di Telecomunicazion (Italy)
Advocacy group representing Italian telecommunications users.
Web: http://www.anuit.it/

APCUG Association of Personal Computer User Groups (USA)
International organization for computer user groups.
Web: http://www.apcug.org/

APPN Advanced Peer-to-Peer Networking Consortium (USA)
Develops and promotes APPN and SNA (Systems Network Architecture) standards and internetworking products.
Web: http://www.networking.ibm.com/app/aiwhome.htm

APT Alliance for Public Technology (USA)
Advocacy group promoting broad public access to affordable communication services and technology.
Web: http://apt.org/apt/index.html

ATM (Asynchronous Transfer Mode) Forum (USA)
Industry organization promoting the use and development of ATM products and services.
Web: http://www.atmforum.com/

ATUG Australian Telecommunications Users Group
Advocacy group for both private and professional telecommunications consumers.
Web: http://www.sofcom.com.au/atug/index.html

American Association of Domain Names (USA)
Provides information and assistance to domain name holders.
Web: http://www.domains.org/

BMUG Berkeley Macintosh Users Group (USA)
The world's largest advocacy group for Macintosh computer users.
Web: http://www.bmug.org/

CDMA Development Group (USA)
Professional organization promoting the use of CDMA (Code Division Multiple Access) technology in wireless communications.
Web: http://www.cdg.org/

INTEREST GROUPS, con't.

CDPD (Cellular Digital Packet Data) Forum (USA)
Professional group promoting the international advancement of open cellular data technologies.
Web: http://www.cdpd.com/

CIX Commercial Internet eXchange (USA)
Forum for the exchange of ideas and information among public data internetworking service providers.
Web: http://www.cix.org/

CRA Computing Research Association (USA)
Advocacy group for computing research professionals.
Web: http://www.cra.org/

CSPP Computer Systems Policy Project (USA)
Organization of major information technology companies developing public policy positions on trade and technology issues.
Web: http://www.cspp.org/

Center for Software Development, The (USA)
Advocates innovation in software development by providing technical and business resources to software developers.
Web: http://www.center.org/

Center for Telecommunications at Stanford, The (USA)
Focuses on excellence in telecommunications research and education.
Web: http://telecom.stanford.edu/

DAVIC Digital Audio Visual Interoperability Council (USA)
International advocacy group for digital audio-visual applications and services.
Web: http://www.davic.org/

DSTC Distributed Systems Technology Centre (Australia)
Coalition of industrial and government organizations working to develop technologies that further the growth of the global information infrastructure.
Web: http://www.dstc.edu.au/

DTV Digital TV Team (USA)
An alliance of Intel, Compaq, and Microsoft to promote the growth of the digital television industry.
Web: http://dtv.org/

EBU European Broadcasting Union (Switzerland)
Largest industry group in Europe promoting the development of new broadcasting
technologies such as HDTV.
Web: http://www.ebu.ch/

EEMA European Electronic Messaging Association (European Union)
Industry organization promoting the development of electronic messaging in the European Community.
Web: http://www.eema.org/

EFF Electronic Frontier Foundation (USA)
Advocacy group working in the public interest to protect privacy, free speech, and access to public resources and online information resources.
Web: http://www.eff.org/

EMF European Multimedia Forum (European Union)
Industry group concerned with the multimedia technology and standards used in the European Community.
Web: http://www.emf.be/

FCA Fibre Channel Association (USA)
Industry group promoting the use of fibre channel technology in high speed networks.
Web: http://www.amdahl.com/ext/carp/fca/fca.html

FMMC Foundation for MultiMedia Communications (Japan)
Organization working to advance new generation multimedia networks.
Web: http://www.iijnet.or.jp/fmmc/indexe.html

FRF Frame Relay Forum (USA)
International professional group promoting the implementation of Frame Relay technology in networks.
Web: http://www.frforum.com/index.html

Gigabit Ethernet Alliance (USA)
Industry group promoting the development of high-speed Ethernet as a standard for networks.
Web: http://www.gigabit-ethernet.org/

HIPPI (High-Performance Parallel Interface) Networking Forum (USA)
International forum to advance the HIPPI switched networking standard.
Web: http://www.esscom.com/hnf/index.html

HKCS Hong Kong Computer Society, The
Industry body promoting the benefits and uses of information technology.
Web: http://www.hkcs.org.hk

IAB Internet Architecture Board (USA)
National group responsible for defining the overall architecture of the Internet.
Web: http://www.isi.edu/iab/

INTEREST GROUPS, con't.

IANA Internet Assigned Numbers Authority (USA)
Organization in charge of allocating IP addresses and other unique
identifying numbers used to configure computers on the Internet.
Web: http://www.iana.org/iana/

ICS Industrial Computing Society (USA)
Promotes improving the quality of computer technology in industrial
applications.
Web: http://www2.ics.org/ics/

IEEE Computer Society (USA)
One of the leading international organizations of computing profession-
als.
Web: http://www.computer.org/
Web: http://www.comsoc.org/

IESG Internet Engineering Steering Group (USA)
International technical development group that has final approval
regarding Internet standards.
Web: http://www.ietf.org/iesg.html

IETF Internet Engineering Task Force (USA)
International community of interested designers, programmers, scien-
tists, and engineers, concerned with the development and operation of
Internet architecture.
Web: http://www.ietf.org/

IFIP International Federation for Information Processing (Austria)
United Nations-sponsored research organization encouraging and promoting the development of information technology for the benefit of all
people.
Web: http://www.ifip.or.at/

IISP Information Infrastructure Standards Panel (USA)
ANSI-sponsored organization developing standards critical to the
growth of the Global Information Infrastructure (GII).
Web: http://www.ansi.org/iisp/iisphome.html

IMTC International Multimedia Teleconferencing Consortium (USA)
Industry consortium of major technology companies promoting the
adoption of universal interoperability standards in the multimedia teleconferencing industry.
Web: http://www.imtc.org/imtc/

INTUG International Telecommunications Users Group (European Union)
Advocacy group for users of telecommunication services in the
European Community.
Web: http://www.lamp.ac.uk/~ewan/intug/

ISC Internet Software Consortium (USA)
International organization promoting open software standards and universal access on the Internet.
Web: http://www.vix.com/isc/

ISOC Internet Society, The (USA)
International organization of Internet experts who guide the global development of the Internet.
Web: http://www.isoc.org/

Information Society, The (European Union)
European Union initiative to promote the growth of trans-european networks, services, applications and content.
Web: http://www.ispo.cec.be/infosoc/infosoc.html

Internet Telephony Consortium (USA)
Organization researching issues arising from using the Internet on the public switched telephone network.
Web: http://itel.mit.edu/

InterNIC, The (USA)
Central organization managing registration and DNS (domain name services) for the Internet community.
Web: http://www.internic.net/

JEMA Japan Electronic Messaging Association
Industry group promoting the widespread diffusion of secure electronic messaging in Japan.
Web: http://www.iijnet.or.jp/fmmc/jemae.html

JFRF Japan Frame Relay Forum
Industry group promoting the development and use of frame relay technology in Japan.
Web: http://www.iijnet.or.jp/fmmc/jfrf/index-e.html

NCHPC National Consortium for High Performance Computing (USA)
Promotes the design and use of scaleable systems for the U.S. National Information Infrastructure (NII).
Web: http://www.nchpc.lcs.mit.edu/

NCSA National Computer Security Association (USA)
Industry association dedicated to improving the quality of computer security by means of product certification.
Web: http://www.ncsa.com/

NTD National Technology Databank of Singapore (Singapore)
A resource for locating local and foreign information technology expertise.
Web: http://ntd.intro.nus.sg/

INTEREST GROUPS, con't.

PCCA Portable Computer and Communications Association (USA)
Advocacy association for those interested in portable computer communications.
Web: http://www.outlook.com/pcca/

PTC Pacific Telecommunications Council (Hawaii)
Coordinates telecommunications policy, services, and infrastructure for North, Central, and South America, Asia, and Oceania.
Web: http://www.ptc.org/

RIPE Réseaux IP Européens (European Union)
Industry group that manages the local Internet in Europe and acts as the regional Internet registry for Europe.
Web: http://www.ripe.net/

RIPN Russian Institute for Public Networks (Russia)
Organization promoting the use of networked communications in the interest of research and education.
Web: http://www.ripn.net:8081/ripnhomepage.html

SMDS Interest Group (USA)
International industry association promoting the expansion of SMDS (Switched Multimegabit Data Services) products and applications.
Web: http://www.smds-ig.org/

SIF SONET Interoperability Forum (USA)
ATIS-sponsored industry group promoting the implementation of SONET technology in the Internet infrastructure.
Web: http://www.atis.org/atis/sif/sifhom.htm

SIGCAT ACM Special Interest Group on CD-ROM Applications and Technology (USA)
Interest group concerned with the growth of CD-ROM technology.
Web: http://www.sigcat.org/

SIGCOMM ACM Special Interest Group on Data Communications (USA)
Interest group concerned with the growth of data communication networks.
Web: http://www.acm.org/sigcomm/

SIGGRAPH ACM Special Interest Group on Computer Graphics (USA)
Forum concerned with the application and technology of computer-generated graphics.
Web: http://www.siggraph.org/

SIGLINK ACM Special Interest Group on Hypertext and Hypermedia (USA)
Interest group concerned with the technology and development of hypermedia systems and the interactive representation of knowledge.
Web: http://info.acm.org/siglink/

SIGMM ACM Special Interest Group on Multimedia Systems (USA)
Forum for multimedia practitioners concerned with the application and technology of multimedia computing.
Web: http://info.acm.org/sigmm/

SISA Supporters of Interoperable Systems in Australia
Group promoting open and interoperable systems.
Web: http://www.sisa.org.au/

SMCC Sociedad Mexicana de Ciencia de la Computación (Mexico)
Organization promoting the use of information technology in Mexico.
Web: http://www.lania.mx/spanish/smcc/

SOCATEL La Société Centrafricaine de Télécommunications (Central African Republic)
Government development group dedicated to producing services, managing infrastructure, and expanding the role of telecommunications technology in Central Africa.
Web: http://socatel.intnet.cf/

SPIE International Society for Optical Engineering (USA)
Professional society promoting growth in the field of optics, photonics, imaging, and electronics.
Web: http://www.spie.org/

T1 Telecommunications (USA)
ATIS-sponsored organization responsible for developing network interconnection and interoperability standards for the United States.
Web: http://www.t1.org/

TERENA Trans-European Research and Education Networking Association (European Union)
Promotes the development of an international information and telecommunications infrastructure for the benefit of research and education. Created from the merger of RARE (Réseaux Associés pour la Recherche Européenne) and EARN (European Academic and Research Network).
Web: http://www.rare.nl/

TIF Telecoms Infotech Forum (Hong Kong)
Central clearinghouse for telecommunications industry information in the Greater China and Asia Pacific region.
Web: http://www.lawhk.hku.hk/TIF/homepage

TINA-C Telecommunications Information Networking Architecture-Consortium (USA)
An international consortium of telecommunications and information technology companies working to develop an open software architecture for information services.
Web: http://www.tinac.com/

INTEREST GROUPS, con't.

TUANZ Telecommunications Users Association of New Zealand
Industry association representing business, government, educational,
and private users. similar to ACM
Web: http://www.tuanz.gen.nz/

Technical Committee on Computer Communications (USA)
IEEE-sponsored group concerned with the technical aspects of comput-
er communication systems.
Web: http://www-net.cs.umass.edu/tccc/tccc.html

Technical Committee on Gigabit Networking (USA)
IEEE-sponsored forum concerned with high-speed networking tech-
nologies.
Web: http://www.ccrc.wustl.edu/pub/ieee-tcgn/tcgn.html

VRML Consortium, The (USA)
Association promoting the use of the VRML (Virtual Reality Modeling
Language) graphics standard on the World Wide Web.
Web: http://vag.vrml.org/

Voice over IP (VoIP) Forum (USA)
Organization establishing guidelines for the implementation of voice
communications over the Internet.
Web: http://www.imtc.org:80/imtc/i/activity/i_voip.htm

W3 World Wide Web Organization (Switzerland)
Major international body in charge of developing the universal proto-
cols and standards used in the World Wide Web.
Web: http://www.w3.org/pub/WWW/

XIWT Cross-Industry Working Team (USA)
CNRI-sponsored coalition of industry representatives responsible for
determining the requirements of the NII (National Information
Infrastructure).
Web: http://www.cnri.reston.va.us:3000/xiwt/public.html

APPENDIX G
INTERNATIONAL STANDARDS ORGANIZATIONS

ABNT Associaçao Brasileira de Normas Técnicas
National standards body of Brazil.
Av. 13 de Maio, no 13, 28o andar
20003-900 - Rio de Janeiro-RJ
Brazil
Phone: + 55 21 210 31 22, Fax: + 55 21 532 21 43
Internet: abnt@embratel.net.br
Web: http://www.abnt.org.br/

ACM-TSC Association for Computing Machinery - Technical Standards Committee
ACM is the largest information technology organization in the United States. It sponsors several special interest groups (SIGs); for example, SIGART (Artificial Intelligence), SIGCOMM (Data Communications), and SIGGRAPH (Computer-generated graphics).
1515 Broadway, 17th Floor
New York, NY 10036-5701
USA
Phone: 1 800 342 6626, Fax: 1 212 944 1318
Web: http://www.acm.org/tsc/

Advanced Television Systems Committee: See ATSC.

AFNOR Association française de normalisation
National standards body of France.
Tour Europe-Cedex 7
F-92080 Paris La Defence
France
Phone: +33 1 42 91 58 07, Fax: + 33 1 42 91 56 56
Web: http://www.afnor.fr/

AIIM Association for Information and Image Management
Worldwide association determining document imaging and interoperability standards.
AIIM International
1100 Wayne Avenue
Suite 1100
Silver Springs, Maryland 20910
USA
Phone: 1 301 587 8202
Web: http://www.aiim.org/

Alliance for Telecommunications Industry Solutions: See ATIS.

American National Standards Institute: See ANSI.

ANSI American National Standards Institute
The main organization in the United States charged with administering and coordinating efforts toward voluntary standardization.
11 West 42nd Street
New York, New York 10036
USA
Phone: 1 212 642 4900, Fax: 1 212 398 0023
Web: http://wwwe.ansi.org/

Associaçao Brasileir de Normas Técnicas: See ABNT.

Association for Computing Machinery - Technical Standards Committee: See ACM-TSC.

Association française de normalisation: See AFNOR.

Association for Information and Image Management: See AIIM.

Asynchronous Transfer Mode Forum: See ATM Forum.

ATIS Alliance for Telecommunications Industry Solutions, The
National ANSI-certified body in charge of reconciling national and international telecommunications standards issues. Promotes open industry standards for service providers and equipment manufacturers in North America and the Caribbean. (Formerly, Exchange Carriers Standards Association.)
1200 G Street, NW, Suite 500
Washington, DC 20005
USA
Phone: 1 202 628 6380, Fax: 1 202 393 5453
Web: http://www.atis.org/

ATM Forum
Major international organization working on the standardization of ATM (Asynchronous Transfer Mode) technology and services.
World Headquarters:
2570 West El Camino Real, Suite 304
Mountain View, CA 94040-1313
Phone: 1 415 949 6700, Fax: 1 415 949 6705
Web: http://www.atmforum.com/

ATSC Advanced Television Systems Committee
Establishes voluntary technical standards including those for HDTV (high definition television).
1750 K Street, NW, Suite 800
Washington, DC 20006
USA
Phone: 1 202 828 3130, Fax: 1 202 828 3131
Web: http://www.atsc.org/

British Standards Institution: See BSI.

BSI British Standards Institution
National standards body of Great Britain
British Standards House
389 Chiswick High Road
London
W4 4AL
United Kingdom
Phone: +44 (0) 181-996 9000, Fax: +44 (0) 181-996 7400
Web: http://www.bsi.org.uk/

CEN Committe Européen de Normalisation
CEN is one of three regional organizations responsible for voluntary standardization in the European Union. It is responsible for all standards except Electro-technical (CENELEC) and Telecommunications (ETSI).
36, Rue de Strassart
B-1050 Brussels
Belgium
Phone: +32 2 519 68 11, Fax: +32 2 519 68 19
Web: http://www.stri.is/cen/

CIE Commission Internationale de L'Éclairage
International standards body for the technology of lighting and color.
Kegelgasse 27, A-1030 Wien
Austria
Phone: +43 7143187-0, Fax: +43(1) 713 0838 18
e-mail: ciecb@ping.at
Web: http://www.cie.co.at/cie/

Commission Internationale de L'Éclairage: See CIE.

Committee Européen de Normilisation: See CEN.

Dansk Standard: See DS.

Data Interchange Standards Asociation: See DISA.

DAVIC Digital Audio Visual Interoperability Council
International organization developing open digital audio-visual standards.
DAVIC Secretariat
The Digital Audio-Visual Council
C/o Me Jean-Pierre Jacquemoud
2, rue Bellot
CH-1206 Geneve
Switzerland
Web: http://www.davic.org/

Department of Standards Malaysia: See DSM.

Deutsches Institut für Normung: See DIN.

DGN Dirección General de Normas
National standards body of Mexico.
Calle Puente de Tecamachalco No 6
Lomas de Tecamachalco
Sección Fuentes
Naucalpan de Jauárez
53 950 Mexico
Mexico
Phone: + 52 5 729 93 00, Fax: + 52 5 729 94 84
Web: http://www.secofi.gob.mx/

Digital Audio Visual Interoperability Council: See DAVIC.

DIN Deutsches Institut für Normung
National standards body of Germany.
Burggrafenstraáe 6
Postfach 11 07
10787 Berlin
Germany
Phone: + 49 30 2601 2344, Fax: + 49 30 2601 1231
Web: http://www.din.de/

Dirección Genral de Normas: See #DGN.

DISA Data Interchange Standards Association
ANSI-sponsored organization developing EDI standards for electronic commerce.
1800 Diagonal Road, Suite 200
Alexandria, VA 22314
USA
Phone: 1 703 548 7005
Web: http://www.disa.org/

DS Dansk Standard
National standards body of Denmark.
Kollegievej 6 - DK-2920 Charlottenlund
Denmark
Phone: + 45 39 96 61 01, Fax: + 45 39 96 61 02
Web: http://www.ds.dk/

DSM Department of Standards Malaysia
21st Floor, Wisma MPSA
Persiaran Perbandaran
40675 Shah Alam
Selangor Darul Ehsan
Malaysia
Phone: + 60 3 559 80 33, Fax: + 60 3 559 24 97
Web: http://www.mastic.gov.my/

ECMA European Computer Manufacturers' Association
European industrial association dedicated to the regional standardization of information and communication systems.
114 Rue du Rhône
CH 1204 Geneva
Switzerland
Fax: 022 7865231
Web: http://www.ecma.ch/

ELOT Hellenic Organization for Standardization
National standards body for Greece.
313 Acharnon Str.
111 45, Athens
Greece
Phone: + 30 1 228 0001
Fax: + 30 1 228 3034
Web: www. http://elot.gr/

Ente Nazionale Italiano di Unificazione: See UNI.

ETSI European Telecommunications Standards Indstitute
European Union organization in charge of coordinating the establishment of European telecommunications, broadcasting, and office information technology standards.
06921 Sophia Antipolis Cedex
France
Phone: + 33 (0)4 92 94 42 22
Fax: + 33 (0)4 92 94 43 33
e-mail: infocentre@etsi.fr
Web: http://www.etsi.fr/

European Computer Manufacturers' Association: See ECMA.

European Telecommunications Standards Institute: See ETSI.

FCC Federal Communications Commission (USA)
Government agency in charge of regulating the communications market in the United States.
1919 M Street NW
Washington, DC 20554
USA
Phone: 1 888 225 5322
Fax: 1 202 418 0232
e-mail: fccinfo@fcc.gov
Web: http://www.fcc.gov/

Federal Communications Commission (USA): See FCC.

Hellenic Organization for Standardization: See ELOT.

IEC International Electrotechnical Commission
Major international standards and conformity assessment body concerned with all fields of electrotechnology.
3, rue de Varembé • PO Box 131
1211 Geneva 20
Switzerland
Phone: + 41 22 919 02 11, Fax: + 41 22 919 03 00
Web: http://www.iec.ch/

IEEE Institute of Electrical And Electronics Engineers
World's largest technical professional society for engineers.
1828 L St. NW Washington, DC 20036-5104
USA
Phone: 1 800 678 IEEE or 1 202 785 0017
e-mail: stds.info@ieee.org
Web: http://www.ieee.org/

IETF Internet Engineering Task Force, The (USA)
International community of networking professionals, vendors, and researchers working to establish infrastructure protocol standards for the Internet.
IETF Secretariat
c/o Corporation for National Research Initiatives
1895 Preston White Drive, Suite 100
Reston, VA 20191-5434
USA
Tel: 1 703 620 8990
Fax: 1 703 758 5913
e-mail: ietf-info@ietf.org
Web: http://www.ietf.cnri.reston.va.us/home.html

Institute of Electrical And Electronics Engineers: See IEEE.

Instituto Argentino de Normalizatción: See IRAM.

Instrument Society of America: See ISA.

Intelsat
A cooperative of more than 135 member nations working together to establish technical standards for satellite earth stations.
3400 International Drive NW
Washington, DC 20008-3098
USA
Phone: 1 202 944 6800
Web: http://www.intelsat.int/

International Electrotechnical Commission: See IEC.

International Standards Organization: See ISO.

International Telecommunication Union: ITU International Telecommunication Union: See ITU.

Internet Engineering Task Force, The (USA): See IETF.

Internet SOCiety: See ISOC.

InterNIC (Netwlrk Information Center)
A cooperative effort sponsored by the National Science Foundation, AT&T, and Network Solutions, Inc., to provide domain name registration and IP network number assignment services to the Internet community.
Network Solutions, Inc.
Attn: InterNIC Registration Services
505 Huntmar Park Dr.
Herndon, VA 20170
USA
Phone: 1 703 742 4777
Fax: 1 703 742 9552
Web: http://ds.internic.net/

IRAM Instituto Argentino de Normalizacion
National standards body of Argentina.
Chile 1192
1098 Buesnos Aires
Argentina
Phone: + 54 1 383 37 51
e-mail: postmaster@iram.org.ar
Web: http://www.iram.org.ar/

ISA Instrument Society of America
International engineering society developing standards for measurement and control for computers and telecommunications devices.
PO Box 12277
Research Triangle Park, NC 27709
USA
Phone: 1 919 549 8411
Fax: 1 919 549 8288
e-mail: info@isa.org
Web: http://www.isa.org/

ISO International Standards Organization
Major international federation of standards bodies responsible for global cooperation in the development of technical standards.
1, rue de Varembé
Case postale 56
CH-1211 Genéve 20
Switzerland
Phone: + 41 22 749 01 11
Fax: + 41 22 733 34 30
Telex: 41 22 05 iso ch
e-mail: central@iso.ch
Web: http://www.iso.ch/

ISOC Internet SOCiety, The
International organization steering the global coordination of internet-working technologies and applications as they apply to the Internet.
Internet Society International Secretariat
12020 Sunrise Valley Drive
Suite 210
Reston, Virginia 20191
USA
Phone: 1 703 648 9888
Fax: 1 703 648 9887
e-mail: isoc@isoc.org
Web: http://www.isoc.org/

ITU International Telecommunications Union
Intergovernmental orgainization chartered by the United Nations which coordinates global effors toward standardizing telecommunications technology (formerly, CCITT).
Place des Nations
1211 Geneval 20
Switzerland
Phone: +41 22 730 51 11
Fax: +41 22 733 7256
e-mail: itumail@itu.int
Web: http://info.itu.ch/

National Committee for Information Technology Standards: See NCITS.

National Electrical Manufacturers Association: See NEMA.

National Information Standards Organizaitons: See NISO.

National Institute of Standards and Technology: See NIST.

National Standards Authority of Ireland: See NSAI.

NCITS National Committee for Information Technology Standards:
ANSI-sponsored committee to oversee the development of voluntary standards in the information technology field (formerly,X3).
NCITS Secretariat
1250 I Street. N.W. Suite 200,
Washington, DC 20005
USA
Phone: 1-202-737-8888
Fax: 1-202-638-4922
e-mail: NCITS@itic.nw.dc.us
Web: http://www.x3.org/

Nederlands Normailisatie-Institute: See NNI.

NEMA National Electrical Manufacturers Association
Develops and promotes positions on standards and government regulations.
1300 North 17th Street, Suite 1847
Rosslyn, Virginia 22209
USA
Phone: 1 703 841 3200, Fax: 1 703 841 3300
e-mail: http://www.nema.org/nema/contact/
Web: http://www.nema.org/

Network Information Center: *See* InterNIC.

NISO National Information Standards Organization
Develops techincal standards for the electronic exchange of documents.
PO Box 338
Oxon Hill, MD 207450-0338
USA
Phone: 1-301-654-2512, Fax: 1-301-654-1721
e-mail: nisohq@cni.org
Web: http://www.niso.org/

NIST National Institute of Standars and Techology
Department of Commerce agency promoting US economic growth by working with industry to develop and apply technology standards.
Pubic inquiries Unit
Admin. A903
Gaithersburg, MD 20899-0001
USA
Phone: 1-301-975-3058
e-mail: inquires@enh.nist.gov
Web: http://www.nist.gov/

NNI Nederlands Normalisatie-Institute
National standards body of the Netherlands.
PO Box 5059
NL-2600 GB Delft
Nederland
Phone: +31 15 269 0192, Fax: +31 15 269 0242
Web: http://www.nni.nl/

Norges Standardiseringsforbund: See NSF.

NSAI National Standards Authority of Ireland
National standards body of Ireland.
Glasnevin, Dublin 9
Ireland
Phone: +353 1 807 38 00, Fax: +353 1 807 38 38
Web: http://www.nsai.ie/

NSF Norges Standardiseringsforbund
National standards body of Norway.
Drammensveien 145 A
Postboks 353 Skoyen
N-0212 Osio
Norway
Phone: +47 22 04 92 00, Fax: +47 22 04 92 11
Web: http://www.standard.no/

ODMG Object Database Management Group
An OMG-sponsored collective of object-oriented database mangement
system (ODBMS) vendors developing a universal standard for object
technology.
14041 Burnhaven Drive, Suite 105
Burnsville, MN 55337
USA
Phone: 1 612 953 7250, Fax: 1 612 397 7146
e-mail: question@odmg.org.
Web: http://www.odmg.org/

Object Database Management Group. See ODMG.

Object Management Group: See OMG.

OMG Object Management Group
Group steering the international development of object technology
using the CORBA (Common Object Request Broker Architecture) spec-
ification.
492 Old Connecticut Path
Framingham, MA 01701
USA
Phone: 1 508 820 4300, Fax: 1 508 820 4303
e-mail: info@omg.org
Web: http://www.omg.org/

The Open Group
Organization dedicated to the implementation of the Open Systems
specification (formerly, X/Open Corp. and the Open Software
Foundation).
11 Cambridge Center
Cambridge, MA 02142
USA
Phone: 1 617 621 8700, Fax: 1 617 621 0631
Web: http://www.opengroup.org/

SAA Standards Australia
National standards organization of Australia.
PO Box 1055, Strathfield NSW 2135
Australia
Phone: 1 800 029 955 or 61 9746 4600, Fax: 61 9746 3333
Web: http://www.standards.com.au/~sicsaa/

SCC Standards Council of Canada
National standards organization of Canada.
Suite 1200, 45 O'Connor Street
Ottawa, Ontario
K1P 6N7
Canada
Phone: 613 238 3222, Fax: 613 995 4564
Web: http://www.scc.ca/indexe.html

SFS Suomen Standardisoimisliitto
National standards organization of Finland.
PL 116 Maistraatinportti 2
00240 Helsinki
Finland
Phone: +358 0 149 93 31, Fax: +358 0 146 49 25
Web: http://www.sfs.fi/

SIRIM (Standards and Industrial Research Institute of Malaysia) Berhad
National standards body of Malaysia.
No. 1, Persiaran Dato' Menteri
Seksyen 2, 40000 Shah Alam
Selangor Darul Ehsan
Malaysia
Phone: 603 5592601/5591630
Fax: 603 5508095
Web: http://www.sirim.my/

SIS Standardiseringen i Sverige
National standards body of Sweden.
Box 6455, SE-113 82 Stockholm
Sweden
Phone: +46 8 610 30 00, Fax: +46 8 30 77 57
e-mail: info@sis.se
Web: http://www.sis.se/

Standardiseringen I Sverige: See SIS.

Standards Australia: See SAA.

Standards Council of Canada: See SCC.

Standards and Industrial Research Institute of Malaysia Berhad: See SIRIM.

Standards New Zealand
National standards body of New Zealand.
Standards House
155 The Terrace
Wellington 6001
New Zealand
Phone: (04) 498 5992
Web: http://www.standards.co.nz/

Suomen Standardisoimisliitto: See SFS.

T1 Committee
Committee formed by ANSI and ATIS that is charged with developing
network interoperability standards in the United States.
C/o Alliance for Telecommunications Industry Solutions
1200 G Street, NW, Suite 500
Washington, DC 20005
USA
Phone: 1 202 434 8845, Fax: 1 202 347 7125
Web: http://www.t1.org/

TCIF Telecommunications Industry Forum
ATIS committee in charge of developing guidelines for global standards
for electronic data exchange and electronic commerce.
Alliance for Telecommunications Industry Solutions
1200 G Street, NW, Suite 500
Washington, DC 20005
USA
Phone: 1 202 628 6380, Fax: 1 202 393 5453

Telecommunications Industry Association: See TIA.

Telecommunications Industry Forum: See TCIF.

TIA Telecommunications Industry Association
The main body representing the industry on public policy issues.
2500 Wilson Blvd., Suite 300
Arlington, VA 22201
USA
Phone: 1 703 907 7714
Fax: 1 703 907 7728
Web: http://www.industry.net/

UNI Ente Nazionale Italiano di Unificazione
National standards body of Italy.
via Battistotti Sassi 11/b
20133 MILANO MI
Italy
Phone: +39 2 700241, Fax: +39 2 70106106
Web: http://www.unicei.it/uni/english/

The Unicode Consortium
International organization supporting the establishment of a universal
text display standard.
PO Box 700519
San Jose, CA 95170-0519
Phone: 1 408 777 5870, Fax: 1 408 777 5082
e-mail: unicode-inc@unicode.org
Web: http://www.cam.spyglass.com/unicode.html

VESA Video Electronics Standard Association
International organization developing video graphics and interface standards for the information technology industry.
2150 North First Street, Suite 440
San Jose, CA 95131-2029
USA
Phone: 1 408 435 0333
Fax: 1 408 435 8225
Web: http://www.vesa.org/

Video Electronics Standard Association: See VESA.

W3 World Wide Web Consortium
MIT, INRIA, and CERN-sponsored international community developing open standards to enhance the growth and smooth operation of the World Wide Web.
Massachusetts Institute of Technology Branch
Laboratory for Computer Science
545 Technology Square
Cambridge, MA 02139
USA
Phone: 1 617 253 2613
Fax: 1 617 258 5999
e-mail: admin@w3.org
Web: http://www.w3.org/pub/www/

WIPO World Intellectual Property Organization
United Nations organization administering intellectual property protection treaties.
34 chemin des Colombettes, Geneva
Switzerland
Phone: +41-22 338 91 11
Fax: +41-22 733 54 28
Web: http://www.wipo.int

World Intellectual Property Organization: See WIPO.

W3 World Wide Web Consortium: See W3.